# Take Our Moments and Our Days

# Take Our Moments and Our Days

AN ANABAPTIST PRAYER BOOK

Volume 2

ADVENT THROUGH PENTECOST

Prepared by
Arthur Paul Boers ◆ Barbara Nelson Gingerich
Eleanor Kreider ◆ John Rempel ◆ Mary H. Schertz

Herald Press

**Library of Congress Cataloging-in-Publication Data**
Take our moments and our days : an Anabaptist prayer book : Advent through Pentecost / prepared by Arthur Paul Boers ... [et al].
p. cm.
"Published in collaboration with Institute of Mennonite Studies, Associated Mennonite Biblical Seminary, Elkhart, Indiana, USA."
"Vol. 2."
Includes bibliographical references and index.
ISBN 978-0-8361-9449-4 (hardback : alk. paper)
1. Church year—Prayers and devotions. 2. Mennonites—Prayers and devotions. 3. Anabaptists—Prayers and devotions. I. Boers, Arthur P. (Arthur Paul), 1957-
BV30.T34 2010
264'.09707—dc22

2010035375

Published in collaboration with Institute of Mennonite Studies, Associated Mennonite Biblical Seminary, Elkhart, Indiana, USA


Library of Congress Catalog Card Number: 2010035375
International Standard Book Number: 978-0-8361-9449-4
Printed in Canada

Book design by Gwen Stamm; cover design by Merrill Miller

15 14 13 12 11 10 10 9 8 7 6 5 4 3 2 1

To order or request information, please call
1-800-245-7894, or visit www.heraldpress.com.

We offer this prayer book
in the spirit of the compilers of the Ausbund,
a sixteenth-century Anabaptist hymnbook,
who dedicated their work
"in an unpartisan way"
for use by any and all Christians.

*"Allen und jeden Christen*
*welcher Religion sie seyen,*
*unpartheyisch fast nützlich."*

# Contents

# Preface

Recent years have seen the publication of many new prayer books. Do we need yet another? And why an Anabaptist-Mennonite one?

Although some Anabaptists centuries ago compiled prayer books, developing such resources now may seem a departure from our traditions and priorities. But we have discovered that many Mennonite pastors, church leaders, spiritual directors, scholars, and other believers are vitally interested in this form of prayer and now use prayer books from various sources. They are tapping into a time-honored practice of Christian daily prayer, and some are looking for resources that reflect the strengths of the radical reformation tradition. This growing Mennonite interest in morning and evening prayer practices provided the initial impetus for this project.

As we began posting on the Web site www.ambs.edu/prayerbook earlier drafts of the prayers collected in this and the previous volume, we were amazed and humbled to discover the extent of interest in Anabaptist-Mennonite prayer resources among Christians of other traditions. Repeatedly, we received messages from people of many denominations around the globe, expressing enthusiasm for the project and telling us about their experiences with this way of praying.

Grassroots users of the draft first volume of the prayer book, for ordinary time, provided helpful insight into what worked well and what needed more refinement. We weighed carefully their thoughtful responses and shaped these prayers for the seasons of the church year, Advent through Pentecost, accordingly. Most of all, respondents' words of appreciation provided much encouragement for our labors and sustained our sense that the project addresses a vital need.

We offer this second volume of prayers as a gift to fellow Christians. Our desire is that use of these services will enrich the prayer of the church and its members. In the words of the old hymn, we pray that God will take our moments and our days and "let them flow in ceaseless praise."[1]

**Finding biblical clues**

The Psalms include frequent references to praying morning and evening. But the psalmist does not intend that believers limit their praying to those times of day. Rather, praying at certain times fosters being prayerful all the time. Consider the repeated phrase in the first chapter of Genesis, "And there was evening and there was morning ..." This shorthand denotes not

---

1 "Take my life"; text by Frances R. Havergal, *Songs of Grace and Glory,* Appendix, 1874.

just evening and morning but the passage of the whole day. In like manner, the psalmist's words, "From the rising of the sun to its setting the name of the LORD is to be praised" (Ps 113.3), indicate an aspiration to perpetual prayer.

Jesus made a similar recommendation. His parable about the persistent widow may puzzle us, but one point is plain: the story addresses his followers' need "to pray always and not to lose heart" (Lk 18.1).

The New Testament epistles pick up this theme. Paul urges believers to "rejoice always, pray without ceasing, give thanks in all circumstances" (1 Thess 5.16-18). We are told to "pray in the Spirit at all times" (Eph 6.18); "devote yourselves to prayer" (Col 4.2); "persevere in prayer" (Rom 12.12).

**Praying without ceasing**

The biblical counsel to "pray without ceasing" is clear, but how we do so is less apparent. A few believers have tried literally to live on prayer alone—without working, eating, sleeping—but Christian tradition sensibly cautions against such distortions. Christians today are more likely to say that our work or service is prayer. This approach to unceasing prayer may have more to commend it, but is it adequate? A few Christians live and work with steady awareness of God, but most of us need help to do so. Saying that everything we do is prayer may mean that in fact we rarely pray with conscious intention.

Our Sunday giving reminds us that all we have belongs to God; offerings make us mindful that all the ways we use money and other resources express our faith. In a similar way, morning and evening prayers remind us that all our time belongs to God. Morning and evening prayer is not about praying only at those times of day, any more than tithing is about granting God's ownership of just ten percent of our money.

Morning and evening symbolize all time. They are key daily moments when we set our direction, remember our purpose, review how God is at work, and recall where we missed God's priorities. Regular, disciplined prayers at particular times encourage us to be prayerful always.

**Supporting one another in prayer**

Many Christians struggle with prayer. We may not know how or when to pray, what to say, how to start, or when we are finished. Some have never settled into habits of prayer. Others have ceased to pray for a variety of reasons. Because challenges of busyness are pressing spiritual issues today, we may have trouble finding time for prayer. Patterned prayer helps many of us pray—or pray again. Some who learn this way of praying report, "Until now I was not able to pray."

Prayer books can give us the encouragement of praying with others. Here as elsewhere, we experience the truth of the Anabaptist conviction that we need the body of Christ. Given our society's individualism, we may tend to think it noble for each person always to pray freely, spontaneously, alone, one's own way, according to one's own inspirations. But the current narrow emphasis on private prayer was not characteristic of Bible times or of the church in the early centuries. And the truth is, constancy in prayer—like all faithful living—typically relies on the help and support of other believers.

Morning and evening prayer touches on issues that run throughout Christian history: the relationship of individual and corporate prayer, unplanned and set prayers, fixed-time and unceasing prayer. All have value, not as ends in themselves but to the extent that they lead us to God. Our hope is that through these morning and evening prayers, believers may experience the truth of the psalmist's words of praise: "You make the gateways of the morning and the evening shout for joy" (Ps 65.8).

# Acknowledgments

From its inception, this project has relied on the generous contributions of many, and our circle of benefactors continues to expand.

A group of North American Mennonite leaders came together, initially to dream about the project and later to evaluate what we learned from response to the first two draft versions of the first volume of *Take Our Moments and Our Days*. J. Nelson Kraybill, then president of Associated Mennonite Biblical Seminary (AMBS), enthusiastically supported this venture and helped fund that early consultation through the Presidential Vision Fund. From then on, our work was generously underwritten by The Anabaptist Foundation, Vancouver, British Columbia, and its president, J. Evan Kreider.

The Institute of Mennonite Studies at AMBS endorsed the project and made staff time available to help bring it to fruition. From her expertise in church music, Associate Professor of Worship and the Arts Rebecca Slough proposed a wealth of song selections. Out of his deep love and vast knowledge of scripture, Professor Emeritus of New Testament Willard M. Swartley aided our committee with discernment about text selections. With her customary skill and grace, Director of Communications Mary E. Klassen has provided invaluable help with publicity and maintenance of the prayer book Web pages.

Mennonite Church USA and Mennonite Church Canada created Web links to previous versions of the prayers, which helped connect us with believers in far-flung places. The responses of these users have assisted and encouraged our work in more ways than we can say.

Prayerful poets enriched the services by composing collects to complete each day's intercessory prayer. Our thanks to Mary Schertz for morning and evening collects for Advent and (with Barbara Nelson Gingerich) for December 24 through December 30, John Rempel for December 31, Eleanor Kreider for January 1 through January 5, Rachel Miller Jacobs with Ben Miller Jacobs for Epiphany, Samantha Lioi for Lent, Laura Kraybill for Holy Week, Adam Tice for Easter, Janeen Bertsche Johnson for the first week of Pentecost, and Rachel Miller Jacobs for the second week of Pentecost.

Tireless and multitalented volunteer James Nelson Gingerich formatted the book. He has also provided critical assistance to the project by refining and maintaining our scripture selection database, begun through the efforts of AMBS student Christine Guth.

We are grateful for the AMBS community that has nurtured this project, for its prayerful engagement with scripture, which seeks to form lives suited to witness to God's extravagant and costly love for the world.

And we thank God for colleagues whose good humor, varied abilities—as liturgists, theologians, scripture scholars, editors—and common passion for prayer have made collaborating on this project a source of so much satisfaction and joy.

# Introduction

A threefold pattern of praising, listening, and responding is how Christians pray. We honor God and give thanks. Then we listen to God through Bible readings, in quiet moments of intentional waiting for God's voice, or sometimes through other people's words. And finally we respond to God, giving the love of our hearts and the renewed dedication of our lives, interceding for others, and receiving a blessing. Whether we are young or old, in families or as individuals, accustomed to formal prayers or spontaneous ones, Christians naturally pray in this three-part form. *Take Our Moments and Our Days* reflects this familiar way of praying.

## Scripture-saturated prayer

The words of these prayers are taken directly from the Bible or use words minimally adapted from it.[1] In each service we read a psalm portion (or, in some cases, another passage of Hebrew poetry or a prophetic oracle), a Gospel text, and another scripture passage. The structure of the services, the three calls—to praise, discipleship,

[1] See indexes for a list of all scripture references. Bible readings are from the New Revised Standard Version; Psalm portions use *The Psalms: An Inclusive Language Version Based on the Grail Translation from the Hebrew* (Chicago: GIA Publications, Inc., 2000). Where it is different from the Grail's, NRSV versification appears in brackets.

and intercession—use scripture words, as do the words of thanksgiving and (in the evening) confession. Every service includes a song from scripture (canticle). A selection of canticles appears on pages 12–25. In each service we pray the Lord's Prayer and hear a biblical benediction or charge.

Early Anabaptists learned much scripture by heart; we hope that those who use these services will be inspired to do the same. We trust that by praying these scripture-saturated prayers, you will find your days and nights suffused with "the remembered Word," a hallmark of Anabaptist spirituality.

## Anabaptist coloration

At the beginning of each season's services, you will find a brief introduction to the season and an explanation of the approach taken to selecting the scriptures. The scriptures chosen reflect intensive work by the editorial committee to identify foundational texts of early Anabaptists as well as those important to Anabaptists today.

The biblical songs—canticles—that shape these prayers include joyful recognition of God's mercy in surprising reversals; comforting and challenging reflection on Jesus, who suffered and died for us; creedal affirmation from the earliest church; and exalted praise of the risen Christ. The titles and opening sentences unfold the week's canticle, line by line, Sunday through

Saturday. Each day the entire passage serves as the canticle. We commend prayerful immersion in these canticles as you move through the seasons of the year. We believe that together they resonate with a foundational Anabaptist theme, that of following Jesus in life through the Spirit's empowerment, both as individuals and as communities of faith.

# Notes on using *Take Our Moments and Our Days*

Try to set a regular time for prayer. Few of us find time for sustained prayer both morning and evening, so adopt either pattern. If possible, create a physical setting conducive to praying. You might want to have a visual focus—an open Bible, a cross, candle, symbol, or picture.

If you are praying in a group, any designated person can lead the services. Leader parts are in regular type; others present respond by reading the bold italic type. If a scripture text is very brief, reading it a second time may help you memorize it.

An overarching scripture text for each week provides title lines and opening sentences and sets the tone for the week's thematically linked Bible readings. Organizing texts for the seasons are the canticles found on pages 12–25.

The services have a simple three-part form—praise, listen, respond—which is evident in the three calls: call to praise, call to discipleship, call to intercession. Proceed through these parts at an unhurried pace that allows ample time—breathing space—for meditation.

## Call to praise

The first section of each service features praise of God through psalm prayer, personal thanksgiving, and song. The opening sentence is a line from the canticle for the week and shapes the choices of the Psalm and readings in the service.

After the call to praise, the word "Glory …" signals a traditional Christian outburst of praise directed toward God. We provide two forms of this doxology on page 11 or invite you to use another expression of praise. Several sung and spoken doxologies are also listed there.

The psalm may be prayed in alternating voices (leader and congregation, or responsively by two parts of the gathered group) as indicated with regular and bold italic type.

Verses from the Psalms frame open space for brief spontaneous prayers of thanksgiving.

Songs in the first section address God with our praise and thanksgiving. Numbers listed refer to songs in these resources: *Hymnal: A Worship Book* (Scottdale, PA: Mennonite Publishing House, 1992); *Sing the Journey* (Scottdale, PA: Faith & Life Resources, 2005); and *Sing the Story* (Scottdale, PA: Faith & Life Resources, 2007). Many of these hymns appear in other hymnals. You may substitute or add songs from other sources. Some people enjoy reading the hymn texts as devotional poetry instead of singing them.

In the evening the first section ends with scripture words of confession and assurance, which surround moments of silent confession.

## Call to discipleship

The second section is a call to listen to the voice of Jesus, and to express our desire to follow in his way. In each service these words anchor us to the heart of Jesus' vocation and message.

Gospel readings follow the week's theme as indicated in the opening sentences of each service. The Bible reading that accompanies the Gospel text may be drawn from either the Old or the New Testament. You may wish to omit, substitute, or add a reading. The thematically chosen Bible readings in these services are not meant to supplant other forms of daily reading of the Bible. These readings will stimulate reflection, praise, and application to life—all forms of prayer different from the benefits of linear Bible reading.

During the brief reflection on the readings, you may pause in silence, simply repeat a word or phrase from the reading, or comment on a connection between the readings or with events of the day. This is not a time for discussion but rather for heartfelt response to the readings. Anabaptist tradition is characterized by a conviction that the Spirit may illumine scripture through any participant's comment.

The songs listed after the readings reflect the day's theme and provide opportunity to respond in gratitude, affirmation of faith, and self-dedication. Again, the hymn texts may be sung or spoken.

The canticles (biblical songs) that shape these prayers are printed on pages 12–25. You may recite these in unison or in a responsorial way. Our hope is that frequent repetition of these vital texts will help you learn them by heart, in all the rich meanings of that phrase.

## Call to intercession

In the third section, we continue to respond to the reading of scripture by praying for ourselves and those dear to us, for our community, for the church, for the world, and for other concerns.

As each of the five subjects for intercession is introduced, allow plenty of opportunity for open, free prayers before concluding with the simple responsive phrase provided. Morning and evening intercessions are usually the same on any given day, and their imagery is drawn from the morning and evening readings for the day. Note that the petitions for the church and the world change each day throughout the week. If you use only one service for a particular day, notice the content of these intercessions on the other days; you may want to combine or adapt the materials to suit your occasion.

A brief prayer (loosely following the traditional form known as a "collect") draws the intercessions to a close and creates a bridge to the Lord's Prayer. Three forms of the Lord's Prayer are printed on pages 26 and 27.

The benedictions are all scriptural. Some groups conclude their prayer service with a period of silence, a simple song of peace and blessing, or by extending the peace of Christ to one another.

## Flexible adaptation of the services

You may use these materials to lead public worship. Adapt them by adding spontaneous elements, songs, longer Bible readings, meditation on the readings, readings by spiritual writers, more silence, additional canticles, a sermon, testimony, or free prayers.

You may shorten the services as well. For example, you may memorize the three calls and pray them by heart amid the activities of your day. Then add your personal petitions and finish by praying the Lord's Prayer. However you adapt the services, keep the threefold structure—praise, listen, respond—clear.

But don't feel slavishly bound to every detail. For example, you may use the entire Psalm indicated, not just the printed verses. You might add a line to the bidding prayers to make your intercessions more specific to your setting. You may choose to read just one of the Bible readings, or substitute another reading that better suits your occasion.

If you are not used to reading prayers, you may still find something of value here. In each service, you will find Psalm verses and words or stories of Jesus that can provide a setting for your informal prayers. After reading the Bible passages, you can put the book aside and pray freely. You may wish to return for the benediction.

The services are suited to group or individual prayers. Even when you pray alone, you know that your prayers join the prayers of many others.

## Other resources

A companion volume of morning and evening prayers for ordinary time (a four-week cycle) is available from Herald Press. For information on volume 1 (Ordinary Time) of *Take Our Moments and Our Days: An Anabaptist Prayer Book,* and for other prayer resources, see http://www.mpn.net/takeourmoments.

Especially illuminating as background for using *Take Our Moments and Our Days: An Anabaptist Prayer Book* is a scholarly but accessible study of Anabaptist spirituality by C. Arnold Snyder: *Following in the Footsteps of Christ: The Anabaptist Tradition* (Maryknoll, NY: Orbis Books, 2004).

A recently revised and expanded book by Arthur Paul Boers, *Day by Day These Things*

*We Pray: Uncovering Ancient Rhythms of Prayer* (Scottdale, PA: Herald Press, 2010), is a thoughtful and accessible introduction to the practice of daily prayer and a good guide for those wondering about or eager to begin the spiritual journey of corporate praying. It includes a useful list of resources, along with suggestions for preparing a prayer space and enriching your practice of prayer.

# Repeated elements

## Glory ...

***Glory to the Father,***
***and to the Son,***
***and to the Holy Spirit:***
***as it was in the beginning,***
***is now,***
***and will be for ever. Amen.***[1]

## Praise God ...

***Praise God, the Abba bearing love;***
***Praise God, the Servant from above;***
***Praise God, the Paraclete we share:***
***O triune God, receive our prayer.***[2]

### Sung doxologies[3]

Praise God, the Source of life (H95)
Praise God from whom (H118, H119)
To God, with the Lamb (H125)
Glory be to the Father (H127)

---

1 This translation of the Gloria Patri was prepared by the English Language Liturgical Consultation (ELLC), 1988.

2 Gail Ramshaw-Schmidt, "Naming the Trinity: Orthodoxy and Inclusivity," *Worship* 60, no. 6 (November 1986): 497–98.

3 Numbers refer to *Hymnal: A Worship Book* (Scottdale, PA: Mennonite Publishing House, 1992). Many hymns end with a doxological verse; see, for example, the final verses of the following: 22, 48, 52, 85, 86, 121, 177, 179, 183, 236, 256, 264, 441, 492, 650, 658.

## Mary's song

My soul proclaims the greatness of the Lord,
my spirit rejoices in God my Savior,
***who has looked with favor***
***on his lowly servant.***
From this day
all generations will call me blessed:
***the Almighty has done great things for me***
***and holy is his name.***
God has mercy on those who fear him,
from generation to generation.
***The Lord has shown strength with his arm***
***and scattered the proud in their conceit,***
casting down the mighty from their thrones
and lifting up the lowly.
***God has filled the hungry with good things***
***and sent the rich away empty.***
He has come to the aid of his servant Israel,
to remember the promise of mercy,
***the promise made to our forebears,***
***to Abraham and his children for ever.***[4]

### Spoken settings for responsive reading

An ELLC version (H840)
A version using direct address to God (H715)

---

[4] This translation of Luke 1:46-55 was prepared by the English Language Liturgical Consultation (ELLC), 1988.

## Mary's song

*My soul magnifies the Lord;*
*my spirit exults in God my Savior.*
*You, Lord, have noticed the humiliation*
*of your servant;*
*from now on all generations will count me*
*blessed.*
*Mighty One, you have done great things for*
*me,*
*and holy is your name.*
*your mercy is on all who fear you*
*from generation to generation.*
*You have shown strength with your arm,*
*and dispersed the haughty*
*in the scheming of their minds.*
*You have unseated tyrants from their thrones*
*and lifted high the lowly.*
*You have filled the hungry with good things*
*and sent the rich ones away empty.*
*You have come to the aid of Israel your ser-*
*vant;*
*you have remembered your mercy,*
*just as you promised our ancestors,*
*Abraham and Sarah and all their descendents*
*forever.*[5]

---

[5] This translation of Luke 1:46-55 was prepared by Mary H. Schertz.

## Sung settings of Mary's song

My soul proclaims (H179, accompaniment book)
My soul proclaims with wonder (H181)
My soul is filled with joy (SJ13)
Sing we a song of high revolt (SS13)
My soul cries out (SS124)

## Sung settings of Zechariah's song

Bless'd be the God of Israel (H174)
Blessed be the Lord (H179)

## Zechariah's song

Blessed be the Lord, the God of Israel,
who has come to his people and set them free.
***The Lord has raised up for us a mighty Savior,***
***born of the house of his servant David.***
Through the holy prophets, God promised of old
to save us from our enemies,
from the hands of all who hate us,
***to show mercy to our forebears,***
***and to remember his holy covenant.***
This was the oath God swore
  to our father Abraham:
to set us free from the hands of our enemies,
***free to worship him without fear,***
***holy and righteous before him,***
***all the days of our life.***

And you, child, shall be called
  the prophet of the Most High,
for you will go before the Lord to prepare his way,
***to give his people knowledge of salvation***
***by the forgiveness of their sins.***
In the tender compassion of our God
the dawn from on high shall break upon us,
***to shine on those who dwell in darkness***
  ***and the shadow of death,***
***and to guide our feet into the way of peace.***[6]

---

[6] This translation of Luke 1:68-79 was prepared by the English Language Liturgical Consultation (ELLC), 1988.

## Zechariah's song

Blessed are you, Lord, the God of Israel,
you have come to your people and set them free.
***You have raised up for us a mighty Savior,***
***born of the house of your servant David.***
Through your holy prophets, you promised of old
to save us from our enemies,
from the hands of all who hate us,
***to show mercy to our forebears,***
***and to remember your holy covenant.***
This was the oath you swore
to our father Abraham:
to set us free from the hands of our enemies,
***free to worship you without fear,***
***holy and righteous before you,***
***all the days of our life.***

And you, child, shall be called the prophet
of the Most High,
for you will go before the Lord to prepare the way,
***to give God's people knowledge of salvation***
***by the forgiveness of their sins.***
In the tender compassion of our God
the dawn from on high shall break upon us,
***to shine on those who dwell in darkness***
***and the shadow of death,***
***and to guide our feet into the way of peace.***[7]

---

[7] This alternative version of Luke 1:68-79 was prepared by the English Language Liturgical Consultation (ELLC), 1988.

## Colossians 1.15-20

He is the image of the invisible God,
the firstborn of all creation;
***for in him all things in heaven and on earth were created,***
***things visible and invisible,***
whether thrones or dominions or rulers or powers—
all things have been created through him and for him.
***He himself is before all things,***
***and in him all things hold together.***
He is the head of the body, the church;
he is the beginning, the firstborn from the dead,
so that he might come to have first place in everything.
***For in him all the fullness of God was pleased to dwell,***
and through him God was pleased to reconcile to himself all things,
***whether on earth or in heaven,***
***by making peace through the blood of his cross.***

## Simeon's song

*Now, Lord, you let your servant go in peace:*
*your word has been fulfilled.*
*My own eyes have seen the salvation*
*which you have prepared*
*in the sight of every people:*
*a light to reveal you to the nations*
*and the glory of your people Israel.*[8]

### Sung settings of Simeon's song

Lord, bid your servant go (H179, accompaniment book)

### Spoken settings of Simeon's song

NRSV version (H771)

[8] This translation of Luke 2.29-32 was prepared by the English Language Liturgical Consultation (ELLC), 1988.

## 1 Peter 2.21-24

For to this you have been called,
because Christ also suffered for you,
*leaving you an example,*
*so that you should follow in his steps.*
"He committed no sin,
and no deceit was found in his mouth."
*When he was abused, he did not return abuse;*
*when he suffered, he did not threaten;*
but he entrusted himself to the one who
judges justly.
*He himself bore our sins in his body on the*
*cross,*
so that, free from sins, we might live for
righteousness;
*by his wounds you have been healed.*

## 1 Peter 2.21-24

*For to this you have been called:*
*because Christ also suffered for you.*
*He left an example for you,*
*that you should follow in his steps.*
*He committed no sin;*
*no trickery was found on his lips.*
*When he was insulted, he did not insult in return.*
*When he was threatened, he did not threaten.*
*Instead, he trusted himself to the one who judges justly.*
*He himself bore our sins in his body on the tree*
*so that we might die to sin and live for justice.*
*By his wounds you have been healed.*[9]

[9] This translation was prepared by Mary H. Schertz.

## Philippians 2.5-8

Let the same mind be in you that was in
  Christ Jesus,
*who, though he was in the form of God,*
*did not regard equality with God*
*as something to be exploited,*
but emptied himself,
taking the form of a slave,
being born in human likeness.
*And being found in human form,*
*he humbled himself*
and became obedient to the point of death—
*even death on a cross.*

## Philippians 2.5-8

*Have the same frame of mind in you*
*that was also in Christ Jesus.*
*He existed in the form of God,*
*but he did not consider equality with God*
  *something to exploit.*
*Instead he emptied himself,*
*assuming the form of a slave.*
*He was born in the image of a human being;*
*and being found in the design of a human*
  *being, he humbled himself,*
*and he became obedient unto death,*
*even death on a cross.*[10]

[10] This translation was prepared by Mary H. Schertz.

## Philippians 2.5-11

Let the same mind be in you that was
in Christ Jesus,
***who, though he was in the form of God,***
***did not regard equality with God***
***as something to be exploited,***
but emptied himself,
taking the form of a slave,
being born in human likeness.
***And being found in human form,***
***he humbled himself***
and became obedient to the point of death—
even death on a cross.

***Therefore God also highly exalted him***
***and gave him the name that is above every name,***
so that at the name of Jesus every knee should bend,
in heaven and on earth and under the earth,
***and every tongue should confess***
***that Jesus Christ is Lord,***
***to the glory of God the Father.***

## Philippians 2.5-11

*Have the same frame of mind in you*
*that was also in Christ Jesus.*
*He existed in the form of God,*
*but he did not consider equality with God*
  *something to exploit.*
*Instead he emptied himself,*
*assuming the form of a slave.*
*He was born in the image of a human being;*
*and being found in the design of a human*
  *being, he humbled himself,*
*and he became obedient unto death,*
*even death on a cross.*
*Therefore God lifted him high*
*and granted freely to him the name above*
  *every name,*
*so that in the name of Jesus*
*every knee would bend,*
*in heaven, on earth, under the earth,*
*and every tongue consent*
*that Jesus Christ is Lord—*
*to the glory of God the Father.*[11]

### Sung setting of Philippians 2.5-11

Christ, who is in the form of God (H333)

---

[11] This translation was prepared by Mary H. Schertz.

## Ephesians 2.17-22

Christ Jesus came and proclaimed peace
to you who were far off
and peace to those who were near;
***for through him both of us have access***
***in one Spirit to the Father.***
So then you are no longer strangers and
aliens,
but you are citizens with the saints
***and also members of the household of God,***
***built upon the foundation of the apostles and***
***prophets,***
***with Christ Jesus himself as the cornerstone.***
In him the whole structure is joined together
and grows into a holy temple in the Lord;
***in whom you also are built together spiritu-***
***ally***
***into a dwelling place for God.***

## 1 Thessalonians 5.16-24

Rejoice always,
pray without ceasing,
give thanks in all circumstances;
for this is the will of God in Christ Jesus for you.
***Do not quench the Spirit.***
***Do not despise the words of prophets,***
***but test everything;***
hold fast to what is good;
abstain from every form of evil.
***May the God of peace sanctify you entirely;***
and may your spirit and soul and body
be kept sound and blameless
at the coming of our Lord Jesus Christ.
***The one who calls you is faithful and will do this.***[12]

---

12 NRSV (alt.)

## Our Father in heaven

***Our Father in heaven,***
***hallowed be your name,***
***your kingdom come,***
***your will be done,***
***on earth as in heaven.***
***Give us today our daily bread.***
***Forgive us our sins***
***as we forgive those who sin against us.***
***Save us from the time of trial***
***and deliver us from evil.***
***For the kingdom, the power, and the glory***
***are yours***
***now and forever. Amen.***[13]

### Sung settings of the Lord's Prayer

Our Father, which art in heaven (SJ48)
Our Father who art in heaven (H228)
Our Father who art in heaven (H351)
Our Father who art in heaven (H554, with verses)
Our Father, which art in heaven (SS42)

### Spoken settings of the Lord's Prayer

The ELLC version (H731)

---

[13] This translation of the Lord's Prayer was prepared by the English Language Liturgical Consultation (ELLC), 1988.

## Our Father who art in heaven

*Our Father who art in heaven,*
*hallowed be thy name.*
*Thy kingdom come, thy will be done*
*on earth as it is in heaven.*
*Give us this day our daily bread,*
*and forgive us our debts,*
*as we forgive our debtors.*
*And lead us not into temptation,*
*but deliver us from evil,*
*for thine is the kingdom, and the power,*
*and the glory forever. Amen.*

## Our Father in heaven

*Our Father in heaven,*
*hallowed be your name.*
*Your kingdom come.*
*Your will be done, on earth as it is in heaven.*
*Give us this day our daily bread.*
*And forgive us our debts,*
*as we also have forgiven our debtors.*
*And do not bring us to the time of trial,*
*but rescue us from the evil one.*[14]

---

[14] Matthew 6.9-13.

# Advent

## Introduction to the Advent prayers

*Advent* simply means "coming." It is the season of yearning and hoping; its cry is "Come, Lord Jesus." The last of the seasons of the church year to develop, Advent began as the period of preparation before Christmas, just as Lent is preparation for Easter. Advent begins on the fourth Sunday before Christmas Day and lasts through Christmas Eve day. From the beginning it has been a time of both repentance and hope, a time we enter in a spirit both of self-examination and of anticipation.

In choosing texts for Advent, we were drawn to the Magnificat for the titles, opening sentences, and canticle, because it represents our sense that Mary's pregnancy is still the most profound symbol we have of the divine grace and human courage at the heart of incarnation.

The scriptures calling us to praise were chosen from the great texts of yearning that are such a rich gift of Isaiah. With the biblical people of Israel, we proclaim that despite evidence of deep hopelessness among the nations, we will keep faith. With Isaiah, we restate our trust that God is "about to do a new thing."

Most of the Gospel readings are from Luke, the evangelist who lingers longest with the raw and tender story of incarnation. The second readings bring other canonical voices into conversation with the texts of yearning and the Gospel narrative of this strange and wondrous partnership of divine and human. There are Old Testament texts that remind us of how this unique "coming One" is embedded in the history of his people's sojourn with God. There are New Testament texts that remind us that the lowly birth this season anticipates became in the end a wellspring of joy and love and holy power inseparable from the cross and resurrection. The theme of peace in the readings and benedictions expresses a foundational tenet of Anabaptist spirituality—that the gospel of Jesus Christ is the gospel of peace, and that the longed-for incarnation is the gift of the God of peace.

This week of services can be used throughout the Advent season.

# My soul magnifies the Lord

## ADVENT SUNDAY MORNING

**Opening sentence**

My soul magnifies the Lord;
***my spirit exults in God my Savior.***

## Call to praise

I wait for you, Lord, my soul waits,
and in your word I hope.
***My soul waits for you, Lord,***
***more than sentries watch for dawn.***

*Glory ...*

**Isaiah 52.7-10**

How beautiful upon the mountains
are the feet of the messenger who announces
peace,
***who brings good news,***
***who announces salvation,***
***who says to Zion, "Your God reigns."***
Listen! Your sentinels lift up their voices,
together they sing for joy;
***for in plain sight they see***
***the return of the LORD to Zion.***
Break forth together into singing,
you ruins of Jerusalem;

***for the LORD has comforted his people,***
***he has redeemed Jerusalem.***
The LORD has bared his holy arm
before the eyes of all the nations;
***and all the ends of the earth shall see***
***the salvation of our God.***

**Thanksgiving**

With joy we will draw water
from the wells of salvation.
***We give thanks to you, Lord;***
***we call on your name.***
*(free prayers of thanksgiving)*
You are the Lord for whom we have waited;
***we are glad and rejoice in your salvation.***
***Amen.***

**Song**

Earth and all stars (H47, vv. 1, 3, 5)
Lord, with devotion we pray (H79)
Santo, santo, santo (H400)

## Call to discipleship

No one can lay any foundation
other than the one that has been laid;
***that foundation is Jesus Christ.***

**Matthew 4.12-17**

Now when Jesus heard that John had been arrested, he withdrew to Galilee. He left Nazareth and made his home in Capernaum by the sea, in the territory of Zebulun and Naphtali, so that what had been spoken through the prophet Isaiah might be fulfilled:

"Land of Zebulun, land of Naphtali,
on the road by the sea, across the Jordan,
Galilee of the Gentiles—
the people who sat in darkness
have seen a great light,
and for those who sat in the region and shadow of death
light has dawned."

From that time Jesus began to proclaim, "Repent, for the kingdom of heaven has come near."

**Ephesians 6.15**

As shoes for your feet put on whatever will make you ready to proclaim the gospel of peace.

**Silent or spoken reflection on the readings**

**Song**

Hark! the glad sound (H184)
Blessed be the Lord (H179)
Oh, for a thousand tongues to sing (H110)

**Mary's song**

## Call to intercession

We pray to you, Lord;
our prayer rises with the sun.
***At dawn we plead our case and watch for you.***

God of our salvation, all our longing is known to you, our sighing is not hidden from you. In your mercy,
***Lord, hear our prayer.***

You comfort your people. We pray for ourselves and those dear to us.
*(open prayers)*
In your mercy,
***Lord, hear our prayer.***

Your reign draws near. We pray for our community and for our neighbors.
*(open prayers)*
In your mercy,
***Lord, hear our prayer.***

You come to us with the good news of peace. We pray for the church in all places, that we may be one.
*(open prayers)*
In your mercy,
***Lord, hear our prayer.***

Your salvation reaches to the ends of the earth.
We pray for the world, that your reign may come and your will be done on earth.
*(open prayers)*
In your mercy,
***Lord, hear our prayer.***

We offer you other concerns we carry in our hearts.
*(open prayers)*
In your mercy,
***Lord, hear our prayer.***

Incarnate God,
holding tenderly all things human,
you became one of us.
Lighten our hearts
with Mary's vision of your just mercy,
that we may be gentled into joining you
in the hard and holy work
of releasing peace on earth.
In Jesus' name we pray:

***Our Father …***

**Benediction**

***May the God of hope fill us***
***with all joy and peace in believing,***
***so that we may abound in hope***
***by the power of the Holy Spirit. Amen.***

# My spirit exults in God my Savior

## ADVENT SUNDAY EVENING

**Opening sentence**

My soul magnifies the Lord;
***my spirit exults in God my Savior.***

## Call to praise

The glory of the Lord shall be revealed,
***and all people shall see it together.***

***Glory …***

**Isaiah 35.1-6**

The wilderness and the dry land shall be glad,
the desert shall rejoice and blossom;
***like the crocus it shall blossom abundantly,***
***and rejoice with joy and singing.***
The glory of Lebanon shall be given to it,
the majesty of Carmel and Sharon.
***They shall see the glory of the LORD,***
***the majesty of our God.***

Strengthen the weak hands,
and make firm the feeble knees.
***Say to those who are of a fearful heart,***
***"Be strong, do not fear!***
***Here is your God.***

He will come with vengeance,
with terrible recompense.
He will come and save you."

***Then the eyes of the blind shall be opened,***
***and the ears of the deaf unstopped;***
then the lame shall leap like a deer,
and the tongue of the speechless sing for joy.
***For waters shall break forth in the wilderness,***
***and streams in the desert.***

**Thanksgiving**

I will tell of your gracious deeds, O Lord,
***giving thanks for your unfailing love.***
*(free prayers of thanksgiving)*
You are the Lord for whom we have waited;
***we are glad and rejoice in your salvation.***
***Amen.***

**Song**

Let the heavens be glad (H187)
Praise the One who breaks the darkness (SS1)
I'll praise my Maker (H166)

**Confession**

You desire truth in my inward being;
***teach me wisdom in my secret heart.***
*(silence)*
In your goodness, O God, have mercy on me;
***with gentleness wipe away my faults. Amen.***

## Call to discipleship

Jesus calls to those are weary
and carrying heavy burdens:
Come to me, and I will give you rest.
***I am gentle and humble in heart,***
***and you will find rest for your souls.***

**Luke 7.18-23**

John summoned two of his disciples and sent them to the Lord to ask, "Are you the one who is to come, or are we to wait for another?" When the men had come to him, they said, "John the Baptist has sent us to you to ask, 'Are you the one who is to come, or are we to wait for another?'" Jesus had just then cured many people of diseases, plagues, and evil spirits, and had given sight to many who were blind. And he answered them, "Go and tell John what you have seen and heard: the blind receive their sight, the lame walk, the lepers are cleansed, the deaf hear, the dead are raised, the poor have good news brought to them. And blessed is anyone who takes no offense at me."

**Acts 3.1-10**

One day Peter and John were going up to the temple at the hour of prayer, at three o'clock in the afternoon. And a man lame from birth was being carried in. People would lay him daily at the gate of the temple called the Beautiful Gate so that he could ask for alms from those entering the temple. When he saw Peter and John about to go into the temple, he asked them for alms. Peter looked intently at him, as did John, and said, "Look at us." And he fixed his attention on them, expecting to receive something from them. But Peter said, "I have no silver or gold, but what I have I give you; in the name of Jesus Christ of Nazareth, stand up and walk." And he took him by the right hand and raised him up; and immediately his feet and ankles were made strong. Jumping up, he stood and began to walk, and he entered the temple with them, walking and leaping and praising God. All the people saw him walking and praising God, and they recognized him as the one who used to sit and ask for alms at the Beautiful Gate of the temple; and they were filled with wonder and amazement at what had happened to him.

**Silent or spoken reflection on the readings**

**Song**

Rejoice, rejoice, the Savior comes (SS4)
Heal us, Immanuel, here we are (H375)
Healer of our every ill (H377)

**Mary's song**

## Call to intercession

We seek you, Lord, while you may be found,
***we call upon you while you are near.***

Restore us, O God; let your face shine, that we may be saved. In your mercy,
***Lord, hear our prayer.***

You comfort your people. We pray for ourselves and those dear to us.
*(open prayers)*
In your mercy,
***Lord, hear our prayer.***

Your reign draws near. We pray for our community and for our neighbors.
*(open prayers)*
In your mercy,
***Lord, hear our prayer.***

You come to us with the good news of peace. We pray for the church in all places, that we may be one.
*(open prayers)*
In your mercy,
***Lord, hear our prayer.***

Your salvation reaches to the ends of the earth. We pray for the world, that your reign may come and your will be done on earth.
*(open prayers)*

In your mercy,
***Lord, hear our prayer.***

We offer you other concerns we carry in our hearts.
*(open prayers)*
In your mercy,
***Lord, hear our prayer.***

Incarnate God,
you fill the deepest blue of world and soul.
Help us to claim the sturdy hope
that Mary held in her heart
and sang out in witness,
that we too may rejoice to be disciples
of the one coming as dawn from on high.
We pray in his name:

***Our Father …***

**Benediction**

***May the God of peace sanctify us entirely;***
***and may our spirit and soul and body***
***be kept sound and blameless***
***at the coming of our Lord Jesus Christ.***
***The one who calls us is faithful,***
***and will do this. Amen.***

# God has noticed

## ADVENT MONDAY MORNING

**Opening sentence**

You, Lord, have noticed
the humiliation of your servant;
***from now on all generations***
***will count me blessed.***

## Call to praise

I wait for you, Lord, my soul waits,
and in your word I hope.
***My soul waits for you, Lord,***
***more than sentries watch for dawn.***

***Glory …***

**Isaiah 61.10-11**

I will greatly rejoice in the LORD,
my whole being shall exult in my God;
for he has clothed me with the garments of salvation,
***he has covered me with the robe of righteousness,***
***as a bridegroom decks himself with a garland,***
***and as a bride adorns herself with her jewels.***

For as the earth brings forth its shoots,
and as a garden causes what is sown in it
to spring up,
***so the Lord GOD will cause righteousness
and praise
to spring up before all the nations.***

**Thanksgiving**

With joy we will draw water
from the wells of salvation.
***We give thanks to you, Lord;
we call on your name.***
*(free prayers of thanksgiving)*
You are the Lord for whom we have waited;
***we are glad and rejoice in your salvation.
Amen.***

**Song**

Joyful, joyful, we adore thee (H71)
Lord, with devotion we pray (H79)
O bless the Lord, my soul (H80)

## Call to discipleship

No one can lay any foundation
other than the one that has been laid;
***that foundation is Jesus Christ.***

**Luke 1.5-7**

In the days of King Herod of Judea, there was a priest named Zechariah, who belonged to the priestly order of Abijah. His wife was a descendant of Aaron, and her name was Elizabeth. Both of them were righteous before God, living blamelessly according to all the commandments and regulations of the Lord. But they had no children, because Elizabeth was barren, and both were getting on in years.

**Philippians 4.4-9**

Rejoice in the Lord always; again I will say, Rejoice. Let your gentleness be known to everyone. The Lord is near. Do not worry about anything, but in everything by prayer and supplication with thanksgiving let your requests be made known to God. And the peace of God, which surpasses all understanding, will guard your hearts and your minds in Christ Jesus.

Finally, beloved, whatever is true, whatever is honorable, whatever is just, whatever is pure, whatever is pleasing, whatever is commendable, if there is any excellence and if there is anything worthy of praise, think about these things. Keep on doing the things that you have learned and received and heard and seen in me, and the God of peace will be with you.

**Silent or spoken reflection on the readings**

**Song**

Beloved, God's chosen (SJ38)
Confitemini Domino (Come and fill our hearts) (SJ59)
Jesus, help us live in peace (SJ52)
Praise the Lord (H52)
Ehane he'ama (Father God, you are holy) (H78)
Help us to help each other (H362)
Prepare the way of the Lord (SS14)

**Mary's song**

## Call to intercession

We pray to you, Lord;
our prayer rises with the sun.
***At dawn we plead our case and watch for you.***

God of our salvation, all our longing is known to you, our sighing is not hidden from you. In your mercy,
***Lord, hear our prayer.***

You comfort us as a mother comforts her child. We pray for ourselves and those dear to us.
*(open prayers)*
In your mercy,
***Lord, hear our prayer.***

You are God of astounding promises. We pray for our community and for our neighbors.
*(open prayers)*
In your mercy,
***Lord, hear our prayer.***

Your peace guards our hearts and minds. We pray for the church in all places, that we may know the freedom of life in the Spirit.
*(open prayers)*
In your mercy,
***Lord, hear our prayer.***

You cause righteousness and praise to spring up. We pray for the world and for all who care for creation.
*(open prayers)*
In your mercy,
***Lord, hear our prayer.***

We offer you other concerns we carry in our hearts.
*(open prayers)*
In your mercy,
***Lord, hear our prayer.***

Incarnate God,
holding tenderly all things human,
you became one of us.
Lighten our hearts
with Mary's vision of your just mercy,
that we may be gentled into joining you

in the hard and holy work
of releasing peace on earth.
In Jesus' name we pray:

***Our Father ...***

**Benediction**

***May the God of hope fill us
with all joy and peace in believing,
so that we may abound in hope
by the power of the Holy Spirit. Amen.***

# All generations will count me blessed

## ADVENT MONDAY EVENING

**Opening sentence**

You, Lord, have noticed
the humiliation of your servant;
***from now on all generations***
***will count me blessed.***

## Call to praise

The glory of the Lord shall be revealed,
***and all people shall see it together.***

*Glory ...*

**Isaiah 66.10-14**

Rejoice with Jerusalem, and be glad for her,
all you who love her;
***rejoice with her in joy,***
***all you who mourn over her—***
that you may nurse and be satisfied
from her consoling breast;
***that you may drink deeply with delight***
***from her glorious bosom.***

For thus says the LORD:
I will extend prosperity to her like a river,

and the wealth of the nations like an overflowing stream;
***and you shall nurse and be carried on her arm,***
***and dandled on her knees.***
As a mother comforts her child,
so I will comfort you;
you shall be comforted in Jerusalem.
***You shall see, and your heart shall rejoice;***
***your bodies shall flourish like the grass.***

## Thanksgiving

I will tell of your gracious deeds, O Lord,
***giving thanks for your unfailing love.***
*(free prayers of thanksgiving)*
You are the Lord for whom we have waited;
***we are glad and rejoice in your salvation.***
***Amen.***

## Song

Sing praise to God who reigns (H59)
Let the heavens be glad (H187)
Let all creation dance (SS122)
O Savior, rend the heavens (H175)

## Confession

You desire truth in my inward being;
***teach me wisdom in my secret heart.***
*(silence)*
In your goodness, O God, have mercy on me;
***with gentleness wipe away my faults. Amen.***

## Call to discipleship

Jesus calls to those are weary
and carrying heavy burdens:
Come to me, and I will give you rest.
***I am gentle and humble in heart,***
***and you will find rest for your souls.***

**Luke 1.8-17**

Once when [Zechariah] was serving as priest before God and his section was on duty, he was chosen by lot, according to the custom of the priesthood, to enter the sanctuary of the Lord and offer incense. Now at the time of the incense offering, the whole assembly of the people was praying outside. Then there appeared to him an angel of the Lord, standing at the right side of the altar of incense. When Zechariah saw him, he was terrified; and fear overwhelmed him. But the angel said to him, "Do not be afraid, Zechariah, for your prayer has been heard. Your wife Elizabeth will bear you a son, and you will name him John. You will have joy and gladness, and many will rejoice at his birth, for he will be great in the sight of the Lord. He must never drink wine or strong drink; even before his birth he will be filled with the Holy Spirit. He will turn many of the people of Israel to the Lord their God.

With the spirit and power of Elijah he will go before him, to turn the hearts of parents to their children, and the disobedient to the wisdom of the righteous, to make ready a people prepared for the Lord."

**1 Peter 1.17-23**

If you invoke as Father the one who judges all people impartially according to their deeds, live in reverent fear during the time of your exile. You know that you were ransomed from the futile ways inherited from your ancestors, not with perishable things like silver or gold, but with the precious blood of Christ, like that of a lamb without defect or blemish. He was destined before the foundation of the world, but was revealed at the end of the ages for your sake. Through him you have come to trust in God, who raised him from the dead and gave him glory, so that your faith and hope are set on God.

Now that you have purified your souls by your obedience to the truth so that you have genuine mutual love, love one another deeply from the heart. You have been born anew, not of perishable but of imperishable seed, through the living and enduring word of God.

**Silent or spoken reflection on the readings**

**Song**

Don't be afraid (SJ105)
Ubi caritas et amor (H452)
Ubi Caritas (Where true love) (SJ39)
Holy Spirit, come to us (SS79)
Of the Father's love begotten (H104)
Christ, who is in the form of God (H333)
How good a thing it is (H310)

**Mary's song**

## Call to intercession

We seek you, Lord, while you may be found,
***we call upon you while you are near.***

Restore us, O God; let your face shine, that we may be saved. In your mercy,
***Lord, hear our prayer.***

You comfort us as a mother comforts her child. We pray for ourselves and those dear to us.
*(open prayers)*
In your mercy,
***Lord, hear our prayer.***

You are God of astounding promises. We pray for our community and for our neighbors.
*(open prayers)*
In your mercy,
***Lord, hear our prayer.***

Your peace guards our hearts and minds. We pray for the church in all places, that we may know the freedom of life in the Spirit.
*(open prayers)*
In your mercy,
***Lord, hear our prayer.***

You cause righteousness and praise to spring up. We pray for the world and for all who care for creation.
*(open prayers)*
In your mercy,
***Lord, hear our prayer.***

We offer you other concerns we carry in our hearts.
*(open prayers)*
In your mercy,
***Lord, hear our prayer.***

Incarnate God,
you fill the deepest blue of world and soul.
Help us to claim the sturdy hope
that Mary held in her heart
and sang out in witness,
that we too may rejoice to be disciples
of the one coming as dawn from on high.
We pray in his name:

***Our Father …***

**Benediction**

*May the God of peace sanctify us entirely;*
*and may our spirit and soul and body*
*be kept sound and blameless*
*at the coming of our Lord Jesus Christ.*
*The one who calls us is faithful,*
*and will do this. Amen.*

# The Mighty One has done great things

## ADVENT TUESDAY MORNING

**Opening sentence**

Mighty One,
you have done great things for me,
***and holy is your name.***

## Call to praise

I wait for you, Lord, my soul waits,
and in your word I hope.
***My soul waits for you, Lord,***
***more than sentries watch for dawn.***

*Glory …*

**Isaiah 12.2-6**

Surely God is my salvation;
I will trust, and will not be afraid,
***for the LORD GOD is my strength and my might;***
***he has become my salvation.***

With joy you will draw water from the wells of salvation. And you will say in that day:
Give thanks to the LORD,
call on his name;

***make known his deeds among the nations;***
***proclaim that his name is exalted.***

Sing praises to the LORD, for he has done gloriously;
let this be known in all the earth.
***Shout aloud and sing for joy, O royal Zion,***
***for great in your midst is the Holy One of Israel.***

**Thanksgiving**

With joy we will draw water
from the wells of salvation.
***We give thanks to you, Lord;***
***we call on your name.***
*(free prayers of thanksgiving)*
You are the Lord for whom we have waited;
***we are glad and rejoice in your salvation.***
***Amen.***

**Song**

Asithi: Amen (Sing amen) (H64)
Praise, my soul, the God of heaven (H63)
Jubilate Deo omnis terra (H103)

# Call to discipleship

No one can lay any foundation
other than the one that has been laid;
***that foundation is Jesus Christ.***

**Luke 1.18-20**

Zechariah said to the angel, "How will I know that this [prophecy] is so? For I am an old man, and my wife is getting on in years." The angel replied, "I am Gabriel. I stand in the presence of God, and I have been sent to speak to you and to bring you this good news. But now, because you did not believe my words, which will be fulfilled in their time, you will become mute, unable to speak, until the day these things occur."

**Daniel 9.20-23**

While I was speaking, and was praying and confessing my sin and the sin of my people Israel, and presenting my supplication before the LORD my God on behalf of the holy mountain of my God—while I was speaking in prayer, the man Gabriel, whom I had seen before in a vision, came to me in swift flight at the time of the evening sacrifice. He came and said to me, "Daniel, I have now come out to give you wisdom and understanding. At the beginning of your supplications a word went out, and I have come to declare it, for you are greatly beloved. So consider the word and understand the vision."

**Silent or spoken reflection on the readings**

**Song**

Open, Lord, my inward ear (H140)
Open my eyes, that I may see (H517)
Abre mis ojos (Open my eyes) (SS65, vv. 1, 2, 3, 5)

**Mary's song**

# Call to intercession

We pray to you, Lord;
our prayer rises with the sun.
***At dawn we plead our case and watch for you.***

God of our salvation, all our longing is known to you, our sighing is not hidden from you. In your mercy,
***Lord, hear our prayer.***

You are God, our salvation. We pray for ourselves and those dear to us.
*(open prayers)*
In your mercy,
***Lord, hear our prayer.***

You give wisdom and understanding. We pray for our community and for our neighbors.
*(open prayers)*
In your mercy,
***Lord, hear our prayer.***

You make rivers in the desert and provide drink for your people. We pray for the church

in all places, that we may reflect your faithful love.
*(open prayers)*
In your mercy,
***Lord, hear our prayer.***

You are about to do a new thing. We pray for the world, for those who are in need.
*(open prayers)*
In your mercy,
***Lord, hear our prayer.***

We offer you other concerns we carry in our hearts.
*(open prayers)*
In your mercy,
***Lord, hear our prayer.***

Incarnate God,
holding tenderly all things human,
you became one of us.
Lighten our hearts
with Mary's vision of your just mercy,
that we may be gentled into joining you
in the hard and holy work
of releasing peace on earth.
In Jesus' name we pray:

***Our Father …***

**Benediction**

*May the God of hope fill us*
*with all joy and peace in believing,*
*so that we may abound in hope*
*by the power of the Holy Spirit. Amen.*

# Holy is God's name

## ADVENT TUESDAY EVENING

**Opening sentence**

Mighty One,
you have done great things for me,
***and holy is your name.***

## Call to praise

The glory of the Lord shall be revealed,
***and all people shall see it together.***

*Glory …*

**Isaiah 43.15-21**

I am the LORD, your Holy One,
the Creator of Israel, your King.
*Thus says the LORD,*
*who makes a way in the sea,*
*a path in the mighty waters,*
who brings out chariot and horse,
army and warrior;
*they lie down, they cannot rise,*
*they are extinguished, quenched like a wick:*
Do not remember the former things,
or consider the things of old.
*I am about to do a new thing;*
*now it springs forth, do you not perceive it?*

I will make a way in the wilderness
and rivers in the desert.
***The wild animals will honor me,***
***the jackals and the ostriches;***
for I give water in the wilderness,
rivers in the desert,
to give drink to my chosen people,
***the people whom I formed for myself***
***so that they might declare my praise.***

### Thanksgiving

I will tell of your gracious deeds, O Lord,
***giving thanks for your unfailing love.***
*(free prayers of thanksgiving)*
You are the Lord for whom we have waited;
***we are glad and rejoice in your salvation.***
***Amen.***

### Song

Heilig, heilig, heilig (H75)
Great is the Lord (H87)
This is a day of new beginnings (H640)
New earth, heavens new (H299)

### Confession

You desire truth in my inward being;
***teach me wisdom in my secret heart.***
*(silence)*
In your goodness, O God, have mercy on me;
***with gentleness wipe away my faults. Amen.***

## Call to discipleship

Jesus calls to those are weary
and carrying heavy burdens:
Come to me, and I will give you rest.
***I am gentle and humble in heart,***
***and you will find rest for your souls.***

**Luke 1.21-25**

The people were waiting for Zechariah, and wondered at his delay in the sanctuary. When he did come out, he could not speak to them, and they realized that he had seen a vision in the sanctuary. He kept motioning to them and remained unable to speak. When his time of service was ended, he went to his home.

After those days his wife Elizabeth conceived, and for five months she remained in seclusion. She said, "This is what the Lord has done for me when he looked favorably on me and took away the disgrace I have endured among my people."

**Matthew 13.31-33**

[Jesus] put before them another parable: "The kingdom of heaven is like a mustard seed that someone took and sowed in his field; it is the smallest of all the seeds, but when it has grown it is the greatest of shrubs and becomes a tree, so that the birds of the air come and make nests in its branches."

He told them another parable: "The kingdom of heaven is like yeast that a woman took and mixed in with three measures of flour until all of it was leavened."

**Silent or spoken reflection on the readings**

**Song**

My soul cries out (SS124, verses 1, 2)
Who is so great a God (H62)
The kingdom of God (H224)

**Mary's song**

## Call to intercession

We seek you, Lord, while you may be found,
***we call upon you while you are near.***

Restore us, O God; let your face shine, that we may be saved. In your mercy,
***Lord, hear our prayer.***

You are God, our salvation. We pray for ourselves and those dear to us.
*(open prayers)*
In your mercy,
***Lord, hear our prayer.***

You give wisdom and understanding. We pray for our community and for our neighbors.
*(open prayers)*
In your mercy,
***Lord, hear our prayer.***

You make rivers in the desert and provide drink for your people. We pray for the church in all places, that we may reflect your faithful love.
*(open prayers)*
In your mercy,
***Lord, hear our prayer.***

You are about to do a new thing. We pray for the world, for those who are in need.
*(open prayers)*
In your mercy,
***Lord, hear our prayer.***

We offer you other concerns we carry in our hearts.
*(open prayers)*
In your mercy,
***Lord, hear our prayer.***

Incarnate God,
you fill the deepest blue of world and soul.
Help us to claim the sturdy hope
that Mary held in her heart
and sang out in witness,
that we too may rejoice to be disciples

of the one coming as dawn from on high.
We pray in his name:

*Our Father ...*

**Benediction**

*May the God of peace sanctify us entirely;*
*and may our spirit and soul and body*
*be kept sound and blameless*
*at the coming of our Lord Jesus Christ.*
*The one who calls us is faithful,*
*and will do this. Amen.*

# God's mercy is on all

## ADVENT WEDNESDAY MORNING

**Opening sentence**

Your mercy is on all who fear you
***from generation to generation.***

## Call to praise

I wait for you, Lord, my soul waits,
and in your word I hope.
***My soul waits for you, Lord,***
***more than sentries watch for dawn.***

***Glory …***

**Isaiah 11.1-9**

A shoot shall come out from the stump of
Jesse,
and a branch shall grow out of his roots.
***The spirit of the LORD shall rest on him,***
***the spirit of wisdom and understanding,***
the spirit of counsel and might,
the spirit of knowledge and the fear of the
LORD.
***His delight shall be in the fear of the LORD.***

He shall not judge by what his eyes see,
or decide by what his ears hear;

***but with righteousness he shall judge the poor,***
***and decide with equity for the meek of the earth;***
he shall strike the earth with the rod of his mouth,
and with the breath of his lips he shall kill the wicked.
***Righteousness shall be the belt around his waist,***
***and faithfulness the belt around his loins.***

The wolf shall live with the lamb,
the leopard shall lie down with the kid,
***the calf and the lion and the fatling together,***
***and a little child shall lead them.***
The cow and the bear shall graze,
their young shall lie down together;
and the lion shall eat straw like the ox.
***The nursing child shall play over the hole of the asp,***
***and the weaned child shall put its hand on the adder's den.***
They will not hurt or destroy
on all my holy mountain;
***for the earth will be full of the knowledge of the LORD***
***as the waters cover the sea.***

**Thanksgiving**

With joy we will draw water
from the wells of salvation.

***We give thanks to you, Lord;***
***we call on your name.***
*(free prayers of thanksgiving)*
You are the Lord for whom we have waited;
***we are glad and rejoice in your salvation.***
***Amen.***

**Song**

Lord, I am fondly, earnestly (H514)
God is working his purpose out (H638)
O day of peace (H408)

## Call to discipleship

No one can lay any foundation
other than the one that has been laid;
***that foundation is Jesus Christ.***

**Luke 1.26-38**

In the sixth month the angel Gabriel was sent by God to a town in Galilee called Nazareth, to a virgin engaged to a man whose name was Joseph, of the house of David. The virgin's name was Mary. And he came to her and said, "Greetings, favored one! The Lord is with you." But she was much perplexed by his words and pondered what sort of greeting this might be. The angel said to her, "Do not be afraid, Mary, for you have found favor with God. And now, you will conceive in your womb and bear a son, and you will name him Jesus. He will be great, and will be called the Son of the Most High, and the Lord God will give to him the throne of his ancestor David. He will reign over the house of Jacob forever, and of his kingdom there will be no end." Mary said to the angel, "How can this be, since I am a virgin?" The angel said to her, "The Holy Spirit will come upon you, and the power of the Most High will overshadow you; therefore the child to be born will be holy; he will be called Son of God. And now, your relative Elizabeth in her old age has also conceived a son; and this is the sixth month for her who was said to be barren. For nothing will be impossible with God." Then Mary said, "Here am I, the servant of the Lord; let it be with me according to your word." Then the angel departed from her.

**1 Samuel 2.1-10**

Hannah prayed and said,
"My heart exults in the LORD;
my strength is exalted in my God.
My mouth derides my enemies,
because I rejoice in my victory.

"There is no Holy One like the LORD,
no one besides you;
there is no Rock like our God.
Talk no more so very proudly,

let not arrogance come from your mouth;
for the LORD is a God of knowledge,
and by him actions are weighed.
The bows of the mighty are broken,
but the feeble gird on strength.

Those who were full have hired themselves out for bread,
but those who were hungry are fat with spoil.
The barren has borne seven,
but she who has many children is forlorn.
The LORD kills and brings to life;
he brings down to Sheol and raises up.
The LORD makes poor and makes rich;
he brings low, he also exalts.
He raises up the poor from the dust;
he lifts the needy from the ash heap,
to make them sit with princes
and inherit a seat of honor.
For the pillars of the earth are the LORD's,
and on them he has set the world.

"He will guard the feet of his faithful ones,
but the wicked shall be cut off in darkness;
for not by might does one prevail.
The LORD! His adversaries shall be shattered;
the Most High will thunder in heaven.
The LORD will judge the ends of the earth;

he will give strength to his king,
and exalt the power of his anointed."

**Silent or spoken reflection on the readings**

**Song**

My soul is filled with joy (SJ13)
My soul proclaims with wonder (H181)
No wind at the window (SS11)

**Mary's song**

## Call to intercession

We pray to you, Lord;
our prayer rises with the sun.
***At dawn we plead our case and watch for you.***

God of our salvation, all our longing is known to you, our sighing is not hidden from you. In your mercy,
***Lord, hear our prayer.***

You give promises and signs. We pray for ourselves and those dear to us.
*(open prayers)*
In your mercy,
***Lord, hear our prayer.***

You decide with equity for the meek of the earth. We pray for our community and for our neighbors.

*(open prayers)*
In your mercy,
***Lord, hear our prayer.***

You guard your faithful ones. We pray for the church in all places, that we may bear witness to your reign of justice, peace, and joy.
*(open prayers)*
In your mercy,
***Lord, hear our prayer.***

There is no Holy One, no Rock, like you. We pray for the world, for all who are ensnared in greed, violence, and oppression.
*(open prayers)*
In your mercy,
***Lord, hear our prayer.***

We offer you other concerns we carry in our hearts.
*(open prayers)*
In your mercy,
***Lord, hear our prayer.***

Incarnate God,
holding tenderly all things human,
you became one of us.
Lighten our hearts
with Mary's vision of your just mercy,
that we may be gentled into joining you
in the hard and holy work

of releasing peace on earth.
In Jesus' name we pray:

*Our Father ...*

**Benediction**

*May the God of hope fill us*
*with all joy and peace in believing,*
*so that we may abound in hope*
*by the power of the Holy Spirit. Amen.*

# God has shown strength

## ADVENT WEDNESDAY EVENING

**Opening sentence**

You have shown strength with your arm,
***and dispersed the haughty***
***in the scheming of their minds.***

## Call to praise

The glory of the Lord shall be revealed,
***and all people shall see it together.***

***Glory …***

**Isaiah 7.14-15**

Therefore the Lord himself will give you a sign.
Look, the young woman is with child and shall bear a son,
and shall name him Immanuel.
***He shall eat curds and honey***
***by the time he knows how to refuse the evil***
***and choose the good.***

**Thanksgiving**

I will tell of your gracious deeds, O Lord,
***giving thanks for your unfailing love.***
*(free prayers of thanksgiving)*

You are the Lord for whom we have waited;
***we are glad and rejoice in your salvation. Amen.***

**Song**

Oh, how shall I receive thee (H182)
O come, O come, Immanuel (H172, vv. 1–3)

**Confession**

You desire truth in my inward being;
***teach me wisdom in my secret heart.***
*(silence)*
In your goodness, O God, have mercy on me;
***with gentleness wipe away my faults. Amen.***

## Call to discipleship

Jesus calls to those are weary
and carrying heavy burdens:
Come to me, and I will give you rest.
***I am gentle and humble in heart,***
***and you will find rest for your souls.***

**Matthew 1.18-25**

Now the birth of Jesus the Messiah took place in this way. When his mother Mary had been engaged to Joseph, but before they lived together, she was found to be with child from the Holy Spirit. Her husband Joseph, being a righteous man and unwilling to expose her to public disgrace, planned to dismiss her quietly. But just when he had resolved to do this, an angel of the Lord appeared to him in a dream and said, "Joseph, son of David, do not be afraid to take Mary as your wife, for the child conceived in her is from the Holy Spirit. She will bear a son, and you are to name him Jesus, for he will save his people from their sins." All this took place to fulfill what had been spoken by the Lord through the prophet:

> "Look, the virgin shall conceive and bear
> a son,
> and they shall name him Emmanuel,"

which means, "God is with us." When Joseph awoke from sleep, he did as the angel of the Lord commanded him; he took her as his wife, but had no marital relations with her until she had borne a son; and he named him Jesus.

**Romans 1.1-8**

Paul, a servant of Jesus Christ, called to be an apostle, set apart for the gospel of God, which he promised beforehand through his prophets in the holy scriptures, the gospel concerning his Son, who was descended from David according to the flesh and was declared to be Son of God with power according to the spirit of holiness by resurrection from the dead, Jesus Christ our Lord, through whom we have received grace and apostleship to bring about the obedience of faith among all the Gentiles for the sake of his name, including yourselves who are called to belong to Jesus Christ,

To all God's beloved in Rome, who are called to be saints:

Grace to you and peace from God our Father and the Lord Jesus Christ.

**Silent or spoken reflection on the readings**

**Song**

Bless'd be the God of Israel (H174)
Come, thou long-expected Jesus (H178)
Lo, how a Rose e'er blooming (H211)

**Mary's song**

## Call to intercession

We seek you, Lord, while you may be found,
***we call upon you while you are near.***

Restore us, O God; let your face shine, that we may be saved. In your mercy,
***Lord, hear our prayer.***

You give promises and signs. We pray for ourselves and those dear to us.
*(open prayers)*

In your mercy,
***Lord, hear our prayer.***

You decide with equity for the meek of the earth. We pray for our community and for our neighbors.
*(open prayers)*
In your mercy,
***Lord, hear our prayer.***

You guard your faithful ones. We pray for the church in all places, that we may bear witness to your reign of justice, peace, and joy.
*(open prayers)*
In your mercy,
***Lord, hear our prayer.***

There is no Holy One, no Rock, like you. We pray for the world, for all who are ensnared in greed, violence, and oppression.
*(open prayers)*
In your mercy,
***Lord, hear our prayer.***

We offer you other concerns we carry in our hearts.
*(open prayers)*
In your mercy,
***Lord, hear our prayer.***

Incarnate God,
you fill the deepest blue of world and soul.

Help us to claim the sturdy hope
that Mary held in her heart
and sang out in witness,
that we too may rejoice to be disciples
of the one coming as dawn from on high.
We pray in his name:

*Our Father ...*

**Benediction**

*May the God of peace sanctify us entirely;
and may our spirit and soul and body
be kept sound and blameless
at the coming of our Lord Jesus Christ.
The one who calls us is faithful,
and will do this. Amen.*

# God has lifted up the lowly

## ADVENT THURSDAY MORNING

**Opening sentence**

You have unseated tyrants from their thrones
***and lifted high the lowly.***

## Call to praise

I wait for you, Lord, my soul waits,
and in your word I hope.
***My soul waits for you, Lord,***
***more than sentries watch for dawn.***

*Glory ...*

**Isaiah 9.2-7**

The people who walked in darkness
have seen a great light;
***those who lived in a land of deep darkness—***
***on them light has shined.***
You have multiplied the nation,
you have increased its joy;
***they rejoice before you***
***as with joy at the harvest,***
***as people exult when dividing plunder.***
For the yoke of their burden,
and the bar across their shoulders,

***the rod of their oppressor,***
***you have broken as on the day of Midian.***
For all the boots of the tramping warriors
and all the garments rolled in blood
shall be burned as fuel for the fire.
***For a child has been born for us,***
***a son given to us;***
***authority rests upon his shoulders;***
and he is named
Wonderful Counselor, Mighty God,
Everlasting Father, Prince of Peace.
***His authority shall grow continually,***
***and there shall be endless peace***
***for the throne of David and his kingdom.***
He will establish and uphold it
with justice and with righteousness
from this time onward and forevermore.
***The zeal of the LORD of hosts will do this.***

**Thanksgiving**

With joy we will draw water
from the wells of salvation.
***We give thanks to you, Lord;***
***we call on your name.***
*(free prayers of thanksgiving)*
You are the Lord for whom we have waited;
***we are glad and rejoice in your salvation.***
***Amen.***

**Song**

Fling wide the door, unbar the gate (H186)
To us a Child of hope is born (H189)
Hail to the Lord's anointed (H185)

## Call to discipleship

No one can lay any foundation
other than the one that has been laid;
***that foundation is Jesus Christ.***

**Luke 1.39-45**

In those days Mary set out and went with haste to a Judean town in the hill country, where she entered the house of Zechariah and greeted Elizabeth. When Elizabeth heard Mary's greeting, the child leaped in her womb. And Elizabeth was filled with the Holy Spirit and exclaimed with a loud cry, "Blessed are you among women, and blessed is the fruit of your womb. And why has this happened to me, that the mother of my Lord comes to me? For as soon as I heard the sound of your greeting, the child in my womb leaped for joy. And blessed is she who believed that there would be a fulfillment of what was spoken to her by the Lord."

**Romans 16.25-27**

Now to God who is able to strengthen you according to my gospel and the proclamation of Jesus Christ, according to the revelation of the mystery that was kept secret for long ages but is now disclosed, and through the prophetic writings is made known to all the Gentiles, according to the command of the eternal God, to bring about the obedience of faith—to the only wise God, through Jesus Christ, to whom be the glory forever! Amen.

**Silent or spoken reflection on the readings**

**Song**

Who now would follow Christ (H535)
Lead me, Lord (H538)
My Lord, he is a-comin' soon (SS112)
He comes to us as one unknown (H498, vv. 1, 4, 5)

**Mary's song**

## Call to intercession

We pray to you, Lord;
our prayer rises with the sun.
***At dawn we plead our case and watch for you.***

God of our salvation, all our longing is known to you, our sighing is not hidden from you. In your mercy,
***Lord, hear our prayer.***

You remind us not to be afraid. We pray for ourselves and those dear to us.
*(open prayers)*
In your mercy,
***Lord, hear our prayer.***

You gather the outcast and change their shame into praise. We pray for our community and for our neighbors.
*(open prayers)*
In your mercy,
***Lord, hear our prayer.***

You renew your people in your love. We pray for the church in all places, that we may daily follow in the footsteps of Christ.
*(open prayers)*
In your mercy,
***Lord, hear our prayer.***

You break the rod of the oppressor. We pray for the world, for those in positions of power and authority.
*(open prayers)*
In your mercy,
***Lord, hear our prayer.***

We offer you other concerns we carry in our hearts.
*(open prayers)*
In your mercy,
***Lord, hear our prayer.***

Incarnate God,
holding tenderly all things human,
you became one of us.
Lighten our hearts
with Mary's vision of your just mercy,
that we may be gentled into joining you
in the hard and holy work
of releasing peace on earth.
In Jesus' name we pray:

***Our Father …***

**Benediction**

***May the God of hope fill us***
***with all joy and peace in believing,***
***so that we may abound in hope***
***by the power of the Holy Spirit. Amen.***

# God has filled the hungry

## ADVENT THURSDAY EVENING

**Opening sentence**

You have filled the hungry with good things
***and sent the rich ones away empty.***

## Call to praise

The glory of the Lord shall be revealed,
***and all people shall see it together.***

*Glory ...*

**Isaiah 40.9-11**

Get you up to a high mountain,
O Zion, herald of good tidings;
***lift up your voice with strength,***
***O Jerusalem, herald of good tidings,***
lift it up, do not fear;
***say to the cities of Judah,***
***"Here is your God!"***
See, the Lord GOD comes with might,
and his arm rules for him;
***his reward is with him,***
***and his recompense before him.***
He will feed his flock like a shepherd;
he will gather the lambs in his arms,

***and carry them in his bosom,***
***and gently lead the mother sheep.***

**Thanksgiving**

I will tell of your gracious deeds, O Lord,
***giving thanks for your unfailing love.***
*(free prayers of thanksgiving)*
You are the Lord for whom we have waited;
***we are glad and rejoice in your salvation.***
***Amen.***

**Song**

Bless'd be the God of Israel (H174)
Comfort, comfort, O my people (H176)
My Shepherd will supply my need (H589)
Glorious things of thee are spoken (H619)

**Confession**

You desire truth in my inward being;
***teach me wisdom in my secret heart.***
*(silence)*
In your goodness, O God, have mercy on me;
***with gentleness wipe away my faults. Amen.***

## Call to discipleship

Jesus calls to those are weary
and carrying heavy burdens:
Come to me, and I will give you rest.

***I am gentle and humble in heart,***
***and you will find rest for your souls.***

**Luke 1.57-67, 80**

Now the time came for Elizabeth to give birth, and she bore a son. Her neighbors and relatives heard that the Lord had shown his great mercy to her, and they rejoiced with her.

On the eighth day they came to circumcise the child, and they were going to name him Zechariah after his father. But his mother said, "No; he is to be called John." They said to her, "None of your relatives has this name." Then they began motioning to his father to find out what name he wanted to give him. He asked for a writing tablet and wrote, "His name is John." And all of them were amazed. Immediately his mouth was opened and his tongue freed, and he began to speak, praising God. Fear came over all their neighbors, and all these things were talked about throughout the entire hill country of Judea. All who heard them pondered them and said, "What then will this child become?" For, indeed, the hand of the Lord was with him.

Then his father Zechariah was filled with the Holy Spirit....

The child grew and became strong in spirit,
and he was in the wilderness until the day he
appeared publicly to Israel.

**Zephaniah 3.14-20**

Sing aloud, O daughter Zion;
shout, O Israel!
Rejoice and exult with all your heart,
O daughter Jerusalem!
The LORD has taken away the judgments
against you,
he has turned away your enemies.
The king of Israel, the LORD, is in your midst;
you shall fear disaster no more.
On that day it shall be said to Jerusalem:
Do not fear, O Zion;
do not let your hands grow weak.
The LORD, your God, is in your midst,
a warrior who gives victory;
he will rejoice over you with gladness,
he will renew you in his love;
he will exult over you with loud singing
as on a day of festival.
I will remove disaster from you,
so that you will not bear reproach for it.
I will deal with all your oppressors at that
time.
And I will save the lame
and gather the outcast,
and I will change their shame into praise

and renown in all the earth.
At that time I will bring you home,
at the time when I gather you;
for I will make you renowned and praised
among all the peoples of the earth,
when I restore your fortunes before your eyes,
says the LORD.

**Silent or spoken reflection on the readings**

**Song**

When all thy mercies, O my God (H72)
Creator of the stars of night (H177)
I will come to you in the silence (SS49)

**Mary's song**

## Call to intercession

We seek you, Lord, while you may be found,
***we call upon you while you are near.***

Restore us, O God; let your face shine, that we may be saved. In your mercy,
***Lord, hear our prayer.***

You remind us not to be afraid. We pray for ourselves and those dear to us.
*(open prayers)*
In your mercy,
***Lord, hear our prayer.***

You gather the outcast and change their shame into praise. We pray for our community and for our neighbors.
*(open prayers)*
In your mercy,
***Lord, hear our prayer.***

You renew your people in your love. We pray for the church in all places, that we may daily follow in the footsteps of Christ.
*(open prayers)*
In your mercy,
***Lord, hear our prayer.***

You break the rod of the oppressor. We pray for the world, for those in positions of power and authority.
*(open prayers)*
In your mercy,
***Lord, hear our prayer.***

We offer you other concerns we carry in our hearts.
*(open prayers)*
In your mercy,
***Lord, hear our prayer.***

Incarnate God,
you fill the deepest blue of world and soul.
Help us to claim the sturdy hope
that Mary held in her heart
and sang out in witness,

that we too may rejoice to be disciples
of the one coming as dawn from on high.
We pray in his name:

*Our Father ...*

**Benediction**

*May the God of peace sanctify us entirely;
and may our spirit and soul and body
be kept sound and blameless
at the coming of our Lord Jesus Christ.
The one who calls us is faithful,
and will do this. Amen.*

# God has come to our aid

## ADVENT FRIDAY MORNING

**Opening sentence**

You have come to the aid of Israel your servant;
***you have remembered your mercy.***

## Call to praise

I wait for you, Lord, my soul waits,
and in your word I hope.
***My soul waits for you, Lord,***
***more than sentries watch for dawn.***

*Glory ...*

**Isaiah 49.8-11**

Thus says the LORD:
In a time of favor I have answered you,
on a day of salvation I have helped you;
***I have kept you and given you***
***as a covenant to the people,***
to establish the land,
to apportion the desolate heritages;
***saying to the prisoners, "Come out,"***
***to those who are in darkness, "Show yourselves."***
They shall feed along the ways,
on all the bare heights shall be their pasture;

***they shall not hunger or thirst,***
***neither scorching wind nor sun shall strike***
***them down,***
for he who has pity on them will lead them,
and by springs of water will guide them.
***And I will turn all my mountains into a road,***
***and my highways shall be raised up.***

**Thanksgiving**

With joy we will draw water
from the wells of salvation.
***We give thanks to you, Lord;***
***we call on your name.***
*(free prayers of thanksgiving)*
You are the Lord for whom we have waited;
***we are glad and rejoice in your salvation.***
***Amen.***

**Song**

I sing the mighty power of God (H46)
Oh, for a thousand tongues to sing (H110)
Come! Walk in the light (SS10, vv. 1–4, 6)

## Call to discipleship

No one can lay any foundation
other than the one that has been laid;
***that foundation is Jesus Christ.***

**Luke 3.1-6**

In the fifteenth year of the reign of Emperor Tiberius, when Pontius Pilate was governor of Judea, and Herod was ruler of Galilee, and his brother Philip ruler of the region of Ituraea and Trachonitis, and Lysanias ruler of Abilene, during the high priesthood of Annas and Caiaphas, the word of God came to John son of Zechariah in the wilderness. He went into all the region around the Jordan, proclaiming a baptism of repentance for the forgiveness of sins, as it is written in the book of the words of the prophet Isaiah,

> "The voice of one crying out in the
> wilderness:
> 'Prepare the way of the Lord,
> make his paths straight.
> Every valley shall be filled,
> and every mountain and hill shall be made
> low,
> and the crooked shall be made straight,
> and the rough ways made smooth;
> and all flesh shall see the salvation of
> God.'"

**Malachi 3.1-4**

See, I [the Lord] am sending my messenger to prepare the way before me, and the Lord whom you seek will suddenly come to his temple. The messenger of the covenant in whom you delight—indeed, he is coming, says the LORD of hosts. But who can endure the day of his coming, and who can stand when he appears?

For he is like a refiner's fire and like fullers' soap; he will sit as a refiner and purifier of silver, and he will purify the descendants of Levi and refine them like gold and silver, until they present offerings to the LORD in righteousness. Then the offering of Judah and Jerusalem will be pleasing to the LORD as in the days of old and as in former years.

**Silent or spoken reflection on the readings**

**Song**

On Jordan's bank the Baptist's cry (H183)
Wild and lone the prophet's voice (SS8)
God, whose purpose is to kindle (H135)

**Mary's song**

## Call to intercession

We pray to you, Lord;
our prayer rises with the sun.
***At dawn we plead our case and watch for you.***

God of our salvation, all our longing is known to you, our sighing is not hidden from you. In your mercy,
***Lord, hear our prayer.***

You take us by the hand and keep us. We pray for ourselves and those dear to us.
*(open prayers)*
In your mercy,
***Lord, hear our prayer.***

You ask those who have plenty to share with those who have none. We pray for our community and for our neighbors.
*(open prayers)*
In your mercy,
***Lord, hear our prayer.***

Like a refiner of gold and silver, you refine and purify your people. We pray for the church in all places, that we may speak boldly for Christ.
*(open prayers)*
In your mercy,
***Lord, hear our prayer.***

Your word will not return to you empty, but will succeed in your purpose. We pray for the world, for all who do justice and love mercy.
*(open prayers)*
In your mercy,
***Lord, hear our prayer.***

We offer you other concerns we carry in our hearts.
*(open prayers)*
In your mercy,
***Lord, hear our prayer.***

Incarnate God,
holding tenderly all things human,
you became one of us.
Lighten our hearts
with Mary's vision of your just mercy,
that we may be gentled into joining you
in the hard and holy work
of releasing peace on earth.
In Jesus' name we pray:

***Our Father …***

**Benediction**

***May the God of hope fill us***
***with all joy and peace in believing,***
***so that we may abound in hope***
***by the power of the Holy Spirit. Amen.***

# God has remembered mercy

## ADVENT FRIDAY EVENING

**Opening sentence**

You have come to the aid of Israel your servant;
*you have remembered your mercy.*

## Call to praise

The glory of the Lord shall be revealed,
*and all people shall see it together.*

*Glory ...*

**Isaiah 55.6-11**

Seek the LORD while he may be found,
call upon him while he is near;
*let the wicked forsake their way,*
*and the unrighteous their thoughts;*
let them return to the LORD, that he may have mercy on them,
*and to our God, for he will abundantly pardon.*
For my thoughts are not your thoughts,
nor are your ways my ways, says the LORD.
*For as the heavens are higher than the earth,*
*so are my ways higher than your ways*
*and my thoughts than your thoughts.*

For as the rain and the snow come down from heaven,
and do not return there until they have watered the earth,
***making it bring forth and sprout,***
***giving seed to the sower and bread to the eater,***
so shall my word be that goes out from my mouth;
it shall not return to me empty,
***but it shall accomplish that which I purpose,***
***and succeed in the thing for which I sent it.***

**Thanksgiving**

I will tell of your gracious deeds, O Lord,
***giving thanks for your unfailing love.***
*(free prayers of thanksgiving)*
You are the Lord for whom we have waited;
***we are glad and rejoice in your salvation.***
***Amen.***

**Song**

Great God of wonders (H149)
O bless the Lord, my soul (H600)
The word of God is solid ground (H314, vv. 1, 3)
There's a wideness in God's mercy (H145)

**Confession**

You desire truth in my inward being;
***teach me wisdom in my secret heart.***
*(silence)*

In your goodness, O God, have mercy on me;
***with gentleness wipe away my faults. Amen.***

## Call to discipleship

Jesus calls to those are weary
and carrying heavy burdens:
Come to me, and I will give you rest.
***I am gentle and humble in heart,***
***and you will find rest for your souls.***

**Luke 3.7-18**

John said to the crowds that came out to be baptized by him, "You brood of vipers! Who warned you to flee from the wrath to come? Bear fruits worthy of repentance. Do not begin to say to yourselves, 'We have Abraham as our ancestor'; for I tell you, God is able from these stones to raise up children to Abraham. Even now the ax is lying at the root of the trees; every tree therefore that does not bear good fruit is cut down and thrown into the fire."

And the crowds asked him, "What then should we do?" In reply he said to them, "Whoever has two coats must share with anyone who has none; and whoever has food must do likewise." Even tax collectors came to be baptized, and they asked him, "Teacher, what should we do?" He said to them, "Collect no more than the amount prescribed for you." Soldiers also asked him, "And we, what should we do?" He said to them, "Do not extort money from anyone by threats or false accusation, and be satisfied with your wages."

As the people were filled with expectation, and all were questioning in their hearts concerning John, whether he might be the Messiah, John answered all of them by saying, "I baptize you with water; but one who is more powerful than I is coming; I am not worthy to untie the thong of his sandals. He will baptize you with the Holy Spirit and fire. His winnowing fork is in his hand, to clear his threshing floor and to gather the wheat into his granary; but the chaff he will burn with unquenchable fire."

So, with many other exhortations, he proclaimed the good news to the people.

**1 Thessalonians 3.9-13**

How can we [Paul, Sylvanus, and Timothy] thank God enough for you in return for all the joy that we feel before our God because of you? Night and day we pray most earnestly that we may see you face to face and restore whatever is lacking in your faith.

Now may our God and Father himself and our Lord Jesus direct our way to you. And may the

Lord make you increase and abound in love for one another and for all, just as we abound in love for you. And may he so strengthen your hearts in holiness that you may be blameless before our God and Father at the coming of our Lord Jesus with all his saints.

**Silent or spoken reflection on the readings**

**Song**

I bind my heart this tide (H411)
Help us to help each other (H362)
Let justice roll like a river (SS33)
What does the Lord require of you? (SS54)
God, whose purpose is to kindle (H135)

**Mary's song**

## Call to intercession

We seek you, Lord, while you may be found,
***we call upon you while you are near.***

Restore us, O God; let your face shine, that we may be saved. In your mercy,
***Lord, hear our prayer.***

You take us by the hand and keep us. We pray for ourselves and those dear to us.
*(open prayers)*

In your mercy,
***Lord, hear our prayer.***

You ask those who have plenty to share with those who have none. We pray for our community and for our neighbors.
*(open prayers)*
In your mercy,
***Lord, hear our prayer.***

Like a refiner of gold and silver, you refine and purify your people. We pray for the church in all places, that we may speak boldly for Christ.
*(open prayers)*
In your mercy,
***Lord, hear our prayer.***

Your word will not return to you empty, but will succeed in your purpose. We pray for the world, for all who do justice and love mercy.
*(open prayers)*
In your mercy,
***Lord, hear our prayer.***

We offer you other concerns we carry in our hearts.
*(open prayers)*
In your mercy,
***Lord, hear our prayer.***

Incarnate God,
you fill the deepest blue of world and soul.

Help us to claim the sturdy hope
that Mary held in her heart
and sang out in witness,
that we too may rejoice to be disciples
of the one coming as dawn from on high.
We pray in his name:

*Our Father ...*

**Benediction**

*May the God of peace sanctify us entirely;*
*and may our spirit and soul and body*
*be kept sound and blameless*
*at the coming of our Lord Jesus Christ.*
*The one who calls us is faithful,*
*and will do this. Amen.*

# As God promised our ancestors

## ADVENT SATURDAY MORNING

**Opening sentence**

You have remembered your mercy,
***just as you promised our ancestors.***

## Call to praise

I wait for you, Lord, my soul waits,
and in your word I hope.
***My soul waits for you, Lord,***
***more than sentries watch for dawn.***

*Glory …*

**Isaiah 60.4-5**

Lift up your eyes and look around;
they all gather together, they come to you;
***your sons shall come from far away,***
***and your daughters shall be carried on their nurses' arms.***
Then you shall see and be radiant;
your heart shall thrill and rejoice,
***because the abundance of the sea shall be brought to you,***
***the wealth of the nations shall come to you.***

**Thanksgiving**

With joy we will draw water
from the wells of salvation.
***We give thanks to you, Lord;***
***we call on your name.***
*(free prayers of thanksgiving)*
You are the Lord for whom we have waited;
***we are glad and rejoice in your salvation.***
***Amen.***

**Song**

Holy, holy, holy (H120)
Holy God, we praise thy name (H121)
Gloria, gloria, gloria (SS23)
I will stand in the congregation (SS113)

# Call to discipleship

No one can lay any foundation
other than the one that has been laid;
***that foundation is Jesus Christ.***

**Luke 21.5-11**

When some were speaking about the temple, how it was adorned with beautiful stones and gifts dedicated to God, [Jesus] said, "As for these things that you see, the days will come when not one stone will be left upon another; all will be thrown down."

They asked him, "Teacher, when will this be, and what will be the sign that this is about to take place?" And he said, "Beware that you are not led astray; for many will come in my name and say, 'I am he!' and, 'The time is near!' Do not go after them.

"When you hear of wars and insurrections, do not be terrified; for these things must take place first, but the end will not follow immediately." Then he said to them, "Nation will rise against nation, and kingdom against kingdom; there will be great earthquakes, and in various places famines and plagues; and there will be dreadful portents and great signs from heaven."

**James 5.7-11**

Be patient, therefore, beloved, until the coming of the Lord. The farmer waits for the precious crop from the earth, being patient with it until it receives the early and the late rains. You also must be patient. Strengthen your hearts, for the coming of the Lord is near. Beloved, do not grumble against one another, so that you may not be judged. See, the Judge is standing at the doors! As an example of suffering and patience, beloved, take the prophets who spoke in the name of the Lord. Indeed we call blessed those who showed endurance. You have heard of the endurance of Job, and you have seen the purpose of the Lord, how the Lord is compassionate and merciful.

**Silent or spoken reflection on the readings**

**Song**

Longing for light (SJ54)
They that wait upon the Lord (H584)
If you but trust in God (H576)

**Mary's song**

## Call to intercession

We pray to you, Lord;
our prayer rises with the sun.
***At dawn we plead our case and watch for you.***

God of our salvation, all our longing is known to you, our sighing is not hidden from you. In your mercy,
***Lord, hear our prayer.***

You teach us your ways. We pray for ourselves and those dear to us.
*(open prayers)*
In your mercy,
***Lord, hear our prayer.***

You are compassionate and merciful. We pray for our community and for our neighbors.
*(open prayers)*

In your mercy,
***Lord, hear our prayer.***

Your day is near. We pray for the church in all places, that we may be faithful in solidarity across generations and geography.
*(open prayers)*
In your mercy,
***Lord, hear our prayer.***

Your glory will appear over the nations. We pray for the world, for our enemies and for those who are in conflict.
*(open prayers)*
In your mercy,
***Lord, hear our prayer.***

We offer you other concerns we carry in our hearts.
*(open prayers)*
In your mercy,
***Lord, hear our prayer.***

Incarnate God,
holding tenderly all things human,
you became one of us.
Lighten our hearts
with Mary's vision of your just mercy,
that we may be gentled into joining you
in the hard and holy work
of releasing peace on earth.
In Jesus' name we pray:

*Our Father …*

**Benediction**

*May the God of hope fill us*
*with all joy and peace in believing,*
*so that we may abound in hope*
*by the power of the Holy Spirit. Amen.*

# Abraham and Sarah and all their descendants forever

## ADVENT SATURDAY EVENING

**Opening sentence**

You have remembered your mercy,
just as you promised our ancestors,
***Abraham and Sarah***
***and all their descendants forever.***

## Call to praise

The glory of the Lord shall be revealed,
***and all people shall see it together.***

***Glory …***

**Isaiah 54.11-14**

O afflicted one, storm-tossed, and not comforted,
I am about to set your stones in antimony,
and lay your foundations with sapphires.
***I will make your pinnacles of rubies,***
***your gates of jewels,***
***and all your wall of precious stones.***
All your children shall be taught by the Lord,
and great shall be the prosperity of your children.

***In righteousness you shall be established;***
***you shall be far from oppression, for you shall not fear;***
***and from terror, for it shall not come near you.***

**Thanksgiving**

I will tell of your gracious deeds, O Lord,
***giving thanks for your unfailing love.***
*(free prayers of thanksgiving)*
You are the Lord for whom we have waited;
***we are glad and rejoice in your salvation. Amen.***

**Song**

Christ is the world's true light (H334)
Oh, for a thousand tongues to sing (H81)
We are often tossed and driv'n (SS72)
How firm a foundation (H567)

**Confession**

You desire truth in my inward being;
***teach me wisdom in my secret heart.***
*(silence)*
In your goodness, O God, have mercy on me;
***with gentleness wipe away my faults. Amen.***

## Call to discipleship

Jesus calls to those are weary
and carrying heavy burdens:
Come to me, and I will give you rest.
***I am gentle and humble in heart,***
***and you will find rest for your souls.***

**Luke 21.25-36**

[Jesus said,] "There will be signs in the sun, the moon, and the stars, and on the earth distress among nations confused by the roaring of the sea and the waves. People will faint from fear and foreboding of what is coming upon the world, for the powers of the heavens will be shaken. Then they will see 'the Son of Man coming in a cloud' with power and great glory. Now when these things begin to take place, stand up and raise your heads, because your redemption is drawing near."

Then he told them a parable: "Look at the fig tree and all the trees; as soon as they sprout leaves you can see for yourselves and know that summer is already near. So also, when you see these things taking place, you know that the kingdom of God is near. Truly I tell you, this generation will not pass away until all things have taken place. Heaven and earth will pass away, but my words will not pass away.

"Be on guard so that your hearts are not weighed down with dissipation and drunkenness and the worries of this life, and that day catch you unexpectedly, like a trap. For it will come upon all who live on the face of the whole earth. Be alert at all times, praying that you may have the strength to escape all these things that will take place, and to stand before the Son of Man."

**Romans 13.11-14**

Besides this, you know what time it is, how it is now the moment for you to wake from sleep. For salvation is nearer to us now than when we became believers; the night is far gone, the day is near. Let us then lay aside the works of darkness and put on the armor of light; let us live honorably as in the day, not in reveling and drunkenness, not in debauchery and licentiousness, not in quarreling and jealousy. Instead, put on the Lord Jesus Christ, and make no provision for the flesh, to gratify its desires.

**Silent or spoken reflection on the readings**

**Song**

You are salt for the earth (H226)

Sleepers, wake (H188)
Sing praise to God who reigns (H59)
Maranatha, come (SS2)

**Mary's song**

## Call to intercession

We seek you, Lord, while you may be found,
***we call upon you while you are near.***

Restore us, O God; let your face shine, that we may be saved. In your mercy,
***Lord, hear our prayer.***

You teach us your ways. We pray for ourselves and those dear to us.
*(open prayers)*
In your mercy,
***Lord, hear our prayer.***

You are compassionate and merciful. We pray for our community and for our neighbors.
*(open prayers)*
In your mercy,
***Lord, hear our prayer.***

Your day is near. We pray for the church in all places, that we may be faithful in solidarity across generations and geography.
*(open prayers)*

In your mercy,
***Lord, hear our prayer.***

Your glory will appear over the nations. We pray for the world, for our enemies and for those who are in conflict.
*(open prayers)*
In your mercy,
***Lord, hear our prayer.***

We offer you other concerns we carry in our hearts.
*(open prayers)*
In your mercy,
***Lord, hear our prayer.***

Incarnate God,
you fill the deepest blue of world and soul.
Help us to claim the sturdy hope
that Mary held in her heart
and sang out in witness,
that we too may rejoice to be disciples
of the one coming as dawn from on high.
We pray in his name:

***Our Father …***

**Benediction**

***May the God of peace sanctify us entirely;***
***and may our spirit and soul and body***
***be kept sound and blameless***
***at the coming of our Lord Jesus Christ.***

*The one who calls us is faithful,*
*and will do this. Amen.*

# Christmas

## Introduction to the Christmas prayers

The celebration of the birth of Jesus as a separate feast is first recorded early in the fourth century. Both the traditional date of the announcement of Jesus' birth to Mary (March 25) and the winter solstice feast of light seem to have influenced the choice in the West of December 25. The narrative focus was on the birth of Jesus and the adoration of the shepherds; the theological focus was on Jesus as the Light and on the mystery of incarnation. Added soon thereafter were a period of preparation before Christmas (see Advent, above), and after Christmas day a continuation of the narrative (including the slaughter of the innocent children, and Jesus' circumcision) for eleven days, concluding with the celebration of Epiphany on January 6. The latter came to be called the Christmas cycle, parallel to the Easter cycle that had been established. Traditional Protestant practice has made New Year's Eve and New Year's Day services part of the Christmas season.

For the titles, opening sentences, and canticle of the first week of Christmas, we chose Zechariah's poignant song. This hymn articulates a profound hope that human liberation, the dawn breaking from on high, is rooted in the mercy of Israel's God. In company with the Benedictus, Anabaptist spirituality holds humility and justice in paradoxical tension, and this pairing is also reflected in our choice of Christmas readings. The narrative thread from the Gospels of Luke and Matthew reflects Jesus' social status as a refugee child. He and his family are on the move and under duress. The call to praise and the second readings surround this narrative of an implausibly lowly Messianic birth with expressions of God's passion for justice. The God who has compassion for the suffering and attends the poor is the God who offers this child as the hope of the world.

The services and scriptures for the turning of the year provide a change of pace, an opportunity to rest in a contemplative space with considerations of our mortality and the immortal love of God that upholds our frail selves. The central text, reflected in both the frame of the services and the readings, is Jesus' words from the mountain about letting God "clothe" us.

The second week of Christmas moves from the narrative of Jesus' birth to early reflections on the significance of this birth. We chose the powerful Christological hymn of Colossians 1 for the titles, opening sentences, and canticle. The mystery and the joy of incarnation is that the lowly child is also the reconciling fullness of God making peace through the blood of the cross. The primary scripture text for these services is a continuous reading of the word symphony of John 1, with its overture in which the Word becomes flesh and tents among us. That reading is supported by exuberant royal psalms and second readings that remind us that allegiance to and worship of the God who gave us Jesus is our Christmas thanksgiving.

# Blessed are you, Lord

## DECEMBER 24 EVENING

**Opening sentence**

Blessed are you, Lord, the God of Israel,
***you have come to your people***
***and set them free.***

## Call to praise

Emmanuel! God is with us.
***Glory to God in the highest heaven,***
***and on earth, peace, goodwill among people.***

***Glory …***

**Psalm 68.5-12 [4-11]**

O sing to the LORD, make music to God's name;
make a highway for the One who rides on the clouds.
***Rejoice in the LORD, exult before God.***

Father of the orphan, defender of the widow,
such is God in the holy place.
***God gives the lonely a home to live in;***
***and leads the prisoners forth into freedom;***
***but rebels must dwell in a parched land.***

When you went forth, O God, at the head of
your people,
*when you marched across the desert, the earth
trembled,*
the heavens melted at the presence of God,
at the presence of God, Israel's God.
*You poured down, O God, a generous rain;*
*when your people were starved you gave them
new life.*
It was there that your people found a home,
prepared in your goodness, O God, for the
poor.

*The LORD gives the word to the bearers of
good tidings.*

**Thanksgiving**

This is the day you have made, Lord;
*we rejoice and are glad in it.*
*(free prayers of thanksgiving)*
We give thanks to you, Lord, for you are good;
*your steadfast love endures forever. Amen.*

**Song**

Fling wide the door, unbar the gate (H186)
Jubilate Deo omnis terra (H103)
Gloria, gloria, gloria (SS23)

**Confession**

You, O Lord, are a God of justice.
*Blessed are all who wait for you.*

*(silence)*
You wait to be gracious to us;
***you will rise up to show mercy to us. Amen.***

## Call to discipleship

Every generous act of giving,
every perfect gift, is from above.
***It comes down from the Father of lights.***

**Luke 2.1-7**

In those days a decree went out from Emperor Augustus that all the world should be registered. This was the first registration and was taken while Quirinius was governor of Syria. All went to their own towns to be registered. Joseph also went from the town of Nazareth in Galilee to Judea, to the city of David called Bethlehem, because he was descended from the house and family of David. He went to be registered with Mary, to whom he was engaged and who was expecting a child. While they were there, the time came for her to deliver her child. And she gave birth to her firstborn son and wrapped him in bands of cloth, and laid him in a manger, because there was no place for them in the inn.

**2 Corinthians 8.9**

For you know the generous act of our Lord Jesus Christ, that though he was rich, yet for your sakes he became poor, so that by his poverty you might become rich.

**Silent or spoken reflection on the readings**

**Song**

From heaven above to earth I come (H205)
Where is this stupendous Stranger (H200)
O little town of Bethlehem (H191)
Hacia Belén se en caminan (Walking slowly unto Bethl'em) (SS20)
Oh, how joyfully (H209)

**Zechariah's song**

## Call to intercession

O God, you grant justice to your chosen ones, who cry to you day and night,
***so we pray always, and do not lose heart.***

Generous God, you come among us bringing peace to earth. In your mercy,
***Lord, hear our prayer.***

You come to us in humility. We pray for ourselves and those dear to us.
*(open prayers)*

In your mercy,
***Lord, hear our prayer.***

In your goodness you prepare a home for the poor. We pray for our community and for our neighbors.
*(open prayers)*
In your mercy,
***Lord, hear our prayer.***

You became poor so that we may be rich. We pray for the church in all places, that we may be one.
*(open prayers)*
In your mercy,
***Lord, hear our prayer.***

You give new life to those who are starving. We pray for the world, that your reign may come and your will be done on earth.
*(open prayers)*
In your mercy,
***Lord, hear our prayer.***

We offer you other concerns we carry in our hearts.
*(open prayers)*
In your mercy,
***Lord, hear our prayer.***

God of prophetic promise,
your radiance penetrates our wintry night.

Come to us in tender compassion,
that we too may walk the path of peace
in holiness and without fear.
We pray in the name of the One
whose birth a heavenly host heralded:

*Our Father ...*

**Benediction**

*May God strengthen us*
*according to the proclamation of Jesus Christ,*
*according to the revelation of the mystery*
*that was kept secret for long ages*
*but is now disclosed. Amen.*

# You have come to your people

## DECEMBER 25 MORNING

**Opening sentence**

Blessed are you, Lord, the God of Israel,
*you have come to your people*
*and set them free.*

## Call to praise

The Word became flesh and lived among us,
full of grace and truth.
*In him was life,*
*and the life was the light of all.*

*Glory ...*

**Ezekiel 34.25-28**

I will make with them a covenant of peace
and banish wild animals from the land,
*so that they may live in the wild*
*and sleep in the woods securely.*
I will make them and the region around my
hill a blessing;
*and I will send down the showers in their season;*
*they shall be showers of blessing.*
The trees of the field shall yield their fruit,
and the earth shall yield its increase.

***They shall be secure on their soil;***
***and they shall know that I am the LORD,***
when I break the bars of their yoke,
and save them from the hands
of those who enslaved them.
***They shall no more be plunder for the nations,***
***nor shall the animals of the land devour them;***
they shall live in safety,
***and no one shall make them afraid.***

### Thanksgiving

We remember your great goodness to us, Lord.
***It was no messenger or angel***
***but your very presence that saved us.***
*(free prayers of thanksgiving)*
In love and pity you redeemed us;
***you lift us up and carry us all our days. Amen.***

### Song

Let our gladness have no end (H198)
Gloria, gloria, gloria (SS23)
Alleluia (SJ41)
O Savior, rend the heavens (H175)
To us a Child of hope is born (H189)

## Call to discipleship

Beloved, let us love one another,
because love is from God;

*everyone who loves is born of God*
*and knows God.*

**Luke 2.8-14**

In that region there were shepherds living in the fields, keeping watch over their flock by night. Then an angel of the Lord stood before them, and the glory of the Lord shone around them, and they were terrified. But the angel said to them, "Do not be afraid; for see—I am bringing you good news of great joy for all the people: to you is born this day in the city of David a Savior, who is the Messiah, the Lord. This will be a sign for you: you will find a child wrapped in bands of cloth and lying in a manger." And suddenly there was with the angel a multitude of the heavenly host, praising God and saying,

"Glory to God in the highest heaven,
and on earth peace among those whom he
favors!"

**1 John 4.7-12**

Beloved, let us love one another, because love is from God; everyone who loves is born of God and knows God. Whoever does not love does not know God, for God is love. God's love was revealed among us in this way: God sent his only Son into the world so that we might live through him. In this is love, not that we loved God but that he loved us and sent his Son to be the atoning sacrifice for our sins. Beloved, since God loved us so much, we also ought to love one another. No one has ever seen God; if we love one another, God lives in us, and his love is perfected in us.

**Silent or spoken reflection on the readings**

**Song**

Break forth, O beauteous heavenly (H203)
While shepherds watched (H196)
Holy Child within the manger (SS28)
Hark! the herald angels sing (H201)
Gloria (H204)

**Zechariah's song**

## Call to intercession

Lord, you fulfill the desire of all who fear you;
***you hear their cry, and save them.***

Incarnate God, you comfort your people and have compassion on your suffering ones. In your mercy,
***Lord, hear our prayer.***

You live in us when we love one another. We pray for ourselves and those dear to us.
*(open prayers)*

In your mercy,
***Lord, hear our prayer.***

You bring good news of great joy. We pray for our community and for our neighbors.
*(open prayers)*
In your mercy,
***Lord, hear our prayer.***

You establish your covenant of peace. We pray for the church in all places, that we may know the freedom of life in the Spirit.
*(open prayers)*
In your mercy,
***Lord, hear our prayer.***

You will judge the peoples with truth. We pray for the world and for all who care for creation.
*(open prayers)*
In your mercy,
***Lord, hear our prayer.***

We offer you other concerns we carry in our hearts.
*(open prayers)*
In your mercy,
***Lord, hear our prayer.***

God of breaking dawn,
you dance the earth into day.
Grant us that awareness of forgiveness
with which Zechariah ended his silence,

that we too might rejoice
to proclaim the good news of your salvation.
We pray in the name of the Messiah
who came to set us free:

*Our Father ...*

**Benediction**

*May grace and peace be ours in abundance
in the knowledge of God
and of Jesus our Lord. Amen.*

# You have raised up for us a mighty Savior

## DECEMBER 25 EVENING

**Opening sentence**

You have raised up for us a mighty Savior,
***born of the house of your servant David.***

## Call to praise

Emmanuel! God is with us.
***Glory to God in the highest heaven,***
***and on earth, peace, goodwill among people.***

*Glory ...*

**Psalm 96**

O sing a new song to the LORD,
sing to the LORD all the earth.
O sing to the LORD, bless his name.

***Proclaim God's help day by day,***
***tell among the nations his glory***
***and his wonders among all the peoples.***

The LORD is great and worthy of praise,
to be feared above all gods;
the gods of the heathens are naught.

***It was the LORD who made the heavens,***
***his are majesty and honor and power***
***and splendor in the holy place.***

Give the LORD, you families of peoples,
give the LORD glory and power;
give the LORD the glory of his name.

***Bring an offering and enter God's courts,***
***worship the LORD in the temple.***
***O earth, stand in fear of the LORD.***

Proclaim to the nations: "God is king."
The world was made firm in its place;
God will judge the people in fairness.

***Let the heavens rejoice and earth be glad,***
***let the sea and all within it thunder praise,***
let the land and all it bears rejoice,
all the trees of the wood shout for joy

***at the presence of the LORD who comes,***
***who comes to rule the earth,***
comes with justice to rule the world,
***and to judge the peoples with truth.***

**Thanksgiving**

This is the day you have made, Lord;
***we rejoice and are glad in it.***
*(free prayers of thanksgiving)*
We give thanks to you, Lord, for you are good;
***your steadfast love endures forever. Amen.***

**Song**

Great is the Lord (H87)
On this day earth shall ring (H192)
Let all together praise our God (H213)
Alleluia (SS24)

**Confession**

You, O Lord, are a God of justice.
***Blessed are all who wait for you.***
*(silence)*
You wait to be gracious to us;
***you will rise up to show mercy to us. Amen.***

## Call to discipleship

Every generous act of giving,
every perfect gift, is from above.
***It comes down from the Father of lights.***

**Luke 2.15-20**

When the angels had left them and gone into heaven, the shepherds said to one another, "Let us go now to Bethlehem and see this thing that has taken place, which the Lord has made known to us." So they went with haste and found Mary and Joseph, and the child lying in the manger. When they saw this, they made known what had been told them about this child; and all who heard it were amazed at what the shepherds told them. But Mary treasured all these words and pondered them in her heart. The shepherds returned, glorifying and praising God for all they had heard and seen, as it had been told them.

**Micah 5.2**

But you, O Bethlehem of Ephrathah,
who are one of the little clans of Judah,
from you shall come forth for me
one who is to rule in Israel,
whose origin is from of old, from ancient days.

**Silent or spoken reflection on the readings**

**Song**

Jesus, Jesus, oh, what a wonderful child (SS19)
A stable lamp is lighted (SS25)
Niño lindo (Child so lovely) (H207)
Gloria, gloria, gloria (SS23)

**Zechariah's song**

## Call to intercession

O God, you grant justice to your chosen ones, who cry to you day and night,
***so we pray always, and do not lose heart.***

Incarnate God, you come among us bringing peace to earth. In your mercy,
***Lord, hear our prayer.***

You live in us when we love one another. We pray for ourselves and those dear to us.
*(open prayers)*
In your mercy,
***Lord, hear our prayer.***

You bring good news of great joy. We pray for our community and for our neighbors.
*(open prayers)*
In your mercy,
***Lord, hear our prayer.***

You establish your covenant of peace. We pray for the church in all places, that we may know the freedom of life in the Spirit.
*(open prayers)*
In your mercy,
***Lord, hear our prayer.***

You will judge the peoples with truth. We pray for the world and for all who care for creation.
*(open prayers)*
In your mercy,
***Lord, hear our prayer.***

We offer you other concerns we carry in our hearts.
*(open prayers)*
In your mercy,
***Lord, hear our prayer.***

God of prophetic promise,
your radiance penetrates our wintry night.
Come to us in tender compassion,
that we too may walk the path of peace
in holiness and without fear.
We pray in the name of the One
whose birth a heavenly host heralded:

*Our Father ...*

**Benediction**

*May God strengthen us*
*according to the proclamation of Jesus Christ,*
*according to the revelation of the mystery*
*that was kept secret for long ages*
*but is now disclosed. Amen.*

# You promised of old to save us

## DECEMBER 26 MORNING

**Opening sentence**

Through your holy prophets,
you promised of old
to save us from our enemies,
***from the hands of all who hate us.***

## Call to praise

The Word became flesh and lived among us,
full of grace and truth.
***In him was life,***
***and the life was the light of all.***

***Glory …***

**Micah 4.6-10**

In that day, says the LORD,
I will assemble the lame
***and gather those who have been driven away,***
***and those whom I have afflicted.***
The lame I will make the remnant,
and those who were cast off, a strong nation;
***and the LORD will reign over them in Mount Zion***
***now and forevermore.***

And you, O tower of the flock,
hill of daughter Zion,
to you it shall come,
***the former dominion shall come,***
***the sovereignty of daughter Jerusalem.***

Now why do you cry aloud?
Is there no king in you?
***Has your counselor perished,***
***that pangs have seized you like a woman in labor?***
Writhe and groan, O daughter Zion,
like a woman in labor;
***for now you shall go forth from the city***
***and camp in the open country;***
you shall go to Babylon.
There you shall be rescued,
***there the LORD will redeem you***
***from the hands of your enemies.***

**Thanksgiving**

We remember your great goodness to us, Lord.
***It was no messenger or angel***
***but your very presence that saved us.***
*(free prayers of thanksgiving)*
In love and pity you redeemed us;
***you lift us up and carry us all our days. Amen.***

**Song**

Arise, your light is come! (SS30)
How brightly beams the morning (H222)

Alleluia (SS24)
To us a Child of hope is born (H189)

## Call to discipleship

Beloved, let us love one another,
because love is from God;
***everyone who loves is born of God***
***and knows God.***

**Luke 2.21-24**

After eight days had passed, it was time to circumcise the child; and he was called Jesus, the name given by the angel before he was conceived in the womb.

When the time came for their purification according to the law of Moses, they brought him up to Jerusalem to present him to the Lord (as it is written in the law of the Lord, "Every firstborn male shall be designated as holy to the Lord"), and they offered a sacrifice according to what is stated in the law of the Lord, "a pair of turtledoves or two young pigeons."

**Exodus 13.1-2, 11-16**

The Lord said to Moses: Consecrate to me all the firstborn; whatever is the first to open the womb among the Israelites, of human beings and animals, is mine. Moses said to the people, …

"When the LORD has brought you into the land of the Canaanites, as he swore to you and your ancestors, and has given it to you, you shall set apart to the LORD all that first opens the womb. All the firstborn of your livestock that are males shall be the LORD's. But every firstborn donkey you shall redeem with a sheep; if you do not redeem it, you must break its neck. Every firstborn male among your children you shall redeem. When in the future your child asks you, 'What does this mean?' you shall answer, 'By strength of hand the LORD brought us out of Egypt, from the house of slavery. When Pharaoh stubbornly refused to let us go, the LORD killed all the firstborn in the land of Egypt, from human firstborn to the firstborn of animals. Therefore I sacrifice to the LORD every male that first opens the womb, but every firstborn of my sons I redeem.' It shall serve as a sign on your hand and as an emblem on your forehead that by strength of hand the LORD brought us out of Egypt."

**Silent or spoken reflection on the readings**

**Song**

Lord of all good (SJ60)

Heart and mind, possessions, Lord (H392)
As saints of old (H386)

**Zechariah's song**

## Call to intercession

Lord, you fulfill the desire of all who fear you;
***you hear their cry, and save them.***

Faithful God, you comfort your people and have compassion on your suffering ones. In your mercy,
***Lord, hear our prayer.***

In you is life, the light of all people. We pray for ourselves and those dear to us.
*(open prayers)*
In your mercy,
***Lord, hear our prayer.***

You gather those who have been driven away. We pray for our community and for our neighbors.
*(open prayers)*
In your mercy,
***Lord, hear our prayer.***

You have given your people as a light for the nations. We pray for the church in all places, that we may reflect your faithful love.
*(open prayers)*

In your mercy,
***Lord, hear our prayer.***

You have made known your salvation. We pray for the world, for those who are in need.
*(open prayers)*
In your mercy,
***Lord, hear our prayer.***

We offer you other concerns we carry in our hearts.
*(open prayers)*
In your mercy,
***Lord, hear our prayer.***

God of breaking dawn,
you dance the earth into day.
Grant us that awareness of forgiveness
with which Zechariah ended his silence,
that we too might rejoice
to proclaim the good news of your salvation.
We pray in the name of the Messiah
who came to set us free:

***Our Father …***

**Benediction**

***May grace and peace be ours in abundance***
***in the knowledge of God***
***and of Jesus our Lord. Amen.***

# You promised of old to show mercy

## DECEMBER 26 EVENING

**Opening sentence**

Through your holy prophets,
you promised of old
to save us from our enemies,
from the hands of all who hate us,
***to show mercy to our forebears,***
***and to remember your holy covenant.***

## Call to praise

Emmanuel! God is with us.
***Glory to God in the highest heaven,***
***and on earth, peace, goodwill among people.***

***Glory …***

**Isaiah 30.18-21**

Therefore the LORD waits to be gracious to you;
therefore he will rise up to show mercy to you.
***For the LORD is a God of justice;***
***blessed are all those who wait for him.***

Truly, O people in Zion, inhabitants of
Jerusalem,
you shall weep no more.

***He will surely be gracious to you at the sound of your cry;***
***when he hears it, he will answer you.***
Though the Lord may give you the bread of adversity
and the water of affliction,
***yet your Teacher will not hide himself any more,***
***but your eyes shall see your Teacher.***
And when you turn to the right
or when you turn to the left,
***your ears shall hear a word behind you,***
***saying, "This is the way; walk in it."***

## Thanksgiving

This is the day you have made, Lord;
***we rejoice and are glad in it.***
*(free prayers of thanksgiving)*
We give thanks to you, Lord, for you are good;
***your steadfast love endures forever. Amen.***

## Song

Come! Walk in the light (SS10, with verses)
Abre mis ojos (Open my eyes) (SS65)
Som'landela (We will follow) (SS40)
Sizohamba naye (We will walk with God) (SJ78)

## Confession

You, O Lord, are a God of justice.
***Blessed are all who wait for you.***

*(silence)*
You wait to be gracious to us;
***you will rise up to show mercy to us. Amen.***

## Call to discipleship

Every generous act of giving,
every perfect gift, is from above.
***It comes down from the Father of lights.***

**Luke 2.25-32**

Now there was a man in Jerusalem whose name was Simeon; this man was righteous and devout, looking forward to the consolation of Israel, and the Holy Spirit rested on him. It had been revealed to him by the Holy Spirit that he would not see death before he had seen the Lord's Messiah. Guided by the Spirit, Simeon came into the temple; and when the parents brought in the child Jesus, to do for him what was customary under the law, Simeon took him in his arms and praised God, saying,

"Master, now you are dismissing your servant in peace,
according to your word;
for my eyes have seen your salvation,
which you have prepared in the presence of all peoples,

a light for revelation to the Gentiles
and for glory to your people Israel."

**Isaiah 42.6-9**

I am the LORD, I have called you in righteousness,
I have taken you by the hand and kept you;
I have given you as a covenant to the people,
a light to the nations,
to open the eyes that are blind,
to bring out the prisoners from the dungeon,
from the prison those who sit in darkness.
I am the LORD, that is my name;
my glory I give to no other,
nor my praise to idols.
See, the former things have come to pass,
and new things I now declare;
before they spring forth,
I tell you of them.

**Silent or spoken reflection on the readings**

**Song**

I will come to you in the silence (SS49)
My soul cries out (SS124)
O God, who gives us life (H483)

**Zechariah's song**

## Call to intercession

O God, you grant justice to your chosen ones,
who cry to you day and night,
***so we pray always, and do not lose heart.***

Faithful God, you come among us bringing peace to earth. In your mercy,
***Lord, hear our prayer.***

In you is life, the light of all people. We pray for ourselves and those dear to us.
*(open prayers)*
In your mercy,
***Lord, hear our prayer.***

You gather those who have been driven away. We pray for our community and for our neighbors.
*(open prayers)*
In your mercy,
***Lord, hear our prayer.***

You have given your people as a light for the nations. We pray for the church in all places, that we may reflect your faithful love.
*(open prayers)*
In your mercy,
***Lord, hear our prayer.***

You have made known your salvation. We pray for the world, for those who are in need.

*(open prayers)*
In your mercy,
***Lord, hear our prayer.***

We offer you other concerns we carry in our hearts.
*(open prayers)*
In your mercy,
***Lord, hear our prayer.***

God of prophetic promise,
your radiance penetrates our wintry night.
Come to us in tender compassion,
that we too may walk the path of peace
in holiness and without fear.
We pray in the name of the One
whose birth a heavenly host heralded:

***Our Father …***

**Benediction**

***May God strengthen us
according to the proclamation of Jesus Christ,
according to the revelation of the mystery
that was kept secret for long ages
but is now disclosed. Amen.***

# You swore an oath to set us free

## DECEMBER 27 MORNING

**Opening sentence**

This was the oath you swore
to our father Abraham:
***to set us free from the hands of our enemies.***

## Call to praise

The Word became flesh and lived among us,
full of grace and truth.
***In him was life,***
***and the life was the light of all.***

***Glory …***

**Psalm 102.16-23 [15-22]**

The nations shall fear the name of the LORD
and all the earth's kings your glory,
***when the LORD shall build up Zion again***
***and appear resplendent in glory.***
The LORD will turn to the prayers of the helpless;
and will not despise their prayers.

***Let this be written for ages to come***
***that a people yet unborn may praise the LORD;***

for the LORD leaned down from the sanctuary
on high,
and looked down from heaven to the earth
***in order to hear the groans of the prisoners***
***and free those condemned to die.***

Our descendants shall dwell untroubled
***and our children endure before you***
that the name of the LORD may be proclaimed
in Zion
and God's praise in the heart of Jerusalem,
***when peoples and kingdoms are gathered***
***together***
***to pay their homage to the LORD.***

**Thanksgiving**

We remember your great goodness to us, Lord.
***It was no messenger or angel***
***but your very presence that saved us.***
*(free prayers of thanksgiving)*
In love and pity you redeemed us;
***you lift us up and carry us all our days. Amen.***

**Song**

Sing praise to God who reigns (H59)
Praise the One who breaks the darkness (SS1)
It came upon a midnight clear (H195)
Glorious things of thee are spoken (H619)

## Call to discipleship

Beloved, let us love one another,
because love is from God;
***everyone who loves is born of God***
***and knows God.***

**Luke 2.33-35**

And the child [Jesus'] father and mother were amazed at what was being said about him. Then Simeon blessed them and said to his mother Mary, "This child is destined for the falling and the rising of many in Israel, and to be a sign that will be opposed so that the inner thoughts of many will be revealed—and a sword will pierce your own soul too."

**Isaiah 49.6**

[The LORD] says,
"It is too light a thing that you should be my servant
to raise up the tribes of Jacob
and to restore the survivors of Israel;
I will give you as a light to the nations,
that my salvation may reach to the end of the earth."

**Silent or spoken reflection on the readings**

**Song**

The Lord is my light (SJ97)
Christ is the world's true light (H334)
A stable lamp is lighted (SS25)
Joyful is the dark (H233)

**Zechariah's song**

## Call to intercession

Lord, you fulfill the desire of all who fear you;
***you hear their cry, and save them.***

Protecting God, you comfort your people and have compassion on your suffering ones. In your mercy,
***Lord, hear our prayer.***

You call us to trust and not be afraid. We pray for ourselves and those dear to us.
*(open prayers)*
In your mercy,
***Lord, hear our prayer.***

You strengthen the hearts of the poor. We pray for our community and for our neighbors.
*(open prayers)*
In your mercy,
***Lord, hear our prayer.***

In your love and pity you have redeemed your people. We pray for the church in all places,

that we may bear witness to your reign of justice, peace, and joy.
*(open prayers)*
In your mercy,
***Lord, hear our prayer.***

You establish equity and justice. We pray for the world, for all who are ensnared in greed, violence, and oppression.
*(open prayers)*
In your mercy,
***Lord, hear our prayer.***

We offer you other concerns we carry in our hearts.
*(open prayers)*
In your mercy,
***Lord, hear our prayer.***

God of breaking dawn,
you dance the earth into day.
Grant us that awareness of forgiveness
with which Zechariah ended his silence,
that we too might rejoice
to proclaim the good news of your salvation.
We pray in the name of the Messiah
who came to set us free:

***Our Father …***

**Benediction**

*May grace and peace be ours in abundance*
*in the knowledge of God*
*and of Jesus our Lord. Amen.*

# Free to worship you without fear

DECEMBER 27 EVENING

**Opening sentence**

This was the oath you swore
to our father Abraham:
to set us free from the hands of our enemies.
***free to worship you without fear,***
***holy and righteous before you,***
***all the days of our life.***

## Call to praise

Emmanuel! God is with us.
***Glory to God in the highest heaven,***
***and on earth, peace, goodwill among people.***

***Glory ...***

**Isaiah 63.7-9**

I will recount the gracious deeds of the LORD,
the praiseworthy acts of the LORD,
***because of all that the LORD has done for us,***
***and the great favor to the house of Israel***
that he has shown them according to his mercy,
according to the abundance of his steadfast love.

*For he said, "Surely they are my people,*
*children who will not deal falsely";*
*and he became their savior in all their distress.*
It was no messenger or angel
but his presence that saved them;
*in his love and in his pity he redeemed them;*
*he lifted them up and carried them all the days of old.*

### Thanksgiving

This is the day you have made, Lord;
*we rejoice and are glad in it.*
*(free prayers of thanksgiving)*
We give thanks to you, Lord, for you are good;
*your steadfast love endures forever. Amen.*

### Song

For God so loved us (H167)
We would extol thee (H74)
Who is so great a God (H62)
Had God brought us out (SS96)

### Confession

You, O Lord, are a God of justice.
*Blessed are all who wait for you.*
*(silence)*
You wait to be gracious to us;
*you will rise up to show mercy to us. Amen.*

## Call to discipleship

Every generous act of giving,
every perfect gift, is from above.
***It comes down from the Father of lights.***

**Luke 2.36-38**

There was also a prophet, Anna the daughter of Phanuel, of the tribe of Asher. She was of a great age, having lived with her husband for seven years after her marriage, then as a widow to the age of eighty-four. She never left the temple but worshiped there with fasting and prayer night and day. At that moment she came, and began to praise God and to speak about the child to all who were looking for the redemption of Jerusalem.

**Isaiah 12.1-2**

You will say in that day:
I will give thanks to you, O LORD,
for though you were angry with me,
your anger turned away,
and you comforted me.
Surely God is my salvation;
I will trust, and will not be afraid,
for the LORD GOD is my strength and my
  might;
he has become my salvation.

**Silent or spoken reflection on the readings**

**Song**

Lo, how a Rose e'er blooming (H211)
Worship the Lord in the beauty (H220)
To us a Child of hope is born (H189)
Peace before us (SS16)

**Zechariah's song**

## Call to intercession

O God, you grant justice to your chosen ones, who cry to you day and night,
***so we pray always, and do not lose heart.***

Protecting God, you come among us bringing peace to earth. In your mercy,
***Lord, hear our prayer.***

You call us to trust and not be afraid. We pray for ourselves and those dear to us.
*(open prayers)*
In your mercy,
***Lord, hear our prayer.***

You strengthen the hearts of the poor. We pray for our community and for our neighbors.
*(open prayers)*
In your mercy,
***Lord, hear our prayer.***

In your love and pity you have redeemed your people. We pray for the church in all places, that we may bear witness to your reign of justice, peace, and joy.
*(open prayers)*
In your mercy,
***Lord, hear our prayer.***

You establish equity and justice. We pray for the world, for all who are ensnared in greed, violence, and oppression.
*(open prayers)*
In your mercy,
***Lord, hear our prayer.***

We offer you other concerns we carry in our hearts.
*(open prayers)*
In your mercy,
***Lord, hear our prayer.***

God of prophetic promise,
your radiance penetrates our wintry night.
Come to us in tender compassion,
that we too may walk the path of peace
in holiness and without fear.
We pray in the name of the One
whose birth a heavenly host heralded:

***Our Father …***

**Benediction**

*May God strengthen us*
*according to the proclamation of Jesus Christ,*
*according to the revelation of the mystery*
*that was kept secret for long ages*
*but is now disclosed. Amen.*

# You, child, shall be called prophet

## DECEMBER 28 MORNING

**Opening sentence**

And you, child, shall be called
the prophet of the Most High,
***for you will go before the Lord***
***to prepare the way.***

## Call to praise

The Word became flesh and lived among us,
full of grace and truth.
***In him was life,***
***and the life was the light of all.***

***Glory …***

**Psalm 114**

Alleluia!

When Israel came forth from Egypt,
Jacob's family from an alien people,
***Judah became the LORD's temple,***
***Israel became God's kingdom.***

The sea fled at the sight,
the Jordan turned back on its course,

***the mountains leapt like rams***
***and the hills like yearling sheep.***

Why was it, sea, that you fled,
that you turned back, Jordan, on your course?
***Mountains, that you leapt like rams;***
***hills, like yearling sheep?***

Tremble, O earth, before the LORD,
in the presence of the God of Jacob,
***who turns the rock into a pool***
***and flint into a spring of water.***

**Thanksgiving**

We remember your great goodness to us, Lord.
***It was no messenger or angel***
***but your very presence that saved us.***
*(free prayers of thanksgiving)*
In love and pity you redeemed us;
***you lift us up and carry us all our days. Amen.***

**Song**

Let all creation bless the Lord (H61)
Alleluia (SS24)
Praise, praise, praise the Lord! (SJ11)
Oh, that I had a thousand voices (H84)
Gloria, gloria, gloria (SS23)

## Call to discipleship

Beloved, let us love one another,
because love is from God;
***everyone who loves is born of God***
***and knows God.***

**Matthew 2.13-15**

Now after [the wise men] had left, an angel of the Lord appeared to Joseph in a dream and said, "Get up, take the child and his mother, and flee to Egypt, and remain there until I tell you; for Herod is about to search for the child, to destroy him." Then Joseph got up, took the child and his mother by night, and went to Egypt, and remained there until the death of Herod. This was to fulfill what had been spoken by the Lord through the prophet, "Out of Egypt I have called my son."

**Isaiah 49.13-15**

Sing for joy, O heavens, and exult, O earth;
break forth, O mountains, into singing!
For the LORD has comforted his people,
and will have compassion on his suffering
ones.

But Zion said, "The LORD has forsaken me,
my Lord has forgotten me.'
Can a woman forget her nursing child,

or show no compassion for the child of her
womb?
Even these may forget,
yet I will not forget you."

**Silent or spoken reflection on the readings**

**Song**

Don't be afraid (SJ105)
Love came down at Christmas (H208)
What Child is this (H215)
Sing a different song (SS27)

**Zechariah's song**

## Call to intercession

Lord, you fulfill the desire of all who fear you;
***you hear their cry, and save them.***

God of promises, you comfort your people and have compassion on your suffering ones. In your mercy,
***Lord, hear our prayer.***

You see not our outward appearance but our hearts. We pray for ourselves and those dear to us.
*(open prayers)*
In your mercy,
***Lord, hear our prayer.***

You promise hope for the future. We pray for our community and for our neighbors.
*(open prayers)*
In your mercy,
***Lord, hear our prayer.***

You have comforted your people. We pray for the church in all places, that we may daily follow in the footsteps of Christ.
*(open prayers)*
In your mercy,
***Lord, hear our prayer.***

You turn rocks and flint into springs and pools of water. We pray for the world, for those in positions of power and authority.
*(open prayers)*
In your mercy,
***Lord, hear our prayer.***

We offer you other concerns we carry in our hearts.
*(open prayers)*
In your mercy,
***Lord, hear our prayer.***

God of breaking dawn,
you dance the earth into day.
Grant us that awareness of forgiveness
with which Zechariah ended his silence,
that we too might rejoice
to proclaim the good news of your salvation.

We pray in the name of the Messiah
who came to set us free:

*Our Father ...*

**Benediction**

*May grace and peace be ours in abundance
in the knowledge of God
and of Jesus our Lord. Amen.*

# You will go before the Lord

DECEMBER 28 EVENING

**Opening sentence**

And you, child, shall be called
the prophet of the Most High,
***for you will go before the Lord***
***to prepare the way.***

## Call to praise

Emmanuel! God is with us.
***Glory to God in the highest heaven,***
***and on earth, peace, goodwill among people.***

***Glory …***

**Jeremiah 31.15-17**

Thus says the LORD:
A voice is heard in Ramah,
lamentation and bitter weeping.
***Rachel is weeping for her children;***
***she refuses to be comforted for her children,***
***because they are no more.***
Thus says the LORD:
Keep your voice from weeping,
and your eyes from tears;
for there is a reward for your work, says the
LORD:

***they shall come back from the land of the enemy;***
***there is hope for your future, says the Lord:***
***your children shall come back to their own country.***

**Thanksgiving**

This is the day you have made, Lord;
***we rejoice and are glad in it.***
*(free prayers of thanksgiving)*
We give thanks to you, Lord, for you are good;
***your steadfast love endures forever. Amen.***

**Song**

Comfort, comfort, O my people (H176)
All will be well (SJ98)
Sizohamba naye (We will walk with God) (SJ78)

**Confession**

You, O Lord, are a God of justice.
***Blessed are all who wait for you.***
*(silence)*
You wait to be gracious to us;
***you will rise up to show mercy to us. Amen.***

## Call to discipleship

Every generous act of giving,
every perfect gift, is from above.
***It comes down from the Father of lights.***

**Matthew 2.16-18**

When Herod saw that he had been tricked by the wise men, he was infuriated, and he sent and killed all the children in and around Bethlehem who were two years old or under, according to the time that he had learned from the wise men. Then was fulfilled what had been spoken through the prophet Jeremiah:

"A voice was heard in Ramah,
wailing and loud lamentation,
Rachel weeping for her children;
she refused to be consoled, because they
are no more."

**1 Peter 4.12-19**

Beloved, do not be surprised at the fiery ordeal that is taking place among you to test you, as though something strange were happening to you. But rejoice insofar as you are sharing Christ's sufferings, so that you may also be glad and shout for joy when his glory is revealed. If you are reviled for the name of Christ, you are blessed, because the spirit of glory, which is the Spirit of God, is resting on you. But let none of you suffer as a murderer, a thief, a criminal, or even as a mischief maker. Yet if any of you suffers as a Christian, do not consider it a disgrace, but glorify God because you bear this name. For the time has come for judgment to begin with the household of God; if it begins with us, what will be the end for those who do not obey the gospel of God? And

"If it is hard for the righteous to be saved,
what will become of the ungodly and the
sinners?"

Therefore, let those suffering in accordance with God's will entrust themselves to a faithful Creator, while continuing to do good.

**Silent or spoken reflection on the readings**

**Song**

Living and dying with Jesus (H550)
Nada te turbe (H562)
What Child is this (H215)
If you but trust in God (H576, vv. 1, 3, 4)

**Zechariah's song**

## Call to intercession

O God, you grant justice to your chosen ones,
who cry to you day and night,
***so we pray always, and do not lose heart.***

God of promises, you come among us bringing peace to earth. In your mercy,
***Lord, hear our prayer.***

You see not our outward appearance but our hearts. We pray for ourselves and those dear to us.
*(open prayers)*
In your mercy,
***Lord, hear our prayer.***

You promise hope for the future. We pray for our community and for our neighbors.
*(open prayers)*
In your mercy,
***Lord, hear our prayer.***

You have comforted your people. We pray for the church in all places, that we may daily follow in the footsteps of Christ.
*(open prayers)*
In your mercy,
***Lord, hear our prayer.***

You turn rocks and flint into springs and pools of water. We pray for the world, for those in positions of power and authority.
*(open prayers)*
In your mercy,
***Lord, hear our prayer.***

We offer you other concerns we carry in our hearts.
*(open prayers)*
In your mercy,
***Lord, hear our prayer.***

God of prophetic promise,
your radiance penetrates our wintry night.
Come to us in tender compassion,
that we too may walk the path of peace
in holiness and without fear.
We pray in the name of the One
whose birth a heavenly host heralded:

***Our Father …***

**Benediction**

***May God strengthen us***
***according to the proclamation of Jesus Christ,***
***according to the revelation of the mystery***
***that was kept secret for long ages***
***but is now disclosed. Amen.***

# You will go before the Lord to give knowledge of salvation

## DECEMBER 29 MORNING

**Opening sentence**

You will go before the Lord
to prepare the way,
***to give God's people knowledge of salvation***
***by the forgiveness of their sins.***

## Call to praise

The Word became flesh and lived among us,
full of grace and truth.
***In him was life,***
***and the life was the light of all.***

***Glory ...***

**Psalm 85.2-8 [1-7]**

O LORD, you once favored your land
and revived the fortunes of Jacob,
***you forgave the guilt of your people***
***and covered all their sins.***
You averted all your rage,
you calmed the heat of your anger.

***Revive us now, God, our helper!***
***Put an end to your grievance against us.***

Will you be angry with us for ever,
will your anger never cease?

***Will you not restore again our life***
***that your people may rejoice in you?***
Let us see, O LORD, your mercy
***and give us your saving help.***

**Thanksgiving**

We remember your great goodness to us, Lord.
***It was no messenger or angel***
***but your very presence that saved us.***
*(free prayers of thanksgiving)*
In love and pity you redeemed us;
***you lift us up and carry us all our days. Amen.***

**Song**

You are all we have (SJ29)
Save us, O Lord (SS6, v. 1)
O bless the Lord, my soul (H600)

## Call to discipleship

Beloved, let us love one another,
because love is from God;
***everyone who loves is born of God***
***and knows God.***

**Matthew 2.19-23**

When Herod died, an angel of the Lord suddenly appeared in a dream to Joseph in Egypt and said, "Get up, take the child and his mother, and go to the land of Israel, for those who were seeking the child's life are dead." Then Joseph got up, took the child and his mother, and went to the land of Israel. But when he heard that Archelaus was ruling over Judea in place of his father Herod, he was afraid to go there. And after being warned in a dream, he went away to the district of Galilee. There he made his home in a town called Nazareth, so that what had been spoken through the prophets might be fulfilled, "He will be called a Nazorean."

**Ephesians 1.3-10**

Blessed be the God and Father of our Lord Jesus Christ, who has blessed us in Christ with every spiritual blessing in the heavenly places, just as he chose us in Christ before the foundation of the world to be holy and blameless before him in love. He destined us for adoption as his children through Jesus Christ, according to the good pleasure of his will, to the praise of his glorious grace that he freely bestowed on us in the Beloved. In him we have redemption through his blood, the forgiveness of our trespasses, according to the riches of his grace that he lavished on us. With all wisdom and insight he has made known to us the mystery of his will, according to his good pleasure that he set forth in Christ, as a plan for the fullness of time, to gather up all things in him, things in heaven and things on earth.

**Silent or spoken reflection on the readings**

**Song**

Hark! the herald angels sing (H201)
Holy Child within the manger (SS28)
If Christ is mine (H331)

**Zechariah's song**

## Call to intercession

Lord, you fulfill the desire of all who fear you;
***you hear their cry, and save them.***

Saving God, you comfort your people and have compassion on your suffering ones. In your mercy,
***Lord, hear our prayer.***

You call us to live in harmony and love. We pray for ourselves and those dear to us.
*(open prayers)*
In your mercy,
***Lord, hear our prayer.***

You reach out in tender compassion. We pray for our community and for our neighbors.

*(open prayers)*
In your mercy,
***Lord, hear our prayer.***

You equip your people for our struggle. We pray for the church in all places, that we may speak boldly for Christ.
*(open prayers)*
In your mercy,
***Lord, hear our prayer.***

You come with justice to rule the world. We pray for the world, for all who do justice and love mercy.
*(open prayers)*
In your mercy,
***Lord, hear our prayer.***

We offer you other concerns we carry in our hearts.
*(open prayers)*
In your mercy,
***Lord, hear our prayer.***

God of breaking dawn,
you dance the earth into day.
Grant us that awareness of forgiveness
with which Zechariah ended his silence,
that we too might rejoice
to proclaim the good news of your salvation.
We pray in the name of the Messiah
who came to set us free:

*Our Father ...*

**Benediction**

*May grace and peace be ours in abundance*
*in the knowledge of God*
*and of Jesus our Lord. Amen.*

# The dawn from on high shall break

## DECEMBER 29 EVENING

**Opening sentence**

In the tender compassion of our God
***the dawn from on high shall break upon us.***

## Call to praise

Emmanuel! God is with us.
***Glory to God in the highest heaven,***
***and on earth, peace, goodwill among people.***

***Glory …***

**Psalm 97.6-12**

The skies proclaim God's justice;
all peoples see God's glory.

***Let those who serve idols be ashamed,***
***those who boast of their worthless gods.***
***All you spirits, worship the Lord.***

Zion hears and is glad;
the people of Judah rejoice
because of your judgments, O LORD.

***For you indeed are the LORD***
***most high above all the earth,***
***exalted far above all spirits.***

The LORD loves those who hate evil,
guards the souls of the saints,
and sets them free from the wicked.

***Light shines forth for the just***
***and joy for the upright of heart.***
Rejoice, you just, in the LORD;
***give glory to God's holy name.***

**Thanksgiving**

This is the day you have made, Lord;
***we rejoice and are glad in it.***
*(free prayers of thanksgiving)*
We give thanks to you, Lord, for you are good;
***your steadfast love endures forever. Amen.***

**Song**

Immortal, invisible, God only wise (H70)
Praise the Lord who reigns above (H54)
The Lord is my light (SJ97)
The God of Abraham praise (H162)

**Confession**

You, O Lord, are a God of justice.
***Blessed are all who wait for you.***
*(silence)*
You wait to be gracious to us;
***you will rise up to show mercy to us. Amen.***

## Call to discipleship

Every generous act of giving,
every perfect gift, is from above.
***It comes down from the Father of lights.***

**Luke 2.39-40**

When [Jesus' parents] had finished everything required by the law of the Lord, they returned to Galilee, to their own town of Nazareth. The child grew and became strong, filled with wisdom; and the favor of God was upon him.

**Hosea 6.1-3**

"Come, let us return to the LORD;
for it is he who has torn, and he will heal us;
he has struck down, and he will bind us up.
After two days he will revive us;
on the third day he will raise us up,
that we may live before him.
Let us know, let us press on to know the LORD;
his appearing is as sure as the dawn;
he will come to us like the showers,
like the spring rains that water the earth."

**Silent or spoken reflection on the readings**

**Song**

Great is thy faithfulness (H327, vv. 1, 3)

Keep me safe, O God (SJ50)
Peace before us (SS16)

**Zechariah's song**

## Call to intercession

O God, you grant justice to your chosen ones, who cry to you day and night,
***so we pray always, and do not lose heart.***

Saving God, you come among us bringing peace to earth. In your mercy,
***Lord, hear our prayer.***

You call us to live in harmony and love. We pray for ourselves and those dear to us.
*(open prayers)*
In your mercy,
***Lord, hear our prayer.***

You reach out in tender compassion. We pray for our community and for our neighbors.
*(open prayers)*
In your mercy,
***Lord, hear our prayer.***

You equip your people for our struggle. We pray for the church in all places, that we may speak boldly for Christ.
*(open prayers)*

In your mercy,
***Lord, hear our prayer.***

You come with justice to rule the world. We pray for the world, for all who do justice and love mercy.
*(open prayers)*
In your mercy,
***Lord, hear our prayer.***

We offer you other concerns we carry in our hearts.
*(open prayers)*
In your mercy,
***Lord, hear our prayer.***

God of prophetic promise,
your radiance penetrates our wintry night.
Come to us in tender compassion,
that we too may walk the path of peace
in holiness and without fear.
We pray in the name of the One
whose birth a heavenly host heralded:

***Our Father …***

**Benediction**

***May God strengthen us***
***according to the proclamation of Jesus Christ,***
***according to the revelation of the mystery***
***that was kept secret for long ages***
***but is now disclosed. Amen.***

# The dawn will shine on those in darkness

DECEMBER 30 MORNING

**Opening sentence**

The dawn from on high shall break upon us
***to shine on those who dwell in darkness***
***and the shadow of death.***

## Call to praise

The Word became flesh and lived among us,
full of grace and truth.
***In him was life,***
***and the life was the light of all.***

*Glory ...*

**Isaiah 9.1-5**

But there will be no gloom
for those who were in anguish.
***In the former time he brought into contempt***
***the land of Zebulun and the land of Naphtali,***
but in the latter time he will make glorious
  the way of the sea,
the land beyond the Jordan, Galilee of the
  nations.
***The people who walked in darkness***
***have seen a great light;***

those who lived in a land of deep darkness—
on them light has shined.
***You have multiplied the nation,***
***you have increased its joy;***
they rejoice before you
as with joy at the harvest,
as people exult when dividing plunder.
***For the yoke of their burden,***
***and the bar across their shoulders,***
the rod of their oppressor,
you have broken as on the day of Midian.
***For all the boots of the tramping warriors***
***and all the garments rolled in blood***
***shall be burned as fuel for the fire.***

**Thanksgiving**

We remember your great goodness to us, Lord.
***It was no messenger or angel***
***but your very presence that saved us.***
*(free prayers of thanksgiving)*
In love and pity you redeemed us;
***you lift us up and carry us all our days. Amen.***

**Song**

Come! Walk in the light (SS10)
Christ is the world's true light (H334)
O Splendor of God's glory bright (H646, vv. 1, 4, 5)

## Call to discipleship

Beloved, let us love one another,
because love is from God;
***everyone who loves is born of God***
***and knows God.***

**Luke 2.41-47**

Now every year [Jesus'] parents went to Jerusalem for the festival of the Passover. And when he was twelve years old, they went up as usual for the festival. When the festival was ended and they started to return, the boy Jesus stayed behind in Jerusalem, but his parents did not know it. Assuming that he was in the group of travelers, they went a day's journey. Then they started to look for him among their relatives and friends. When they did not find him, they returned to Jerusalem to search for him. After three days they found him in the temple, sitting among the teachers, listening to them and asking them questions. And all who heard him were amazed at his understanding and his answers.

**Revelation 11.15-18**

Then the seventh angel blew his trumpet, and there were loud voices in heaven, saying,
"The kingdom of the world has become
the kingdom of our Lord

and of his Messiah,
and he will reign forever and ever."

Then the twenty-four elders who sit on their thrones before God fell on their faces and worshiped God, singing,

"We give you thanks, Lord God Almighty,
who are and who were,
for you have taken your great power
and begun to reign.
The nations raged,
but your wrath has come,
and the time for judging the dead,
for rewarding your servants, the prophets
and saints and all who fear your name,
both small and great,
and for destroying those who destroy the
earth."

**Silent or spoken reflection on the readings**

**Song**

Blessing and honor and glory (H108)
All hail the power of Jesus' name (H106, H285)
Jesus shall reign (H319)
Joy to the world (H318)
When Jesus worked here on earth (SS38)
Blessing and honor (SS109)
Alleluia! Gracious Jesus! (SS110, verses 1, 4)
I will stand in the congregation (SS113)

## Zechariah's song

# Call to intercession

Lord, you fulfill the desire of all who fear you;
***you hear their cry, and save them.***

Guiding God, you comfort your people and have compassion on your suffering ones. In your mercy,
***Lord, hear our prayer.***

You call us to generous acts of giving. We pray for ourselves and those dear to us.
*(open prayers)*
In your mercy,
***Lord, hear our prayer.***

In you there is no gloom or anguish. We pray for our community and for our neighbors.
*(open prayers)*
In your mercy,
***Lord, hear our prayer.***

You guide your people into the way of peace. We pray for the church in all places, that we may be faithful in solidarity across generations and geography.
*(open prayers)*
In your mercy,
***Lord, hear our prayer.***

Your zeal will establish endless peace with justice. We pray for the world, for our enemies and for those who are in conflict.
*(open prayers)*
In your mercy,
***Lord, hear our prayer.***

We offer you other concerns we carry in our hearts.
*(open prayers)*
In your mercy,
***Lord, hear our prayer.***

God of breaking dawn,
you dance the earth into day.
Grant us that awareness of forgiveness
with which Zechariah ended his silence,
that we too might rejoice
to proclaim the good news of your salvation.
We pray in the name of the Messiah
who came to set us free:

***Our Father …***

**Benediction**

***May grace and peace be ours in abundance***
***in the knowledge of God***
***and of Jesus our Lord. Amen.***

# To guide our feet into the way of peace

## DECEMBER 30 EVENING

**Opening sentence**

The dawn from on high shall break upon us
to shine on those who dwell in darkness
and the shadow of death
***and to guide our feet into the way of peace.***

## Call to praise

Emmanuel! God is with us.
***Glory to God in the highest heaven,***
***and on earth, peace, goodwill among people.***

***Glory …***

**Isaiah 9.6-7**

For a child has been born for us,
a son given to us;
authority rests upon his shoulders;
***and he is named***
***Wonderful Counselor, Mighty God,***
***Everlasting Father, Prince of Peace.***
His authority shall grow continually,
***and there shall be endless peace***
***for the throne of David and his kingdom.***

He will establish and uphold it
with justice and with righteousness
from this time onward and forevermore.
***The zeal of the LORD of hosts will do this.***

**Thanksgiving**

This is the day you have made, Lord;
***we rejoice and are glad in it.***
*(free prayers of thanksgiving)*
We give thanks to you, Lord, for you are good;
***your steadfast love endures forever. Amen.***

**Song**

To us a Child of hope is born (H189)
Joy to the world (H318)
Alleluia (SS24)
Gloria, gloria, gloria (SS23)

**Confession**

You, O Lord, are a God of justice.
***Blessed are all who wait for you.***
*(silence)*
You wait to be gracious to us;
***you will rise up to show mercy to us. Amen.***

## Call to discipleship

Every generous act of giving,
every perfect gift, is from above.
***It comes down from the Father of lights.***

**Luke 2.48-52**

When [Jesus'] parents saw him they were astonished; and his mother said to him, "Child, why have you treated us like this? Look, your father and I have been searching for you in great anxiety." He said to them, "Why were you searching for me? Did you not know that I must be in my Father's house?" But they did not understand what he said to them. Then he went down with them and came to Nazareth, and was obedient to them. His mother treasured all these things in her heart.

And Jesus increased in wisdom and in years, and in divine and human favor.

**Nahum 1.15**

Look! On the mountains the feet of one
who brings good tidings,
who proclaims peace!
Celebrate your festivals, O Judah,
fulfill your vows,
for never again shall the wicked invade you;
they are utterly cut off.

**Silent or spoken reflection on the readings**

**Song**

Jesus came—the heavens adoring (H297, vv. 1–4)

He came down (SJ31)
Heri ni jina (Blessed be the name) (SS75)

**Zechariah's song**

## Call to intercession

O God, you grant justice to your chosen ones,
who cry to you day and night,
***so we pray always, and do not lose heart.***

Guiding God, you come among us bringing peace to earth. In your mercy,
***Lord, hear our prayer.***

You call us to generous acts of giving. We pray for ourselves and those dear to us.
*(open prayers)*
In your mercy,
***Lord, hear our prayer.***

In you there is no gloom or anguish. We pray for our community and for our neighbors.
*(open prayers)*
In your mercy,
***Lord, hear our prayer.***

You guide your people into the way of peace. We pray for the church in all places, that we may be faithful in solidarity across generations and geography.
*(open prayers)*

In your mercy,
***Lord, hear our prayer.***

Your zeal will establish endless peace with justice. We pray for the world, for our enemies and for those who are in conflict.
*(open prayers)*
In your mercy,
***Lord, hear our prayer.***

We offer you other concerns we carry in our hearts.
*(open prayers)*
In your mercy,
***Lord, hear our prayer.***

God of prophetic promise,
your radiance penetrates our wintry night.
Come to us in tender compassion,
that we too may walk the path of peace
in holiness and without fear.
We pray in the name of the One
whose birth a heavenly host heralded:

***Our Father …***

**Benediction**

***May God strengthen us***
***according to the proclamation of Jesus Christ,***
***according to the revelation of the mystery***
***that was kept secret for long ages***
***but is now disclosed. Amen.***

# There your heart will be

## DECEMBER 31 MORNING

**Opening sentence**

Store up for yourselves treasures in heaven,
where neither moth nor rust consumes
and where thieves do not break in and steal.
*For where your treasure is,*
*there your heart will be also.*

## Call to praise

Lord, you have been our dwelling-place
in all generations.
*Before the mountains were brought forth,*
*or ever you had formed the earth*
*and the world,*
*from everlasting to everlasting you are God.*

*Glory ...*

**Psalm 90.11-14**

Who understands the power of your anger
and fears the strength of your fury?

*Make us know the shortness of our life*
*that we may gain wisdom of heart.*
LORD, relent! Is your anger for ever?
Show pity to your servants.

***In the morning, fill us with your love;***
***we shall exult and rejoice all our days.***

**Thanksgiving**

By day you send loving kindness;
***by night I will praise you, God of my life.***
*(free prayers of thanksgiving)*
I hope in you, O God.
***I praise you, my savior and my God. Amen.***

**Song**

O God, our help in ages past (H328)
God is our refuge and strength (SJ26)
O God, your constant care (H481)

## Call to discipleship

Do not worry about your life,
what you will eat or what you will drink,
or about your body, what you will wear.
***Is not life more than food,***
***and the body more than clothing?***

**Matthew 6.19-21**

"Do not store up for yourselves treasures on earth, where moth and rust consume and where thieves break in and steal; but store up for yourselves treasures in heaven, where neither moth nor rust consumes and where thieves do not break in and steal. For where your treasure is, there your heart will be also."

**James 4.13-15**

Come now, you who say, "Today or tomorrow we will go to such and such a town and spend a year there, doing business and making money." Yet you do not even know what tomorrow will bring. What is your life? For you are a mist that appears for a little while and then vanishes. Instead you ought to say, "If the Lord wishes, we will live and do this or that."

**Silent or spoken reflection on the readings**

**Song**

Today I live (H607)
Teach me the measure of my days (H485)
From time beyond my memory (H484, vv. 1, 3)
You are all we have (SJ29)

**Zechariah's song**

## Call to intercession

Can a woman forget her nursing child,
or show no compassion
for the child of her womb?

***Even these may forget,***
***yet God will not forget us.***
***We are inscribed on the palms of God's hands.***

Mothering God, you are more willing to answer than we are to ask. In your mercy,
***Lord, hear our prayer.***

Your tender care enfolds us. We pray for ourselves and those dear to us.
*(open prayers)*
In your mercy,
***Lord, hear our prayer.***

You never forget those you have made. We pray for our community and for our neighbors.
*(open prayers)*
In your mercy,
***Lord, hear our prayer.***

Your love is strong for all who revere you. We pray for the church in all places, that we may be one.
*(open prayers)*
In your mercy,
***Lord, hear our prayer.***

You promise justice for those who are oppressed. We pray for the world, that your reign may come and your will be done on earth.
*(open prayers)*

In your mercy,
***Lord, hear our prayer.***

We offer you other concerns we carry in our hearts.
*(open prayers)*
In your mercy,
***Lord, hear our prayer.***

Eternal God,
you gave your people of old a cloud by day
and a pillar of fire by night.
Guide us as you guided them
with your counsel,
and afterward receive us with honor,
so that, although our flesh and heart may fail,
you may be our strength
and our portion forever.
With confidence, we pray as Jesus taught us:

***Our Father …***

**Benediction**

***The Lord will keep us from all evil.***
***The Lord will keep our life.***
***The Lord will keep our going out***
***and our coming in***
***from this time on and forevermore. Amen.***

# If God so clothes the grass of the field

## DECEMBER 31 EVENING

**Opening sentence**

If God so clothes the grass of the field,
which is alive today
and tomorrow is thrown into the oven,
***will God not much more clothe you?***

## Call to praise

Lord, you have been our dwelling-place
in all generations.
***Before the mountains were brought forth,***
***or ever you had formed the earth***
***and the world,***
***from everlasting to everlasting you are God.***

***Glory ...***

**Psalm 103.6-15**

The LORD does deeds of justice,
gives judgment for all who are oppressed.
***The Lord's ways were made known to Moses;***
***the Lord's deeds to Israel's children.***

The LORD is compassion and love,
slow to anger and rich in mercy.

***The* Lord *will not always chide,***
***will not be angry forever.***
God does not treat us according to our sins
nor repay us according to our faults.

***For as the heavens are high above the earth***
***so strong is God's love for the God-fearing.***
As far as the east is from the west
so far does he remove our sins.

***As parents have compassion on their children,***
***the* Lord *has pity on those who are God-fearing***
for he knows of what we are made,
and remembers that we are dust.

***As for us, our days are like grass;***
***we flower like the flower of the field.***

**Thanksgiving**

By day you send loving kindness;
***by night I will praise you, God of my life.***
*(free prayers of thanksgiving)*
I hope in you, O God.
***I praise you, my savior and my God. Amen.***

**Song**

Praise, my soul, the God of heaven (H63)
Great is thy faithfulness (H327)
O bless the Lord, my soul (H600)
Sithi bonga (We sing praise) (SS94)

**Confession**

O Lord, you have searched me and know me.
You are acquainted with all my ways.
***Where can I go from your spirit?***
***Or where can I flee from your presence?***
*(silence)*
Search me, O God, and know my heart;
test me and know my thoughts.
***See if there is any hurtful way in me,***
***and lead me in the way everlasting. Amen.***

## Call to discipleship

Do not worry about your life,
what you will eat or what you will drink,
or about your body, what you will wear.
***Is not life more than food,***
***and the body more than clothing?***

**Matthew 6.26-33**

"Look at the birds of the air; they neither sow nor reap nor gather into barns, and yet your heavenly Father feeds them. Are you not of more value than they? And can any of you by worrying add a single hour to your span of life? And why do you worry about clothing? Consider the lilies of the field, how they grow; they neither toil nor spin, yet I tell you, even Solomon in all his glory was not clothed like one of these. But if God so clothes the grass of the field, which is alive today and tomorrow is thrown into the oven, will he not much more clothe you—you of little faith? Therefore do not worry, saying, 'What will we eat?' or 'What will we drink?' or 'What will we wear?' For it is the Gentiles who strive for all these things; and indeed your heavenly Father knows that you need all these things. But strive first for the kingdom of God and his righteousness, and all these things will be given to you as well."

**Romans 8.31-39**

What then are we to say about these things? If God is for us, who is against us? He who did not withhold his own Son, but gave him up for all of us, will he not with him also give us everything else? Who will bring any charge against God's elect? It is God who justifies. Who is to condemn? It is Christ Jesus, who died, yes, who was raised, who is at the right hand of God, who indeed intercedes for us. Who will separate us from the love of Christ? Will hardship, or distress, or persecution, or famine, or nakedness, or peril, or sword? As it is written,

"For your sake we are being killed all day
long;
we are accounted as sheep to be
slaughtered."

No, in all these things we are more than conquerors through him who loved us. For I am convinced that neither death, nor life, nor angels, nor rulers, nor things present, nor things to come, nor powers, nor height, nor depth, nor anything else in all creation, will be able to separate us from the love of God in Christ Jesus our Lord.

**Silent or spoken reflection on the readings**

**Song**

Seek ye first the kingdom of God (H324)
O Power of love (H593)
For God so loved us (H167)
I am trusting thee, Lord Jesus (H564)

**Mary's or Simeon's song**

## Call to intercession

Can a woman forget her nursing child,
or show no compassion
for the child of her womb?
***Even these may forget,***
***yet God will not forget us.***
***We are inscribed on the palms of God's hands.***

Mothering God, you are more willing to answer than we are to ask. In your mercy,
***Lord, hear our prayer.***

Your tender care enfolds us. We pray for ourselves and those dear to us.
*(open prayers)*
In your mercy,
***Lord, hear our prayer.***

You never forget those you have made. We pray for our community and for our neighbors.
*(open prayers)*
In your mercy,
***Lord, hear our prayer.***

Your love is strong for all who revere you. We pray for the church in all places, that we may be one.
*(open prayers)*
In your mercy,
***Lord, hear our prayer.***

You promise justice for those who are oppressed. We pray for the world, that your reign may come and your will be done on earth.
*(open prayers)*
In your mercy,
***Lord, hear our prayer.***

We offer you other concerns we carry in our hearts.
*(open prayers)*
In your mercy,
***Lord, hear our prayer.***

Eternal God,
you gave your people of old a cloud by day
and a pillar of fire by night.
Guide us as you guided them
with your counsel,
and afterward receive us with honor,
so that, although our flesh and heart may fail,
you may be our strength
and our portion forever.
With confidence, we pray as Jesus taught us:

*Our Father ...*

**Benediction**

***The Lord will keep us from all evil.***
***The Lord will keep our life.***
***The Lord will keep our going out***
***and our coming in***
***from this time on and forevermore. Amen.***

# He is the image of the invisible God

## JANUARY 1 MORNING

**Opening sentence**

He is the image of the invisible God,
the firstborn of all creation.
***In him all things in heaven***
***and on earth were created,***
***things visible and invisible.***

## Call to praise

O God, may your way be known upon earth,
your saving power among all nations.
***Let the peoples praise you, O God;***
***let all the peoples praise you.***

***Glory …***

**Psalm 102.25-28 [24-28]**

I say to God: "Do not take me away
before my days are complete,
you, whose days last from age to age.

***Long ago you founded the earth***
***and the heavens are the work of your hands.***
They will perish but you will remain.
They will all wear out like a garment.

*You will change them like clothes that are changed.*
*But you neither change, nor have an end."*

**Thanksgiving**

The Word became flesh and lived among us,
and we have seen his glory,
***the glory as of a father's only son,***
***full of grace and truth.***
*(free prayers of thanksgiving)*
The light shines in the darkness
***and the darkness has not overcome it. Amen.***

**Song**

O God, our help in ages past (H328)
God of our life (H486)
God moves in a mysterious way (SJ104)
I was there to hear your borning cry (SJ89)

## Call to discipleship

God sent the only begotten Son into the world
so that we might live through him.
***Beloved, since God loved us so much,***
***we also ought to love one another.***

**John 1.1-9**

In the beginning was the Word, and the Word was with God, and the Word was God. He was in the beginning with God. All things came into being through him, and without him not one thing came into being. What has come into being in him was life, and the life was the light of all people. The light shines in the darkness, and the darkness did not overcome it.

There was a man sent from God, whose name was John. He came as a witness to testify to the light, so that all might believe through him. He himself was not the light, but he came to testify to the light. The true light, which enlightens everyone, was coming into the world.

**Genesis 1.1-5**

In the beginning when God created the heavens and the earth, the earth was a formless void and darkness covered the face of the deep, while a wind from God swept over the face of the waters. Then God said, "Let there be light"; and there was light. And God saw that the light was good; and God separated the light from the darkness. God called the light Day, and the darkness he called Night. And there was evening and there was morning, the first day.

**Silent or spoken reflection on the readings**

**Song**

Of the Father's love begotten (H104)

Arise, your light is come! (SS30)
We are people of God's peace (H407)

**Colossians 1.15-20**

## Call to intercession

Morning, noon, and night
call out to God, who hears your cry.
***Give your burden to the Lord,***
***who will be your support.***

God of creation and new creation, we bring our prayers to you because you know well what we are made of. In your mercy,
***Lord, hear our prayer.***

You hold our lives in your hands. We pray for ourselves and those dear to us.
*(open prayers)*
In your mercy,
***Lord, hear our prayer.***

You give joy to balance affliction. We pray for our community and for our neighbors.
*(open prayers)*
In your mercy,
***Lord, hear our prayer.***

You let your glory shine on your people. We pray for the church in all places, that we may know the freedom of life in the Spirit.

*(open prayers)*
In your mercy,
***Lord, hear our prayer.***

You sent the true light, which enlightens everyone, into the world. We pray for the world and for all who care for creation.
*(open prayers)*
In your mercy,
***Lord, hear our prayer.***

We offer you other concerns we carry in our hearts.
*(open prayers)*
In your mercy,
***Lord, hear our prayer.***

Unseen God,
you were pleased to dwell in Christ,
to fill him with all your fullness.
Open our eyes to see your glory
shining supremely in Emmanuel, God with us,
so that we, with all of creation,
may shout praise and honor
to the One in whose name we pray:

***Our Father …***

**Benediction**

***May grace and peace be ours in abundance***
***in the knowledge of God***
***and of Jesus our Lord. Amen.***

# In him all things were created

## JANUARY 1 EVENING

**Opening sentence**

He is the image of the invisible God,
the firstborn of all creation.
***In him all things in heaven***
***and on earth were created,***
***things visible and invisible.***

## Call to praise

Sing a new song to the Lord.
Sing praise in the assembly of the faithful.
***Let the faithful exult. Let them sing for joy!***

***Glory …***

**Psalm 90.15-17**

Give us joy to balance our affliction
for the years when we knew misfortune.

***Show forth your work to your servants;***
***let your glory shine on their children.***
Let the favor of the LORD be upon us:
***give success to the work of our hands***
***(give success to the work of our hands).***

**Thanksgiving**

When the fullness of time had come,
you sent your Son,
***so that we might receive adoption as children.***
*(free prayers of thanksgiving)*
Thanks be to you, O God;
***you have given us an indescribable gift! Amen.***

**Song**

Great is thy faithfulness (H327)
O God, who gives us life (H483)
I will stand in the congregation (SS113)

**Confession**

Lord, you are good and just;
***you guide those who stray.***
*(silence)*
You forgive our sins, though great,
***and you teach the humble your way. Amen.***

## Call to discipleship

Let the word of Christ dwell in you richly;
teach and admonish one another
in all wisdom;
***and with gratitude in your hearts***
***sing psalms, hymns, and spiritual songs to God.***

**John 1.9-13**

The true light, which enlightens everyone, was coming into the world.

He was in the world, and the world came into being through him; yet the world did not know him. He came to what was his own, and his own people did not accept him. But to all who received him, who believed in his name, he gave power to become children of God, who were born, not of blood or of the will of the flesh or of the will of man, but of God.

**1 John 2.29–3.2**

If you know that he is righteous, you may be sure that everyone who does right has been born of him. See what love the Father has given us, that we should be called children of God; and that is what we are. The reason the world does not know us is that it did not know him. Beloved, we are God's children now; what we will be has not yet been revealed. What we do know is this: when he is revealed, we will be like him, for we will see him as he is.

**Silent or spoken reflection on the readings**

**Song**

I want to walk as a child of the light (SJ95)

Where charity and love prevail (H305)
Love the Lord your God (SS55)

**Colossians 1.15-20**

## Call to intercession

Jesus said, If you abide in me,
and my words abide in you,
ask whatever you wish,
and it will be done for you.
***The Father will give you***
***whatever you ask in my name.***

God of creation and new creation, you know how to give good gifts to your children. In your mercy,
***Lord, hear our prayer.***

You hold our lives in your hands. We pray for ourselves and those dear to us.
*(open prayers)*
In your mercy,
***Lord, hear our prayer.***

You give joy to balance affliction. We pray for our community and for our neighbors.
*(open prayers)*
In your mercy,
***Lord, hear our prayer.***

You let your glory shine on your people. We pray for the church in all places, that we may know the freedom of life in the Spirit.
*(open prayers)*
In your mercy,
***Lord, hear our prayer.***

You sent the true light, which enlightens everyone, into the world. We pray for the world and for all who care for creation.
*(open prayers)*
In your mercy,
***Lord, hear our prayer.***

We offer you other concerns we carry in our hearts.
*(open prayers)*
In your mercy,
***Lord, hear our prayer.***

O God, you hold all things together in Christ.
Come to our fractured world;
be pleased to dwell with us
as through Christ you reconcile
all that is in heaven and earth.
In his name we pray:

***Our Father …***

**Benediction**

***The Lord will keep us from all evil.***
***The Lord will keep our life.***

*The Lord will keep our going out*
*and our coming in*
*from this time on and forevermore. Amen.*

# All things were created through him and for him

JANUARY 2 MORNING

**Opening sentence**

Whether thrones or dominions
or rulers or powers—
***all things have been created through him***
***and for him.***

## Call to praise

O God, may your way be known upon earth,
your saving power among all nations.
***Let the peoples praise you, O God;***
***let all the peoples praise you.***

***Glory ...***

**Psalm 91.1-6**

Those who dwell in the shelter of the Most
High
and abide in the shade of the Almighty
***say to the LORD: "My refuge,***
***my stronghold, my God in whom I trust!"***

It is God who will free you from the snare
of the fowler who seeks to destroy you;

***God will conceal you with his pinions,***
***and under his wings you will find refuge.***

You will not fear the terror of the night
nor the arrow that flies by day,
***nor the plague that prowls in the darkness***
***nor the scourge that lays waste at noon.***

**Thanksgiving**

The Word became flesh and lived among us,
and we have seen his glory,
***the glory as of a father's only son,***
***full of grace and truth.***
*(free prayers of thanksgiving)*
The light shines in the darkness
***and the darkness has not overcome it. Amen.***

**Song**

For mornings bright (SJ113)
Who is so great a God (H62)
And I will raise you up (H596)

## Call to discipleship

God sent the only begotten Son into the world
so that we might live through him.
***Beloved, since God loved us so much,***
***we also ought to love one another.***

**John 1.14-18**

And the Word became flesh and lived among us, and we have seen his glory, the glory as of a father's only son, full of grace and truth. (John testified to him and cried out, "This was he of whom I said, 'He who comes after me ranks ahead of me because he was before me.'") From his fullness we have all received, grace upon grace. The law indeed was given through Moses; grace and truth came through Jesus Christ. No one has ever seen God. It is God the only Son, who is close to the Father's heart, who has made him known.

**Ezekiel 37.26-28**

I will make a covenant of peace with them; it shall be an everlasting covenant with them; and I will bless them and multiply them, and will set my sanctuary among them forevermore. My dwelling place shall be with them; and I will be their God, and they shall be my people. Then the nations shall know that I the LORD sanctify Israel, when my sanctuary is among them forevermore.

**Silent or spoken reflection on the readings**

**Song**

Let all together praise our God (H213)
Where is this stupendous Stranger (H200)
All glory be to God on high (H122)

O God, who gives us life (H483)
Gloria, gloria, gloria (SS23)

**Colossians 1.15-20**

## Call to intercession

Morning, noon, and night
call out to God, who hears your cry.
***Give your burden to the Lord,***
***who will be your support.***

Loving God, we bring our prayers to you
because you know well what we are made of.
In your mercy,
***Lord, hear our prayer.***

You come to us anew in Christ, full of grace
and truth. We pray for ourselves and those
dear to us.
*(open prayers)*
In your mercy,
***Lord, hear our prayer.***

You offer refuge under your wings. We pray
for our community and for our neighbors.
*(open prayers)*
In your mercy,
***Lord, hear our prayer.***

You give grace upon grace. We pray for the church in all places, that we may reflect your faithful love.
*(open prayers)*
In your mercy,
***Lord, hear our prayer.***

You desire to establish an everlasting covenant of peace. We pray for the world, for those who are in need.
*(open prayers)*
In your mercy,
***Lord, hear our prayer.***

We offer you other concerns we carry in our hearts.
*(open prayers)*
In your mercy,
***Lord, hear our prayer.***

Unseen God,
you were pleased to dwell in Christ,
to fill him with all your fullness.
Open our eyes to see your glory
shining supremely in Emmanuel, God with us,
so that we, with all of creation,
may shout praise and honor
to the One in whose name we pray:

***Our Father …***

**Benediction**

*May grace and peace be ours in abundance*
*in the knowledge of God*
*and of Jesus our Lord. Amen.*

# All things were created through him and for him

## JANUARY 2 EVENING

**Opening sentence**

Whether thrones or dominions
or rulers or powers—
*all things have been created through him*
*and for him.*

## Call to praise

Sing a new song to the Lord.
Sing praise in the assembly of the faithful.
*Let the faithful exult. Let them sing for joy!*

*Glory ...*

**Psalm 91.8-17**

Your eyes have only to look
to see how the wicked are repaid,
*you who have said: "LORD, my refuge!"*
*and have made the Most High your dwelling.*

Upon you no evil shall fall,
no plague approach where you dwell.
*For you God has commanded the angels,*
*to keep you in all your ways.*

They shall bear you upon their hands
lest you strike your foot against a stone.
***On the lion and the viper you will tread***
***and trample the young lion and the dragon.***

You set your love on me so I will save you,
protect you for you know my name.
***When you call I shall answer: "I am with you,"***
***I will save you in distress and give you glory.***

With length of days I will content you;
***I shall let you see my saving power.***

**Thanksgiving**

When the fullness of time had come,
you sent your Son,
***so that we might receive adoption as children.***
*(free prayers of thanksgiving)*
Thanks be to you, O God;
***you have given us an indescribable gift! Amen.***

**Song**

I to the hills will lift my eyes (H169, 563)
And I will raise you up (H596)
You are all we have (SJ29)

**Confession**

Lord, you are good and just;
***you guide those who stray.***
*(silence)*

You forgive our sins, though great,
***and you teach the humble your way. Amen.***

## Call to discipleship

Let the word of Christ dwell in you richly;
teach and admonish one another
in all wisdom;
***and with gratitude in your hearts***
***sing psalms, hymns, and spiritual songs to God.***

**John 1.19-23**

This is the testimony given by John when the Jews sent priests and Levites from Jerusalem to ask him, "Who are you?" He confessed and did not deny it, but confessed, "I am not the Messiah." And they asked him, "What then? Are you Elijah?" He said, "I am not." "Are you the prophet?" He answered, "No." Then they said to him, "Who are you? Let us have an answer for those who sent us. What do you say about yourself?" He said,

"I am the voice of one crying out in the wilderness,
'Make straight the way of the Lord,'"

as the prophet Isaiah said.

**Isaiah 40.3**

A voice cries out:
"In the wilderness prepare the way of the
 LORD,
make straight in the desert a highway for our
 God."

**Silent or spoken reflection on the readings**

**Song**

Prepare the way of the Lord (SS14)
Wild and lone the prophet's voice (SS8)
My Lord, he is a-comin' soon (SS112)
Comfort, comfort, O my people (H176)

**Colossians 1.15-20**

## Call to intercession

Jesus said, If you abide in me,
and my words abide in you,
ask whatever you wish,
and it will be done for you.
***The Father will give you***
***whatever you ask in my name.***

Loving God, you know how to give good gifts
to your children. In your mercy,
***Lord, hear our prayer.***

You come to us anew in Christ, full of grace and truth. We pray for ourselves and those dear to us.
*(open prayers)*
In your mercy,
***Lord, hear our prayer.***

You offer refuge under your wings. We pray for our community and for our neighbors.
*(open prayers)*
In your mercy,
***Lord, hear our prayer.***

You give grace upon grace. We pray for the church in all places, that we may reflect your faithful love.
*(open prayers)*
In your mercy,
***Lord, hear our prayer.***

You desire to establish an everlasting covenant of peace. We pray for the world, for those who are in need.
*(open prayers)*
In your mercy,
***Lord, hear our prayer.***

We offer you other concerns we carry in our hearts.
*(open prayers)*
In your mercy,
***Lord, hear our prayer.***

O God, you hold all things together in Christ.
Come to our fractured world;
be pleased to dwell with us
as through Christ you reconcile
all that is in heaven and earth.
In his name we pray:

*Our Father …*

**Benediction**

*The Lord will keep us from all evil.*
*The Lord will keep our life.*
*The Lord will keep our going out*
*and our coming in*
*from this time on and forevermore. Amen.*

# In him all things hold together

JANUARY 3 MORNING

**Opening sentence**

He himself is before all things,
***and in him all things hold together.***

## Call to praise

O God, may your way be known upon earth,
your saving power among all nations.
***Let the peoples praise you, O God;***
***let all the peoples praise you.***

*Glory …*

**Psalm 95.1-7**

Come, ring out our joy to the LORD;
hail the rock who saves us.
***Let us come before God, giving thanks,***
***with songs let us hail the LORD.***

A mighty God is the LORD,
a great king above all gods,
***in whose hands are the depths of the earth;***
***the heights of the mountains as well.***
The sea belongs to God, who made it
and the dry land shaped by his hands.

***Come in; let us bow and bend low;***
***let us kneel before the God who made us***
for this is our God and we
the people who belong to his pasture,
***the flock that is led by his hand.***

**Thanksgiving**

The Word became flesh and lived among us,
and we have seen his glory,
***the glory as of a father's only son,***
***full of grace and truth.***
*(free prayers of thanksgiving)*
The light shines in the darkness
***and the darkness has not overcome it. Amen.***

**Song**

We worship God the Rock (SJ28)
Cantemos al Señor (Let's sing unto the Lord)
(H55)
O worship the King (H66)

## Call to discipleship

God sent the only begotten Son into the world
so that we might live through him.
***Beloved, since God loved us so much,***
***we also ought to love one another.***

**John 1.25-28**

[Emissaries of the Pharisees] asked him, "Why then are you baptizing if you are neither the Messiah, nor Elijah, nor the prophet?" John answered them, "I baptize with water. Among you stands one whom you do not know, the one who is coming after me; I am not worthy to untie the thong of his sandal." This took place in Bethany across the Jordan where John was baptizing.

**Deuteronomy 18.15**

The LORD your God will raise up for you a prophet like me from among your own people; you shall heed such a prophet.

**Silent or spoken reflection on the readings**

**Song**

Firstborn of Mary (SS37)
Som'landela (We will follow) (SS40)
O young and fearless Prophet (H374, vv. 1, 4, 5)

**Colossians 1.15-20**

## Call to intercession

Morning, noon, and night
call out to God, who hears your cry.

***Give your burden to the Lord,***
***who will be your support.***

God of truth, we bring our prayers to you because you know well what we are made of.
In your mercy,
***Lord, hear our prayer.***

You put praise and joy in our hearts. We pray for ourselves and those dear to us.
*(open prayers)*
In your mercy,
***Lord, hear our prayer.***

You turn the hearts of parents to their children, and children to their parents. We pray for our community and for our neighbors.
*(open prayers)*
In your mercy,
***Lord, hear our prayer.***

You test and search the hearts of your people. We pray for the church in all places, that we may bear witness to your reign of justice, peace, and joy.
*(open prayers)*
In your mercy,
***Lord, hear our prayer.***

Your steadfast love endures for all you have made. We pray for the world, for all who are ensnared in greed, violence, and oppression.

*(open prayers)*
In your mercy,
***Lord, hear our prayer.***

We offer you other concerns we carry in our hearts.
*(open prayers)*
In your mercy,
***Lord, hear our prayer.***

Unseen God,
you were pleased to dwell in Christ,
to fill him with all your fullness.
Open our eyes to see your glory
shining supremely in Emmanuel, God with us,
so that we, with all of creation,
may shout praise and honor
to the One in whose name we pray:

***Our Father …***

**Benediction**

***May grace and peace be ours in abundance***
***in the knowledge of God***
***and of Jesus our Lord. Amen.***

# In him all things hold together

## JANUARY 3 EVENING

**Opening sentence**

He himself is before all things,
***and in him all things hold together.***

## Call to praise

Sing a new song to the Lord.
Sing praise in the assembly of the faithful.
***Let the faithful exult. Let them sing for joy!***

***Glory …***

**Psalm 136.1-9**

Alleluia!
O give thanks to the LORD who is good,
***whose love endures forever.***
Give thanks to the God of gods,
***whose love endures forever.***
Give thanks to the LORD of lords,
***whose love endures forever;***

who alone has wrought marvelous works,
***whose love endures forever;***
whose wisdom it was made the skies,
***whose love endures forever;***
who fixed the earth firmly on the seas,
***whose love endures forever.***

It was God who made the great lights,
***whose love endures forever;***
the sun to rule in the day,
***whose love endures forever;***
the moon and stars in the night,
***whose love endures forever.***

**Thanksgiving**

When the fullness of time had come,
you sent your Son,
***so that we might receive adoption as children.***
*(free prayers of thanksgiving)*
Thanks be to you, O God;
***you have given us an indescribable gift! Amen.***

**Song**

We give thanks unto you (H161)
Who is so great a God (H62)
Let all creation bless the Lord (H61)

**Confession**

Lord, you are good and just;
***you guide those who stray.***
*(silence)*
You forgive our sins, though great,
***and you teach the humble your way. Amen.***

## Call to discipleship

Let the word of Christ dwell in you richly;
teach and admonish one another
in all wisdom;
***and with gratitude in your hearts***
***sing psalms, hymns, and spiritual songs to God.***

**John 1.29-34**

The next day [John] saw Jesus coming toward him and declared, "Here is the Lamb of God who takes away the sin of the world! This is he of whom I said, 'After me comes a man who ranks ahead of me because he was before me.' I myself did not know him; but I came baptizing with water for this reason, that he might be revealed to Israel." And John testified, "I saw the Spirit descending from heaven like a dove, and it remained on him. I myself did not know him, but the one who sent me to baptize with water said to me, 'He on whom you see the Spirit descend and remain is the one who baptizes with the Holy Spirit.' And I myself have seen and have testified that this is the Son of God."

**Malachi 4.5-6**

Lo, I will send you the prophet Elijah before the great and terrible day of the LORD comes. He will turn the hearts of parents to their children and the hearts of children to their parents, so that I will not come and strike the land with a curse.

**Silent or spoken reflection on the readings**

**Song**

O Christ, the Lamb of God (H153)
I sing with exultation (H438)
Quién dicen que soy yo? (Who do you say that I am?) (SS51)
Lamb of God (SJ21)

**Colossians 1.15-20**

## Call to intercession

Jesus said, If you abide in me,
and my words abide in you,
ask whatever you wish,
and it will be done for you.
***The Father will give you***
***whatever you ask in my name.***

God of truth, you know how to give good gifts to your children. In your mercy,
***Lord, hear our prayer.***

You put praise and joy in our hearts. We pray for ourselves and those dear to us.
*(open prayers)*

In your mercy,
***Lord, hear our prayer.***

You turn the hearts of parents to their children, and children to their parents. We pray for our community and for our neighbors.
*(open prayers)*
In your mercy,
***Lord, hear our prayer.***

You test and search the hearts of your people. We pray for the church in all places, that we may bear witness to your reign of justice, peace, and joy.
*(open prayers)*
In your mercy,
***Lord, hear our prayer.***

Your steadfast love endures for all you have made. We pray for the world, for all who are ensnared in greed, violence, and oppression.
*(open prayers)*
In your mercy,
***Lord, hear our prayer.***

We offer you other concerns we carry in our hearts.
*(open prayers)*
In your mercy,
***Lord, hear our prayer.***

O God, you hold all things together in Christ.
Come to our fractured world;
be pleased to dwell with us
as through Christ you reconcile
all that is in heaven and earth.
In his name we pray:

*Our Father …*

**Benediction**

*The Lord will keep us from all evil.*
*The Lord will keep our life.*
*The Lord will keep our going out*
*and our coming in*
*from this time on and forevermore. Amen.*

# He is the head of the body

JANUARY 4 MORNING

**Opening sentence**

He himself is before all things,
and in him all things hold together.
***He is the head of the body, the church.***

## Call to praise

O God, may your way be known upon earth,
your saving power among all nations.
***Let the peoples praise you, O God;***
***let all the peoples praise you.***

***Glory …***

**Psalm 135.1-7**

Alleluia!

Praise the name of the LORD,
praise, you servants of the LORD,
***who stand in the house of the LORD,***
***in the courts of the house of our God.***

Praise the LORD for the LORD is good.
Praise God's name; God is gracious.
***For Jacob has been chosen by the LORD;***
***Israel for God's own possession.***

For I know the LORD is great,
that our LORD is high above all gods.
***Whatever the LORD wills, the LORD does,***
***in heaven, on earth, in the seas.***

God summons clouds from the ends of the earth;
makes lightning produce the rain;
***and sends forth the wind from the storehouse.***

### Thanksgiving

The Word became flesh and lived among us,
and we have seen his glory,
***the glory as of a father's only son,***
***full of grace and truth.***
*(free prayers of thanksgiving)*
The light shines in the darkness
***and the darkness has not overcome it. Amen.***

### Song

Let the whole creation cry (H51)
Praise the Lord who reigns above (H54)
Asithi: Amen (Sing amen) (H64)

## Call to discipleship

God sent the only begotten Son into the world
so that we might live through him.
***Beloved, since God loved us so much,***
***we also ought to love one another.***

**John 1.35-39**

The next day John again was standing with two of his disciples, and as he watched Jesus walk by, he exclaimed, "Look, here is the Lamb of God!" The two disciples heard him say this, and they followed Jesus. When Jesus turned and saw them following, he said to them, "What are you looking for?" They said to him, "Rabbi" (which translated means Teacher), "where are you staying?" He said to them, "Come and see." They came and saw where he was staying, and they remained with him that day. It was about four o'clock in the afternoon.

**Revelation 5.13-14**

Then I [John] heard every creature in heaven and on earth and under the earth and in the sea, and all that is in them, singing,

> "To the one seated on the throne and to the
> Lamb
> be blessing and honor and glory and might
> forever and ever!"

And the four living creatures said, "Amen!"
And the elders fell down and worshiped.

**Silent or spoken reflection on the readings**

**Song**

Come and see (H20)

Blessing and honor and glory (H108, vv. 1, 3, 4)
To God, with the Lamb (H125)

**Colossians 1.15-20**

## Call to intercession

Morning, noon, and night
call out to God, who hears your cry.
***Give your burden to the Lord,***
***who will be your support.***

Sustaining God, we bring our prayers to you because you know well what we are made of.
In your mercy,
***Lord, hear our prayer.***

You call us to rest in you. We pray for ourselves and those dear to us.
*(open prayers)*
In your mercy,
***Lord, hear our prayer.***

Your love makes all other loves exist. We pray for our community and for our neighbors.
*(open prayers)*
In your mercy,
***Lord, hear our prayer.***

You have set Christ as head of the body, the church. We pray for the church in all places,

that we may daily follow in the footsteps of Christ.
*(open prayers)*
In your mercy,
***Lord, hear our prayer.***

Yours alone is all blessing and honor, glory and might. We pray for the world, for those in positions of power and authority.
*(open prayers)*
In your mercy,
***Lord, hear our prayer.***

We offer you other concerns we carry in our hearts.
*(open prayers)*
In your mercy,
***Lord, hear our prayer.***

Unseen God,
you were pleased to dwell in Christ,
to fill him with all your fullness.
Open our eyes to see your glory
shining supremely in Emmanuel, God with us,
so that we, with all of creation,
may shout praise and honor
to the One in whose name we pray:

***Our Father …***

**Benediction**

*May grace and peace be ours in abundance*
*in the knowledge of God*
*and of Jesus our Lord. Amen.*

# He is the head of the body

JANUARY 4 EVENING

**Opening sentence**

He himself is before all things,
and in him all things hold together.
***He is the head of the body, the church.***

## Call to praise

Sing a new song to the Lord.
Sing praise in the assembly of the faithful.
*Let the faithful exult. Let them sing for joy!*

*Glory ...*

**Psalm 97.1-6**

The LORD is king, let earth rejoice,
let all the coastlands be glad.
***Surrounded by cloud and darkness;
justice and right, God's throne.***

A fire prepares the way;
it burns up foes on every side.
***God's lightnings light up the world,
the earth trembles at the sight.***

The mountains melt like wax
before the LORD of all the earth.

***The skies proclaim God's justice;***
***all peoples see God's glory.***

**Thanksgiving**

When the fullness of time had come,
you sent your Son,
***so that we might receive adoption as children.***
*(free prayers of thanksgiving)*
Thanks be to you, O God;
***you have given us an indescribable gift! Amen.***

**Song**

Open now thy gates of beauty (H19)
O worship the King (H66)
O come, loud anthems let us sing (H68)
Praise, praise, praise the Lord! (SJ11)

**Confession**

Lord, you are good and just;
***you guide those who stray.***
*(silence)*
You forgive our sins, though great,
***and you teach the humble your way. Amen.***

## Call to discipleship

Let the word of Christ dwell in you richly;
teach and admonish one another
in all wisdom;

*and with gratitude in your hearts*
*sing psalms, hymns, and spiritual songs to God.*

**John 1.40-41**

One of the two who heard John speak and followed him was Andrew, Simon Peter's brother. He first found his brother Simon and said to him, "We have found the Messiah" (which is translated Anointed).

**Isaiah 25.9**

It will be said on that day,
Lo, this is our God; we have waited for him, so that he might save us.
This is the LORD for whom we have waited;
let us be glad and rejoice in his salvation.

**Silent or spoken reflection on the readings**

**Song**

'Tis not with eyes of flesh we see (H571)
Joy to the world (H318)
Will you come and follow me (SS39)

**Colossians 1.15-20**

## Call to intercession

Jesus said, If you abide in me,
and my words abide in you,

ask whatever you wish,
and it will be done for you.
***The Father will give you***
***whatever you ask in my name.***

Sustaining God, you know how to give good gifts to your children. In your mercy,
***Lord, hear our prayer.***

You call us to rest in you. We pray for ourselves and those dear to us.
*(open prayers)*
In your mercy,
***Lord, hear our prayer.***

Your love makes all other loves exist. We pray for our community and for our neighbors.
*(open prayers)*
In your mercy,
***Lord, hear our prayer.***

You have set Christ as head of the body, the church. We pray for the church in all places, that we may daily follow in the footsteps of Christ.
*(open prayers)*
In your mercy,
***Lord, hear our prayer.***

Yours alone is all blessing and honor, glory and might. We pray for the world, for those in positions of power and authority.

*(open prayers)*
In your mercy,
***Lord, hear our prayer.***

We offer you other concerns we carry in our hearts.
*(open prayers)*
In your mercy,
***Lord, hear our prayer.***

O God, you hold all things together in Christ.
Come to our fractured world;
be pleased to dwell with us
as through Christ you reconcile
all that is in heaven and earth.
In his name we pray:

***Our Father …***

**Benediction**

***The Lord will keep us from all evil.***
***The Lord will keep our life.***
***The Lord will keep our going out***
***and our coming in***
***from this time on and forevermore. Amen.***

# He is the firstborn from the dead

JANUARY 5 MORNING

**Opening sentence**

He is the beginning,
the firstborn from the dead,
***so that he might come to have first place***
***in everything.***

## Call to praise

O God, may your way be known upon earth,
your saving power among all nations.
***Let the peoples praise you, O God;***
***let all the peoples praise you.***

***Glory …***

**Psalm 98.1-4**

Sing a new song to the LORD
who has worked wonders;
***whose right hand and holy arm***
***have brought salvation.***

The LORD has made known salvation;
has shown justice to the nations;
***has remembered truth and love***
***for the house of Israel.***

All the ends of the earth have seen
the salvation of our God.
***Shout to the Lord, all the earth,***
***ring out your joy.***

**Thanksgiving**

The Word became flesh and lived among us,
and we have seen his glory,
***the glory as of a father's only son,***
***full of grace and truth.***
*(free prayers of thanksgiving)*
The light shines in the darkness
***and the darkness has not overcome it. Amen.***

**Song**

Cantai ao Senhor (O sing to the Lord) (SJ12)
Sithi bonga (We sing praise) (SS94)
O Lord, our Lord, how majestic (H112)

## Call to discipleship

God sent the only begotten Son into the world
so that we might live through him.
***Beloved, since God loved us so much,***
***we also ought to love one another.***

**John 1.42-44**

[Andrew] brought Simon to Jesus, who looked
at him and said, "You are Simon son of John.

You are to be called Cephas" (which is translated Peter).

The next day Jesus decided to go to Galilee. He found Philip and said to him, "Follow me." Now Philip was from Bethsaida, the city of Andrew and Peter.

**Joshua 24.14-15**

"Now therefore revere the LORD, and serve him in sincerity and in faithfulness; put away the gods that your ancestors served beyond the River and in Egypt, and serve the LORD. Now if you are unwilling to serve the LORD, choose this day whom you will serve, whether the gods your ancestors served in the region beyond the River or the gods of the Amorites in whose land you are living; but as for me and my household, we will serve the LORD."

**Silent or spoken reflection on the readings**

**Song**

Tú has venido a la orilla (Lord, you have come to the lakeshore) (H229)
Love the Lord your God (SS55)
Sizohamba naye (We will walk with God) (SJ78)

**Colossians 1.15-20**

## Call to intercession

Morning, noon, and night
call out to God, who hears your cry.
***Give your burden to the Lord,***
***who will be your support.***

God of steadfast love, we bring our prayers to you because you know well what we are made of. In your mercy,
***Lord, hear our prayer.***

You know us through and through. We pray for ourselves and those dear to us.
*(open prayers)*
In your mercy,
***Lord, hear our prayer.***

You long to reveal your salvation. We pray for our community and for our neighbors.
*(open prayers)*
In your mercy,
***Lord, hear our prayer.***

You call us to immeasurable hope for the body of Christ. We pray for the church in all places, that we may speak boldly for Christ.
*(open prayers)*
In your mercy,
***Lord, hear our prayer.***

You show justice, truth, and love to the nations. We pray for the world, for all who do justice and love mercy.
*(open prayers)*
In your mercy,
***Lord, hear our prayer.***

We offer you other concerns we carry in our hearts.
*(open prayers)*
In your mercy,
***Lord, hear our prayer.***

Unseen God,
you were pleased to dwell in Christ,
to fill him with all your fullness.
Open our eyes to see your glory
shining supremely in Emmanuel, God with us,
so that we, with all of creation,
may shout praise and honor
to the One in whose name we pray:

***Our Father …***

**Benediction**

***May grace and peace be ours in abundance***
***in the knowledge of God***
***and of Jesus our Lord. Amen.***

# He is the firstborn from the dead

JANUARY 5 EVENING

**Opening sentence**

He is the beginning,
the firstborn from the dead,
***so that he might come to have first place in everything.***

## Call to praise

Sing a new song to the Lord.
Sing praise in the assembly of the faithful.
***Let the faithful exult. Let them sing for joy!***

***Glory …***

**Psalm 150**

Alleluia!

Praise God in his holy place,
sing praise in the mighty heavens.
***Sing praise for God's powerful deeds,***
***praise God's surpassing greatness.***

Sing praise with the sound of trumpets,
sing praise with lute and harp.
***Sing praise with timbrel and dance,***
***sing praise with strings and pipes.***

Sing praise with resounding cymbals,
sing praise with clashing of cymbals.
***Let everything that lives and that breathes***
***give praise to the LORD. Alleluia!***

**Thanksgiving**

When the fullness of time had come,
you sent your Son,
***so that we might receive adoption as children.***
*(free prayers of thanksgiving)*
Thanks be to you, O God;
***you have given us an indescribable gift! Amen.***

**Song**

When the morning stars together (H34)
When in our music God is glorified (H44, vv. 1, 2, 5)
Praise the Lord who reigns above (H54)

**Confession**

Lord, you are good and just;
***you guide those who stray.***
*(silence)*
You forgive our sins, though great,
***and you teach the humble your way. Amen.***

## Call to discipleship

Let the word of Christ dwell in you richly;
teach and admonish one another
in all wisdom;
***and with gratitude in your hearts***
***sing psalms, hymns, and spiritual songs to God.***

**John 1.45-51**

Philip found Nathanael and said to him, "We have found him about whom Moses in the law and also the prophets wrote, Jesus son of Joseph from Nazareth." Nathanael said to him, "Can anything good come out of Nazareth?" Philip said to him, "Come and see." When Jesus saw Nathanael coming toward him, he said of him, "Here is truly an Israelite in whom there is no deceit!" Nathanael asked him, "Where did you get to know me?" Jesus answered, "I saw you under the fig tree before Philip called you." Nathanael replied, "Rabbi, you are the Son of God! You are the King of Israel!" Jesus answered, "Do you believe because I told you that I saw you under the fig tree? You will see greater things than these." And he said to him, "Very truly, I tell you, you will see heaven opened and the angels of God ascending and descending upon the Son of Man."

**Ephesians 1.17-23**

I pray that the God of our Lord Jesus Christ, the Father of glory, may give you a spirit of wisdom and revelation as you come to know him, so that, with the eyes of your heart enlightened, you may know what is the hope to which he has called you, what are the riches of his glorious inheritance among the saints, and what is the immeasurable greatness of his power for us who believe, according to the working of his great power. God put this power to work in Christ when he raised him from the dead and seated him at his right hand in the heavenly places, far above all rule and authority and power and dominion, and above every name that is named, not only in this age but also in the age to come. And he has put all things under his feet and has made him the head over all things for the church, which is his body, the fullness of him who fills all in all.

**Silent or spoken reflection on the readings**

**Song**

All hail the power of Jesus' name (H106)
At the name of Jesus (H342)
Abre mis ojos (Open my eyes) (SS65)

**Colossians 1.15-20**

## Call to intercession

Jesus said, If you abide in me,
and my words abide in you,
ask whatever you wish,
and it will be done for you.
***The Father will give you***
***whatever you ask in my name.***

God of steadfast love, you know how to give good gifts to your children. In your mercy,
***Lord, hear our prayer.***

You know us through and through. We pray for ourselves and those dear to us.
*(open prayers)*
In your mercy,
***Lord, hear our prayer.***

You long to reveal your salvation. We pray for our community and for our neighbors.
*(open prayers)*
In your mercy,
***Lord, hear our prayer.***

You call us to immeasurable hope for the body of Christ. We pray for the church in all places, that we may speak boldly for Christ.
*(open prayers)*

In your mercy,
***Lord, hear our prayer.***

You show justice, truth, and love to the nations. We pray for the world, for all who do justice and love mercy.
*(open prayers)*
In your mercy,
***Lord, hear our prayer.***

We offer you other concerns we carry in our hearts.
*(open prayers)*
In your mercy,
***Lord, hear our prayer.***

O God, you hold all things together in Christ.
Come to our fractured world;
be pleased to dwell with us
as through Christ you reconcile
all that is in heaven and earth.
In his name we pray:

***Our Father …***

**Benediction**

***The Lord will keep us from all evil.***
***The Lord will keep our life.***
***The Lord will keep our going out***
***and our coming in***
***from this time on and forevermore. Amen.***

# Epiphany

## Introduction to the Epiphany prayers

In the church year, we celebrate Epiphany after Christmas, commemorating either the visit of the Magi (Western tradition) or the baptism of Jesus (Eastern tradition). In this prayer book, the Epiphany day (January 6) services complete the Christmas cycle begun on January 1. In the week of Epiphany services that follow, we expand the celebration to a season by using the concept of epiphany—God revealing the divine self to human beings, through Jesus but also in other times, places, and ways. This week of services can be used until Lent begins on Ash Wednesday.

A central biblical motif for revelation is light. Light imagery floods the language of the calls—to praise, discipleship, and intercession—as well as the other components of the services: light is not overcome by darkness; the windows of heaven are open; the fruit of the light is goodness. The collects address God as the God of light.

For the week of Epiphany services, we chose as scriptures both Old Testament and New Testament epiphanies. With these passages, we give thanks for God's faithfulness in self-revelation over time. These appearances of the divine presence to the patriarchs and matriarchs, to the children of Israel and the prophets and seers, as well as through Jesus, attest to God's yearning to become known to God's people. God's passion for us also blesses us to reach out to others with the light. As Israel, to whom God appeared as a pillar of fire, is called to become a light to the nations, so we too are called to God's mission in the world. Epiphany leads into mission.

For this season, Simeon's song in Luke 2 suggested itself as an appropriate anchor; it is used in the titles and opening sentences, and as canticle for this season. What greater testimony to the power of God's light, as well as the tenacity of human devotion to that light, than this old man's death song, his centered sense of vision claimed and hope fulfilled. With him, we rejoice: "My own eyes have seen the salvation which you have prepared in the sight of every people."

# Through him God was pleased to reconcile all things

## EPIPHANY DAY MORNING

**Opening sentence**

For in him all the fullness of God
was pleased to dwell,
***and through him God was pleased***
***to reconcile to himself all things,***
***whether on earth or in heaven,***
***by making peace***
***through the blood of his cross.***

## Call to praise

Arise, shine; for your light has come
and the glory of the Lord has risen upon you.
***Nations shall come to your light,***
***and kings to the brightness of your dawn.***

***Glory …***

**Isaiah 60.1-3**

Arise, shine; for your light has come,
and the glory of the LORD has risen upon you.
***For darkness shall cover the earth,***
***and thick darkness the peoples;***
but the LORD will arise upon you,
and his glory will appear over you.

***Nations shall come to your light,***
***and kings to the brightness of your dawn.***

**Thanksgiving**

Let the righteous be joyful;
***let them exult before you, O God.***
*(free prayers of thanksgiving)*
Lord, I will sing of your power;
***every morning I will sing of your faithful love.***
***Amen.***

**Song**

Arise, your light is come! (SS30)
Christ is the world's true light (H334)
Awake, awake, fling off the night (H448)

## Call to discipleship

Let us live as children of light,
***for the fruit of the light is found***
***in all that is good and right and true.***

**Matthew 2.1-6**

In the time of King Herod, after Jesus was born in Bethlehem of Judea, wise men from the East came to Jerusalem, asking, "Where is the child who has been born king of the Jews? For we observed his star at its rising, and have come to pay him homage." When King Herod heard this, he was frightened, and all

Jerusalem with him; and calling together all the chief priests and scribes of the people, he inquired of them where the Messiah was to be born. They told him, "In Bethlehem of Judea; for so it has been written by the prophet:

'And you, Bethlehem, in the land of Judah,
are by no means least among the rulers of
Judah;
for from you shall come a ruler
who is to shepherd my people Israel.'"

**Exodus 13.17-22**

When Pharaoh let the people go, God did not lead them by way of the land of the Philistines, although that was nearer; for God thought, "If the people face war, they may change their minds and return to Egypt." So God led the people by the roundabout way of the wilderness toward the Red Sea. The Israelites went up out of the land of Egypt prepared for battle. And Moses took with him the bones of Joseph who had required a solemn oath of the Israelites, saying, "God will surely take notice of you, and then you must carry my bones with you from here." They set out from Succoth, and camped at Etham, on the edge of the wilderness. The LORD went in front of them in a pillar of cloud by day, to lead them along the way, and in a pillar of fire by night, to give them light, so that they might travel by day and by night. Neither the pillar of cloud by day nor the pillar of fire by night left its place in front of the people.

**Silent or spoken reflection on the readings**

**Song**

When Christ's appearing (H217)
Oh, beautiful star of Bethlehem (SS32)
Hail the bless'd morn (H221)
Brightest and best (SS29)
Lead on, O cloud of Presence (H419)

**Colossians 1.15-20**

## Call to intercession

I will open the windows of heaven for you,
says the Lord of hosts,
and pour down an overflowing blessing.
***For those who revere your name, O God,***
***the sun of righteousness will rise,***
***with healing in its wings.***

God of glory, you want the light of your presence to pervade our lives. In your mercy,
***Lord, hear our prayer.***

You fill our lives with the fruit of your light.
We pray for ourselves and those dear to us.
*(open prayers)*

In your mercy,
***Lord, hear our prayer.***

Your steadfast love never ceases. We pray for our community and for our neighbors.
*(open prayers)*
In your mercy,
***Lord, hear our prayer.***

You take notice of your people. We pray for the church in all places, that we may bear witness to your reign of justice, peace, and joy.
*(open prayers)*
In your mercy,
***Lord, hear our prayer.***

Your glory will appear over the nations. We pray for the world, for all who are ensnared in greed, violence, and oppression.
*(open prayers)*
In your mercy,
***Lord, hear our prayer.***

We offer you other concerns we carry in our hearts.
*(open prayers)*
In your mercy,
***Lord, hear our prayer.***

God of light,
your rising reveals all things
in their true proportion.

Illumine our lives,
that we may see rightly,
love deeply, and act justly.
In the example of Jesus,
we pray for the advent of your reign:

***Our Father …***

**Benediction**

***By the tender mercy of our God,***
***the dawn from on high will break upon us,***
***to give light to those who sit in darkness***
***and in the shadow of death,***
***to guide our feet into the way of peace. Amen.***

# Through him God was pleased to reconcile all things

## EPIPHANY DAY EVENING

**Opening sentence**

For in him all the fullness of God
was pleased to dwell,
***and through him God was pleased***
***to reconcile to himself all things,***
***whether on earth or in heaven,***
***by making peace***
***through the blood of his cross.***

## Call to praise

The grace of God has appeared,
bringing salvation to all.
***The light and peace of Jesus Christ be with us.***

***Glory …***

**Isaiah 60.4-6**

Lift up your eyes and look around;
they all gather together, they come to you;
***your sons shall come from far away,***
***and your daughters shall be carried on their nurses' arms.***
Then you shall see and be radiant;
your heart shall thrill and rejoice,

*because the abundance of the sea shall be brought to you,*
*the wealth of the nations shall come to you.*
A multitude of camels shall cover you,
the young camels of Midian and Ephah;
all those from Sheba shall come.
*They shall bring gold and frankincense,*
*and shall proclaim the praise of the LORD.*

**Thanksgiving**

My mouth is filled with your praise, O God,
***and with your glory all day long.***
*(free prayers of thanksgiving)*
Lord, your steadfast love never ceases,
***your mercies never come to an end. Amen.***

**Song**

Alleluia (SS24)
Gloria, gloria, gloria (SS23)
Jubilate Deo omnis terra (H103)
Blessed Savior, we adore thee (H107)

**Confession**

If we confess our sins, O God,
you are faithful and just
and will forgive us our sins,
***and you will cleanse us***
***from all unrighteousness.***
*(silence)*

When we walk in the light
as you are in the light,
we have fellowship with one another,
***and the blood of Jesus cleanses us from all sin.***
***Amen.***

## Call to discipleship

Jesus said, I am the light of the world.
***Whoever follows me***
***will never walk in darkness***
***but will have the light of life.***

**Matthew 2.7-12**

Then Herod secretly called for the wise men and learned from them the exact time when the star had appeared. Then he sent them to Bethlehem, saying, "Go and search diligently for the child; and when you have found him, bring me word so that I may also go and pay him homage." When they had heard the king, they set out; and there, ahead of them, went the star that they had seen at its rising, until it stopped over the place where the child was. When they saw that the star had stopped, they were overwhelmed with joy. On entering the house, they saw the child with Mary his mother; and they knelt down and paid him homage. Then, opening their treasure chests, they offered him gifts of gold, frankincense, and myrrh. And having been warned in a dream not to return to Herod, they left for their own country by another road.

**Ephesians 3.1-6**

This is the reason that I Paul am a prisoner for Christ Jesus for the sake of you Gentiles—for surely you have already heard of the commission of God's grace that was given me for you, and how the mystery was made known to me by revelation, as I wrote above in a few words, a reading of which will enable you to perceive my understanding of the mystery of Christ. In former generations this mystery was not made known to humankind, as it has now been revealed to his holy apostles and prophets by the Spirit: that is, the Gentiles have become fellow heirs, members of the same body, and sharers in the promise in Christ Jesus through the gospel.

**Silent or spoken reflection on the readings**

**Song**

Bright and glorious is the sky (H219)
As with gladness men of old (H218)
Worship the Lord in the beauty (H220)
Holy Child within the manger (SS28)
Jesus, be the center (SS31)

**Colossians 1.15-20**

## Call to intercession

O God, you grant justice to your chosen ones, who cry to you day and night,
***so we pray always, and do not lose heart.***

God of glory, the light of your love cannot be overcome by darkness. In your mercy,
***Lord, hear our prayer.***

You fill our lives with the fruit of your light. We pray for ourselves and those dear to us.
*(open prayers)*
In your mercy,
***Lord, hear our prayer.***

Your steadfast love never ceases. We pray for our community and for our neighbors.
*(open prayers)*
In your mercy,
***Lord, hear our prayer.***

You take notice of your people. We pray for the church in all places, that we may bear witness to your reign of justice, peace, and joy.
*(open prayers)*
In your mercy,
***Lord, hear our prayer.***

Your glory will appear over the nations. We pray for the world, for all who are ensnared in greed, violence, and oppression.
*(open prayers)*
In your mercy,
***Lord, hear our prayer.***

We offer you other concerns we carry in our hearts.
*(open prayers)*
In your mercy,
***Lord, hear our prayer.***

God of light,
your presence illumines
even our darkest shadows.
Gather today's sorrow and pleasure
and remake them, in us,
into generous hope, sober joy, tested faith,
that our lives may be radiant with your love.
In the example of Jesus,
we pray for the advent of your reign:

***Our Father …***

**Benediction**

***May the Lord bless us and keep us.***
***May the face of God shine upon us,***
***and may the Lord be gracious to us.***
***May God's presence embrace us***
***and give us peace. Amen.***

# You let your servant go in peace

## EPIPHANY SUNDAY MORNING

**Opening sentence**

Now, Lord, you let your servant go in peace:
***your word has been fulfilled.***

## Call to praise

Arise, shine; for your light has come
and the glory of the Lord has risen upon you.
***Nations shall come to your light,***
***and kings to the brightness of your dawn.***

***Glory ...***

**Psalm 139.13-18**

For it was you who created my being,
knit me together in my mother's womb.
***I thank you for the wonder of my being,***
***for the wonders of all your creation.***

Already you knew my soul,
my body held no secret from you
***when I was being fashioned in secret***
***and molded in the depths of the earth.***

Your eyes saw all my actions,
they were all of them written in your book;

***every one of my days was decreed***
***before one of them came into being.***

To me, how mysterious your thoughts,
the sum of them not to be numbered!
***If I count them, they are more than the sand;***
***to finish, I must be eternal, like you.***

**Thanksgiving**

Let the righteous be joyful;
***let them exult before you, O God.***
*(free prayers of thanksgiving)*
Lord, I will sing of your power;
***every morning I will sing of your faithful love.***
***Amen.***

**Song**

Christ, whose glory fills the skies (H216)
Je louerai l'Eternel (Praise, I will praise you, Lord) (H76)
O bless the Lord, my soul (H80)
God is here among us (H16)

## Call to discipleship

Let us live as children of light,
***for the fruit of the light is found***
***in all that is good and right and true.***

**Mark 1.4-11**

John the baptizer appeared in the wilderness, proclaiming a baptism of repentance for the forgiveness of sins. And people from the whole Judean countryside and all the people of Jerusalem were going out to him, and were baptized by him in the river Jordan, confessing their sins. Now John was clothed with camel's hair, with a leather belt around his waist, and he ate locusts and wild honey. He proclaimed, "The one who is more powerful than I is coming after me; I am not worthy to stoop down and untie the thong of his sandals. I have baptized you with water; but he will baptize you with the Holy Spirit."

In those days Jesus came from Nazareth of Galilee and was baptized by John in the Jordan. And just as he was coming up out of the water, he saw the heavens torn apart and the Spirit descending like a dove on him. And a voice came from heaven, "You are my Son, the Beloved; with you I am well pleased."

**Jeremiah 1.4-10**

Now the word of the LORD came to me saying,
"Before I formed you in the womb I knew you,
and before you were born I consecrated you;
I appointed you a prophet to the nations."

Then I said, "Ah, Lord GOD! Truly I do not know how to speak, for I am only a boy." But the LORD said to me,

"Do not say, 'I am only a boy';
for you shall go to all to whom I send you,
and you shall speak whatever I command
you,
Do not be afraid of them,
for I am with you to deliver you, says the
LORD."

Then the LORD put out his hand and touched my mouth; and the LORD said to me,

"Now I have put my words in your mouth.
See, today I appoint you over nations and
over kingdoms,
to pluck up and to pull down,
to destroy and to overthrow,
to build and to plant."

**Silent or spoken reflection on the readings**

**Song**

I sing with exultation (H438)
Water has held us (SJ82)
A charge to keep I have (H393)
God has chosen me (SS114)

**Simeon's song**

## Call to intercession

I will open the windows of heaven for you,
says the Lord of hosts,
and pour down an overflowing blessing.
***For those who revere your name, O God,***
***the sun of righteousness will rise,***
***with healing in its wings.***

God of mystery, you want the light of your presence to pervade our lives. In your mercy,
***Lord, hear our prayer.***

You come to us and do not keep silence. We pray for ourselves and those dear to us.
*(open prayers)*
In your mercy,
***Lord, hear our prayer.***

Your light is not overcome by darkness. We pray for our community and for our neighbors.
*(open prayers)*
In your mercy,
***Lord, hear our prayer.***

Your grace has appeared, bringing salvation to all. We pray for the church in all places, that we may be one.
*(open prayers)*
In your mercy,
***Lord, hear our prayer.***

You delight in all that is good and right and true. We pray for the world, that your reign may come and your will be done on earth.
*(open prayers)*
In your mercy,
***Lord, hear our prayer.***

We offer you other concerns we carry in our hearts.
*(open prayers)*
In your mercy,
***Lord, hear our prayer.***

God of light,
your rising reveals all things
in their true proportion.
Illumine our lives,
that we may see rightly,
love deeply, and act justly.
In the example of Jesus,
we pray for the advent of your reign:

***Our Father …***

**Benediction**

***By the tender mercy of our God,***
***the dawn from on high will break upon us,***
***to give light to those who sit in darkness***
***and in the shadow of death,***
***to guide our feet into the way of peace. Amen.***

# You let your servant go in peace

## EPIPHANY SUNDAY EVENING

**Opening sentence**

Now, Lord, you let your servant go in peace:
***your word has been fulfilled.***

## Call to praise

The grace of God has appeared,
bringing salvation to all.
***The light and peace of Jesus Christ be with us.***

***Glory …***

**Psalm 50.1-6**

The God of gods, the LORD,
has spoken and summoned the earth
from the rising of the sun to its setting.
***Out of Zion's perfect beauty God shines.***

***(Our God comes and does not keep silence.)***

Announced by devouring fire,
and surrounded by raging tempest,
***God calls on the heavens and the earth***
***to witness the judgment of his people.***

"Summon before me my people
who made covenant with me by sacrifice!"

*The heavens proclaim God's justice,*
*for God, indeed, is the judge.*

**Thanksgiving**

My mouth is filled with your praise, O God,
***and with your glory all day long.***
*(free prayers of thanksgiving)*
Lord, your steadfast love never ceases,
***your mercies never come to an end. Amen.***

**Song**

Before Jehovah's aweful throne (H18)
All people that on earth do dwell (H42)
From all that dwell below the skies (H49)
O God, who gives us life (H483)

**Confession**

If we confess our sins, O God,
you are faithful and just
and will forgive us our sins,
***and you will cleanse us***
***from all unrighteousness.***
*(silence)*
When we walk in the light
as you are in the light,
we have fellowship with one another,
***and the blood of Jesus cleanses us from all sin.***
***Amen.***

## Call to discipleship

Jesus said, I am the light of the world.
***Whoever follows me***
***will never walk in darkness***
***but will have the light of life.***

**Luke 24.1-11**

But on the first day of the week, at early dawn, [the women] came to the tomb, taking the spices that they had prepared. They found the stone rolled away from the tomb, but when they went in, they did not find the body. While they were perplexed about this, suddenly two men in dazzling clothes stood beside them. The women were terrified and bowed their faces to the ground, but the men said to them, "Why do you look for the living among the dead? He is not here, but has risen. Remember how he told you, while he was still in Galilee, that the Son of Man must be handed over to sinners, and be crucified, and on the third day rise again." Then they remembered his words, and returning from the tomb, they told all this to the eleven and to all the rest. Now it was Mary Magdalene, Joanna, Mary the mother of James, and the other women with them who told this to the apostles. But these words seemed to them an idle tale, and they did not believe them.

**Colossians 3.1-4**

So if you have been raised with Christ, seek the things that are above, where Christ is, seated at the right hand of God. Set your minds on things that are above, not on things that are on earth, for you have died, and your life is hidden with Christ in God. When Christ who is your life is revealed, then you also will be revealed with him in glory.

**Silent or spoken reflection on the readings**

**Song**

We know that Christ is raised (H443)
Christ be with me (H442)
O sons and daughters, let us sing (H274)
Jesus, be the center (SS31)

**Simeon's song**

## Call to intercession

O God, you grant justice to your chosen ones,
who cry to you day and night,
***so we pray always, and do not lose heart.***

God of mystery, the light of your love cannot be overcome by darkness. In your mercy,
***Lord, hear our prayer.***

You come to us and do not keep silence. We pray for ourselves and those dear to us.
*(open prayers)*
In your mercy,
***Lord, hear our prayer.***

Your light is not overcome by darkness. We pray for our community and for our neighbors.
*(open prayers)*
In your mercy,
***Lord, hear our prayer.***

Your grace has appeared, bringing salvation to all. We pray for the church in all places, that we may be one.
*(open prayers)*
In your mercy,
***Lord, hear our prayer.***

You delight in all that is good and right and true. We pray for the world, that your reign may come and your will be done on earth.
*(open prayers)*
In your mercy,
***Lord, hear our prayer.***

We offer you other concerns we carry in our hearts.

*(open prayers)*
In your mercy,
***Lord, hear our prayer.***

God of light,
your presence illumines
even our darkest shadows.
Gather today's sorrow and pleasure
and remake them, in us,
into generous hope, sober joy, tested faith,
that our lives may be radiant with your love.
In the example of Jesus,
we pray for the advent of your reign:

***Our Father …***

**Benediction**

***May the Lord bless us and keep us.***
***May the face of God shine upon us,***
***and may the Lord be gracious to us.***
***May God's presence embrace us***
***and give us peace. Amen.***

# Your word has been fulfilled

## EPIPHANY MONDAY MORNING

**Opening sentence**

Now, Lord, you let your servant go in peace:
*your word has been fulfilled.*

## Call to praise

Arise, shine; for your light has come
and the glory of the Lord has risen upon you.
***Nations shall come to your light,***
***and kings to the brightness of your dawn.***

*Glory ...*

**Isaiah 49.1-6**

The LORD called me before I was born,
while I was in my mother's womb he named me.
***He made my mouth like a sharp sword,***
***in the shadow of his hand he hid me;***
he made me a polished arrow,
in his quiver he hid me away.
***And he said to me, "You are my servant,***
***Israel, in whom I will be glorified."***
But I said, "I have labored in vain,
I have spent my strength for nothing and vanity;

***yet surely my cause is with the LORD,***
***and my reward with my God."***

And now the LORD says,
who formed me in the womb to be his servant,
to bring Jacob back to him,
and that Israel might be gathered to him,
***for I am honored in the sight of the LORD,***
***and my God has become my strength—***
he says,
"It is too light a thing that you should be my servant
to raise up the tribes of Jacob
and to restore the survivors of Israel;
***I will give you as a light to the nations,***
***that my salvation may reach to the end of the earth."***

**Thanksgiving**

Let the righteous be joyful;
***let them exult before you, O God.***
*(free prayers of thanksgiving)*
Lord, I will sing of your power;
***every morning I will sing of your faithful love.***
***Amen.***

**Song**

Morning Star, O cheering sight (H214)
Blessing and honor (SS109)
The Lord is my light (SJ97)

## Call to discipleship

Let us live as children of light,
***for the fruit of the light is found***
***in all that is good and right and true.***

**Genesis 12.1-7**

Now the LORD said to Abram, "Go from your country and your kindred and your father's house to the land that I will show you. I will make of you a great nation, and I will bless you, and make your name great, so that you will be a blessing. I will bless those who bless you, and the one who curses you I will curse; and in you all the families of the earth shall be blessed."

So Abram went, as the LORD had told him; and Lot went with him. Abram was seventy-five years old when he departed from Haran. Abram took his wife Sarai and his brother's son Lot, and all the possessions that they had gathered, and the persons whom they had acquired in Haran; and they set forth to go to the land of Canaan. When they had come to the land of Canaan, Abram passed through the land to the place at Shechem, to the oak of Moreh. At that time the Canaanites were in the land. Then the LORD appeared to Abram, and said, "To your offspring I will give this land."

So he built there an altar to the Lord, who had appeared to him.

**Galatians 3.6-14**

Just as Abraham "believed God, and it was reckoned to him as righteousness," so, you see, those who believe are the descendants of Abraham. And the scripture, foreseeing that God would justify the Gentiles by faith, declared the gospel beforehand to Abraham, saying, "All the Gentiles shall be blessed in you." For this reason, those who believe are blessed with Abraham who believed.

For all who rely on the works of the law are under a curse; for it is written, "Cursed is everyone who does not observe and obey all the things written in the book of the law." Now it is evident that no one is justified before God by the law; for "The one who is righteous will live by faith." But the law does not rest on faith; on the contrary, "Whoever does the works of the law will live by them." Christ redeemed us from the curse of the law by becoming a curse for us—for it is written, "Cursed is everyone who hangs on a tree"—in order that in Christ Jesus the blessing of Abraham might come to the Gentiles, so that we might receive the promise of the Spirit through faith.

**Silent or spoken reflection on the readings**

**Song**

Lord, you sometimes speak (H594)
For me to live is Christ (SS111)

**Simeon's song**

## Call to intercession

I will open the windows of heaven for you,
says the Lord of hosts,
and pour down an overflowing blessing.
***For those who revere your name, O God,***
***the sun of righteousness will rise,***
***with healing in its wings.***

Holy God, you want the light of your presence to pervade our lives. In your mercy,
***Lord, hear our prayer.***

You hide us in the shadow of your hand. We pray for ourselves and those dear to us.
*(open prayers)*
In your mercy,
***Lord, hear our prayer.***

You are able to do what you have promised. We pray for our community and for our neighbors.
*(open prayers)*

In your mercy,
***Lord, hear our prayer.***

You give your people as a light to the nations. We pray for the church in all places, that we may know the freedom of life in the Spirit.
*(open prayers)*
In your mercy,
***Lord, hear our prayer.***

You give life to everything on the earth and in the sea. We pray for the world and for all who care for creation.
*(open prayers)*
In your mercy,
***Lord, hear our prayer.***

We offer you other concerns we carry in our hearts.
*(open prayers)*
In your mercy,
***Lord, hear our prayer.***

God of light,
your rising reveals all things
in their true proportion.
Illumine our lives,
that we may see rightly,
love deeply, and act justly.
In the example of Jesus,
we pray for the advent of your reign:

*Our Father …*

**Benediction**

*By the tender mercy of our God,*
*the dawn from on high will break upon us,*
*to give light to those who sit in darkness*
*and in the shadow of death,*
*to guide our feet into the way of peace. Amen.*

# Your word has been fulfilled

## EPIPHANY MONDAY EVENING

**Opening sentence**

Now, Lord, you let your servant go in peace:
***your word has been fulfilled.***

## Call to praise

The grace of God has appeared,
bringing salvation to all.
***The light and peace of Jesus Christ be with us.***

***Glory …***

**Nehemiah 9.5-8**

Bless the LORD your God
from everlasting to everlasting.
***Blessed be your glorious name,***
***which is exalted above all blessing and praise….***

You are the LORD, you alone;
you have made heaven,
the heaven of heavens, with all their host,
***the earth and all that is on it,***
***the seas and all that is in them.***
To all of them you give life,
and the host of heaven worships you.

***You are the LORD, the God who chose Abram***
***and brought him out of Ur of the Chaldeans***
***and gave him the name Abraham;***
and you found his heart faithful before you,
and made with him a covenant
to give to his descendants the land …
***and you have fulfilled your promise,***
***for you are righteous.***

## Thanksgiving

My mouth is filled with your praise, O God,
***and with your glory all day long.***
*(free prayers of thanksgiving)*
Lord, your steadfast love never ceases,
***your mercies never come to an end. Amen.***

## Song

Let the whole creation cry (H51)
Praise the Lord who reigns above (H54)
Sing praise to God who reigns (H59)

## Confession

If we confess our sins, O God,
you are faithful and just
and will forgive us our sins,
***and you will cleanse us***
***from all unrighteousness.***
*(silence)*
When we walk in the light
as you are in the light,
we have fellowship with one another,

***and the blood of Jesus cleanses us from all sin. Amen.***

## Call to discipleship

Jesus said, I am the light of the world.
***Whoever follows me***
***will never walk in darkness***
***but will have the light of life.***

**Genesis 18.1-14**

The LORD appeared to Abraham by the oaks of Mamre, as he sat at the entrance of his tent in the heat of the day. He looked up and saw three men standing near him. When he saw them, he ran from the tent entrance to meet them, and bowed down to the ground. He said, "My lord, if I find favor with you, do not pass by your servant. Let a little water be brought, and wash your feet, and rest yourselves under the tree. Let me bring a little bread, that you may refresh yourselves, and after that you may pass on—since you have come to your servant." So they said, "Do as you have said." And Abraham hastened into the tent to Sarah, and said, "Make ready quickly three measures of choice flour, knead it, and make cakes." Abraham ran to the herd, and took a calf, tender and good, and gave it to the servant, who hastened to prepare it. Then he took curds and milk and the calf that he had prepared, and set it before them; and he stood by them under the tree while they ate.

They said to him, "Where is your wife Sarah?" And he said, "There, in the tent." Then one said, "I will surely return to you in due season, and your wife Sarah shall have a son." And Sarah was listening at the tent entrance behind him. Now Abraham and Sarah were old, advanced in age; it had ceased to be with Sarah after the manner of women. So Sarah laughed to herself, saying, "After I have grown old, and my husband is old, shall I have pleasure?" The LORD said to Abraham, "Why did Sarah laugh, and say, 'Shall I indeed bear a child, now that I am old?' Is anything too wonderful for the LORD? At the set time I will return to you, in due season, and Sarah shall have a son."

**Romans 4.18-22**

Hoping against hope, [Abraham] believed that he would become "the father of many nations," according to what was said, "So numerous shall your descendants be." He did not weaken in faith when he considered his own body, which was already as good as dead (for he was about a hundred years old), or when he considered the barrenness of Sarah's womb. No distrust made him waver concerning the promise of God, but he grew strong in his faith as he gave glory to God, being fully convinced that God was able to do what he had promised. Therefore his faith "was reckoned to him as righteousness."

**Silent or spoken reflection on the readings**

**Song**

Amazing grace (H143)
If you but trust in God (H576)
Take thou my hand, O Father (H581)

**Simeon's song**

## Call to intercession

O God, you grant justice to your chosen ones,
who cry to you day and night,
***so we pray always, and do not lose heart.***

Holy God, the light of your love cannot be overcome by darkness. In your mercy,
***Lord, hear our prayer.***

You hide us in the shadow of your hand. We pray for ourselves and those dear to us.
*(open prayers)*
In your mercy,
***Lord, hear our prayer.***

You are able to do what you have promised. We pray for our community and for our neighbors.
*(open prayers)*
In your mercy,
***Lord, hear our prayer.***

You give your people as a light to the nations. We pray for the church in all places, that we may know the freedom of life in the Spirit.
*(open prayers)*
In your mercy,
***Lord, hear our prayer.***

You give life to everything on the earth and in the sea. We pray for the world and for all who care for creation.
*(open prayers)*
In your mercy,
***Lord, hear our prayer.***

We offer you other concerns we carry in our hearts.
*(open prayers)*
In your mercy,
***Lord, hear our prayer.***

God of light,
your presence illumines
even our darkest shadows.
Gather today's sorrow and pleasure
and remake them, in us,

into generous hope, sober joy, tested faith,
that our lives may be radiant with your love.
In the example of Jesus,
we pray for the advent of your reign:

*Our Father ...*

**Benediction**

*May the Lord bless us and keep us.*
*May the face of God shine upon us,*
*and may the Lord be gracious to us.*
*May God's presence embrace us*
*and give us peace. Amen.*

# My own eyes have seen the salvation

## EPIPHANY TUESDAY MORNING

**Opening sentence**

My own eyes have seen the salvation
***which you have prepared.***

## Call to praise

Arise, shine; for your light has come
and the glory of the Lord has risen upon you.
***Nations shall come to your light,***
***and kings to the brightness of your dawn.***

***Glory ...***

**Psalm 29**

O give the LORD, you children of God,
give the LORD glory and power;
***give the LORD the glory of his name.***
***Adore the LORD, resplendent and holy.***

The LORD's voice resounding on the waters,
the LORD on the immensity of waters;
***the voice of the LORD, full of power,***
***the voice of the LORD, full of splendor.***

The LORD's voice shattering the cedars,
the LORD shatters the cedars of Lebanon,

***makes Lebanon leap like a calf***
***and Sirion like a young wild ox.***

(The LORD's voice flashes flames of fire.)

***The LORD's voice shaking the wilderness,***
***the LORD shakes the wilderness of Kadesh;***
the LORD's voice rending the oak tree
and stripping the forest bare.

***The God of glory thunders.***
***In his temple they all cry: "Glory!"***
The LORD sat enthroned over the flood;
the LORD sits as king for ever.

***The LORD will give strength to his people,***
***the LORD will bless his people with peace.***

**Thanksgiving**

Let the righteous be joyful;
***let them exult before you, O God.***
*(free prayers of thanksgiving)*
Lord, I will sing of your power;
***every morning I will sing of your faithful love.***
***Amen.***

**Song**

Gloria, gloria, gloria (SS23)
Let the heavens be glad (H187)
Joyful, joyful, we adore thee (H71)

## Call to discipleship

Let us live as children of light,
***for the fruit of the light is found***
***in all that is good and right and true.***

**Genesis 21.15-19**

When the water in the skin was gone, [Hagar] cast the child under one of the bushes. Then she went and sat down opposite him a good way off, about the distance of a bowshot; for she said, "Do not let me look on the death of the child." And as she sat opposite him, she lifted up her voice and wept. And God heard the voice of the boy; and the angel of God called to Hagar from heaven, and said to her, "What troubles you, Hagar? Do not be afraid; for God has heard the voice of the boy where he is. Come, lift up the boy and hold him fast with your hand, for I will make a great nation of him." Then God opened her eyes and she saw a well of water. She went, and filled the skin with water, and gave the boy a drink.

**John 17.20-24**

"I ask not only on behalf of these, but also on behalf of those who will believe in me through their word, that they may all be one. As you, Father, are in me and I am in you, may they also be in us, so that the world may believe that you have sent me. The glory that you have given me I have given them, so that they may be one, as we are one, I in them and you in me, that they may become completely one, so that the world may know that you have sent me and have loved them even as you have loved me. Father, I desire that those also, whom you have given me, may be with me where I am, to see my glory, which you have given me because you loved me before the foundation of the world."

**Silent or spoken reflection on the readings**

**Song**

Great is thy faithfulness (H327)
Thou, O Christ, my Lord and King (SS35)
Don't be afraid (SJ105)

**Simeon's song**

## Call to intercession

I will open the windows of heaven for you,
says the Lord of hosts,
and pour down an overflowing blessing.
***For those who revere your name, O God,***
***the sun of righteousness will rise,***
***with healing in its wings.***

God of blessing, you want the light of your presence to pervade our lives. In your mercy,
***Lord, hear our prayer.***

You know what troubles us and care about what we need. We pray for ourselves and those dear to us.
*(open prayers)*
In your mercy,
***Lord, hear our prayer.***

You desire to draw all people to yourself. We pray for our community and for our neighbors.
*(open prayers)*
In your mercy,
***Lord, hear our prayer.***

You will give strength to your people and bless us with peace. We pray for the church in all places, that we may reflect your faithful love.
*(open prayers)*
In your mercy,
***Lord, hear our prayer.***

You hear the voice of those who weep. We pray for the world, for those who are in need.
*(open prayers)*
In your mercy,
***Lord, hear our prayer.***

We offer you other concerns we carry in our hearts.
*(open prayers)*
In your mercy,
***Lord, hear our prayer.***

God of light,
your rising reveals all things
in their true proportion.
Illumine our lives,
that we may see rightly,
love deeply, and act justly.
In the example of Jesus,
we pray for the advent of your reign:

***Our Father ...***

**Benediction**

***By the tender mercy of our God,***
***the dawn from on high will break upon us,***
***to give light to those who sit in darkness***
***and in the shadow of death,***
***to guide our feet into the way of peace. Amen.***

# My own eyes have seen the salvation

## EPIPHANY TUESDAY EVENING

**Opening sentence**

My own eyes have seen the salvation
***which you have prepared.***

## Call to praise

The grace of God has appeared,
bringing salvation to all.
***The light and peace of Jesus Christ be with us.***

***Glory …***

**Psalm 77.5-16 [4-15]**

You withheld sleep from my eyes.
I was troubled, I could not speak.
***I thought of the days of long ago***
***and remembered the years long past.***
At night I mused within my heart.
I pondered and my spirit questioned.

***"Will the LORD reject us for ever***
***and no longer show favor to us?***
Has God's love vanished for ever?
Has God's promise come to an end?

***Will God forget to be gracious,***
***or in anger withhold compassion?"***

I said: "This is what causes my grief,
that the way of the Most High has changed,"
***I remember the deeds of the LORD,***
***I remember your wonders of old,***
I muse on all your works
and ponder your mighty deeds.

***Your ways, O God, are holy.***
***What god is great as our God?***
You are the God who works wonders.
You showed your power among the peoples.
***Your strong arm redeemed your people,***
***the children of Jacob and Joseph.***

**Thanksgiving**

My mouth is filled with your praise, O God,
***and with your glory all day long.***
*(free prayers of thanksgiving)*
Lord, your steadfast love never ceases,
***your mercies never come to an end. Amen.***

**Song**

Who is so great a God (H62)
O bless the Lord, my soul (H80)
I will stand in the congregation (SS113)

**Confession**

If we confess our sins, O God,
you are faithful and just
and will forgive us our sins,
***and you will cleanse us***
***from all unrighteousness.***
*(silence)*
When we walk in the light
as you are in the light,
we have fellowship with one another,
***and the blood of Jesus cleanses us from all sin.***
***Amen.***

## Call to discipleship

Jesus said, I am the light of the world.
***Whoever follows me***
***will never walk in darkness***
***but will have the light of life.***

**Genesis 32.22-30**

The same night [Jacob] got up and took his two wives, his two maids, and his eleven children, and crossed the ford of the Jabbok. He took them and sent them across the stream, and likewise everything that he had. Jacob was left alone; and a man wrestled with him until daybreak. When the man saw that he did not prevail against Jacob, he struck him on the hip socket; and Jacob's hip was put out of joint as he wrestled with him. Then he said, "Let me go, for the day is breaking." But Jacob said, "I will not let you go, unless you bless me." So he said to him, "What is your name?" And he said, "Jacob." Then the man said, "You shall no longer be called Jacob, but Israel, for you have striven with God and with humans, and have prevailed." Then Jacob asked him, "Please tell me your name." But he said, "Why is it that you ask my name?" And there he blessed him. So Jacob called the place Peniel, saying, "For I have seen God face to face, and yet my life is preserved."

**John 12.27-32**

"Now my soul is troubled. And what should I say—'Father, save me from this hour'? No, it is for this reason that I have come to this hour. Father, glorify your name." Then a voice came from heaven, "I have glorified it, and I will glorify it again." The crowd standing there heard it and said that it was thunder. Others said, "An angel has spoken to him." Jesus answered, "This voice has come for your sake, not for mine. Now is the judgment of this world; now the ruler of this world will be driven out. And I, when I am lifted up from the earth, will draw all people to myself."

**Silent or spoken reflection on the readings**

**Song**

Come, O thou Traveler unknown (H503, vv. 1, 2, 8–11)
Love divine, all loves excelling (H592)
Take, O take me as I am (SJ81)

**Simeon's song**

## Call to intercession

O God, you grant justice to your chosen ones,
who cry to you day and night,
***so we pray always, and do not lose heart.***

God of blessing, the light of your love cannot be overcome by darkness. In your mercy,
***Lord, hear our prayer.***

You know what troubles us and care about what we need. We pray for ourselves and those dear to us.
*(open prayers)*
In your mercy,
***Lord, hear our prayer.***

You desire to draw all people to yourself. We pray for our community and for our neighbors.
*(open prayers)*
In your mercy,
***Lord, hear our prayer.***

You will give strength to your people and bless us with peace. We pray for the church in all places, that we may reflect your faithful love.
*(open prayers)*
In your mercy,
***Lord, hear our prayer.***

You hear the voice of those who weep. We pray for the world, for those who are in need.
*(open prayers)*
In your mercy,
***Lord, hear our prayer.***

We offer you other concerns we carry in our hearts.
*(open prayers)*
In your mercy,
***Lord, hear our prayer.***

God of light,
your presence illumines
even our darkest shadows.
Gather today's sorrow and pleasure
and remake them, in us,
into generous hope, sober joy, tested faith,
that our lives may be radiant with your love.
In the example of Jesus,
we pray for the advent of your reign:

***Our Father …***

**Benediction**

*May the Lord bless us and keep us.*
*May the face of God shine upon us,*
*and may the Lord be gracious to us.*
*May God's presence embrace us*
*and give us peace. Amen.*

# The salvation you have prepared

## EPIPHANY WEDNESDAY MORNING

**Opening sentence**

My own eyes have seen the salvation
***which you have prepared.***

## Call to praise

Arise, shine; for your light has come
and the glory of the Lord has risen upon you.
***Nations shall come to your light,***
***and kings to the brightness of your dawn.***

*Glory ...*

**Psalm 133**

How good and how pleasant it is,
when people live in unity!

***It is like precious oil upon the head,***
***running down upon the beard,***
***running down upon Aaron's beard,***
***upon the collar of his robes.***

It is like the dew of Hermon which falls
on the heights of Zion.
***For there the LORD gives blessing,***
***life for ever.***

**Thanksgiving**

Let the righteous be joyful;
***let them exult before you, O God.***
*(free prayers of thanksgiving)*
Lord, I will sing of your power;
***every morning I will sing of your faithful love.***
***Amen.***

**Song**

Christ is the world's true light (H334)
Praise the One who breaks the darkness (SS1)
Miren qué bueno (Behold, how pleasant) (SJ37)

## Call to discipleship

Let us live as children of light,
***for the fruit of the light is found***
***in all that is good and right and true.***

**Genesis 33.1-10**

Now Jacob looked up and saw Esau coming, and four hundred men with him. So he divided the children among Leah and Rachel and the two maids. He put the maids with their children in front, then Leah with her children, and Rachel and Joseph last of all. He himself went on ahead of them, bowing himself to the ground seven times, until he came near his brother.

But Esau ran to meet him, and embraced him, and fell on his neck and kissed him, and they wept. When Esau looked up and saw the women and children, he said, "Who are these with you?" Jacob said, "The children whom God has graciously given your servant." Then the maids drew near, they and their children, and bowed down; Leah likewise and her children drew near and bowed down; and finally Joseph and Rachel drew near, and they bowed down. Esau said, "What do you mean by all this company that I met?" Jacob answered, "To find favor with my lord." But Esau said, "I have enough, my brother; keep what you have for yourself." Jacob said, "No, please; if I find favor with you, then accept my present from my hand; for truly to see your face is like seeing the face of God—since you have received me with such favor."

**John 13.31-35**

When [Judas] had gone out, Jesus said, "Now the Son of Man has been glorified, and God has been glorified in him. If God has been glorified in him, God will also glorify him in himself and will glorify him at once. Little children, I am with you only a little longer. You will look for me; and as I said to the Jews so now I say to you, 'Where I am going, you cannot come.' I give you a new commandment, that you love one another. Just as I have loved you, you also should love one another. By this everyone will know that you are my disciples, if you have love for one another."

**Silent or spoken reflection on the readings**

**Song**

How good a thing it is (H310)
Somos el cuerpo de Cristo (We are the body of Christ) (SJ64, vv. 1, 3)
Where charity and love prevail (H305)
Ubi Caritas (Where true love) (SJ39)

**Simeon's song**

## Call to intercession

I will open the windows of heaven for you,
says the Lord of hosts,
and pour down an overflowing blessing.
***For those who revere your name, O God,***
***the sun of righteousness will rise,***
***with healing in its wings.***

Gracious God, you want the light of your presence to pervade our lives. In your mercy,
***Lord, hear our prayer.***

You will show us the path of life. We pray for ourselves and those dear to us.

*(open prayers)*
In your mercy,
***Lord, hear our prayer.***

You rejoice when people are reconciled.
We pray for our community and for our neighbors.
*(open prayers)*
In your mercy,
***Lord, hear our prayer.***

You desire that your followers love one another. We pray for the church in all places, that we may bear witness to your reign of justice, peace, and joy.
*(open prayers)*
In your mercy,
***Lord, hear our prayer.***

Where your Spirit is, there is freedom. We pray for the world, for all who are ensnared in greed, violence, and oppression.
*(open prayers)*
In your mercy,
***Lord, hear our prayer.***

We offer you other concerns we carry in our hearts.
*(open prayers)*
In your mercy,
***Lord, hear our prayer.***

God of light,
your rising reveals all things
in their true proportion.
Illumine our lives,
that we may see rightly,
love deeply, and act justly.
In the example of Jesus,
we pray for the advent of your reign:

*Our Father ...*

**Benediction**

*By the tender mercy of our God,*
*the dawn from on high will break upon us,*
*to give light to those who sit in darkness*
*and in the shadow of death,*
*to guide our feet into the way of peace. Amen.*

# The salvation you have prepared

## EPIPHANY WEDNESDAY EVENING

**Opening sentence**

My own eyes have seen the salvation
***which you have prepared.***

## Call to praise

The grace of God has appeared,
bringing salvation to all.
***The light and peace of Jesus Christ be with us.***

*Glory ...*

**Psalm 16.7-11**

I will bless you, LORD, you give me counsel,
and even at night direct my heart.
***I keep you, LORD, ever in my sight;***
***since you are at my right hand, I shall stand firm.***

And so my heart rejoices, my soul is glad;
even my body shall rest in safety.
***For you will not leave my soul among the dead,***
***nor let your beloved know decay.***

You will show me the path of life,
the fullness of joy in your presence,
***at your right hand happiness for ever.***

**Thanksgiving**

My mouth is filled with your praise, O God,
***and with your glory all day long.***
*(free prayers of thanksgiving)*
Lord, your steadfast love never ceases,
***your mercies never come to an end. Amen.***

**Song**

Praise, my soul, the God of heaven (H63)
The Lord is King (H69)
Praise, praise, praise the Lord! (SJ11)
All praise to thee my God (H658)
Sun of my soul (H654)

**Confession**

If we confess our sins, O God,
you are faithful and just
and will forgive us our sins,
***and you will cleanse us***
***from all unrighteousness.***
*(silence)*
When we walk in the light
as you are in the light,
we have fellowship with one another,
***and the blood of Jesus cleanses us from all sin.***
***Amen.***

## Call to discipleship

Jesus said, I am the light of the world.
***Whoever follows me***
***will never walk in darkness***
***but will have the light of life.***

**Exodus 33.17-22**

The LORD said to Moses, "I will do the very thing that you have asked; for you have found favor in my sight, and I know you by name." Moses said, "Show me your glory, I pray." And he said, "I will make all my goodness pass before you, and will proclaim before you the name, 'The LORD'; and I will be gracious to whom I will be gracious, and will show mercy on whom I will show mercy. But," he said, "you cannot see my face; for no one shall see me and live." And the LORD continued, "See, there is a place by me where you shall stand on the rock; and while my glory passes by I will put you in a cleft of the rock, and I will cover you with my hand until I have passed by; then I will take away my hand, and you shall see my back; but my face shall not be seen."

**2 Corinthians 3.12-13, 16-18**

Since, then, we have such a hope, we act with great boldness, not like Moses, who put a veil over his face to keep the people of Israel from gazing at the end of the glory that was being set aside.... But when one turns to the Lord, the veil is removed. Now the Lord is the Spirit, and where the Spirit of the Lord is, there is freedom. And all of us, with unveiled faces, seeing the glory of the Lord as though reflected in a mirror, are being transformed into the same image from one degree of glory to another; for this comes from the Lord, the Spirit.

**Silent or spoken reflection on the readings**

**Song**

O worship the Lord (H124)
Gloria (H204)
Lord Jesus Christ, be present now (H22)
Love divine, all loves excelling (H592)

**Simeon's song**

## Call to intercession

O God, you grant justice to your chosen ones,
who cry to you day and night,
***so we pray always, and do not lose heart.***

Gracious God, the light of your love cannot be overcome by darkness. In your mercy,
***Lord, hear our prayer.***

You will show us the path of life. We pray for ourselves and those dear to us.
*(open prayers)*
In your mercy,
***Lord, hear our prayer.***

You rejoice when people are reconciled. We pray for our community and for our neighbors.
*(open prayers)*
In your mercy,
***Lord, hear our prayer.***

You desire that your followers love one another. We pray for the church in all places, that we may bear witness to your reign of justice, peace, and joy.
*(open prayers)*
In your mercy,
***Lord, hear our prayer.***

Where your Spirit is, there is freedom. We pray for the world, for all who are ensnared in greed, violence, and oppression.
*(open prayers)*
In your mercy,
***Lord, hear our prayer.***

We offer you other concerns we carry in our hearts.
*(open prayers)*

In your mercy,
***Lord, hear our prayer.***

God of light,
your presence illumines
even our darkest shadows.
Gather today's sorrow and pleasure
and remake them, in us,
into generous hope, sober joy, tested faith,
that our lives may be radiant with your love.
In the example of Jesus,
we pray for the advent of your reign:

***Our Father …***

**Benediction**

***May the Lord bless us and keep us.***
***May the face of God shine upon us,***
***and may the Lord be gracious to us.***
***May God's presence embrace us***
***and give us peace. Amen.***

# In the sight of every people

## EPIPHANY THURSDAY MORNING

**Opening sentence**

My own eyes have seen the salvation
***which you have prepared***
***in the sight of every people.***

## Call to praise

Arise, shine; for your light has come
and the glory of the Lord has risen upon you.
***Nations shall come to your light,***
***and kings to the brightness of your dawn.***

*Glory ...*

**Psalm 138.1-5**

I thank you, Lord, with all my heart,
you have heard the words of my mouth.
***In the presence of the angels I will bless you.***
***I will adore before your holy temple.***

I thank you for your faithfulness and love
which excel all we ever knew of you.
***On the day I called, you answered;***
***you increased the strength of my soul.***

All the rulers on earth shall thank you
when they hear the words of my mouth.

*They shall sing of the LORD's ways:*
*"How great is the glory of the Lord!"*

**Thanksgiving**

Let the righteous be joyful;
***let them exult before you, O God.***
*(free prayers of thanksgiving)*
Lord, I will sing of your power;
***every morning I will sing of your faithful love.***
***Amen.***

**Song**

Holy God, we praise thy name (H121)
All glory be to God on high (H122)
How wondrous great (H126)
Love the Lord your God (SS55)

## Call to discipleship

Let us live as children of light,
***for the fruit of the light is found***
***in all that is good and right and true.***

**Exodus 34.29-35**

Moses came down from Mount Sinai. As he came down from the mountain with the two tablets of the covenant in his hand, Moses did not know that the skin of his face shone because he had been talking with God. When Aaron and all the Israelites saw Moses, the skin of his face was shining, and they were afraid to come near him. But Moses called to them; and Aaron and all the leaders of the congregation returned to him, and Moses spoke with them. Afterward all the Israelites came near, and he gave them in commandment all that the LORD had spoken with him on Mount Sinai. When Moses had finished speaking with them, he put a veil on his face; but whenever Moses went in before the LORD to speak with him, he would take the veil off, until he came out; and when he came out, and told the Israelites what he had been commanded, the Israelites would see the face of Moses, that the skin of his face was shining; and Moses would put the veil on his face again, until he went in to speak with him.

**Acts 9.1-9**

Meanwhile Saul, still breathing threats and murder against the disciples of the Lord, went to the high priest and asked him for letters to the synagogues at Damascus, so that if he found any who belonged to the Way, men or women, he might bring them bound to Jerusalem. Now as he was going along and approaching Damascus, suddenly a light from heaven flashed around him. He fell to the ground and heard a voice saying to him, "Saul, Saul, why do you persecute me?" He asked, "Who are you, Lord?" The reply came, "I am Jesus, whom you are persecuting. But get up and enter the city, and you will be told what you are to do." The men who were traveling with him stood speechless because they heard the voice but saw no one. Saul got up from the ground, and though his eyes were open, he could see nothing; so they led him by the hand and brought him into Damascus. For three days he was without sight, and neither ate nor drank.

**Silent or spoken reflection on the readings**

**Song**

Eternal Light, shine in my heart (H518)
Longing for light (SJ54, vv. 1, 2, 5)
I want to walk as a child of the light (SJ95)

**Simeon's song**

## Call to intercession

I will open the windows of heaven for you,
says the Lord of hosts,
and pour down an overflowing blessing.
***For those who revere your name, O God,***
***the sun of righteousness will rise,***
***with healing in its wings.***

God of salvation, you want the light of your presence to pervade our lives. In your mercy,
***Lord, hear our prayer.***

You increase the strength of our souls. We pray for ourselves and those dear to us.
*(open prayers)*
In your mercy,
***Lord, hear our prayer.***

You promise the light of life. We pray for our community and for our neighbors.
*(open prayers)*
In your mercy,
***Lord, hear our prayer.***

You shed your light on your people, so all may learn your saving help. We pray for the church in all places, that we may daily follow in the footsteps of Christ.
*(open prayers)*
In your mercy,
***Lord, hear our prayer.***

You have prepared salvation in the sight of all people. We pray for the world, for those in positions of power and authority.
*(open prayers)*
In your mercy,
***Lord, hear our prayer.***

We offer you other concerns we carry in our hearts.
*(open prayers)*
In your mercy,
***Lord, hear our prayer.***

God of light,
your rising reveals all things
in their true proportion.
Illumine our lives,
that we may see rightly,
love deeply, and act justly.
In the example of Jesus,
we pray for the advent of your reign:

***Our Father …***

**Benediction**

***By the tender mercy of our God,***
***the dawn from on high will break upon us,***
***to give light to those who sit in darkness***
***and in the shadow of death,***
***to guide our feet into the way of peace. Amen.***

# In the sight of every people

## EPIPHANY THURSDAY EVENING

**Opening sentence**

My own eyes have seen the salvation
***which you have prepared***
***in the sight of every people.***

## Call to praise

The grace of God has appeared,
bringing salvation to all.
***The light and peace of Jesus Christ be with us.***

*Glory ...*

**Psalm 67**

O God, be gracious and bless us
and let your face shed its light upon us.
So will your ways be known upon earth
and all nations learn your saving help.

***Let the peoples praise you, O God;***
***let all the peoples praise you.***

Let the nations be glad and exult
for you rule the world with justice.
With fairness you rule the peoples,
you guide the nations on earth.

***Let the peoples praise you, O God;***
***let all the peoples praise you.***

The earth has yielded its fruit
for God, our God, has blessed us.
May God still give us blessing
till the ends of the earth stand in awe.

***Let the peoples praise you, O God;***
***let all the peoples praise you.***

**Thanksgiving**

My mouth is filled with your praise, O God,
***and with your glory all day long.***
*(free prayers of thanksgiving)*
Lord, your steadfast love never ceases,
***your mercies never come to an end. Amen.***

**Song**

God, be merciful and gracious (H424)
Asithi: Amen (Sing amen) (H64)
Alleluia (SJ41)
Blessing and honor (SS109)

**Confession**

If we confess our sins, O God,
you are faithful and just
and will forgive us our sins,
***and you will cleanse us***
***from all unrighteousness.***
*(silence)*

When we walk in the light
as you are in the light,
we have fellowship with one another,
***and the blood of Jesus cleanses us from all sin.***
***Amen.***

## Call to discipleship

Jesus said, I am the light of the world.
***Whoever follows me***
***will never walk in darkness***
***but will have the light of life.***

**Isaiah 6.1-8**

In the year that King Uzziah died, I saw the Lord sitting on a throne, high and lofty; and the hem of his robe filled the temple. Seraphs were in attendance above him; each had six wings: with two they covered their faces, and with two they covered their feet, and with two they flew. And one called to another and said:

"Holy, holy, holy is the LORD of hosts;
the whole earth is full of his glory."

The pivots on the thresholds shook at the voices of those who called, and the house filled with smoke. And I said: "Woe is me! I am lost, for I am a man of unclean lips, and I live among a people of unclean lips; yet my eyes have seen the King, the LORD of hosts!"

Then one of the seraphs flew to me, holding a live coal that had been taken from the altar with a pair of tongs. The seraph touched my mouth with it and said: "Now that this has touched your lips, your guilt has departed and your sin is blotted out." Then I heard the voice of the LORD saying, "Whom shall I send, and who will go for us?" And I said, "Here am I; send me!"

**Acts 9.10-18**

Now there was a disciple in Damascus named Ananias. The Lord said to him in a vision, "Ananias." He answered, "Here I am, Lord." The Lord said to him, "Get up and go to the street called Straight, and at the house of Judas look for a man of Tarsus named Saul. At this moment he is praying, and he has seen in a vision a man named Ananias come in and lay his hands on him so that he might regain his sight." But Ananias answered, "Lord, I have heard from many about this man, how much evil he has done to your saints in Jerusalem; and here he has authority from the chief priests to bind all who invoke your name." But the Lord said to him, "Go, for he is an instrument whom I have chosen to bring my name before Gentiles and kings and before the people of Israel; I myself will show him how much he must suffer for the sake of my name."

So Ananias went and entered the house. He laid his hands on Saul and said, "Brother Saul, the Lord Jesus, who appeared to you on your way here, has sent me so that you may regain your sight and be filled with the Holy Spirit." And immediately something like scales fell from his eyes, and his sight was restored.

**Silent or spoken reflection on the readings**

**Song**

Let all mortal flesh keep silence (H463)
Here I am, Lord (H395)
'Tis not with eyes of flesh we see (H571)
Abre mis ojos (Open my eyes) (SS65)
Open my eyes, that I may see (H517)

**Simeon's song**

## Call to intercession

O God, you grant justice to your chosen ones, who cry to you day and night,
***so we pray always, and do not lose heart.***

God of salvation, the light of your love cannot be overcome by darkness. In your mercy,
***Lord, hear our prayer.***

You increase the strength of our souls. We pray for ourselves and those dear to us.

*(open prayers)*
In your mercy,
***Lord, hear our prayer.***

You promise the light of life. We pray for our community and for our neighbors.
*(open prayers)*
In your mercy,
***Lord, hear our prayer.***

You shed your light on your people, so all may learn your saving help. We pray for the church in all places, that we may daily follow in the footsteps of Christ.
*(open prayers)*
In your mercy,
***Lord, hear our prayer.***

You have prepared salvation in the sight of all people. We pray for the world, for those in positions of power and authority.
*(open prayers)*
In your mercy,
***Lord, hear our prayer.***

We offer you other concerns we carry in our hearts.
*(open prayers)*
In your mercy,
***Lord, hear our prayer.***

God of light,
your presence illumines
even our darkest shadows.
Gather today's sorrow and pleasure
and remake them, in us,
into generous hope, sober joy, tested faith,
that our lives may be radiant with your love.
In the example of Jesus,
we pray for the advent of your reign:

*Our Father ...*

**Benediction**

*May the Lord bless us and keep us.*
*May the face of God shine upon us,*
*and may the Lord be gracious to us.*
*May God's presence embrace us*
*and give us peace. Amen.*

# A light to reveal you

EPIPHANY FRIDAY MORNING

**Opening sentence**

My own eyes have seen the salvation
which you have prepared
in the sight of every people:
***a light to reveal you to the nations.***

## Call to praise

Arise, shine; for your light has come
and the glory of the Lord has risen upon you.
***Nations shall come to your light,***
***and kings to the brightness of your dawn.***

*Glory ...*

**1 Chronicles 16.23-31**

Sing to the LORD, all the earth.
Tell of his salvation from day to day.
***Declare his glory among the nations,***
***his marvelous works among all the peoples.***
For great is the LORD, and greatly to be
praised;
he is to be revered above all gods.
***For all the gods of the peoples are idols,***
***but the LORD made the heavens.***

Honor and majesty are before him;
strength and joy are in his place.

***Ascribe to the LORD, O families of the peoples,***
***ascribe to the LORD glory and strength.***
Ascribe to the Lord the glory due his name;
bring an offering, and come before him.
***Worship the LORD in holy splendor;***
***tremble before him, all the earth.***
The world is firmly established; it shall never be moved.
***Let the heavens be glad, and let the earth rejoice,***
***and let them say among the nations, "The LORD is king!"***

**Thanksgiving**

Let the righteous be joyful;
***let them exult before you, O God.***
*(free prayers of thanksgiving)*
Lord, I will sing of your power;
***every morning I will sing of your faithful love.***
***Amen.***

**Song**

The Lord is King (H69)
Cantai ao Senhor (O sing to the Lord) (SJ12)
From all that dwell below the skies (H49)

## Call to discipleship

Let us live as children of light,
***for the fruit of the light is found***
***in all that is good and right and true.***

**Ezekiel 43.1-7**

Then [the Lord] brought me to the gate, the gate facing east. And there, the glory of the God of Israel was coming from the east; the sound was like the sound of mighty waters; and the earth shone with his glory. The vision I saw was like the vision that I had seen when he came to destroy the city, and like the vision that I had seen by the river Chebar; and I fell upon my face. As the glory of the LORD entered the temple by the gate facing east, the spirit lifted me up, and brought me into the inner court; and the glory of the LORD filled the temple.

While the man was standing beside me, I heard someone speaking to me out of the temple. He said to me: Mortal, this is the place of my throne and the place for the soles of my feet, where I will reside among the people of Israel forever.

**2 Corinthians 4.5-15**

For we do not proclaim ourselves; we proclaim Jesus Christ as Lord and ourselves as your slaves for Jesus' sake. For it is the God who said, "Let light shine out of darkness," who has shone in our hearts to give the light of the knowledge of the glory of God in the face of Jesus Christ.

But we have this treasure in clay jars, so that it may be made clear that this extraordinary power belongs to God and does not come from us. We are afflicted in every way, but not crushed; perplexed, but not driven to despair; persecuted, but not forsaken; struck down, but not destroyed; always carrying in the body the death of Jesus, so that the life of Jesus may also be made visible in our bodies. For while we live, we are always being given up to death for Jesus' sake, so that the life of Jesus may be made visible in our mortal flesh. So death is at work in us, but life in you.

But just as we have the same spirit of faith that is in accordance with scripture—"I believed, and so I spoke"—we also believe, and so we speak, because we know that the one who raised the Lord Jesus will raise us also with Jesus, and will bring us with you into his presence. Yes, everything is for your sake, so that grace, as it extends to more and more people, may increase thanksgiving, to the glory of God.

**Silent or spoken reflection on the readings**

**Song**

O Splendor of God's glory bright (H646)
Oh, have you not heard (H606)
The Lord is my light (SJ97)

**Simeon's song**

## Call to intercession

I will open the windows of heaven for you,
says the Lord of hosts,
and pour down an overflowing blessing.
***For those who revere your name, O God,***
***the sun of righteousness will rise,***
***with healing in its wings.***

Renewing God, you want the light of your presence to pervade our lives. In your mercy,
***Lord, hear our prayer.***

You place your treasure in clay vessels. We pray for ourselves and those dear to us.
*(open prayers)*
In your mercy,
***Lord, hear our prayer.***

Your sun of righteousness rises with healing in its wings. We pray for our community and for our neighbors.
*(open prayers)*
In your mercy,
***Lord, hear our prayer.***

You will live among your people forever. We pray for the church in all places, that we may speak boldly for Christ.
*(open prayers)*
In your mercy,
***Lord, hear our prayer.***

When you teach us your ways, nation will not lift up sword against nation. We pray for the world, for all who do justice and love mercy.
*(open prayers)*
In your mercy,
***Lord, hear our prayer.***

We offer you other concerns we carry in our hearts.
*(open prayers)*
In your mercy,
***Lord, hear our prayer.***

God of light,
your rising reveals all things
in their true proportion.
Illumine our lives,
that we may see rightly,

love deeply, and act justly.
In the example of Jesus,
we pray for the advent of your reign:

*Our Father ...*

**Benediction**

*By the tender mercy of our God,*
*the dawn from on high will break upon us,*
*to give light to those who sit in darkness*
*and in the shadow of death,*
*to guide our feet into the way of peace. Amen.*

# A light to reveal you

## EPIPHANY FRIDAY EVENING

**Opening sentence**

My own eyes have seen the salvation
which you have prepared
in the sight of every people:
***a light to reveal you to the nations.***

## Call to praise

The grace of God has appeared,
bringing salvation to all.
***The light and peace of Jesus Christ be with us.***

*Glory …*

**Isaiah 2.2-4**

In days to come
the mountain of the LORD's house
shall be established as the highest of the
mountains,
***and shall be raised above the hills;***
***all the nations shall stream to it.***
Many peoples shall come and say,
"Come, let us go up to the mountain of the
LORD,
to the house of the God of Jacob;

***that he may teach us his ways***
***and that we may walk in his paths."***
For out of Zion shall go forth instruction,
and the word of the LORD from Jerusalem.
***He shall judge between the nations,***
***and shall arbitrate for many peoples;***
they shall beat their swords into plowshares,
and their spears into pruning hooks;
***nation shall not lift up sword against nation,***
***neither shall they learn war any more.***

**Thanksgiving**

My mouth is filled with your praise, O God,
***and with your glory all day long.***
*(free prayers of thanksgiving)*
Lord, your steadfast love never ceases,
***your mercies never come to an end. Amen.***

**Song**

Christ is the world's true light (H334)
Come! Walk in the light (SS10)
Arise, your light is come! (SS30)

**Confession**

If we confess our sins, O God,
you are faithful and just
and will forgive us our sins,
***and you will cleanse us***
***from all unrighteousness.***
*(silence)*

When we walk in the light
as you are in the light,
we have fellowship with one another,
***and the blood of Jesus cleanses us from all sin.***
***Amen.***

## Call to discipleship

Jesus said, I am the light of the world.
***Whoever follows me***
***will never walk in darkness***
***but will have the light of life.***

**Daniel 7.13-14**

As I watched in the night visions,
I saw one like a human being [Son of Man]
coming with the clouds of heaven.
And he came to the Ancient One
and was presented before him.
To him was given dominion
and glory and kingship,
that all peoples, nations, and languages
should serve him.
His dominion is an everlasting dominion
that shall not pass away,
and his kingship is one
that shall never be destroyed.

**Revelation 1.12-20**

Then I turned to see whose voice it was that spoke to me, and on turning I saw seven golden lampstands, and in the midst of the lampstands I saw one like the Son of Man, clothed with a long robe and with a golden sash across his chest. His head and his hair were white as white wool, white as snow; his eyes were like a flame of fire, his feet were like burnished bronze, refined as in a furnace, and his voice was like the sound of many waters. In his right hand he held seven stars, and from his mouth came a sharp, two-edged sword, and his face was like the sun shining with full force.

When I saw him, I fell at his feet as though dead. But he placed his right hand on me, saying, "Do not be afraid; I am the first and the last, and the living one. I was dead, and see, I am alive forever and ever; and I have the keys of Death and of Hades. Now write what you have seen, what is, and what is to take place after this. As for the mystery of the seven stars that you saw in my right hand, and the seven golden lampstands: the seven stars are the angels of the seven churches, and the seven lampstands are the seven churches."

**Silent or spoken reflection on the readings**

**Song**

How wondrous great (H126)
Alleluia! Gracious Jesus! (SS110)
Blessing and honor and glory (H108, vv. 1, 3, 4)

**Simeon's song**

## Call to intercession

O God, you grant justice to your chosen ones,
who cry to you day and night,
***so we pray always, and do not lose heart.***

Renewing God, the light of your love cannot be overcome by darkness. In your mercy,
***Lord, hear our prayer.***

You place your treasure in clay vessels. We pray for ourselves and those dear to us.
*(open prayers)*
In your mercy,
***Lord, hear our prayer.***

Your sun of righteousness rises with healing in its wings. We pray for our community and for our neighbors.
*(open prayers)*
In your mercy,
***Lord, hear our prayer.***

You will live among your people forever. We pray for the church in all places, that we may speak boldly for Christ.
*(open prayers)*
In your mercy,
***Lord, hear our prayer.***

When you teach us your ways, nation will not lift up sword against nation. We pray for the world, for all who do justice and love mercy.
*(open prayers)*
In your mercy,
***Lord, hear our prayer.***

We offer you other concerns we carry in our hearts.
*(open prayers)*
In your mercy,
***Lord, hear our prayer.***

God of light,
your presence illumines
even our darkest shadows.
Gather today's sorrow and pleasure
and remake them, in us,
into generous hope, sober joy, tested faith,
that our lives may be radiant with your love.
In the example of Jesus,
we pray for the advent of your reign:

***Our Father …***

**Benediction**

*May the Lord bless us and keep us.*
*May the face of God shine upon us,*
*and may the Lord be gracious to us.*
*May God's presence embrace us*
*and give us peace. Amen.*

# To the nations and to your people

EPIPHANY SATURDAY MORNING

**Opening sentence**

My own eyes have seen the salvation
which you have prepared
in the sight of every people:
***a light to reveal you to the nations***
***and the glory of your people Israel.***

## Call to praise

Arise, shine; for your light has come
and the glory of the Lord has risen upon you.
***Nations shall come to your light,***
***and kings to the brightness of your dawn.***

***Glory …***

**Isaiah 43.1-3**

But now thus says the LORD,
***he who created you, O Jacob,***
***he who formed you, O Israel:***
Do not fear, for I have redeemed you;
I have called you by name, you are mine.
***When you pass through the waters, I will be with you;***
***and through the rivers, they shall not overwhelm you;***

when you walk through fire you shall not be burned,
and the flame shall not consume you.
***For I am the LORD your God,***
***the Holy One of Israel, your Savior.***

**Thanksgiving**

Let the righteous be joyful;
***let them exult before you, O God.***
*(free prayers of thanksgiving)*
Lord, I will sing of your power;
***every morning I will sing of your faithful love.***
***Amen.***

**Song**

Por la mañana (At break of day) (H647)
How firm a foundation (H567)
I will come to you in the silence (SS49)

## Call to discipleship

Let us live as children of light,
***for the fruit of the light is found***
***in all that is good and right and true.***

**Matthew 17.1-8**

Six days later, Jesus took with him Peter and James and his brother John and led them up a high mountain, by themselves. And he was transfigured before them, and his face shone like the sun, and his clothes became dazzling white. Suddenly there appeared to them Moses and Elijah, talking with him. Then Peter said to Jesus, "Lord, it is good for us to be here; if you wish, I will make three dwellings here, one for you, one for Moses, and one for Elijah." While he was still speaking, suddenly a bright cloud overshadowed them, and from the cloud a voice said, "This is my Son, the Beloved; with him I am well pleased; listen to him!" When the disciples heard this, they fell to the ground and were overcome by fear. But Jesus came and touched them, saying, "Get up and do not be afraid." And when they looked up, they saw no one except Jesus himself alone.

**Exodus 3.1-12**

Moses was keeping the flock of his father-in-law Jethro, the priest of Midian; he led his flock beyond the wilderness, and came to Horeb, the mountain of God. There the angel of the LORD appeared to him in a flame of fire out of a bush; he looked, and the bush was blazing, yet it was not consumed. Then Moses said, "I must turn aside and look at this great sight, and see why the bush is not burned up." When the LORD saw that he had turned aside to see, God called to him out of the bush, "Moses, Moses!" And he said, "Here I am."

Then he said, "Come no closer! Remove the sandals from your feet, for the place on which you are standing is holy ground." He said further, "I am the God of your father, the God of Abraham, the God of Isaac, and the God of Jacob." And Moses hid his face, for he was afraid to look at God.

Then the LORD said, "I have observed the misery of my people who are in Egypt; I have heard their cry on account of their taskmasters. Indeed, I know their sufferings, and I have come down to deliver them from the Egyptians, and to bring them up out of that land to a good and broad land, a land flowing with milk and honey, to the country of the Canaanites, the Hittites, the Amorites, the Perizzites, the Hivites, and the Jebusites. The cry of the Israelites has now come to me; I have also seen how the Egyptians oppress them. So come, I will send you to Pharaoh to bring my people, the Israelites, out of Egypt." But Moses said to God, "Who am I that I should go to Pharaoh, and bring the Israelites out of Egypt?" He said, "I will be with you; and this shall be the sign for you that it is I who sent you: when you have brought the people out of Egypt, you shall worship God on this mountain."

**Silent or spoken reflection on the readings**

**Song**

Christ upon the mountain peak (H232)
When Israel was in Egypt's land (H164)

**Simeon's song**

## Call to intercession

I will open the windows of heaven for you,
says the Lord of hosts,
and pour down an overflowing blessing.
***For those who revere your name, O God,***
***the sun of righteousness will rise,***
***with healing in its wings.***

God of hope, you want the light of your presence to pervade our lives. In your mercy,
***Lord, hear our prayer.***

You call us by name; we are yours. We pray for ourselves and those dear to us.
*(open prayers)*
In your mercy,
***Lord, hear our prayer.***

You are with those who pass through deep waters. We pray for our community and for our neighbors.
*(open prayers)*
In your mercy,
***Lord, hear our prayer.***

You have redeemed us, so we need not fear. We pray for the church in all places, that we may be faithful in solidarity across generations and geography.
*(open prayers)*
In your mercy,
***Lord, hear our prayer.***

You see the misery of those who are oppressed. We pray for the world, for our enemies and for those who are in conflict.
*(open prayers)*
In your mercy,
***Lord, hear our prayer.***

We offer you other concerns we carry in our hearts.
*(open prayers)*
In your mercy,
***Lord, hear our prayer.***

God of light,
your rising reveals all things
in their true proportion.
Illumine our lives,
that we may see rightly,
love deeply, and act justly.
In the example of Jesus,
we pray for the advent of your reign:

***Our Father ...***

**Benediction**

*By the tender mercy of our God,*
*the dawn from on high will break upon us,*
*to give light to those who sit in darkness*
*and in the shadow of death,*
*to guide our feet into the way of peace. Amen.*

# To the nations and to your people

## EPIPHANY SATURDAY EVENING

**Opening sentence**

My own eyes have seen the salvation
which you have prepared
in the sight of every people:
***a light to reveal you to the nations***
***and the glory of your people Israel.***

## Call to praise

The grace of God has appeared,
bringing salvation to all.
***The light and peace of Jesus Christ be with us.***

*Glory ...*

**Psalm 2.1-8**

Why this tumult among the nations,
among peoples this useless murmuring?
***They arise, the kings of the earth,***
***princes plot against the LORD and his***
***Anointed,***
"Come, let us break their fetters,
come, let us cast off their yoke."

***God who sits in the heavens laughs,***
***the Lord is laughing them to scorn.***

Then God will speak in anger,
and in rage will strike them with terror.
***"It is I who have set up my king***
***on Zion, my holy mountain."***

(I will announce the decree of the LORD.)

The Lord said to me: "You are my Son.
It is I who have begotten you this day.
***Ask and I shall bequeath you the nations,***
***put the ends of the earth in your possession."***

**Thanksgiving**

My mouth is filled with your praise, O God,
***and with your glory all day long.***
*(free prayers of thanksgiving)*
Lord, your steadfast love never ceases,
***your mercies never come to an end. Amen.***

**Song**

Blessed Savior, we adore thee (H107)
All hail the power of Jesus' name (H106)
Christ, we do all adore thee (H105)

**Confession**

If we confess our sins, O God,
you are faithful and just
and will forgive us our sins,
***and you will cleanse us***
***from all unrighteousness.***
*(silence)*

When we walk in the light
as you are in the light,
we have fellowship with one another,
***and the blood of Jesus cleanses us from all sin.***
***Amen.***

## Call to discipleship

Jesus said, I am the light of the world.
***Whoever follows me***
***will never walk in darkness***
***but will have the light of life.***

**Matthew 17.9-13**

As [Jesus and the disciples] were coming down the mountain, Jesus ordered them, "Tell no one about the vision until after the Son of Man has been raised from the dead." And the disciples asked him, "Why, then, do the scribes say that Elijah must come first?" He replied, "Elijah is indeed coming and will restore all things; but I tell you that Elijah has already come, and they did not recognize him, but they did to him whatever they pleased. So also the Son of Man is about to suffer at their hands." Then the disciples understood that he was speaking to them about John the Baptist.

**1 Kings 19.9-12**

[Elijah] came to a cave, and spent the night there.

Then the word of the LORD came to him, saying, "What are you doing here, Elijah?" He answered, "I have been very zealous for the LORD, the God of hosts; for the Israelites have forsaken your covenant, thrown down your altars, and killed your prophets with the sword. I alone am left, and they are seeking my life, to take it away."

He said, "Go out and stand on the mountain before the LORD, for the LORD is about to pass by." Now there was a great wind, so strong that it was splitting mountains and breaking rocks in pieces before the LORD, but the LORD was not in the wind; and after the wind an earthquake, but the LORD was not in the earthquake; and after the earthquake a fire, but the LORD was not in the fire; and after the fire a sound of sheer silence.

**Silent or spoken reflection on the readings**

**Song**

Cast thy burden upon the Lord (H586)
Lo, a gleam from yonder heaven (H591)
Don't be afraid (SJ105)

By gracious powers (H552)
Nada te turbe (H562)

**Simeon's song**

## Call to intercession

O God, you grant justice to your chosen ones,
who cry to you day and night,
***so we pray always, and do not lose heart.***

God of hope, the light of your love cannot be overcome by darkness. In your mercy,
***Lord, hear our prayer.***

You call us by name; we are yours. We pray for ourselves and those dear to us.
*(open prayers)*
In your mercy,
***Lord, hear our prayer.***

You are with those who pass through deep waters. We pray for our community and for our neighbors.
*(open prayers)*
In your mercy,
***Lord, hear our prayer.***

You have redeemed us, so we need not fear. We pray for the church in all places, that we may be faithful in solidarity across generations and geography.

*(open prayers)*
In your mercy,
***Lord, hear our prayer.***

You see the misery of those who are oppressed. We pray for the world, for our enemies and for those who are in conflict.
*(open prayers)*
In your mercy,
***Lord, hear our prayer.***

We offer you other concerns we carry in our hearts.
*(open prayers)*
In your mercy,
***Lord, hear our prayer.***

God of light,
your presence illumines
even our darkest shadows.
Gather today's sorrow and pleasure
and remake them, in us,
into generous hope, sober joy, tested faith,
that our lives may be radiant with your love.
In the example of Jesus,
we pray for the advent of your reign:

***Our Father …***

**Benediction**

***May the Lord bless us and keep us.***
***May the face of God shine upon us,***

*and may the Lord be gracious to us.*
*May God's presence embrace us*
*and give us peace. Amen.*

# Lent

## Introduction to the Lent prayers

Christian observance of Lent began late in the third century, as the time to prepare candidates for baptism at Easter. In imitation of Jesus, who spent forty days in the wilderness before beginning his ministry, Christians devote the forty days of Lent to disciplines of prayer and fasting, and in caring for those in need.

This prayer book treats Lent and Holy Week as a unity, albeit with their own emphases. In both sets of prayers, we move ourselves into Jesus' spirituality by reflecting on the biblical resources we know he used. The Gospel writers remember Jesus with the Torah and the Psalms on his mind and heart from the beginning in the wilderness through his prayer at Olivet and as he took his last breath.

In both Lent and Holy Week, we also made an effort to reflect a biblical and Anabaptist view of the cross and the atoning work of Jesus. Minimally that means viewing Jesus' life poured out for us on the cross together with his life and his ministry of teaching, preaching, and healing. To that end, we chose scriptures that honor both the Old Testament foundations for understanding the work of the cross as well as this new initiative of God. We tried to be both theological and Christological in our choices.

For Lent, the choice of Luke's reversal theme for the Gospel readings is a reminder that Jesus' course toward the cross is most immediately a consequence of his particular obedience to God in caring for the poor and loving his enemies. The title lines and opening sentences for these Lenten prayers are taken from 1 Peter 2.21-24, a text that reflects an early Christian understanding of the cross, in which Jesus' bearing of our sins and his refusal to retaliate are inseparable. The 1 Peter hymn also serves as the canticle during this season. This passage was chosen because of its powerful understanding of the healing of our wounds precisely through Jesus' refusal to retaliate; rather he entrusts himself to his faithful Creator. Together the Lukan reversal theme and the Petrine understanding of the cross, both beloved in Anabaptist spirituality, keep our Lenten prayers grounded in God's grace and Jesus' nonviolent obedience.

This week of services can be used from Ash Wednesday up to the beginning of Holy Week, on Palm Sunday.

# Return to the Lord, your God

## ASH WEDNESDAY MORNING

**Opening sentence**

Return to the Lord, your God,
who is gracious and merciful;
***God is slow to anger***
***and abounding in steadfast love.***

## Call to praise

The Lord is my light and my salvation;
whom shall I fear?
***The Lord is the stronghold of my life;***
***of whom shall I be afraid?***

***Glory ...***

**Isaiah 58.1-5**

Shout out, do not hold back!
Lift up your voice like a trumpet!
***Announce to my people their rebellion,***
***to the house of Jacob their sins.***
Yet day after day they seek me
and delight to know my ways,
***as if they were a nation that practiced righteousness***
***and did not forsake the ordinance of their God;***

they ask of me righteous judgments,
they delight to draw near to God.
***"Why do we fast, but you do not see?***
***Why humble ourselves, but you do not notice?"***
Look, you serve your own interest on your fast-day,
and oppress all your workers.
***Look, you fast only to quarrel and to fight***
***and to strike with a wicked fist.***
Such fasting as you do today
will not make your voice heard on high.
***Is such the fast that I choose,***
***a day to humble oneself?***
Is it to bow down the head like a bulrush,
and to lie in sackcloth and ashes?
***Will you call this a fast,***
***a day acceptable to the Lord?***

**Thanksgiving**

Our souls are waiting for God,
our help and our shield.
***Our hearts are glad in you, Lord,***
***because we trust in your holy name.***
*(free prayers of thanksgiving)*
Let your steadfast love, O Lord, be upon us,
***even as we wait for you. Amen.***

**Song**

The glory of these forty days (H225)

Teach me the measure of my days (H485)
What does the Lord require (H409)
O God, to whom then shall I turn? (SS61)

## Call to discipleship

One does not live by bread alone,
but by every word
that comes from the mouth of God.
***Let us worship the Lord our God,***
***and serve God alone.***

**Matthew 6.1-6**

"Beware of practicing your piety before others in order to be seen by them; for then you have no reward from your Father in heaven.

"So whenever you give alms, do not sound a trumpet before you, as the hypocrites do in the synagogues and in the streets, so that they may be praised by others. Truly I tell you, they have received their reward. But when you give alms, do not let your left hand know what your right hand is doing, so that your alms may be done in secret; and your Father who sees in secret will reward you.

"And whenever you pray, do not be like the hypocrites; for they love to stand and pray in the synagogues and at the street corners, so that they may be seen by others. Truly I tell you, they have received their reward. But whenever you pray, go into your room and shut the door and pray to your Father who is in secret; and your Father who sees in secret will reward you."

**2 Corinthians 5.20-21**

We entreat you on behalf of Christ, be reconciled to God. For our sake he made him to be sin who knew no sin, so that in him we might become the righteousness of God.

**Silent or spoken reflection on the readings**

**Song**

Lord, teach us how to pray aright (H350)
What mercy and divine compassion (H524)
Savior of my soul (H549)
Prayer is the soul's sincere desire (H572)
Ya hamalaLah (O Lamb of God) (SS69)

**1 Peter 2.21-24**

## Call to intercession

Wait for the Lord;
be strong, and let your heart take courage.
***Hear, O Lord, when we cry aloud,***
***be gracious to us and answer us!***

God who brings release to troubled spirits, we offer our prayers in the name of Jesus. In your mercy,
***Lord, hear our prayer.***

The fast you choose ushers in light and healing. We pray for ourselves and those dear to us.
*(open prayers)*
In your mercy,
***Lord, hear our prayer.***

The fast you command brings relief for those who are oppressed. We pray for our community and for our neighbors.
*(open prayers)*
In your mercy,
***Lord, hear our prayer.***

In the fast you choose, we share our bread with those who are hungry. We pray for the church in all places, that we may bear witness to your reign of justice, peace, and joy.
*(open prayers)*
In your mercy,
***Lord, hear our prayer.***

The fast you desire looses the bonds of injustice. We pray for the world, for all who are ensnared in greed, violence, and oppression.
*(open prayers)*

In your mercy,
***Lord, hear our prayer.***

We offer you other concerns we carry in our hearts.
*(open prayers)*
In your mercy,
***Lord, hear our prayer.***

God our only hope,
you seat us at the table with our enemies,
breathing in our fears.
Feed us from your mouth,
that our bread may be to do your will,
in the strength of your Anointed,
who taught us to pray:

***Our Father …***

**Benediction**

***Now may our Lord Jesus Christ himself***
***and God the Father,***
***who has loved us and through grace***
***has given us eternal comfort and good hope,***
***comfort and strengthen our hearts***
***in every good work and word. Amen.***

# Return to the Lord, your God

## ASH WEDNESDAY EVENING

**Opening sentence**

Return to the Lord, your God,
who is gracious and merciful;
***God is slow to anger***
***and abounding in steadfast love.***

## Call to praise

Make me know your ways, O God;
Lead me in your truth, and teach me,
***for you are the God of my salvation;***
***for you I wait all day long.***

***Glory …***

**Isaiah 58.6-12**

Is not this the fast that I choose:
to loose the bonds of injustice,
to undo the thongs of the yoke,
***to let the oppressed go free,***
***and to break every yoke?***
Is it not to share your bread with the hungry,
and bring the homeless poor into your house;
***when you see the naked, to cover them,***
***and not to hide yourself from your own kin?***

Then your light shall break forth like the dawn,
and your healing shall spring up quickly;
***your vindicator shall go before you,***
***the glory of the LORD shall be your rearguard.***
Then you shall call, and the LORD will answer;
you shall cry for help, and he will say, Here I am.

***If you remove the yoke from among you,***
***the pointing of the finger, the speaking of evil,***
if you offer your food to the hungry
and satisfy the needs of the afflicted,
***then your light shall rise in the darkness***
***and your gloom be like the noonday.***
The LORD will guide you continually,
and satisfy your needs in parched places,
and make your bones strong;
***and you shall be like a watered garden,***
***like a spring of water,***
***whose waters never fail.***
Your ancient ruins shall be rebuilt;
you shall raise up the foundations of many generations;
***you shall be called the repairer of the breach,***
***the restorer of streets to live in.***

**Thanksgiving**

I am bound by my promises to you, O God;
***I will offer you my thanks.***
*(free prayers of thanksgiving)*

You deliver my soul from death,
and my feet from falling,
***so that I may walk before you***
***in the light of life. Amen.***

**Song**

God, whose purpose is to kindle (H135)
Brothers and sisters of mine (H142)
I'll praise my Maker (H166)
Praise with joy the world's Creator (SJ16)

**Confession**

Remember your mercy, O Lord,
and the love you have shown from of old.
***Do not remember my sins;***
***in your love remember me.***
*(silence)*
You relieve the troubles of my heart,
and bring me out of my distress.
***You consider my affliction and my trouble,***
***and forgive all my sins. Amen.***

## Call to discipleship

Jesus said, Unless a grain of wheat falls
into the earth and dies,
it remains just a single grain;
but if it dies, it bears much fruit.
***Whoever serves me must follow me,***
***and where I am, there will my servant be also.***

**Matthew 6.16-21**

"And whenever you fast, do not look dismal, like the hypocrites, for they disfigure their faces so as to show others that they are fasting. Truly I tell you, they have received their reward. But when you fast, put oil on your head and wash your face, so that your fasting may be seen not by others but by your Father who is in secret; and your Father who sees in secret will reward you.

"Do not store up for yourselves treasures on earth, where moth and rust consume and where thieves break in and steal; but store up for yourselves treasures in heaven, where neither moth nor rust consumes and where thieves do not break in and steal. For where your treasure is, there your heart will be also."

**2 Corinthians 6.1-2**

As we work together with him, we urge you also not to accept the grace of God in vain. For he says,

> "At an acceptable time I have listened to
> you,
> and on a day of salvation I have helped
> you."

See, now is the acceptable time; see, now is the day of salvation!

**Silent or spoken reflection on the readings**

**Song**

Whatsoever you do (SS52)
O Love of God (H326)
I know not why God's wondrous (H338)
What mercy and divine compassion (H524)

**1 Peter 2.21-24**

## Call to intercession

The Spirit helps us in our weakness;
for we do not know how to pray as we ought,
***but that very Spirit intercedes***
***with sighs too deep for words.***

God who brings release to troubled spirits, we offer our prayers in the name of Jesus. In your mercy,
***Lord, hear our prayer.***

The fast you choose ushers in light and healing. We pray for ourselves and those dear to us.
*(open prayers)*
In your mercy,
***Lord, hear our prayer.***

The fast you command brings relief for those who are oppressed. We pray for our community and for our neighbors.
*(open prayers)*

In your mercy,
***Lord, hear our prayer.***

In the fast you choose, we share our bread with those who are hungry. We pray for the church in all places, that we may bear witness to your reign of justice, peace, and joy.
*(open prayers)*
In your mercy,
***Lord, hear our prayer.***

The fast you desire looses the bonds of injustice. We pray for the world, for all who are ensnared in greed, violence, and oppression.
*(open prayers)*
In your mercy,
***Lord, hear our prayer.***

We offer you other concerns we carry in our hearts.
*(open prayers)*
In your mercy,
***Lord, hear our prayer.***

Hungry Christ,
your body is broken
in the rocky soil of human vengeance.
Lovingly tend and till us,
that we may, at this day's dying,
entrust ourselves into the hands
of the Merciful One, praying as you taught us:

*Our Father ...*

**Benediction**

*Now may our Lord Jesus Christ himself*
*and God the Father,*
*who has loved us and through grace*
*has given us eternal comfort and good hope,*
*comfort and strengthen our hearts*
*in every good work and word. Amen.*

# To this you have been called

## LENT SUNDAY MORNING

**Opening sentence**

For to this you have been called:
***because Christ also suffered for you.***

## Call to praise

The Lord is my light and my salvation;
whom shall I fear?
***The Lord is the stronghold of my life;***
***of whom shall I be afraid?***

***Glory …***

**Psalm 82**

God stands in the divine assembly,
and gives judgment in the midst of the gods.

***"How long will you judge unjustly***
***and favor the cause of the wicked?***
Do justice for the weak and the orphan,
defend the afflicted and the needy.
***Rescue the weak and the poor;***
***set them free from the hand of the wicked."***

Unperceiving, they grope in the darkness
and the order of the world is shaken.

***I have said: "You are gods,***
***and all of you, children of the Most High,***
and yet, you shall die like mortals,
you shall fall like any earthly ruler."

***Arise, O God, judge the earth,***
***for you rule all the nations.***

**Thanksgiving**

Our souls are waiting for God,
our help and our shield.
***Our hearts are glad in you, Lord,***
***because we trust in your holy name.***
*(free prayers of thanksgiving)*
Let your steadfast love, O Lord, be upon us,
***even as we wait for you. Amen.***

**Song**

From all that dwell below the skies (H49)
I'll praise my Maker (H166)

## Call to discipleship

One does not live by bread alone,
but by every word
that comes from the mouth of God.
***Let us worship the Lord our God,***
***and serve God alone.***

**Luke 4.17-19**

And the scroll of the prophet Isaiah was given to [Jesus]. He unrolled the scroll and found the place where it was written:

"The Spirit of the Lord is upon me,
because he has anointed me to bring good
news to the poor.
He has sent me to proclaim release to the
captives
and recovery of sight to the blind,
to let the oppressed go free,
to proclaim the year of the Lord's favor."

**Leviticus 19.9-10**

When you reap the harvest of your land, you shall not reap to the very edges of your field, or gather the gleanings of your harvest. You shall not strip your vineyard bare, or gather the fallen grapes of your vineyard; you shall leave them for the poor and the alien: I am the LORD your God.

**Silent or spoken reflection on the readings**

**Song**

I bind my heart this tide (H411)
Who has known the mind of Jesus? (SJ58)
O young and fearless Prophet (H374)

**1 Peter 2.21-24**

## Call to intercession

Wait for the Lord;
be strong, and let your heart take courage.
***Hear, O Lord, when we cry aloud,***
***be gracious to us and answer us!***

Attentive God, we bring our prayers to you because we trust you to protect and provide.
In your mercy,
***Lord, hear our prayer.***

You lead us with your light and truth. We pray for ourselves and those dear to us.
*(open prayers)*
In your mercy,
***Lord, hear our prayer.***

You provide for the poor and the stranger. We pray for our community and for our neighbors.
*(open prayers)*
In your mercy,
***Lord, hear our prayer.***

You are the help and hope of your people. We pray for the church in all places, that we may be one.
*(open prayers)*
In your mercy,
***Lord, hear our prayer.***

All the nations belong to you. We pray for the world, that your reign may come and your will be done on earth.
*(open prayers)*
In your mercy,
***Lord, hear our prayer.***

We offer you other concerns we carry in our hearts.
*(open prayers)*
In your mercy,
***Lord, hear our prayer.***

God our only hope,
you seat us at the table with our enemies,
breathing in our fears.
Feed us from your mouth,
that our bread may be to do your will,
in the strength of your Anointed,
who taught us to pray:

***Our Father ...***

**Benediction**

***May God our Savior,***
***through Jesus Christ our Lord,***
***keep us from falling,***
***and make us stand without blemish***
***in the presence of his glory with rejoicing.***
***Amen.***

# To this you have been called

## LENT SUNDAY EVENING

**Opening sentence**

For to this you have been called:
***because Christ also suffered for you.***

## Call to praise

Make me know your ways, O God;
Lead me in your truth, and teach me,
***for you are the God of my salvation;***
***for you I wait all day long.***

***Glory …***

**Psalm 43**

Defend me, O God, and plead my cause
against a godless nation.
***From a deceitful and cunning people***
***rescue me, O God.***

Since you, O God, are my stronghold,
why have you rejected me?
***Why do I go mourning***
***oppressed by the foe?***

O send forth your light and your truth;
let these be my guide.

***Let them bring me to your holy mountain,***
***to the place where you dwell.***

And I will come to your altar, O God,
the God of my joy.
***My redeemer, I will thank you on the harp,***
***O God, my God.***

Why are you cast down, my soul,
why groan within me?
***Hope in God; I will praise yet again,***
***my savior and my God.***

**Thanksgiving**

I am bound by my promises to you, O God;
***I will offer you my thanks.***
*(free prayers of thanksgiving)*
You deliver my soul from death,
and my feet from falling,
***so that I may walk before you***
***in the light of life. Amen.***

**Song**

Praise the Lord who reigns above (H54)
Cantai ao Senhor (O sing to the Lord) (SJ12, vv. 1–4)
Firstborn of Mary (SS37)

**Confession**

Remember your mercy, O Lord,
and the love you have shown from of old.

***Do not remember my sins;***
***in your love remember me.***
*(silence)*
You relieve the troubles of my heart,
and bring me out of my distress.
***You consider my affliction and my trouble,***
***and forgive all my sins. Amen.***

## Call to discipleship

Jesus said, Unless a grain of wheat
falls into the earth and dies,
it remains just a single grain;
but if it dies, it bears much fruit.
***Whoever serves me must follow me,***
***and where I am, there will my servant be also.***

**Luke 4.24-30**

And [Jesus] said, "Truly I tell you, no prophet is accepted in the prophet's hometown. But the truth is, there were many widows in Israel in the time of Elijah, when the heaven was shut up three years and six months, and there was a severe famine over all the land; yet Elijah was sent to none of them except to a widow at Zarephath in Sidon. There were also many lepers in Israel in the time of the prophet Elisha, and none of them was cleansed except Naaman the Syrian." When they heard this, all in the synagogue were filled with rage.

They got up, drove him out of the town, and led him to the brow of the hill on which their town was built, so that they might hurl him off the cliff. But he passed through the midst of them and went on his way.

**1 Corinthians 1.18-25**

For the message about the cross is foolishness to those who are perishing, but to us who are being saved it is the power of God. For it is written,

> "I will destroy the wisdom of the wise,
> and the discernment of the discerning I
> will thwart."

Where is the one who is wise? Where is the scribe? Where is the debater of this age? Has not God made foolish the wisdom of the world? For since, in the wisdom of God, the world did not know God through wisdom, God decided, through the foolishness of our proclamation, to save those who believe. For Jews demand signs and Greeks desire wisdom, but we proclaim Christ crucified, a stumbling block to Jews and foolishness to Gentiles, but to those who are the called, both Jews and Greeks, Christ the power of God and the wisdom of God. For God's foolishness is wiser than human wisdom, and God's weakness is stronger than human strength.

**Silent or spoken reflection on the readings**

**Song**

Ask ye what great thing I know (H337)
Eternal Light, shine in my heart (H518)

**1 Peter 2.21-24**

## Call to intercession

The Spirit helps us in our weakness;
for we do not know how to pray as we ought,
***but that very Spirit intercedes***
***with sighs too deep for words.***

Sheltering God, we pour out our hearts before you, because you are a refuge for us. In your mercy,
***Lord, hear our prayer.***

You lead us with your light and truth. We pray for ourselves and those dear to us.
*(open prayers)*
In your mercy,
***Lord, hear our prayer.***

You provide for the poor and the stranger. We pray for our community and for our neighbors.
*(open prayers)*

In your mercy,
***Lord, hear our prayer.***

You are the help and hope of your people. We pray for the church in all places, that we may be one.
*(open prayers)*
In your mercy,
***Lord, hear our prayer.***

All the nations belong to you. We pray for the world, that your reign may come and your will be done on earth.
*(open prayers)*
In your mercy,
***Lord, hear our prayer.***

We offer you other concerns we carry in our hearts.
*(open prayers)*
In your mercy,
***Lord, hear our prayer.***

Hungry Christ,
your body is broken
in the rocky soil of human vengeance.
Lovingly tend and till us,
that we may, at this day's dying,
entrust ourselves into the hands
of the Merciful One, praying as you taught us:

***Our Father …***

**Benediction**

*May God our Savior,*
*through Jesus Christ our Lord,*
*keep us from falling,*
*and make us stand without blemish*
*in the presence of his glory with rejoicing.*
*Amen.*

# Christ also suffered for you

## LENT MONDAY MORNING

**Opening sentence**

For to this you have been called:
***because Christ also suffered for you.***

## Call to praise

The Lord is my light and my salvation;
whom shall I fear?
***The Lord is the stronghold of my life;***
***of whom shall I be afraid?***

*Glory ...*

**Psalm 51.3-14 [1-12]**

Have mercy on me, God, in your kindness.
In your compassion blot out my offense.
***O wash me more and more from my guilt***
***and cleanse me from my sin.***

My offenses truly I know them;
my sin is always before me.
***Against you, you alone, have I sinned;***
***what is evil in your sight I have done.***

That you may be justified when you give sentence
and be without reproach when you judge,

***O see, in guilt I was born,***
***a sinner was I conceived.***

Indeed you love truth in the heart;
then in the secret of my heart teach me wisdom.
***O purify me, then I shall be clean;***
***O wash me, I shall be whiter than snow.***

Make me hear rejoicing and gladness
that the bones you have crushed may revive.
***From my sins turn away your face***
***and blot out all my guilt.***

A pure heart create for me, O God,
put a steadfast spirit within me.
***Do not cast me away from your presence,***
***nor deprive me of your holy spirit.***

Give me again the joy of your help;
with a spirit of fervor sustain me,
***that I may teach transgressors your ways***
***and sinners may return to you.***

**Thanksgiving**

Our souls are waiting for God,
our help and our shield.
***Our hearts are glad in you, Lord,***
***because we trust in your holy name.***
*(free prayers of thanksgiving)*
Let your steadfast love, O Lord, be upon us,
***even as we wait for you. Amen.***

**Song**

Je louerai l'Eternel (Praise, I will praise you, Lord) (H76)
Santo (Holy) (SJ15)
What mercy and divine compassion (H524)

## Call to discipleship

One does not live by bread alone,
but by every word
that comes from the mouth of God.
***Let us worship the Lord our God,***
***and serve God alone.***

**Luke 5.18-26**

Just then some men came, carrying a paralyzed man on a bed. They were trying to bring him in and lay him before Jesus; but finding no way to bring him in because of the crowd, they went up on the roof and let him down with his bed through the tiles into the middle of the crowd in front of Jesus. When he saw their faith, he said, "Friend, your sins are forgiven you." Then the scribes and the Pharisees began to question, "Who is this who is speaking blasphemies? Who can forgive sins but God alone?" When Jesus perceived their questionings, he answered them, "Why do you raise such questions in your hearts? Which is easier, to say, 'Your sins are forgiven you,' or to say, 'Stand up and walk'? But so that you may know that the Son of Man has authority on earth to forgive sins"—he said to the one who was paralyzed—"I say to you, stand up and take your bed and go to your home." Immediately he stood up before them, took what he had been lying on, and went to his home, glorifying God. Amazement seized all of them, and they glorified God and were filled with awe, saying, "We have seen strange things today."

**Daniel 9.3-6, 17-19**

Then I turned to the Lord God, to seek an answer by prayer and supplication with fasting and sackcloth and ashes. I prayed to the LORD my God and made confession, saying,

"Ah, Lord, great and awesome God, keeping covenant and steadfast love with those who love you and keep your commandments, we have sinned and done wrong, acted wickedly and rebelled, turning aside from your commandments and ordinances. We have not listened to your servants the prophets, who spoke in your name to our kings, our princes, and our ancestors, and to all the people of the land....

"Now therefore, O our God, listen to the prayer of your servant and to his supplication, and for your own sake, Lord, let your face shine upon your desolated sanctuary. Incline your ear, O my God, and hear. Open your eyes and look at our desolation and the city that bears your name. We do not present our supplication before you on the ground of our righteousness, but on the ground of your great mercies. O Lord, hear; O Lord, forgive; O Lord, listen and act and do not delay! For your own sake, O my God, because your city and your people bear your name!"

**Silent or spoken reflection on the readings**

**Song**

Heal us, Immanuel, here we are (H375)
When Jesus worked here on earth (SS38)
From the depths of sin (H136)

**1 Peter 2.21-24**

## Call to intercession

Wait for the Lord;
be strong, and let your heart take courage.
***Hear, O Lord, when we cry aloud,***
***be gracious to us and answer us!***

Attentive God, we bring our prayers to you because we trust you to protect and provide.

In your mercy,
***Lord, hear our prayer.***

You receive us because of your great mercies. We pray for ourselves and those dear to us.
*(open prayers)*
In your mercy,
***Lord, hear our prayer.***

You rebuke all retaliation. We pray for our community and for our neighbors.
*(open prayers)*
In your mercy,
***Lord, hear our prayer.***

Your people bear your name. We pray for the church in all places, that we may know the freedom of life in the Spirit.
*(open prayers)*
In your mercy,
***Lord, hear our prayer.***

Your face will shine even on earth's desolation. We pray for the world and for all who care for creation.
*(open prayers)*
In your mercy,
***Lord, hear our prayer.***

We offer you other concerns we carry in our hearts.
*(open prayers)*

In your mercy,
***Lord, hear our prayer.***

God our only hope,
you seat us at the table with our enemies,
breathing in our fears.
Feed us from your mouth,
that our bread may be to do your will,
in the strength of your Anointed,
who taught us to pray:

***Our Father …***

**Benediction**

***May God our Savior,***
***through Jesus Christ our Lord,***
***keep us from falling,***
***and make us stand without blemish***
***in the presence of his glory with rejoicing.***
***Amen.***

# Christ also suffered for you

## LENT MONDAY EVENING

**Opening sentence**

For to this you have been called:
***because Christ also suffered for you.***

## Call to praise

Make me know your ways, O God;
Lead me in your truth, and teach me,
***for you are the God of my salvation;***
***for you I wait all day long.***

*Glory …*

**Isaiah 53.1-9**

Who has believed what we have heard?
And to whom has the arm of the LORD been revealed?
***For he grew up before him like a young plant,***
***and like a root out of dry ground;***
he had no form or majesty that we should look at him,
nothing in his appearance that we should desire him.
***He was despised and rejected by others;***
***a man of suffering and acquainted with infirmity;***

and as one from whom others hide their faces
he was despised, and we held him of no
account.

*Surely he has borne our infirmities*
*and carried our diseases;*
yet we accounted him stricken,
struck down by God, and afflicted.
*But he was wounded for our transgressions,*
*crushed for our iniquities;*
upon him was the punishment that made us
whole,
and by his bruises we are healed.
*All we like sheep have gone astray;*
*we have all turned to our own way,*
and the LORD has laid on him
the iniquity of us all.

*He was oppressed, and he was afflicted,*
*yet he did not open his mouth;*
like a lamb that is led to the slaughter,
and like a sheep that before its shearers is
silent,
so he did not open his mouth.
*By a perversion of justice he was taken away.*
*Who could have imagined his future?*
For he was cut off from the land of the living,
stricken for the transgression of my people.
*They made his grave with the wicked*
*and his tomb with the rich,*

although he had done no violence,
and there was no deceit in his mouth.

**Thanksgiving**

I am bound by my promises to you, O God;
***I will offer you my thanks.***
*(free prayers of thanksgiving)*
You deliver my soul from death,
and my feet from falling,
***so that I may walk before you***
***in the light of life. Amen.***

**Song**

What wondrous love is this (H530)
Living and dying with Jesus (H550)

**Confession**

Remember your mercy, O Lord,
and the love you have shown from of old.
***Do not remember my sins;***
***in your love remember me.***
*(silence)*
You relieve the troubles of my heart,
and bring me out of my distress.
***You consider my affliction and my trouble,***
***and forgive all my sins. Amen.***

## Call to discipleship

Jesus said, Unless a grain of wheat
falls into the earth and dies,
it remains just a single grain;
but if it dies, it bears much fruit.
***Whoever serves me must follow me,***
***and where I am, there will my servant be also.***

**Luke 9.51-56**

When the days drew near for [Jesus] to be taken up, he set his face to go to Jerusalem. And he sent messengers ahead of him. On their way they entered a village of the Samaritans to make ready for him; but they did not receive him, because his face was set toward Jerusalem. When his disciples James and John saw it, they said, "Lord, do you want us to command fire to come down from heaven and consume them?" But he turned and rebuked them. Then they went on to another village.

**1 Peter 4.1-6**

Since therefore Christ suffered in the flesh, arm yourselves also with the same intention (for whoever has suffered in the flesh has finished with sin), so as to live for the rest of your earthly life no longer by human desires but by the will of God. You have already spent enough time in doing what the Gentiles like to do, living in licentiousness, passions, drunkenness, revels, carousing, and lawless idolatry. They are surprised that you no longer join them in the same excesses of dissipation, and so they blaspheme. But they will have to give an accounting to him who stands ready to judge the living and the dead. For this is the reason the gospel was proclaimed even to the dead, so that, though they had been judged in the flesh as everyone is judged, they might live in the spirit as God does.

**Silent or spoken reflection on the readings**

**Song**

Take up your cross (H536)
I love thee, Lord (H605)
For me to live is Christ (SS111)

**1 Peter 2.21-24**

## Call to intercession

The Spirit helps us in our weakness;
for we do not know how to pray as we ought,
***but that very Spirit intercedes***
***with sighs too deep for words.***

Sheltering God, we pour out our hearts before you, because you are a refuge for us. In your mercy,
***Lord, hear our prayer.***

You receive us because of your great mercies. We pray for ourselves and those dear to us.
*(open prayers)*
In your mercy,
***Lord, hear our prayer.***

You rebuke all retaliation. We pray for our community and for our neighbors.
*(open prayers)*
In your mercy,
***Lord, hear our prayer.***

Your people bear your name. We pray for the church in all places, that we may know the freedom of life in the Spirit.
*(open prayers)*
In your mercy,
***Lord, hear our prayer.***

Your face will shine even on earth's desolation. We pray for the world and for all who care for creation.
*(open prayers)*
In your mercy,
***Lord, hear our prayer.***

We offer you other concerns we carry in our hearts.
*(open prayers)*
In your mercy,
***Lord, hear our prayer.***

Hungry Christ,
your body is broken
in the rocky soil of human vengeance.
Lovingly tend and till us,
that we may, at this day's dying,
entrust ourselves into the hands
of the Merciful One, praying as you taught us:

***Our Father …***

**Benediction**

***May God our Savior,***
***through Jesus Christ our Lord,***
***keep us from falling,***
***and make us stand without blemish***
***in the presence of his glory with rejoicing.***
***Amen.***

# He left an example for you

## LENT TUESDAY MORNING

**Opening sentence**

He left an example for you,
***that you should follow in his steps.***

## Call to praise

The Lord is my light and my salvation;
whom shall I fear?
***The Lord is the stronghold of my life;***
***of whom shall I be afraid?***

*Glory ...*

**Psalm 1**

Happy indeed are those
who follow not the counsel of the wicked,
***nor linger in the way of sinners***
***nor sit in the company of scorners,***
but whose delight is in the law of the LORD
and who ponder God's law day and night.

***They are like a tree that is planted***
***beside the flowing waters,***
that yields its fruit in due season
and whose leaves shall never fade;
***and all that they do shall prosper.***
***Not so are the wicked, not so!***

For they like winnowed chaff
shall be driven away by the wind.
***When the wicked are judged they shall not stand,***
***nor find room among those who are just;***
for the LORD guards the way of the just
***but the way of the wicked leads to doom.***

**Thanksgiving**

Our souls are waiting for God,
our help and our shield.
***Our hearts are glad in you, Lord,***
***because we trust in your holy name.***
*(free prayers of thanksgiving)*
Let your steadfast love, O Lord, be upon us,
***even as we wait for you. Amen.***

**Song**

Make music to the Lord most high (H73)
I long for your commandments (H543)

## Call to discipleship

One does not live by bread alone,
but by every word
that comes from the mouth of God.
***Let us worship the Lord our God,***
***and serve God alone.***

**Luke 6.20-26**

Then [Jesus] looked up at his disciples and said:

"Blessed are you who are poor,
for yours is the kingdom of God.
"Blessed are you who are hungry now,
for you will be filled.
"Blessed are you who weep now,
for you will laugh.

"Blessed are you when people hate you, and when they exclude you, revile you, and defame you on account of the Son of Man. Rejoice in that day and leap for joy, for surely your reward is great in heaven; for that is what their ancestors did to the prophets.

"But woe to you who are rich,
for you have received your consolation.
"Woe to you who are full now,
for you will be hungry.
"Woe to you who are laughing now,
for you will mourn and weep.

"Woe to you when all speak well of you, for that is what their ancestors did to the false prophets."

**1 Corinthians 12.12-26**

For just as the body is one and has many members, and all the members of the body, though many, are one body, so it is with Christ. For in the one Spirit we were all baptized into one body—Jews or Greeks, slaves or free—and we were all made to drink of one Spirit.

Indeed, the body does not consist of one member but of many. If the foot would say, "Because I am not a hand, I do not belong to the body," that would not make it any less a part of the body. And if the ear would say, "Because I am not an eye, I do not belong to the body," that would not make it any less a part of the body. If the whole body were an eye, where would the hearing be? If the whole body were hearing, where would the sense of smell be? But as it is, God arranged the members in the body, each one of them, as he chose. If all were a single member, where would the body be? As it is, there are many members, yet one body. The eye cannot say to the hand, "I have no need of you," nor again the head to the feet, "I have no need of you." On the contrary, the members of the body that seem to be weaker are indispensable, and those members of the body that we think less honorable we clothe with greater honor, and our less respectable members are treated with greater respect; whereas our more respectable members do not need this. But God has so arranged the body, giving the greater honor to the inferior member, that there may be no dissension within the body, but the members may have the same care for one another. If one member suffers, all suffer together with it; if one member is honored, all rejoice together with it.

**Silent or spoken reflection on the readings**

**Song**

Christ, from whom all blessings (H365)
Blest are they (SJ94)
One is the body (SJ72)

**1 Peter 2.21-24**

## Call to intercession

Wait for the Lord;
be strong, and let your heart take courage.
***Hear, O Lord, when we cry aloud,***
***be gracious to us and answer us!***

Attentive God, we bring our prayers to you
because we trust you to protect and provide.
In your mercy,
***Lord, hear our prayer.***

You are rich in patience. We pray for ourselves
and those dear to us.
*(open prayers)*
In your mercy,
***Lord, hear our prayer.***

You give new life to those who patiently do good. We pray for our community and for our neighbors.
*(open prayers)*
In your mercy,
***Lord, hear our prayer.***

Your kindness is meant to lead us to repentance. We pray for the church in all places, that we may reflect your faithful love.
*(open prayers)*
In your mercy,
***Lord, hear our prayer.***

You show no partiality. We pray for the world, for those who are in need.
*(open prayers)*
In your mercy,
***Lord, hear our prayer.***

We offer you other concerns we carry in our hearts.
*(open prayers)*
In your mercy,
***Lord, hear our prayer.***

God our only hope,
you seat us at the table with our enemies,
breathing in our fears.
Feed us from your mouth,
that our bread may be to do your will,

in the strength of your Anointed,
who taught us to pray:

*Our Father …*

**Benediction**

*The Lord will keep us from all evil.*
*The Lord will keep our life.*
*The Lord will keep our going out*
*and our coming in*
*from this time on and forevermore. Amen.*

# You should follow in his steps

LENT TUESDAY EVENING

**Opening sentence**

He left an example for you,
***that you should follow in his steps.***

## Call to praise

Make me know your ways, O God;
Lead me in your truth, and teach me,
***for you are the God of my salvation;***
***for you I wait all day long.***

***Glory …***

**Psalm 53**

Fools have said in their hearts:
"There is no God above."
***Their deeds are corrupt, depraved;***
***there is no good person left.***

God looks down from heaven
on the peoples of the earth,
***to see if any are wise,***
***if any seek God.***

All have left the right path;
depraved, every one.

***There is no good person left,***
***no, not even one.***

Will the evildoers not understand?
They eat up my people
***as though they were eating bread;***
***they never pray to God.***

See how they tremble with fear,
without cause for fear;
***for God will scatter the bones of the wicked.***
***They are shamed, God rejects them.***

O that Israel's salvation might come from Zion!
***When God delivers the people from bondage,***
***then Jacob will be glad and Israel rejoice.***

**Thanksgiving**

I am bound by my promises to you, O God;
***I will offer you my thanks.***
*(free prayers of thanksgiving)*
You deliver my soul from death,
and my feet from falling,
***so that I may walk before you***
***in the light of life. Amen.***

**Song**

All glory be to God on high (H122)
How bless'd are they (H525)

**Confession**

Remember your mercy, O Lord,
and the love you have shown from of old.
***Do not remember my sins;***
***in your love remember me.***
*(silence)*
You relieve the troubles of my heart,
and bring me out of my distress.
***You consider my affliction and my trouble,***
***and forgive all my sins. Amen.***

## Call to discipleship

Jesus said, Unless a grain of wheat
falls into the earth and dies,
it remains just a single grain;
but if it dies, it bears much fruit.
***Whoever serves me must follow me,***
***and where I am, there will my servant be also.***

**Luke 7.36-50**

One of the Pharisees asked Jesus to eat with him, and he went into the Pharisee's house and took his place at the table. And a woman in the city, who was a sinner, having learned that he was eating in the Pharisee's house, brought an alabaster jar of ointment. She stood behind him at his feet, weeping, and began to bathe his feet with her tears and to dry them with her hair. Then she continued kissing his feet and anointing them with the ointment. Now when the Pharisee who had invited him saw it, he said to himself, "If this man were a prophet, he would have known who and what kind of woman this is who is touching him—that she is a sinner." Jesus spoke up and said to him, "Simon, I have something to say to you." "Teacher," he replied, "Speak." "A certain creditor had two debtors; one owed five hundred denarii, and the other fifty. When they could not pay, he canceled the debts for both of them. Now which of them will love him more?" Simon answered, "I suppose the one for whom he canceled the greater debt." And Jesus said to him, "You have judged rightly." Then turning toward the woman, he said to Simon, "Do you see this woman? I entered your house; you gave me no water for my feet, but she has bathed my feet with her tears and dried them with her hair. You gave me no kiss, but from the time I came in she has not stopped kissing my feet. You did not anoint my head with oil, but she has anointed my feet with ointment. Therefore, I tell you, her sins, which were many, have been forgiven; hence she has shown great love. But the one to whom little is forgiven, loves little." Then he said to her, "Your sins are forgiven." But those who were at the table with him began to say among themselves, "Who is this who even forgives sins?" And he said to the woman, "Your faith has saved you; go in peace."

**Romans 2.1-11**

Therefore you have no excuse, whoever you are, when you judge others; for in passing judgment on another you condemn yourself, because you, the judge, are doing the very same things. You say, "We know that God's judgment on those who do such things is in accordance with truth." Do you imagine, whoever you are, that when you judge those who do such things and yet do them yourself, you will escape the judgment of God? Or do you despise the riches of his kindness and forbearance and patience? Do you not realize that God's kindness is meant to lead you to repentance? But by your hard and impenitent heart you are storing up wrath for yourself on the day of wrath, when God's righteous judgment will be revealed. For he will repay according to each one's deeds: to those who by patiently doing good seek for glory and honor and immortality, he will give eternal life; while for those who are self-seeking and who obey not the truth but wickedness, there will be wrath and fury. There will be anguish and distress for everyone who does evil, the Jew first and also the Greek, but glory and honor and peace for everyone who does good, the Jew first and also the Greek. For God shows no partiality.

**Silent or spoken reflection on the readings**

**Song**

Come down, O Love divine (H501)
Open, Lord, my inward ear (H140)
Forgive our sins as we forgive (H137)

**1 Peter 2.21-24**

## Call to intercession

The Spirit helps us in our weakness;
for we do not know how to pray as we ought,
***but that very Spirit intercedes***
***with sighs too deep for words.***

Sheltering God, we pour out our hearts before you, because you are a refuge for us. In your mercy,
***Lord, hear our prayer.***

You are rich in patience. We pray for ourselves and those dear to us.
*(open prayers)*
In your mercy,
***Lord, hear our prayer.***

You give new life to those who patiently do good. We pray for our community and for our neighbors.
*(open prayers)*
In your mercy,
***Lord, hear our prayer.***

Your kindness is meant to lead us to repentance. We pray for the church in all places, that we may reflect your faithful love.
*(open prayers)*
In your mercy,
***Lord, hear our prayer.***

You show no partiality. We pray for the world, for those who are in need.
*(open prayers)*
In your mercy,
***Lord, hear our prayer.***

We offer you other concerns we carry in our hearts.
*(open prayers)*
In your mercy,
***Lord, hear our prayer.***

Hungry Christ,
your body is broken
in the rocky soil of human vengeance.
Lovingly tend and till us,
that we may, at this day's dying,

entrust ourselves into the hands
of the Merciful One, praying as you taught us:

*Our Father ...*

**Benediction**

*The Lord will keep us from all evil.*
*The Lord will keep our life.*
*The Lord will keep our going out*
*and our coming in*
*from this time on and forevermore. Amen.*

# He committed no sin

## LENT WEDNESDAY MORNING

**Opening sentence**

He committed no sin;
***no trickery was found on his lips.***

## Call to praise

The Lord is my light and my salvation;
whom shall I fear?
***The Lord is the stronghold of my life;***
***of whom shall I be afraid?***

*Glory …*

**Psalm 15**

LORD, who shall be admitted to your tent
and dwell on your holy mountain?

***Those who walk without fault,***
***those who act with justice***
***and speak the truth from their hearts,***
those who do not slander with their tongue,

those who do no wrong to their kindred,
who cast no slur on their neighbors,
***who hold the godless in disdain,***
***but honor those who fear the LORD;***

those who keep their word, come what may,
who take no interest on a loan
and accept no bribes against the innocent.
***Such people will stand firm for ever.***

**Thanksgiving**

Our souls are waiting for God,
our help and our shield.
***Our hearts are glad in you, Lord,***
***because we trust in your holy name.***
*(free prayers of thanksgiving)*
Let your steadfast love, O Lord, be upon us,
***even as we wait for you. Amen.***

**Song**

My soul is filled with joy (SJ13)
Santo, santo, santo (Holy, holy, holy) (H400)

## Call to discipleship

One does not live by bread alone,
but by every word
that comes from the mouth of God.
***Let us worship the Lord our God,***
***and serve God alone.***

**Luke 14.12-14**

[Jesus] said also to the one who had invited him, "When you give a luncheon or a dinner, do not invite your friends or your brothers or your relatives or rich neighbors, in case they may invite you in return, and you would be repaid. But when you give a banquet, invite the poor, the crippled, the lame, and the blind. And you will be blessed, because they cannot repay you, for you will be repaid at the resurrection of the righteous."

**James 2.1-9**

My brothers and sisters, do you with your acts of favoritism really believe in our glorious Lord Jesus Christ? For if a person with gold rings and in fine clothes comes into your assembly, and if a poor person in dirty clothes also comes in, and if you take notice of the one wearing the fine clothes and say, "Have a seat here, please," while to the one who is poor you say, "Stand there," or, "Sit at my feet," have you not made distinctions among yourselves, and become judges with evil thoughts? Listen, my beloved brothers and sisters. Has not God chosen the poor in the world to be rich in faith and to be heirs of the kingdom that he has promised to those who love him? But you have dishonored the poor. Is it not the rich who oppress you? Is it not they who drag you into court? Is it not they who blaspheme the excellent name that was invoked over you?

You do well if you really fulfill the royal law according to the scripture, "You shall love your neighbor as yourself." But if you show partiality, you commit sin and are convicted by the law as transgressors.

**Silent or spoken reflection on the readings**

**Song**

What does the Lord require (H409)
The church of Christ, in every age (H403)
Here to the house of God we come (SS53)

**1 Peter 2.21-24**

## Call to intercession

Wait for the Lord;
be strong, and let your heart take courage.
***Hear, O Lord, when we cry aloud,***
***be gracious to us and answer us!***

Attentive God, we bring our prayers to you
because we trust you to protect and provide.
In your mercy,
***Lord, hear our prayer.***

You are the stronghold of our life. We pray for ourselves and those dear to us.
*(open prayers)*
In your mercy,
***Lord, hear our prayer.***

You relieve the troubles of the heart. We pray for our community and for our neighbors.
*(open prayers)*
In your mercy,
***Lord, hear our prayer.***

You look with favor on the faithful. We pray for the church in all places, that we may bear witness to your reign of justice, peace, and joy.
*(open prayers)*
In your mercy,
***Lord, hear our prayer.***

You have chosen the poor to be rich in faith. We pray for the world, for all who are ensnared in greed, violence, and oppression.
*(open prayers)*
In your mercy,
***Lord, hear our prayer.***

We offer you other concerns we carry in our hearts.
*(open prayers)*
In your mercy,
***Lord, hear our prayer.***

God our only hope,
you seat us at the table with our enemies,
breathing in our fears.
Feed us from your mouth,
that our bread may be to do your will,

in the strength of your Anointed,
who taught us to pray:

*Our Father …*

**Benediction**

*Now may our Lord Jesus Christ himself*
*and God our Father,*
*who has loved us and through grace*
*has given us eternal comfort and good hope,*
*comfort and strengthen our hearts*
*in every good work and word. Amen.*

# No trickery was found on his lips

## LENT WEDNESDAY EVENING

**Opening sentence**

He committed no sin;
***no trickery was found on his lips.***

## Call to praise

Make me know your ways, O God;
Lead me in your truth, and teach me,
***for you are the God of my salvation;***
***for you I wait all day long.***

*Glory …*

**Psalm 101**

My song is of mercy and justice;
I sing to you, O LORD.
***I will walk in the way of perfection.***
***O when, Lord, will you come?***

I will walk with blameless heart
within my house;
***I will not set before my eyes***
***whatever is base.***

I will hate the ways of the crooked;
they shall not be my friends.

***The false-hearted must keep far away;***
***the wicked I disown.***

Those who secretly slander their neighbors
I will bring to silence.
***Those of proud look and haughty heart***
***I will never endure.***

I look to the faithful in the land
that they may dwell with me.
***Those who walk in the way of perfection***
***shall be my friends.***

No one who practices deceit
shall live within my house.
***No one who utters lies shall stand***
***before my eyes.***

Morning by morning I will silence
all the wicked in the land,
***uprooting from the city of the LORD***
***all who do evil.***

**Thanksgiving**

I am bound by my promises to you, O God;
***I will offer you my thanks.***
*(free prayers of thanksgiving)*
You deliver my soul from death,
and my feet from falling,
***so that I may walk before you***
***in the light of life. Amen.***

**Song**

O God, our help in ages past (H328)
Great God, how infinite art thou (H82)
God is our refuge and strength (SJ26)

**Confession**

Remember your mercy, O Lord,
and the love you have shown from of old.
***Do not remember my sins;***
***in your love remember me.***
*(silence)*
You relieve the troubles of my heart,
and bring me out of my distress.
***You consider my affliction and my trouble,***
***and forgive all my sins. Amen.***

## Call to discipleship

Jesus said, Unless a grain of wheat
falls into the earth and dies,
it remains just a single grain;
but if it dies, it bears much fruit.
***Whoever serves me must follow me,***
***and where I am, there will my servant be also.***

**Luke 18.15-17**

People were bringing even infants to [Jesus] that he might touch them; and when the disciples saw it, they sternly ordered them not to do it. But Jesus called for them and said, "Let the little children come to me, and do not stop them; for it is to such as these that the kingdom of God belongs. Truly I tell you, whoever does not receive the kingdom of God as a little child will never enter it."

**Malachi 2.5-6**

My covenant with him was a covenant of life and well-being, which I gave him; this called for reverence, and he revered me and stood in awe of my name. True instruction was in his mouth, and no wrong was found on his lips. He walked with me in integrity and uprightness, and he turned many from iniquity.

**Silent or spoken reflection on the readings**

**Song**

Let the children come to me (SS47)
Strong Son of God, immortal Love (H488)
Come and see (H20)

**1 Peter 2.21-24**

## Call to intercession

The Spirit helps us in our weakness;
for we do not know how to pray as we ought,
***but that very Spirit intercedes***
***with sighs too deep for words.***

Sheltering God, we pour out our hearts before you, because you are a refuge for us. In your mercy,
***Lord, hear our prayer.***

You are the stronghold of our life. We pray for ourselves and those dear to us.
*(open prayers)*
In your mercy,
***Lord, hear our prayer.***

You relieve the troubles of the heart. We pray for our community and for our neighbors.
*(open prayers)*
In your mercy,
***Lord, hear our prayer.***

You look with favor on the faithful. We pray for the church in all places, that we may bear witness to your reign of justice, peace, and joy.
*(open prayers)*
In your mercy,
***Lord, hear our prayer.***

You have chosen the poor to be rich in faith. We pray for the world, for all who are ensnared in greed, violence, and oppression.
*(open prayers)*
In your mercy,
***Lord, hear our prayer.***

We offer you other concerns we carry in our hearts.
*(open prayers)*
In your mercy,
***Lord, hear our prayer.***

Hungry Christ,
your body is broken
in the rocky soil of human vengeance.
Lovingly tend and till us,
that we may, at this day's dying,
entrust ourselves into the hands
of the Merciful One, praying as you taught us:

***Our Father …***

**Benediction**

***Now may our Lord Jesus Christ himself***
***and God our Father,***
***who has loved us and through grace***
***has given us eternal comfort and good hope,***
***comfort and strengthen our hearts***
***in every good work and word. Amen.***

# When he was insulted, he did not insult in return

## LENT THURSDAY MORNING

**Opening sentence**

When he was insulted,
he did not insult in return.
***When he was threatened, he did not threaten.***

## Call to praise

The Lord is my light and my salvation;
whom shall I fear?
***The Lord is the stronghold of my life;***
***of whom shall I be afraid?***

***Glory ...***

**Psalm 75**

We give thanks to you, O God,
we give thanks and call upon your name.
We recount your wonderful deeds.

***"When I reach the appointed time,***
***then I will judge with justice.***
Though the earth and all who dwell in it may rock,
it is I who uphold its pillars.

*To the boastful I say: 'Do not boast,'*
*to the wicked: 'Do not flaunt your strength,*
do not flaunt your strength on high.
Do not speak with insolent pride.'"

*For neither from the east nor from the west,*
*nor from desert or mountains comes judgment,*
but God indeed is the judge.
humbling one and exalting another.

*In the hand of the* LORD *is a cup,*
*full of wine, foaming and spiced.*
God pours it; they drink it to the dregs;
all the wicked on the earth must drain it.

*As for me, I will rejoice for ever*
*and sing psalms to Jacob's God.*
God shall break the power of the wicked,
*but strengthen and exalt the just.*

**Thanksgiving**

Our souls are waiting for God,
our help and our shield.
***Our hearts are glad in you, Lord,***
***because we trust in your holy name.***
*(free prayers of thanksgiving)*
Let your steadfast love, O Lord, be upon us,
***even as we wait for you. Amen.***

**Song**

Sing praise to God who reigns (H59)
My soul proclaims with wonder (H181)

## Call to discipleship

One does not live by bread alone,
but by every word
that comes from the mouth of God.
***Let us worship the Lord our God,***
***and serve God alone.***

**Luke 6.27-31**

"But I say to you that listen, Love your enemies, do good to those who hate you, bless those who curse you, pray for those who abuse you. If anyone strikes you on the cheek, offer the other also; and from anyone who takes away your coat do not withhold even your shirt. Give to everyone who begs from you; and if anyone takes away your goods, do not ask for them again. Do to others as you would have them do to you."

**Romans 5.1-5**

Therefore, since we are justified by faith, we have peace with God through our Lord Jesus Christ, through whom we have obtained access to this grace in which we stand; and we boast in our hope of sharing the glory of God. And not only that, but we also boast in our sufferings, knowing that suffering produces endurance, and endurance produces character, and character produces hope, and hope does not disappoint us, because God's love has been poured into our hearts through the Holy Spirit that has been given to us.

**Silent or spoken reflection on the readings**

**Song**

Spirit of the living God (H349)
Breathe on me, breath of God (H356)
O breathe on me, O breath of God (SJ46)
Blessed are they (SS41)
Herr, füll mich neu (God, fill me now) (SS63)
Gentle God, when we are driven (SS71)
When we are tempted (SS81)

**1 Peter 2.21-24**

## Call to intercession

Wait for the Lord;
be strong, and let your heart take courage.
***Hear, O Lord, when we cry aloud,***
***be gracious to us and answer us!***

Attentive God, we bring our prayers to you because we trust you to protect and provide.
In your mercy,
***Lord, hear our prayer.***

You model kindness and mercy. We pray for ourselves and those dear to us.

*(open prayers)*
In your mercy,
***Lord, hear our prayer.***

You do not refuse any good to those who walk without blame. We pray for our community and for our neighbors.
*(open prayers)*
In your mercy,
***Lord, hear our prayer.***

You call us to love, blessing, and generosity. We pray for the church in all places, that we may daily follow in the footsteps of Christ.
*(open prayers)*
In your mercy,
***Lord, hear our prayer.***

You execute judgment, humbling one and exalting another. We pray for the world, for those in positions of power and authority.
*(open prayers)*
In your mercy,
***Lord, hear our prayer.***

We offer you other concerns we carry in our hearts.
*(open prayers)*
In your mercy,
***Lord, hear our prayer.***

God our only hope,
you seat us at the table with our enemies,
breathing in our fears.
Feed us from your mouth,
that our bread may be to do your will,
in the strength of your Anointed,
who taught us to pray:

*Our Father ...*

**Benediction**

*May God, who supplies seed to the sower
and bread for food,
supply and multiply our seed for sowing
and increase the harvest of our righteousness.
Amen.*

# When he was threatened, he did not threaten

## LENT THURSDAY EVENING

**Opening sentence**

When he was insulted,
he did not insult in return.
***When he was threatened, he did not threaten.***

## Call to praise

Make me know your ways, O God;
Lead me in your truth, and teach me,
***for you are the God of my salvation;***
***for you I wait all day long.***

***Glory …***

**Psalm 84**

How lovely is your dwelling place,
LORD, God of hosts.

***My soul is longing and yearning,***
***is yearning for the courts of the LORD.***
My heart and my soul ring out their joy
to God, the living God.

***The sparrow herself finds a home***
***and the swallow a nest for her brood;***

she lays her young by your altars,
LORD of hosts, my king and my God.

*They are happy, who dwell in your house,*
*for ever singing your praise.*
They are happy, whose strength is in you,
in whose hearts are the roads to Zion.

*As they go through the Bitter Valley*
*they make it a place of springs,*
*(the autumn rain covers it with blessings).*
They walk with ever growing strength,
they will see the God of gods in Zion.

*O LORD God of hosts, hear my prayer,*
*give ear, O God of Jacob.*
Turn your eyes, O God, our shield,
look on the face of your anointed.

*One day within your courts*
*is better than a thousand elsewhere.*
The threshold of the house of God
I prefer to the dwellings of the wicked.

*For the LORD God is a rampart, a shield.*
*The LORD will give us favor and glory.*
The LORD will not refuse any good
to those who walk without blame.

*LORD, God of hosts,*
*happy are those who trust in you.*

**Thanksgiving**

I am bound by my promises to you, O God;
***I will offer you my thanks.***
*(free prayers of thanksgiving)*
You deliver my soul from death,
and my feet from falling,
***so that I may walk before you***
***in the light of life. Amen.***

**Song**

O Lord, our Lord, how majestic (H112)
O come, loud anthems let us sing (H68)

**Confession**

Remember your mercy, O Lord,
and the love you have shown from of old.
***Do not remember my sins;***
***in your love remember me.***
*(silence)*
You relieve the troubles of my heart,
and bring me out of my distress.
***You consider my affliction and my trouble,***
***and forgive all my sins. Amen.***

## Call to discipleship

Jesus said, Unless a grain of wheat
falls into the earth and dies,
it remains just a single grain;
but if it dies, it bears much fruit.

*Whoever serves me must follow me,*
*and where I am, there will my servant be also.*

**Luke 6.32-36**

"If you love those who love you, what credit is that to you? For even sinners love those who love them. If you do good to those who do good to you, what credit is that to you? For even sinners do the same. If you lend to those from whom you hope to receive, what credit is that to you? Even sinners lend to sinners, to receive as much again. But love your enemies, do good, and lend, expecting nothing in return. Your reward will be great, and you will be children of the Most High; for he is kind to the ungrateful and the wicked. Be merciful, just as your Father is merciful."

**Romans 5.6-11**

For while we were still weak, at the right time Christ died for the ungodly. Indeed, rarely will anyone die for a righteous person—though perhaps for a good person someone might actually dare to die. But God proves his love for us in that while we still were sinners Christ died for us. Much more surely then, now that we have been justified by his blood, will we be saved through him from the wrath of God. For if while we were enemies, we were reconciled to God through the death of his Son, much more surely, having been reconciled, will we be saved by his life. But more than that, we even boast in God through our Lord Jesus Christ, through whom we have now received reconciliation.

**Silent or spoken reflection on the readings**

**Song**

Beloved, God's chosen (SJ38)
I know not why God's wondrous (H338)
Beauty for brokenness (SS115)

**1 Peter 2.21-24**

## Call to intercession

The Spirit helps us in our weakness;
for we do not know how to pray as we ought,
***but that very Spirit intercedes***
***with sighs too deep for words.***

Sheltering God, we pour out our hearts before you, because you are a refuge for us. In your mercy,
***Lord, hear our prayer.***

You model kindness and mercy. We pray for ourselves and those dear to us.
*(open prayers)*

In your mercy,
***Lord, hear our prayer.***

You do not refuse any good to those who walk without blame. We pray for our community and for our neighbors.
*(open prayers)*
In your mercy,
***Lord, hear our prayer.***

You call us to love, blessing, and generosity. We pray for the church in all places, that we may daily follow in the footsteps of Christ.
*(open prayers)*
In your mercy,
***Lord, hear our prayer.***

You execute judgment, humbling one and exalting another. We pray for the world, for those in positions of power and authority.
*(open prayers)*
In your mercy,
***Lord, hear our prayer.***

We offer you other concerns we carry in our hearts.
*(open prayers)*
In your mercy,
***Lord, hear our prayer.***

Hungry Christ,
your body is broken

in the rocky soil of human vengeance.
Lovingly tend and till us,
that we may, at this day's dying,
entrust ourselves into the hands
of the Merciful One, praying as you taught us:

*Our Father …*

**Benediction**

*May God, who supplies seed to the sower*
*and bread for food,*
*supply and multiply our seed for sowing*
*and increase the harvest of our righteousness.*
*Amen.*

# He trusted himself to the one who judges justly

## LENT FRIDAY MORNING

**Opening sentence**

Instead, he trusted himself
to the one who judges justly.
***He himself bore our sins***
***in his body on the tree.***

## Call to praise

The Lord is my light and my salvation;
whom shall I fear?
***The Lord is the stronghold of my life;***
***of whom shall I be afraid?***

***Glory …***

**Psalm 91**

Those who dwell in the shelter of the Most
High
and abide in the shade of the Almighty
say to the LORD: "My refuge,
my stronghold, my God in whom I trust!"

***It is God who will free you from the snare***
***of the fowler who seeks to destroy you;***

God will conceal you with his pinions,
and under his wings you will find refuge.

*You will not fear the terror of the night*
*nor the arrow that flies by day,*
nor the plague that prowls in the darkness
nor the scourge that lays waste at noon.

*A thousand may fall at your side,*
*ten thousand fall at your right,*
you, it will never approach;
God's faithfulness is buckler and shield.

*Your eyes have only to look*
*to see how the wicked are repaid,*
you who have said: "LORD, my refuge!"
and have made the Most High your dwelling.

*Upon you no evil shall fall,*
*no plague approach where you dwell.*
For you God has commanded the angels,
to keep you in all your ways.

*They shall bear you upon their hands*
*lest you strike your foot against a stone.*
On the lion and the viper you will tread
and trample the young lion and the dragon.

*You set your love on me, so I will save you,*
*protect you for you know my name.*
When you call I shall answer: "I am with you,"
I will save you in distress and give you glory.

***With length of days I will content you;***
***I shall let you see my saving power.***

**Thanksgiving**

Our souls are waiting for God,
our help and our shield.
***Our hearts are glad in you, Lord,***
***because we trust in your holy name.***
*(free prayers of thanksgiving)*
Let your steadfast love, O Lord, be upon us,
***even as we wait for you. Amen.***

**Song**

Great is thy faithfulness (H327)
We give thanks unto you (H161, verses 1–3, 5)

## Call to discipleship

One does not live by bread alone,
but by every word
that comes from the mouth of God.
***Let us worship the Lord our God,***
***and serve God alone.***

**Luke 12.29-34**

"And do not keep striving for what you are to eat and what you are to drink, and do not keep worrying. For it is the nations of the world that strive after all these things, and your Father knows that you need them.

Instead, strive for his kingdom, and these things will be given to you as well.

"Do not be afraid, little flock, for it is your Father's good pleasure to give you the kingdom. Sell your possessions, and give alms. Make purses for yourselves that do not wear out, an unfailing treasure in heaven, where no thief comes near and no moth destroys. For where your treasure is, there your heart will be also."

**Esther 4.12-16**

When [the messengers] told Mordecai what Esther had said, Mordecai told them to reply to Esther, "Do not think that in the king's palace you will escape any more than all the other Jews. For if you keep silence at such a time as this, relief and deliverance will rise for the Jews from another quarter, but you and your father's family will perish. Who knows? Perhaps you have come to royal dignity for just such a time as this." Then Esther said in reply to Mordecai, "Go, gather all the Jews to be found in Susa, and hold a fast on my behalf, and neither eat nor drink for three days, night or day. I and my maids will also fast as you do. After that I will go to the king, though it is against the law; and if I perish, I perish."

**Silent or spoken reflection on the readings**

**Song**

If you but trust in God (H576)
Lord, thou dost love (H387)
If all you want, Lord (H512)
When we walk with the Lord (H544)

**1 Peter 2.21-24**

## Call to intercession

Wait for the Lord;
be strong, and let your heart take courage.
***Hear, O Lord, when we cry aloud,***
***be gracious to us and answer us!***

Attentive God, we bring our prayers to you
because we trust you to protect and provide.
In your mercy,
***Lord, hear our prayer.***

You know what we need. We pray for ourselves and those dear to us.
*(open prayers)*
In your mercy,
***Lord, hear our prayer.***

You sent your Son into the world that all might find life through him. We pray for our community and for our neighbors.
*(open prayers)*

In your mercy,
***Lord, hear our prayer.***

You guard those who have made you their refuge. We pray for the church in all places, that we may speak boldly for Christ.
*(open prayers)*
In your mercy,
***Lord, hear our prayer.***

You show your salvation to all the ends of the earth. We pray for the world, for all who do justice and love mercy.
*(open prayers)*
In your mercy,
***Lord, hear our prayer.***

We offer you other concerns we carry in our hearts.
*(open prayers)*
In your mercy,
***Lord, hear our prayer.***

God our only hope,
you seat us at the table with our enemies,
breathing in our fears.
Feed us from your mouth,
that our bread may be to do your will,
in the strength of your Anointed,
who taught us to pray:

***Our Father …***

**Benediction**

*And after we have suffered for a little while,*
*the God of all grace,*
*who has called us to eternal glory in Christ,*
*will restore, support, strengthen,*
*and establish us. Amen.*

# He bore our sins in his body on the tree

## LENT FRIDAY EVENING

**Opening sentence**

Instead, he trusted himself
to the one who judges justly.
***He himself bore our sins***
***in his body on the tree.***

## Call to praise

Make me know your ways, O God;
Lead me in your truth, and teach me,
***for you are the God of my salvation;***
***for you I wait all day long.***

***Glory …***

**Isaiah 52.10-15**

The LORD has bared his holy arm
before the eyes of all the nations;
***and all the ends of the earth shall see***
***the salvation of our God.***

Depart, depart, go out from there!
Touch no unclean thing;
***go out from the midst of it, purify yourselves,***
***you who carry the vessels of the LORD.***

For you shall not go out in haste,
and you shall not go in flight;
***for the LORD will go before you,***
***and the God of Israel will be your rear guard.***

See, my servant shall prosper;
he shall be exalted and lifted up,
and shall be very high.
***Just as there were many who were astonished at him***
***—so marred was his appearance, beyond human semblance,***
***and his form beyond that of mortals—***
so he shall startle many nations;
kings shall shut their mouths because of him;
***for that which had not been told them they shall see,***
***and that which they had not heard they shall contemplate.***

**Thanksgiving**

I am bound by my promises to you, O God;
***I will offer you my thanks.***
*(free prayers of thanksgiving)*
You deliver my soul from death,
and my feet from falling,
***so that I may walk before you***
***in the light of life. Amen.***

**Song**

Hail to the Lord's anointed (H185)

All hail the power of Jesus' name (H106)
Sing hallelujah, praise the Lord (H67)

**Confession**

Remember your mercy, O Lord,
and the love you have shown from of old.
***Do not remember my sins;***
***in your love remember me.***
*(silence)*
You relieve the troubles of my heart,
and bring me out of my distress.
***You consider my affliction and my trouble,***
***and forgive all my sins. Amen.***

## Call to discipleship

Jesus said, Unless a grain of wheat
falls into the earth and dies,
it remains just a single grain;
but if it dies, it bears much fruit.
***Whoever serves me must follow me,***
***and where I am, there will my servant be also.***

**Luke 9.23-27**

Then [Jesus] said to them all, "If any want to become my followers, let them deny themselves and take up their cross daily and follow me. For those who want to save their life will lose it, and those who lose their life for my sake will save it. What does it profit them if they gain the whole world, but lose or forfeit themselves? Those who are ashamed of me and of my words, of them the Son of Man will be ashamed when he comes in his glory and the glory of the Father and of the holy angels. But truly I tell you, there are some standing here who will not taste death before they see the kingdom of God."

**1 John 4.7-12**

Beloved, let us love one another, because love is from God; everyone who loves is born of God and knows God. Whoever does not love does not know God, for God is love. God's love was revealed among us in this way: God sent his only Son into the world so that we might live through him. In this is love, not that we loved God but that he loved us and sent his Son to be the atoning sacrifice for our sins. Beloved, since God loved us so much, we also ought to love one another. No one has ever seen God; if we love one another, God lives in us, and his love is perfected in us.

**Silent or spoken reflection on the readings**

**Song**

O Love of God (H326)
Who now would follow Christ (H535)
Holy Spirit, come to us (SS79)

1 Peter 2.21-24

## Call to intercession

The Spirit helps us in our weakness;
for we do not know how to pray as we ought,
***but that very Spirit intercedes***
***with sighs too deep for words.***

Sheltering God, we pour out our hearts before you, because you are a refuge for us. In your mercy,
***Lord, hear our prayer.***

You know what we need. We pray for ourselves and those dear to us.
*(open prayers)*
In your mercy,
***Lord, hear our prayer.***

You sent your Son into the world that all might find life through him. We pray for our community and for our neighbors.
*(open prayers)*
In your mercy,
***Lord, hear our prayer.***

You guard those who have made you their refuge. We pray for the church in all places, that we may speak boldly for Christ.
*(open prayers)*

In your mercy,
***Lord, hear our prayer.***

You show your salvation to all the ends of the earth. We pray for the world, for all who do justice and love mercy.
*(open prayers)*
In your mercy,
***Lord, hear our prayer.***

We offer you other concerns we carry in our hearts.
*(open prayers)*
In your mercy,
***Lord, hear our prayer.***

Hungry Christ,
your body is broken
in the rocky soil of human vengeance.
Lovingly tend and till us,
that we may, at this day's dying,
entrust ourselves into the hands
of the Merciful One, praying as you taught us:

***Our Father …***

**Benediction**

***And after we have suffered for a little while,***
***the God of all grace,***
***who has called us to eternal glory in Christ,***
***will restore, support, strengthen,***
***and establish us. Amen.***

# He bore our sins that we might die to sin and live for justice

## LENT SATURDAY MORNING

**Opening sentence**

He himself bore our sins
in his body on the tree
so that we might die to sin and live for justice.
***By his wounds you have been healed.***

## Call to praise

The Lord is my light and my salvation;
whom shall I fear?
***The Lord is the stronghold of my life;***
***of whom shall I be afraid?***

***Glory …***

**Psalm 146**

My soul, give praise to the LORD;
***I will praise the LORD all my days,***
***make music to my God while I live.***

Put no trust in the powerful,
mere mortals in whom there is no help.
***Take their breath, they return to clay***
***and their plans that day come to nothing.***

They are happy who are helped by Jacob's
God,
whose hope is in the LORD their God,
***who alone made heaven and earth,***
***the seas and all they contain.***

It is the Lord who keeps faith for ever,
who is just to those who are oppressed.
***It is God who gives bread to the hungry,***
***the LORD, who sets prisoners free,***

the LORD who gives sight to the blind,
who raises up those who are bowed down,
***the LORD, who protects the stranger***
***and upholds the widow and orphan.***

It is the LORD who loves the just
but thwarts the path of the wicked.
***The LORD will reign for ever,***
***Zion's God, from age to age.***

**Thanksgiving**

Our souls are waiting for God,
our help and our shield.
***Our hearts are glad in you, Lord,***
***because we trust in your holy name.***
*(free prayers of thanksgiving)*
Let your steadfast love, O Lord, be upon us,
***even as we wait for you. Amen.***

**Song**

Great is the Lord (H87)
Oh, for a thousand tongues to sing (H110)

## Call to discipleship

One does not live by bread alone,
but by every word
that comes from the mouth of God.
***Let us worship the Lord our God,***
***and serve God alone.***

**Luke 19.1-10**

[Jesus] entered Jericho and was passing through it. A man was there named Zacchaeus; he was a chief tax collector and was rich. He was trying to see who Jesus was, but on account of the crowd he could not, because he was short in stature. So he ran ahead and climbed a sycamore tree to see him, because he was going to pass that way. When Jesus came to the place, he looked up and said to him, "Zacchaeus, hurry and come down; for I must stay at your house today." So he hurried down and was happy to welcome him. All who saw it began to grumble and said, "He has gone to be the guest of one who is a sinner." Zacchaeus stood there and said to the Lord, "Look, half of my possessions, Lord, I will give to the poor; and if I have defrauded anyone of anything, I will pay back four times as much." Then Jesus said to him, "Today salvation has come to this house, because he too is a son of Abraham. For the Son of Man came to seek out and to save the lost."

**Micah 6.6-8**

"With what shall I come before the LORD,
and bow myself before God on high?
Shall I come before him with burnt offerings,
with calves a year old?
Will the LORD be pleased with thousands of
  rams,
with ten thousands of rivers of oil?
Shall I give my firstborn for my transgression,
the fruit of my body for the sin of my soul?"
He has told you, O mortal, what is good;
and what does the LORD require of you
but to do justice, and to love kindness,
and to walk humbly with your God?"

**Silent or spoken reflection on the readings**

**Song**

Forgive our sins as we forgive (H137)
There's a wideness in God's mercy (H145)
Prince of peace, control my will (H534)
What does the Lord require of you? (SS54)

**1 Peter 2.21-24**

## Call to intercession

Wait for the Lord;
be strong, and let your heart take courage.
***Hear, O Lord, when we cry aloud,***
***be gracious to us and answer us!***

Attentive God, we bring our prayers to you because we trust you to protect and provide.
In your mercy,
***Lord, hear our prayer.***

You call us to do justice, love kindness, and walk humbly with you. We pray for ourselves and those dear to us.
*(open prayers)*
In your mercy,
***Lord, hear our prayer.***

You are a helper close at hand in times of distress. We pray for our community and for our neighbors.
*(open prayers)*
In your mercy,
***Lord, hear our prayer.***

Your people live by every word that comes from your mouth. We pray for the church in all places, that we may be faithful in solidarity across generations and geography.
*(open prayers)*

In your mercy,
***Lord, hear our prayer.***

You put an end to wars across the earth. We pray for the world, for our enemies and for those who are in conflict.
*(open prayers)*
In your mercy,
***Lord, hear our prayer.***

We offer you other concerns we carry in our hearts.
*(open prayers)*
In your mercy,
***Lord, hear our prayer.***

God our only hope,
you seat us at the table with our enemies,
breathing in our fears.
Feed us from your mouth,
that our bread may be to do your will,
in the strength of your Anointed,
who taught us to pray:

***Our Father …***

**Benediction**

***Neither death, nor life, nor angels, nor rulers,***
***nor things present, nor things to come,***
***nor powers, nor height, nor depth,***
***nor anything else in all creation,***

*can separate us from the love of God*
*in Christ Jesus our Lord. Amen.*

# By his wounds you have been healed

LENT SATURDAY EVENING

**Opening sentence**

He himself bore our sins
in his body on the tree
so that we might die to sin and live for justice.
***By his wounds you have been healed.***

## Call to praise

Make me know your ways, O God;
Lead me in your truth, and teach me,
***for you are the God of my salvation;***
***for you I wait all day long.***

*Glory …*

**Psalm 46**

God is for us a refuge and strength,
a helper close at hand, in time of distress,
***so we shall not fear though the earth should rock,***
***though the mountains fall into the depths of the sea;***
even though its waters rage and foam,
even though the mountains be shaken by its waves.

***The Lord of hosts is with us;***
***the God of Jacob is our stronghold.***

The waters of a river give joy to God's city,
the holy place where the Most High dwells.
***God is within, it cannot be shaken;***
***God will help it at the dawning of the day.***
Nations are in tumult, kingdoms are shaken;
God's voice roars forth, the earth shrinks away.

***The Lord of hosts is with us;***
***the God of Jacob is our stronghold.***

Come, consider the works of the Lord,
the redoubtable deeds God has done on the earth:
***putting an end to wars across the earth;***
***breaking the bow, snapping the spear;***
***[burning the shields with fire.]***
"Be still and know that I am God,
supreme among the nations, supreme on the earth!"

***The Lord of hosts is with us;***
***the God of Jacob is our stronghold.***

**Thanksgiving**

I am bound by my promises to you, O God;
***I will offer you my thanks.***
*(free prayers of thanksgiving)*
You deliver my soul from death,
and my feet from falling,

***so that I may walk before you***
***in the light of life. Amen.***

**Song**

God is our refuge and strength (SJ26)
A mighty fortress is our God (H165)

**Confession**

Remember your mercy, O Lord,
and the love you have shown from of old.
***Do not remember my sins;***
***in your love remember me.***
*(silence)*
You relieve the troubles of my heart,
and bring me out of my distress.
***You consider my affliction and my trouble,***
***and forgive all my sins. Amen.***

## Call to discipleship

Jesus said, Unless a grain of wheat
falls into the earth and dies,
it remains just a single grain;
but if it dies, it bears much fruit.
***Whoever serves me must follow me,***
***and where I am, there will my servant be also.***

**Luke 23.39-43**

One of the criminals who were hanged there
kept deriding [Jesus] and saying, "Are you not

the Messiah? Save yourself and us!" But the other rebuked him, saying, "Do you not fear God, since you are under the same sentence of condemnation? And we indeed have been condemned justly, for we are getting what we deserve for our deeds, but this man has done nothing wrong." Then he said, "Jesus, remember me when you come into your kingdom." He replied, "Truly I tell you, today you will be with me in Paradise."

**Colossians 2.8-15**

See to it that no one takes you captive through philosophy and empty deceit, according to human tradition, according to the elemental spirits of the universe, and not according to Christ. For in him the whole fullness of deity dwells bodily, and you have come to fullness in him, who is the head of every ruler and authority. In him also you were circumcised with a spiritual circumcision, by putting off the body of the flesh in the circumcision of Christ; when you were buried with him in baptism, you were also raised with him through faith in the power of God, who raised him from the dead. And when you were dead in trespasses and the uncircumcision of your flesh, God made you alive together with him, when he forgave us all our trespasses, erasing the record that stood against us with its legal demands. He set this aside, nailing it to the cross. He disarmed the rulers and authorities and made a public example of them, triumphing over them in it.

**Silent or spoken reflection on the readings**

**Song**

All who believe and are baptized (H436)
Jesus, remember me (H247)
I believe in you, Lord Jesus (H440)

**1 Peter 2.21-24**

## Call to intercession

The Spirit helps us in our weakness;
for we do not know how to pray as we ought,
***but that very Spirit intercedes***
***with sighs too deep for words.***

Sheltering God, we pour out our hearts before you, because you are a refuge for us. In your mercy,
***Lord, hear our prayer.***

You call us to do justice, love kindness, and walk humbly with you. We pray for ourselves and those dear to us.
*(open prayers)*

In your mercy,
***Lord, hear our prayer.***

You are a helper close at hand in times of distress. We pray for our community and for our neighbors.
*(open prayers)*
In your mercy,
***Lord, hear our prayer.***

Your people live by every word that comes from your mouth. We pray for the church in all places, that we may be faithful in solidarity across generations and geography.
*(open prayers)*
In your mercy,
***Lord, hear our prayer.***

You put an end to wars across the earth. We pray for the world, for our enemies and for those who are in conflict.
*(open prayers)*
In your mercy,
***Lord, hear our prayer.***

We offer you other concerns we carry in our hearts.
*(open prayers)*
In your mercy,
***Lord, hear our prayer.***

Hungry Christ,
your body is broken
in the rocky soil of human vengeance.
Lovingly tend and till us,
that we may, at this day's dying,
entrust ourselves into the hands
of the Merciful One, praying as you taught us:

*Our Father ...*

**Benediction**

*Neither death, nor life, nor angels, nor rulers,*
*nor things present, nor things to come,*
*nor powers, nor height, nor depth,*
*nor anything else in all creation,*
*can separate us from the love of God*
*in Christ Jesus our Lord. Amen.*

# Holy Week

## Introduction to the Holy Week prayers

Holy Week is the final week of the season of Lent. As the Gospels devote substantial attention to the last week of Jesus' mortal life, so Christians during Holy Week dwell on those final days and enter into his passion. As early as the second century, Christians commemorated the passion, death, and resurrection of Jesus with lengthy observances, perhaps as a single event, eventually over the course of three days, and finally from Palm Sunday until Easter.

In this prayer book we conceived Lent and Holy Week as a unity, albeit with their own emphases. In both seasons, we move ourselves into Jesus' spirituality by reflecting on the biblical resources he had and that we know he used. The Gospel writers remember Jesus with the Torah and the Psalms on his mind and heart from the beginning in the wilderness through his prayer at Olivet and as he took his last breath on the cross. For this season, as part of our effort to honor Jesus' Bible, we have reversed the usual order of the readings, placing the Gospel reading after the Old Testament reading.

In both Lent and Holy Week, we also made an effort to reflect a biblical and Anabaptist view of the cross and the atoning work of Jesus. Minimally that means viewing Jesus' life poured out for us on the cross together with his life and his ministry of teaching, preaching, and healing. To that end, we chose scriptures that honor the Old Testament foundations for understanding the work of the cross as well as this new initiative of God. We tried to be both theological and Christological in our choices.

In these prayers for Holy Week, we dwell on the cross in all its starkness, without moving into the resurrection, which we so properly remember along with the cross every other day of the Christian year. To that end, in the spirit of the Easter Vigil, we focus on the passion along with pre-resurrection (Old Testament) passages that help us reflect on the human dilemma addressed by the cross. We present Luke's version of the narrative as a continuous Gospel reading paired with texts that resonate or provide ironic contrast with the part of the passion story that is the focus of the day's devotion. The Philippians hymn used in titles, opening sentences, and as the week's canticle also helps us attend to the cross.

# Have the same frame of mind in you

## HOLY WEEK SUNDAY MORNING

**Opening sentence**

Have the same frame of mind in you
***that was also in Christ Jesus.***

## Call to praise

Lord, hear me when I cry aloud;
be gracious to me and answer me!
***"Come," my heart says, "seek God's face!"***
***Your face, Lord, do I seek.***

***Glory …***

**Psalm 118.19-29**

Open to me the gates of holiness:
I will enter and give thanks.
***This is the LORD's own gate***
***where the just may enter.***
I will thank you for you have answered
and you are my savior.

***The stone which the builders rejected***
***has become the corner stone.***
This is the work of the LORD,
a marvel in our eyes.

*This day was made by the LORD;*
*we rejoice and are glad.*

O LORD, grant us salvation;
O LORD, grant success.
***Blessed in the name of the LORD***
***is he who comes.***
We bless you from the house of the LORD;
the LORD God is our light.

***Go forward in procession with branches***
***even to the altar.***
You are my God, I thank you.
My God, I praise you.
***Give thanks to the LORD who is good;***
***for God's love endures forever.***

**Thanksgiving**

I pray to you, Lord;
my prayer rises with the sun.
***You hear my words, my groans,***
***my cries for help.***
*(free prayers of thanksgiving)*
Your grace surrounds those
who take refuge in you;
***you protect them***
***and crown them with your favor. Amen.***

**Song**

All glory, laud, and honor (H237)
Hosanna, loud hosanna (H238)

Come, now is the time to worship (SJ9)
Jesus shall reign (H319)

## Call to discipleship

Jesus said, If any want to become my followers,
let them deny themselves
and take up their cross and follow me.
***For those who want to save their life***
***will lose it,***
***and those who lose their life for my sake***
***will save it.***

**Luke 19.29-44**

When [Jesus] had come near Bethphage and Bethany, at the place called the Mount of Olives, he sent two of the disciples, saying, "Go into the village ahead of you, and as you enter it you will find tied there a colt that has never been ridden. Untie it and bring it here. If anyone asks you, 'Why are you untying it?' just say this, 'The Lord needs it.'" So those who were sent departed and found it as he had told them. As they were untying the colt, its owners asked them, "Why are you untying the colt?" They said, "The Lord needs it." Then they brought it to Jesus; and after throwing their cloaks on the colt, they set Jesus on it. As he rode along, people kept spreading their cloaks on the road. As he was now approaching the path down from the Mount of Olives, the whole multitude of the disciples began to praise God joyfully with a loud voice for all the deeds of power that they had seen, saying,

"Blessed is the king
who comes in the name of the Lord!
Peace in heaven,
and glory in the highest heaven!"

Some of the Pharisees in the crowd said to him, "Teacher, order your disciples to stop." He answered, "I tell you, if these were silent, the stones would shout out."

As he came near and saw the city, he wept over it, saying, "If you, even you, had only recognized on this day the things that make for peace! But now they are hidden from your eyes. Indeed, the days will come upon you, when your enemies will set up ramparts around you and surround you, and hem you in on every side. They will crush you to the ground, you and your children within you, and they will not leave within you one stone upon another; because you did not recognize the time of your visitation from God."

**1 Peter 2.4-5**

Come to him, a living stone, though rejected by mortals yet chosen and precious in God's sight, and like living stones, let yourselves be built into a spiritual house, to be a holy priesthood, to offer spiritual sacrifices acceptable to God through Jesus Christ.

**Silent or spoken reflection on the readings**

**Song**

Ride on, ride on in majesty (H239)
Jesus is coming (SS73)
Open are the gifts of God (H255)
At the name of Jesus (H342)
Hosanna! Hosanna! (SS74)

**Philippians 2.5-8**

## Call to intercession

Do not hide your face from us, O God;
you have been our help.
***Do not leave us to the malice of our enemies,***
***O God of our salvation!***

Trustworthy God, we bring our prayers to you because we rely on you to protect and provide.
In your mercy,
***Lord, hear our prayer.***

You keep our feet from falling. We pray for ourselves and those dear to us.
*(open prayers)*
In your mercy,
***Lord, hear our prayer.***

Your grace gives comfort and strength. We pray for our community and for our neighbors.
*(open prayers)*
In your mercy,
***Lord, hear our prayer.***

You build your people into a spiritual home. We pray for the church in all places, that we may be one.
*(open prayers)*
In your mercy,
***Lord, hear our prayer.***

You have made your way known through Jesus Christ. We pray for the world, that your reign may come and your will be done on earth.
*(open prayers)*
In your mercy,
***Lord, hear our prayer.***

We offer you other concerns we carry in our hearts.
*(open prayers)*
In your mercy,
***Lord, hear our prayer.***

God of strength in days of testing,
you deliver us from fear to love.
Pierce our vanity and empty us of pride,
that we may see your image in all humankind
and, like Christ,

embrace both neighbor and enemy.
In the name of Jesus our Savior, we pray:

*Our Father …*

**Benediction**

*Now may our Lord Jesus Christ himself*
*and God our Father,*
*who has loved us and through grace*
*has given us eternal comfort and good hope,*
*comfort and strengthen our hearts*
*in every good work and word. Amen.*

# Have the same frame of mind that was also in Christ Jesus

## HOLY WEEK SUNDAY EVENING

**Opening sentence**

Have the same frame of mind in you
***that was also in Christ Jesus.***

## Call to praise

To you, O Lord, I lift up my soul.
O my God, in you I trust.
***Do not let me be put to shame;***
***do not let my enemies exult over me.***

*Glory ...*

**Psalm 119.41-48**

LORD, let your love come upon me,
the saving help of your promise.
***And I shall answer those who taunt me***
***for I trust in your word.***
Do not take the word of truth from my mouth
for I trust in your decrees.
***I shall keep your law always***
***for ever and ever.***
I shall walk in the path of freedom
for I seek your precepts.

***I will speak of your will before the powerful***
***and not be abashed.***
Your commands have been my delight;
these I have loved.
***I will worship your commands and love them***
***and ponder your statutes.***

**Thanksgiving**

Blessed are you, Lord;
you hear the sound of my pleadings.
***You are my strength and my shield;***
***in you my heart trusts.***
*(free prayers of thanksgiving)*
You have helped me, and my heart exults,
***and with my song I give thanks to you. Amen.***

**Song**

I long for your commandments (H543)
Lamp of our feet (H312)
Lord, I have made thy word (H317)
Rejoice, rejoice in God (H313)

**Confession**

My eyes keep looking to you, Lord,
***spring me from this trap.***
*(silence)*
Turn to me and be gracious to me,
***for I am lonely and afflicted. Amen.***

## Call to discipleship

Jesus said, This is my commandment,
that you love one another as I have loved you.
***No one has greater love than this,***
***to lay down one's life for one's friends.***

**Exodus 13.3-10**

Moses said to the people, "Remember this day on which you came out of Egypt, out of the house of slavery, because the LORD brought you out from there by strength of hand; no leavened bread shall be eaten. Today, in the month of Abib, you are going out. When the LORD brings you into the land of the Canaanites, the Hittites, the Amorites, the Hivites, and the Jebusites, which he swore to your ancestors to give you, a land flowing with milk and honey, you shall keep this observance in this month. Seven days you shall eat unleavened bread, and on the seventh day there shall be a festival to the LORD. Unleavened bread shall be eaten for seven days; no leavened bread shall be seen in your possession, and no leaven shall be seen among you in all your territory. You shall tell your child on that day, 'It is because of what the LORD did for me when I came out of Egypt.' It shall serve for you as a sign on your hand and as a reminder on your forehead, so that the teaching of the LORD may be on your lips; for with a strong hand the LORD brought you out of Egypt. You shall keep this ordinance at its proper time from year to year."

**Luke 21.37–22.13**

Every day [Jesus] was teaching in the temple, and at night he would go out and spend the night on the Mount of Olives, as it was called. And all the people would get up early in the morning to listen to him in the temple.

Now the festival of Unleavened Bread, which is called the Passover, was near. The chief priests and the scribes were looking for a way to put Jesus to death, for they were afraid of the people.

Then Satan entered into Judas called Iscariot, who was one of the twelve; he went away and conferred with the chief priests and officers of the temple police about how he might betray him to them. They were greatly pleased and agreed to give him money. So he consented and began to look for an opportunity to betray him to them when no crowd was present.

Then came the day of Unleavened Bread, on which the Passover lamb had to be sacrificed. So Jesus sent Peter and John, saying, "Go and prepare the Passover meal for us that we may eat it." They asked him, "Where do you want us to make preparations for it?" "Listen," he said to them, "when you have entered the city, a man carrying a jar of water will meet you; follow him into the house he enters and say to the owner of the house, 'The teacher asks you, "Where is the guest room, where I may eat the Passover with my disciples?"' He will show you a large room upstairs, already furnished. Make preparations for us there." So they went and found everything as he had told them; and they prepared the Passover meal.

**Silent or spoken reflection on the readings**

**Song**

We give thanks unto you (H161)
Prepare a room for me (SS76)
Shepherd of souls, refresh (H456, vv. 1–3)
Christ, who is in the form of God (H333)

**Philippians 2.5-8**

## Call to intercession

O God, our God, why are you so far from us?
***Do not stay far off. We have no other help.***

Compassionate God, we pour out our hearts before you, because you are a refuge for us. In your mercy,
***Lord, hear our prayer.***

You keep our feet from falling. We pray for ourselves and those dear to us.
*(open prayers)*
In your mercy,
***Lord, hear our prayer.***

Your grace gives comfort and strength. We pray for our community and for our neighbors.
*(open prayers)*
In your mercy,
***Lord, hear our prayer.***

You build your people into a spiritual home. We pray for the church in all places, that we may be one.
*(open prayers)*
In your mercy,
***Lord, hear our prayer.***

You have made your way known through Jesus Christ. We pray for the world, that your reign may come and your will be done on earth.
*(open prayers)*
In your mercy,
***Lord, hear our prayer.***

We offer you other concerns we carry in our hearts.
*(open prayers)*
In your mercy,
***Lord, hear our prayer.***

God of all sorrows known,
you endured human rejection,
even to the death of your own Son.
Put the same mind in us
that was in Christ Jesus,
that we may walk his path of obedient love.
In his name we pray:

***Our Father …***

**Benediction**

***Neither death, nor life, nor angels, nor rulers,***
***nor things present, nor things to come,***
***nor powers, nor height, nor depth,***
***nor anything else in all creation,***
***can separate us from the love of God***
***in Christ Jesus our Lord. Amen.***

# He existed in the form of God

## HOLY WEEK MONDAY MORNING

**Opening sentence**

He existed in the form of God,
***but he did not consider equality with God***
***something to exploit.***

## Call to praise

Lord, hear me when I cry aloud;
be gracious to me and answer me!
***"Come," my heart says, "seek God's face!"***
***Your face, Lord, do I seek.***

*Glory ...*

**Psalm 119.49-56**

Remember your word to your servant
by which you gave me hope.
***This is my comfort in sorrow:***
***that your promise gives me life.***
Though the proud may utterly deride me
I keep to your law.
***I remember your decrees of old***
***and these, LORD, console me.***
I am seized with indignation at the wicked
who forsake your law.

*Your statutes have become my song*
*in the land of exile.*
I think of your name in the night
and I keep your law.
*This has been my blessing,*
*the keeping of your precepts.*

**Thanksgiving**

I pray to you, Lord;
my prayer rises with the sun.
*You hear my words, my groans,*
*my cries for help.*
*(free prayers of thanksgiving)*
Your grace surrounds those
who take refuge in you;
*you protect them*
*and crown them with your favor. Amen.*

**Song**

O bless the Lord, my soul (H80)
We would extol thee (H74)
Santo (Holy) (SJ15)

## Call to discipleship

Jesus said, If any want to become my followers,
let them deny themselves
and take up their cross and follow me.
*For those who want to save their life*
*will lose it,*

*and those who lose their life for my sake will save it.*

**Exodus 16.9-12**

Then Moses said to Aaron, "Say to the whole congregation of the Israelites, 'Draw near to the LORD, for he has heard your complaining.'" And as Aaron spoke to the whole congregation of the Israelites, they looked toward the wilderness, and the glory of the LORD appeared in the cloud. The LORD spoke to Moses and said, "I have heard the complaining of the Israelites; say to them, 'At twilight you shall eat meat, and in the morning you shall have your fill of bread; then you shall know that I am the LORD your God.'"

**Luke 22.14-20**

When the hour came, [Jesus] took his place at the table, and the apostles with him. He said to them, "I have eagerly desired to eat this Passover with you before I suffer; for I tell you, I will not eat it until it is fulfilled in the kingdom of God." Then he took a cup, and after giving thanks he said, "Take this and divide it among yourselves; for I tell you that from now on I will not drink of the fruit of the vine until the kingdom of God comes." Then he took a loaf of bread, and when he had given thanks, he broke it and gave it to them, saying, "This is my body, which is given for you. Do this in remembrance of me." And he did the same with the cup after supper, saying, "This cup that is poured out for you is the new covenant in my blood."

**Silent or spoken reflection on the readings**

**Song**

Let the hungry come to me (H464)
O Bread of life, for sinners broken (H468)
Taste and see (SJ86)
Here is the bread (SS77)

**Philippians 2.5-8**

## Call to intercession

Do not hide your face from us, O God;
you have been our help.
***Do not leave us to the malice of our enemies,***
***O God of our salvation!***

Trustworthy God, we bring our prayers to you because we rely on you to protect and provide.
In your mercy,
***Lord, hear our prayer.***

You consider our troubles and bring us out of our distress. We pray for ourselves and those dear to us.

*(open prayers)*
In your mercy,
***Lord, hear our prayer.***

Your word brings comfort and hope. We pray for our community and for our neighbors.
*(open prayers)*
In your mercy,
***Lord, hear our prayer.***

Your Spirit intercedes for us. We pray for the church in all places, that we may know the freedom of life in the Spirit.
*(open prayers)*
In your mercy,
***Lord, hear our prayer.***

Your love fills the earth. We pray for the world and for all who care for creation.
*(open prayers)*
In your mercy,
***Lord, hear our prayer.***

We offer you other concerns we carry in our hearts.
*(open prayers)*
In your mercy,
***Lord, hear our prayer.***

God of strength in days of testing,
you deliver us from fear to love.
Pierce our vanity and empty us of pride,

that we may see your image in all humankind
and, like Christ,
embrace both neighbor and enemy.
In the name of Jesus our Savior, we pray:

*Our Father ...*

**Benediction**

*Now may our Lord Jesus Christ himself*
*and God our Father,*
*who has loved us and through grace*
*has given us eternal comfort and good hope,*
*comfort and strengthen our hearts*
*in every good work and word. Amen.*

# He did not consider equality with God something to exploit

## HOLY WEEK MONDAY EVENING

**Opening sentence**

He existed in the form of God,
***but he did not consider equality with God something to exploit.***

## Call to praise

To you, O Lord, I lift up my soul.
O my God, in you I trust.
***Do not let me be put to shame;***
***do not let my enemies exult over me.***

*Glory …*

**Psalm 119.57-64**

My part, I have resolved, O LORD,
is to obey your word.
***With all my heart I implore your favor;***
***show the mercy of your promise.***
I have pondered over my ways
and returned to your will.
***I made haste and did not delay***
***to obey your commands.***
Though the nets of the wicked ensnared me
I remembered your law.

***At midnight I will rise and thank you***
***for your just decrees.***
I am a friend of all who revere you,
who obey your precepts.
***LORD, your love fills the earth.***
***Teach me your statutes.***

**Thanksgiving**

Blessed are you, Lord;
you hear the sound of my pleadings.
***You are my strength and my shield;***
***in you my heart trusts.***
*(free prayers of thanksgiving)*
You have helped me, and my heart exults,
***and with my song I give thanks to you. Amen.***

**Song**

When all thy mercies, O my God (H72)
Sing praise to God who reigns (H59)

**Confession**

My eyes keep looking to you, Lord,
***spring me from this trap.***
*(silence)*
Turn to me and be gracious to me,
***for I am lonely and afflicted. Amen.***

## Call to discipleship

Jesus said, This is my commandment,
that you love one another as I have loved you.
***No one has greater love than this,***
***to lay down one's life for one's friends.***

**Genesis 11.1-4**

Now the whole earth had one language and the same words. And as they migrated from the east, they came upon a plain in the land of Shinar and settled there. And they said to one another, "Come, let us make bricks, and burn them thoroughly." And they had brick for stone, and bitumen for mortar. Then they said, "Come, let us build ourselves a city, and a tower with its top in the heavens, and let us make a name for ourselves; otherwise we shall be scattered abroad upon the face of the whole earth."

**Luke 22.21-30**

[Jesus said,] "But see, the one who betrays me is with me, and his hand is on the table. For the Son of Man is going as it has been determined, but woe to that one by whom he is betrayed!" Then they began to ask one another, which one of them it could be who would do this.

A dispute also arose among them as to which one of them was to be regarded as the greatest. But he said to them, "The kings of the Gentiles lord it over them; and those in authority over them are called benefactors. But not so with you; rather the greatest among you must become like the youngest, and the leader like one who serves. For who is greater, the one who is at the table or the one who serves? Is it not the one at the table? But I am among you as one who serves.

"You are those who have stood by me in my trials; and I confer on you, just as my Father has conferred on me, a kingdom, so that you may eat and drink at my table in my kingdom, and you will sit on thrones judging the twelve tribes of Israel."

**Silent or spoken reflection on the readings**

**Song**

Will you let me be your servant (H307)
Christ, who is in the form of God (H333)
Lord Jesus, as the shadows long (SS78)

**Philippians 2.5-8**

## Call to intercession

O God, our God, why are you so far from us?
***Do not stay far off. We have no other help.***

Compassionate God, we pour out our hearts before you, because you are a refuge for us. In your mercy,
***Lord, hear our prayer.***

You consider our troubles and bring us out of our distress. We pray for ourselves and those dear to us.
*(open prayers)*
In your mercy,
***Lord, hear our prayer.***

Your word brings comfort and hope. We pray for our community and for our neighbors.
*(open prayers)*
In your mercy,
***Lord, hear our prayer.***

Your Spirit intercedes for us. We pray for the church in all places, that we may know the freedom of life in the Spirit.
*(open prayers)*
In your mercy,
***Lord, hear our prayer.***

Your love fills the earth. We pray for the world and for all who care for creation.

*(open prayers)*
In your mercy,
***Lord, hear our prayer.***

We offer you other concerns we carry in our hearts.
*(open prayers)*
In your mercy,
***Lord, hear our prayer.***

God of all sorrows known,
you endured human rejection,
even to the death of your own Son.
Put the same mind in us
that was in Christ Jesus,
that we may walk his path of obedient love.
In his name we pray:

***Our Father ...***

**Benediction**

***Neither death, nor life, nor angels, nor rulers,***
***nor things present, nor things to come,***
***nor powers, nor height, nor depth,***
***nor anything else in all creation,***
***can separate us from the love of God***
***in Christ Jesus our Lord. Amen.***

# Instead he emptied himself

## HOLY WEEK TUESDAY MORNING

**Opening sentence**

Instead he emptied himself,
***assuming the form of a slave.***

## Call to praise

Lord, hear me when I cry aloud;
be gracious to me and answer me!
***"Come," my heart says, "seek God's face!"***
***Your face, Lord, do I seek.***

***Glory ...***

**Isaiah 2.1-5**

In days to come
the mountain of the LORD's house
shall be established as the highest of the mountains,
***and shall be raised above the hills;***
***all the nations shall stream to it.***
Many peoples shall come and say,
"Come, let us go up to the mountain of the LORD,
to the house of the God of Jacob;
***that he may teach us his ways***
***and that we may walk in his paths."***

For out of Zion shall go forth instruction,
and the word of the LORD from Jerusalem.
***He shall judge between the nations,***
***and shall arbitrate for many peoples;***
they shall beat their swords into plowshares,
and their spears into pruning hooks;
***nation shall not lift up sword against nation,***
neither shall they learn war any more.

***O house of Jacob,***
***come, let us walk in the light of the LORD!***

**Thanksgiving**

I pray to you, Lord;
my prayer rises with the sun.
***You hear my words, my groans,***
***my cries for help.***
*(free prayers of thanksgiving)*
Your grace surrounds those
who take refuge in you;
***you protect them***
***and crown them with your favor. Amen.***

**Song**

O Love of God (H326, vv. 1, 2, 4, 6)
From all that dwell below the skies (H49, vv. 1–3)
Let God, who called the worlds (H138)

## Call to discipleship

Jesus said, If any want to become my followers,
let them deny themselves
and take up their cross and follow me.
***For those who want to save their life***
***will lose it,***
***and those who lose their life for my sake***
***will save it.***

**1 Samuel 24.16-20**

When David had finished speaking these words to Saul, Saul said, "Is this your voice, my son David?" Saul lifted up his voice and wept. He said to David, "You are more righteous than I; for you have repaid me good, whereas I have repaid you evil. Today you have explained how you have dealt well with me, in that you did not kill me when the LORD put me into your hands. For who has ever found an enemy, and sent the enemy safely away? So may the LORD reward you with good for what you have done to me this day. Now I know that you shall surely be king, and that the kingdom of Israel shall be established in your hand."

**Luke 22.31-53**

[Jesus said,] "Simon, Simon, listen! Satan has demanded to sift all of you like wheat, but I have prayed for you that your own faith may not fail; and you, when once you have turned back, strengthen your brothers." And he said to him, "Lord, I am ready to go with you to prison and to death!" Jesus said, "I tell you, Peter, the cock will not crow this day, until you have denied three times that you know me."

He said to them, "When I sent you out without a purse, bag, or sandals, did you lack anything?" They said, "No, not a thing." He said to them, "But now, the one who has a purse must take it, and likewise a bag. And the one who has no sword must sell his cloak and buy one. For I tell you, this scripture must be fulfilled in me, 'And he was counted among the lawless'; and indeed what is written about me is being fulfilled." They said, "Lord, look, here are two swords." He replied, "It is enough."

He came out and went, as was his custom, to the Mount of Olives; and the disciples followed him. When he reached the place, he said to them, "Pray that you may not come into the time of trial." Then he withdrew from them about a stone's throw, knelt down, and prayed, "Father, if you are willing, remove this cup from me; yet, not my will but yours be done." Then an angel from heaven appeared to him and gave him strength. In his anguish he prayed more earnestly, and his sweat became like great drops of blood falling down on the ground. When he got up from prayer, he came to the disciples and found them sleeping because of grief, and he said to them, "Why are you sleeping? Get up and pray that you may not come into the time of trial."

While he was still speaking, suddenly a crowd came, and the one called Judas, one of the twelve, was leading them. He approached Jesus to kiss him; but Jesus said to him, "Judas, is it with a kiss that you are betraying the Son of Man?" When those who were around him saw what was coming, they asked, "Lord, should we strike with the sword?" Then one of them struck the slave of the high priest and cut off his right ear. But Jesus said, "No more of this!" And he touched his ear and healed him. Then Jesus said to the chief priests, the officers of the temple police, and the elders who had come for him, "Have you come out with swords and clubs as if I were a bandit? When I was with you day after day in the temple, you did not lay hands on me. But this is your hour, and the power of darkness!"

**Silent or spoken reflection on the readings**

**Song**

'Tis midnight, and on Olive's brow (H241)
Go to dark Gethsemane (H240)
Stay with me (H242)
When we are tempted (SS81)

**Philippians 2.5-8**

## Call to intercession

Do not hide your face from us, O God;
you have been our help.
***Do not leave us to the malice of our enemies,***
***O God of our salvation!***

Trustworthy God, we bring our prayers to you
because we rely on you to protect and provide.
In your mercy,
***Lord, hear our prayer.***

You are gracious and answer us when we call.
We pray for ourselves and those dear to us.
*(open prayers)*
In your mercy,
***Lord, hear our prayer.***

Your judgment brings peace. We pray for our
community and for our neighbors.
*(open prayers)*
In your mercy,
***Lord, hear our prayer.***

Your word is life to your people. We pray for
the church in all places, that we may reflect
your faithful love.
*(open prayers)*

In your mercy,
***Lord, hear our prayer.***

You will teach the nations your ways. We pray for the world, for those who are in need.
*(open prayers)*
In your mercy,
***Lord, hear our prayer.***

We offer you other concerns we carry in our hearts.
*(open prayers)*
In your mercy,
***Lord, hear our prayer.***

God of strength in days of testing,
you deliver us from fear to love.
Pierce our vanity and empty us of pride,
that we may see your image in all humankind
and, like Christ,
embrace both neighbor and enemy.
In the name of Jesus our Savior, we pray:

***Our Father ...***

**Benediction**

***Now may our Lord Jesus Christ himself***
***and God our Father,***
***who has loved us and through grace***
***has given us eternal comfort and good hope,***
***comfort and strengthen our hearts***
***in every good work and word. Amen.***

# He emptied himself, assuming the form of a slave

## HOLY WEEK TUESDAY EVENING

**Opening sentence**

Instead he emptied himself,
***assuming the form of a slave.***

## Call to praise

To you, O Lord, I lift up my soul.
O my God, in you I trust.
***Do not let me be put to shame;***
***do not let my enemies exult over me.***

*Glory …*

**Psalm 41**

Happy those who consider the poor and the weak.
***The LORD will save them in the evil day,***
will guard them, give them life, make them happy in the land
and will not give them up to the will of their foes.
***The LORD will give them strength in their pain,***
***will bring them back from sickness to health.***

As for me, I said: "LORD, have mercy on me,
heal my soul for I have sinned against you."
***My foes are speaking evil against me.***
***They want me to die and my name to perish.***
They come to visit me and speak empty words,
their hearts full of malice, they spread it abroad.

***My enemies whisper together against me.***
***They all weigh up the evil which is on me.***
They say something deadly is fixed upon me
and I will not rise from where I lie.
***Thus even my friend, in whom I trusted,***
***who ate my bread, has turned against me.***

But you, O LORD, have mercy on me.
Let me rise once more and I will repay them.
***By this I shall know that you are my friend,***
***if my foes do not shout in triumph over me.***
If you uphold me I shall be unharmed
and set in your presence for evermore.

***Blessed be the LORD, the God of Israel***
***from age to age. Amen. Amen.***

**Thanksgiving**

Blessed are you, Lord;
you hear the sound of my pleadings.
***You are my strength and my shield;***
***in you my heart trusts.***
*(free prayers of thanksgiving)*

You have helped me, and my heart exults,
***and with my song I give thanks to you. Amen.***

**Song**

Great is thy faithfulness (H327)
O bless the Lord, my soul (H600)
Lord, thou hast searched me (H556)

**Confession**

My eyes keep looking to you, Lord,
***spring me from this trap.***
*(silence)*
Turn to me and be gracious to me,
***for I am lonely and afflicted. Amen.***

## Call to discipleship

Jesus said, This is my commandment,
that you love one another as I have loved you.
***No one has greater love than this,***
***to lay down one's life for one's friends.***

**Exodus 23.1-9**

You shall not spread a false report. You shall not join hands with the wicked to act as a malicious witness. You shall not follow a majority in wrongdoing; when you bear witness in a lawsuit, you shall not side with the majority so as to pervert justice; nor shall you be partial to the poor in a lawsuit.

When you come upon your enemy's ox or donkey going astray, you shall bring it back.

When you see the donkey of one who hates you lying under its burden and you would hold back from setting it free, you must help to set it free.

You shall not pervert the justice due to your poor in their lawsuits. Keep far from a false charge, and do not kill the innocent and those in the right, for I will not acquit the guilty. You shall take no bribe, for a bribe blinds the officials, and subverts the cause of those who are in the right.

You shall not oppress a resident alien; you know the heart of an alien, for you were aliens in the land of Egypt.

**Luke 22.54-62**

Then they seized [Jesus] and led him away, bringing him into the high priest's house. But Peter was following at a distance. When they had kindled a fire in the middle of the courtyard and sat down together, Peter sat among them. Then a servant-girl, seeing him in the firelight, stared at him and said, "This man also was with him." But he denied it, saying, "Woman, I do not know him." A little later someone else, on seeing him, said, "You also are one of them." But Peter said, "Man, I am not!" Then about an hour later still another kept insisting, "Surely this man also was with him; for he is a Galilean." But Peter said, "Man, I do not know what you are talking about!" At that moment, while he was still speaking, the cock crowed. The Lord turned and looked at Peter. Then Peter remembered the word of the Lord, how he had said to him, "Before the cock crows today, you will deny me three times." And he went out and wept bitterly.

**Silent or spoken reflection on the readings**

**Song**

Before the cock crew twice (H243, vv. 1–5)
Christ, who is in the form of God (H333)
By gracious powers (H552)
My faith looks up to thee (H565, vv. 1–3)

**Philippians 2.5-8**

## Call to intercession

O God, our God, why are you so far from us?
***Do not stay far off. We have no other help.***

Compassionate God, we pour out our hearts before you, because you are a refuge for us. In your mercy,
***Lord, hear our prayer.***

You are gracious and answer us when we call. We pray for ourselves and those dear to us.
*(open prayers)*
In your mercy,
***Lord, hear our prayer.***

Your judgment brings peace. We pray for our community and for our neighbors.
*(open prayers)*
In your mercy,
***Lord, hear our prayer.***

Your word is life to your people. We pray for the church in all places, that we may reflect your faithful love.
*(open prayers)*
In your mercy,
***Lord, hear our prayer.***

You will teach the nations your ways. We pray for the world, for those who are in need.
*(open prayers)*
In your mercy,
***Lord, hear our prayer.***

We offer you other concerns we carry in our hearts.
*(open prayers)*
In your mercy,
***Lord, hear our prayer.***

God of all sorrows known,
you endured human rejection,
even to the death of your own Son.
Put the same mind in us
that was in Christ Jesus,
that we may walk his path of obedient love.
In his name we pray:

*Our Father …*

**Benediction**

*Neither death, nor life, nor angels, nor rulers,*
*nor things present, nor things to come,*
*nor powers, nor height, nor depth,*
*nor anything else in all creation,*
*can separate us from the love of God*
*in Christ Jesus our Lord. Amen.*

# He was born in the image of a human being

## HOLY WEEK WEDNESDAY MORNING

**Opening sentence**

He was born in the image of a human being.
***He was born in the image of a human being.***

## Call to praise

Lord, hear me when I cry aloud;
be gracious to me and answer me!
***"Come," my heart says, "seek God's face!"***
***Your face, Lord, do I seek.***

***Glory …***

**Psalm 8.1-9**

How great is your name, O LORD, our God,
through all the earth!

***Your majesty is praised above the heavens;***
***on the lips of children and of babes***
you have found praise to foil your enemy,
to silence the foe and the rebel.

***When I see the heavens, the work of your hands,***
***the moon and the stars which you arranged,***

what are we that you should keep us in mind,
mere mortals that you care for us?

***Yet you have made us little less than gods;***
***and crowned us with glory and honor,***
you gave us power over the work of your hands,
put all things under our feet.

***All of them, sheep and cattle,***
***yes, even the savage beasts,***
birds of the air, and fish
that make their way through the waters.

***How great is your name, O LORD our God,***
***through all the earth!***

**Thanksgiving**

I pray to you, Lord;
my prayer rises with the sun.
***You hear my words, my groans,***
***my cries for help.***
*(free prayers of thanksgiving)*
Your grace surrounds those
who take refuge in you;
***you protect them***
***and crown them with your favor. Amen.***

**Song**

God moves in a mysterious way (SJ104, vv. 1–3, 6)
Lord, our Lord, your glorious name (H157)

O Lord, our Lord, how majestic (H112)
The God of Abraham praise (H162)
Let all creation dance (SS122)

## Call to discipleship

Jesus said, If any want to become my followers,
let them deny themselves
and take up their cross and follow me.
***For those who want to save their life***
***will lose it,***
***and those who lose their life for my sake***
***will save it.***

**Genesis 1.26-27**

Then God said, "Let us make humankind in our image, according to our likeness; and let them have dominion over the fish of the sea, and over the birds of the air, and over the cattle, and over all the wild animals of the earth, and over every creeping thing that creeps upon the earth."

So God created humankind in his image,
in the image of God he created them;
male and female he created them.

**Luke 22.63-71**

Now the men who were holding Jesus began to mock him and beat him; they also blindfolded him and kept asking him, "Prophesy! Who is it that struck you?" They kept heaping many other insults on him.

When day came, the assembly of the elders of the people, both chief priests and scribes, gathered together, and they brought him to their council. They said, "If you are the Messiah, tell us." He replied, "If I tell you, you will not believe; and if I question you, you will not answer. But from now on the Son of Man will be seated at the right hand of the power of God." All of them asked, "Are you, then, the Son of God?" He said to them, "You say that I am." Then they said, "What further testimony do we need? We have heard it ourselves from his own lips!"

**Silent or spoken reflection on the readings**

**Song**

Keep me safe, O God (SJ50)
Give to the winds thy fears (H561)
When the storms of life are raging (H558, vv. 2, 4)
Oh, Lord have mercy (SJ47)
You are all we have (SJ29)

**Philippians 2.5-8**

## Call to intercession

Do not hide your face from us, O God;
you have been our help.
***Do not leave us to the malice of our enemies,***
***O God of our salvation!***

Trustworthy God, we bring our prayers to you because we rely on you to protect and provide.
In your mercy,
***Lord, hear our prayer.***

You have loved us and made us in your image.
We pray for ourselves and those dear to us.
*(open prayers)*
In your mercy,
***Lord, hear our prayer.***

You are mindful and care for all of us. We pray for our community and for our neighbors.
*(open prayers)*
In your mercy,
***Lord, hear our prayer.***

Your word is life to your people. We pray for the church in all places, that we may bear witness to your reign of justice, peace, and joy.
*(open prayers)*
In your mercy,
***Lord, hear our prayer.***

Your heart is grieved by injustice. We pray for the world, for all who are ensnared in greed, violence, and oppression.
*(open prayers)*
In your mercy,
***Lord, hear our prayer.***

We offer you other concerns we carry in our hearts.
*(open prayers)*
In your mercy,
***Lord, hear our prayer.***

God of strength in days of testing,
you deliver us from fear to love.
Pierce our vanity and empty us of pride,
that we may see your image in all humankind
and, like Christ,
embrace both neighbor and enemy.
In the name of Jesus our Savior, we pray:

***Our Father …***

**Benediction**

***Now may our Lord Jesus Christ himself***
***and God our Father,***
***who has loved us and through grace***
***has given us eternal comfort and good hope,***
***comfort and strengthen our hearts***
***in every good work and word. Amen.***

# He was born in the image of a human being

HOLY WEEK WEDNESDAY EVENING

**Opening sentence**

He was born in the image of a human being.
***He was born in the image of a human being.***

## Call to praise

To you, O Lord, I lift up my soul.
O my God, in you I trust.
***Do not let me be put to shame;***
***do not let my enemies exult over me.***

***Glory …***

**Job 31:13-23**

"If I have rejected the cause of my male or female slaves,
when they brought a complaint against me;
what then shall I do when God rises up?
***When he makes inquiry, what shall I answer him?***
***Did not he who made me in the womb make them?***
***And did not one fashion us in the womb?***

"If I have withheld anything that the poor
desired,
or have caused the eyes of the widow to fail,
or have eaten my morsel alone,
and the orphan has not eaten from it—
***for from my youth I reared the orphan like a
father,***
***and from my mother's womb I guided the
widow—***
if I have seen anyone perish for lack of clothing,
or a poor person without covering,
whose loins have not blessed me,
and who was not warmed with the fleece of
my sheep;
***if I have raised my hand against the orphan,***
***because I saw I had supporters at the gate;***
***then let my shoulder blade fall from my shoulder,***
***and let my arm be broken from its socket.***
***For I was in terror of calamity from God,***
***and I could not have faced his majesty."***

**Thanksgiving**

Blessed are you, Lord;
you hear the sound of my pleadings.
***You are my strength and my shield;***
***in you my heart trusts.***
*(free prayers of thanksgiving)*

You have helped me, and my heart exults,
***and with my song I give thanks to you. Amen.***

**Song**

I'll praise my Maker (H166)
Christ, who is in the form of God (H333)
Nothing is lost on the breath of God (SS121)

**Confession**

My eyes keep looking to you, Lord,
***spring me from this trap.***
*(silence)*
Turn to me and be gracious to me,
***for I am lonely and afflicted. Amen.***

## Call to discipleship

Jesus said, This is my commandment,
that you love one another as I have loved you.
***No one has greater love than this,***
***to lay down one's life for one's friends.***

**Hebrews 2.9**

But we do see Jesus, who for a little while was made lower than the angels, now crowned with glory and honor because of the suffering of death, so that by the grace of God he might taste death for everyone.

**Luke 23.1-12**

Then the assembly rose as a body and brought Jesus before Pilate. They began to accuse him, saying, "We found this man perverting our nation, forbidding us to pay taxes to the emperor, and saying that he himself is the Messiah, a king." Then Pilate asked him, "Are you the king of the Jews?" He answered, "You say so." Then Pilate said to the chief priests and the crowds, "I find no basis for an accusation against this man." But they were insistent and said, "He stirs up the people by teaching throughout all Judea, from Galilee where he began even to this place."

When Pilate heard this, he asked whether the man was a Galilean. And when he learned that he was under Herod's jurisdiction, he sent him off to Herod, who was himself in Jerusalem at that time. When Herod saw Jesus, he was very glad, for he had been wanting to see him for a long time, because he had heard about him and was hoping to see him perform some sign. He questioned him at some length, but Jesus gave him no answer. The chief priests and the scribes stood by, vehemently accusing him. Even Herod with his soldiers treated him with contempt and mocked him; then he put an elegant robe on him, and sent him back to Pilate. That same day Herod and Pilate became friends with each other; before this they had been enemies.

**Silent or spoken reflection on the readings**

**Song**

Don't be afraid (SJ105)
O sacred Head, now wounded (H252)
Ah, holy Jesus (H254)
How long, O Lord (SS82)

**Philippians 2.5-8**

## Call to intercession

O God, our God, why are you so far from us?
***Do not stay far off. We have no other help.***

Compassionate God, we pour out our hearts before you, because you are a refuge for us. In your mercy,
***Lord, hear our prayer.***

You have loved us and made us in your image. We pray for ourselves and those dear to us.
*(open prayers)*
In your mercy,
***Lord, hear our prayer.***

You are mindful and care for all of us. We pray for our community and for our neighbors.
*(open prayers)*

In your mercy,
***Lord, hear our prayer.***

Your word is life to your people. We pray for the church in all places, that we may bear witness to your reign of justice, peace, and joy.
*(open prayers)*
In your mercy,
***Lord, hear our prayer.***

Your heart is grieved by injustice. We pray for the world, for all who are ensnared in greed, violence, and oppression.
*(open prayers)*
In your mercy,
***Lord, hear our prayer.***

We offer you other concerns we carry in our hearts.
*(open prayers)*
In your mercy,
***Lord, hear our prayer.***

God of all sorrows known,
you endured human rejection,
even to the death of your own Son.
Put the same mind in us
that was in Christ Jesus,
that we may walk his path of obedient love.
In his name we pray:

***Our Father ...***

**Benediction**

*Neither death, nor life, nor angels, nor rulers,*
*nor things present, nor things to come,*
*nor powers, nor height, nor depth,*
*nor anything else in all creation,*
*can separate us from the love of God*
*in Christ Jesus our Lord. Amen.*

# Being found
# in the design of a human being

## HOLY WEEK THURSDAY MORNING

**Opening sentence**

And being found
in the design of a human being,
***he humbled himself.***

## Call to praise

Lord, hear me when I cry aloud;
be gracious to me and answer me!
***"Come," my heart says, "seek God's face!"***
***Your face, Lord, do I seek.***

*Glory …*

**Psalm 27**

The LORD is my light and my help;
whom shall I fear?
***The LORD is the stronghold of my life;***
***before whom shall I shrink?***

When evildoers draw near
to devour my flesh,
***it is they, my enemies and foes,***
***who stumble and fall.***

Though an army encamp against me
my heart would not fear.
***Though war break out against me***
***even then would I trust.***

There is one thing I ask of the LORD,
for this I long,
to live in the house of the LORD,
all the days of my life,
***to savor the sweetness of the LORD,***
***to behold his temple.***

For God makes me safe in his tent
in the day of evil.
***God hides me in the shelter of his tent,***
***on a rock I am secure.***

And now my head shall be raised
above my foes who surround me
***and I shall offer within God's tent***
***a sacrifice of joy.***

I will sing and make music for the Lord.

***O LORD, hear my voice when I call;***
***have mercy and answer.***
Of you my heart has spoken:
"Seek God's face."

***It is your face, O LORD, that I seek;***
***hide not your face.***
Dismiss not your servant in anger;
you have been my help.

***Do not abandon or forsake me,***
***O God my help!***
Though father and mother forsake me,
the LORD will receive me.

***Instruct me, LORD, in your way;***
***on an even path lead me.***
When they lie in ambush protect me
from my enemies' greed.
***False witnesses rise against me,***
***breathing out fury.***

I am sure I shall see the LORD's goodness
in the land of the living.
***In the LORD, hold firm and take heart.***
***Hope in the LORD!***

**Thanksgiving**

I pray to you, Lord;
my prayer rises with the sun.
***You hear my words, my groans,***
***my cries for help.***
*(free prayers of thanksgiving)*
Your grace surrounds those
who take refuge in you;
***you protect them***
***and crown them with your favor. Amen.***

**Song**

O God, our help in ages past (H328)
I to the hills will lift my eyes (H169)

The Lord's my shepherd (H578)
The Lord's my Shepherd (SS99)

## Call to discipleship

Jesus said, If any want to become my followers,
let them deny themselves
and take up their cross and follow me.
***For those who want to save their life***
***will lose it,***
***and those who lose their life for my sake***
***will save it.***

**Genesis 4.8-16**

Cain said to his brother Abel, "Let us go out to the field." And when they were in the field, Cain rose up against his brother Abel, and killed him. Then the LORD said to Cain, "Where is your brother Abel?" He said, "I do not know; am I my brother's keeper?" And the LORD said, "What have you done? Listen; your brother's blood is crying out to me from the ground! And now you are cursed from the ground, which has opened its mouth to receive your brother's blood from your hand. When you till the ground, it will no longer yield to you its strength; you will be a fugitive and a wanderer on the earth." Cain said to the LORD, "My punishment is greater than I can bear! Today you have driven me away from the soil, and I shall be hidden from your face; I shall be a fugitive and a wanderer on the earth, and anyone who meets me may kill me." Then the LORD said to him, "Not so! Whoever kills Cain will suffer a sevenfold vengeance." And the LORD put a mark on Cain, so that no one who came upon him would kill him. Then Cain went away from the presence of the LORD, and settled in the land of Nod, east of Eden.

**Luke 23.13-25**

Pilate then called together the chief priests, the leaders, and the people, and said to them, "You brought me this man as one who was perverting the people; and here I have examined him in your presence and have not found this man guilty of any of your charges against him. Neither has Herod, for he sent him back to us. Indeed, he has done nothing to deserve death. I will therefore have him flogged and release him."

Then they all shouted out together, "Away with this fellow! Release Barabbas for us!" (This was a man who had been put in prison for an insurrection that had taken place in the city, and for murder.) Pilate, wanting to release Jesus, addressed them again; but they kept shouting, "Crucify, crucify him!" A third time he said to them, "Why, what evil has he done? I have found in him no ground for the sentence of death; I will therefore have him flogged and then release him." But they kept urgently demanding with loud shouts that he should be crucified; and their voices prevailed. So Pilate gave his verdict that their demand should be granted. He released the man they asked for, the one who had been put in prison for insurrection and murder, and he handed Jesus over as they wished.

**Silent or spoken reflection on the readings**

**Song**

Alone thou goest forth (H244, vv. 1–3)
Don't be afraid (SJ105)
Open are the gifts of God (H255)
Jesus walked this lonesome valley (SS80)

**Philippians 2.5-8**

## Call to intercession

Do not hide your face from us, O God;
you have been our help.
***Do not leave us to the malice of our enemies,***
***O God of our salvation!***

Trustworthy God, we bring our prayers to you
because we rely on you to protect and provide.
In your mercy,
***Lord, hear our prayer.***

You call us to walk in integrity. We pray for ourselves and those dear to us.
*(open prayers)*
In your mercy,
***Lord, hear our prayer.***

You promise your goodness in the land of the living. We pray for our community and for our neighbors.
*(open prayers)*
In your mercy,
***Lord, hear our prayer.***

You teach us your way. We pray for the church in all places, that we may daily follow in the footsteps of Christ.
*(open prayers)*
In your mercy,
***Lord, hear our prayer.***

You turn our hearts to peace. We pray for the world, for those in positions of power and authority.
*(open prayers)*
In your mercy,
***Lord, hear our prayer.***

We offer you other concerns we carry in our hearts.
*(open prayers)*
In your mercy,
***Lord, hear our prayer.***

God of strength in days of testing,
you deliver us from fear to love.
Pierce our vanity and empty us of pride,
that we may see your image in all humankind
and, like Christ,
embrace both neighbor and enemy.
In the name of Jesus our Savior, we pray:

***Our Father …***

**Benediction**

***Now may our Lord Jesus Christ himself***
***and God our Father,***
***who has loved us and through grace***
***has given us eternal comfort and good hope,***
***comfort and strengthen our hearts***
***in every good work and word. Amen.***

# He humbled himself

## HOLY WEEK THURSDAY EVENING

**Opening sentence**

And being found
in the design of a human being,
***he humbled himself.***

## Call to praise

To you, O Lord, I lift up my soul.
O my God, in you I trust.
***Do not let me be put to shame;***
***do not let my enemies exult over me.***

*Glory …*

**Psalm 26**

Give judgment for me, O LORD,
for I walk the path of perfection.
***I trust in the LORD; I have not wavered.***

Examine me, LORD, and try me;
O test my heart and my mind,
***for your love is before my eyes***
***and I walk according to your truth.***

I never take my place with liars
and with hypocrites I shall not go.

*I hate the evildoer's company;*
*I will not take my place with the wicked.*

To prove my innocence I wash my hands
and take my place around your altar,
singing a song of thanksgiving,
proclaiming all your wonders.

*O LORD, I love the house where you dwell,*
*the place where your glory abides.*

Do not sweep me away with sinners,
nor my life with bloodthirsty people
*in whose hands are evil plots,*
*whose right hands are filled with gold.*

As for me, I walk the path of perfection.
Redeem me and show me your mercy.
*My foot stands on level ground;*
*I will bless the LORD in the assembly.*

**Thanksgiving**

Blessed are you, Lord;
you hear the sound of my pleadings.
*You are my strength and my shield;*
*in you my heart trusts.*
*(free prayers of thanksgiving)*
You have helped me, and my heart exults,
*and with my song I give thanks to you. Amen.*

**Song**

Out of the depths I cry to you (H133)

Kyrie eleison (H144)
Kyrie (SS68)
Agios o Theos (SJ20)
My life flows on (H580)
Khudaya, rahem kar (Have mercy on us, Lord) (SS67)

**Confession**

My eyes keep looking to you, Lord,
***spring me from this trap.***
*(silence)*
Turn to me and be gracious to me,
***for I am lonely and afflicted. Amen.***

## Call to discipleship

Jesus said, This is my commandment,
that you love one another as I have loved you.
***No one has greater love than this,***
***to lay down one's life for one's friends.***

**Joshua 24.14-15**

"Now therefore revere the LORD, and serve him in sincerity and in faithfulness; put away the gods that your ancestors served beyond the River and in Egypt, and serve the LORD. Now if you are unwilling to serve the LORD, choose this day whom you will serve, whether the gods your ancestors served in the region beyond the River or the gods of the Amorites in whose land you are living; but as for me and my household, we will serve the LORD."

**Luke 23.26-31**

As [the soldiers] led [Jesus] away, they seized a man, Simon of Cyrene, who was coming from the country, and they laid the cross on him, and made him carry it behind Jesus. A great number of the people followed him, and among them were women who were beating their breasts and wailing for him. But Jesus turned to them and said, "Daughters of Jerusalem, do not weep for me, but weep for yourselves and for your children. For the days are surely coming when they will say, 'Blessed are the barren, and the wombs that never bore, and the breasts that never nursed.' Then they will begin to say to the mountains, 'Fall on us'; and to the hills, 'Cover us.' For if they do this when the wood is green, what will happen when it is dry?"

**Silent or spoken reflection on the readings**

**Song**

Don't be afraid (SJ105)
Christ, who is in the form of God (H333)
When Jesus wept, the falling tear (H234)
Ah, holy Jesus (H254)
Cast thy burden upon the Lord (H586)

**Philippians 2.5-8**

## Call to intercession

O God, our God, why are you so far from us?
***Do not stay far off. We have no other help.***

Compassionate God, we pour out our hearts before you, because you are a refuge for us. In your mercy,
***Lord, hear our prayer.***

You call us to walk in integrity. We pray for ourselves and those dear to us.
*(open prayers)*
In your mercy,
***Lord, hear our prayer.***

You promise your goodness in the land of the living. We pray for our community and for our neighbors.
*(open prayers)*
In your mercy,
***Lord, hear our prayer.***

You teach us your way. We pray for the church in all places, that we may daily follow in the footsteps of Christ.
*(open prayers)*
In your mercy,
***Lord, hear our prayer.***

You turn our hearts to peace. We pray for the world, for those in positions of power and authority.
*(open prayers)*
In your mercy,
***Lord, hear our prayer.***

We offer you other concerns we carry in our hearts.
*(open prayers)*
In your mercy,
***Lord, hear our prayer.***

God of all sorrows known,
you endured human rejection,
even to the death of your own Son.
Put the same mind in us
that was in Christ Jesus,
that we may walk his path of obedient love.
In his name we pray:

***Our Father …***

**Benediction**

***Neither death, nor life, nor angels, nor rulers,***
***nor things present, nor things to come,***
***nor powers, nor height, nor depth,***
***nor anything else in all creation,***
***can separate us from the love of God***
***in Christ Jesus our Lord. Amen.***

# He became obedient unto death

## HOLY WEEK FRIDAY MORNING

**Opening sentence**

He humbled himself,
***and he became obedient unto death.***

## Call to praise

Lord, hear me when I cry aloud;
be gracious to me and answer me!
***"Come," my heart says, "seek God's face!"***
***Your face, Lord, do I seek.***

***Glory ...***

**Psalm 22.2-9 [1-8]**

My God, my God, why have you forsaken me?
You are far from my plea and the cry of my
distress.
***O my God, I call by day and you give no reply;***
***I call by night and I find no peace.***

Yet you, O God, are holy,
enthroned on the praises of Israel.
***In you our forebears put their trust;***
***they trusted and you set them free.***
When they cried to you, they escaped.
In you they trusted and never in vain.

***But I am a worm and no man,***
***the butt of all, laughing-stock of the people.***
All who see me deride me.
They curl their lips, they toss their heads.
***"He trusted in the LORD, let him save him,***
***and release him if this is his friend."***

**Thanksgiving**

I pray to you, Lord;
my prayer rises with the sun.
***You hear my words, my groans,***
***my cries for help.***
*(free prayers of thanksgiving)*
Your grace surrounds those
who take refuge in you;
***you protect them***
***and crown them with your favor. Amen.***

**Song**

Kyrie eleison (H144)
Alas! and did my Savior bleed? (H253)
Khudaya, rahem kar (Have mercy on us, Lord) (SS67)
Alone thou goest forth (H244)
When I survey the wondrous cross (H259, H260)

## Call to discipleship

Jesus said, If any want to become my followers,
let them deny themselves
and take up their cross and follow me.
***For those who want to save their life***
***will lose it,***
***and those who lose their life for my sake***
***will save it.***

**Daniel 3.16-18**

Shadrach, Meshach, and Abednego answered the king, "O Nebuchadnezzar, we have no need to present a defense to you in this matter. If our God whom we serve is able to deliver us from the furnace of blazing fire and out of your hand, O king, let him deliver us. But if not, be it known to you, O king, that we will not serve your gods and we will not worship the golden statue that you have set up."

**Luke 23.32-38**

Two others also, who were criminals, were led away to be put to death with [Jesus]. When they came to the place that is called The Skull, they crucified Jesus there with the criminals, one on his right and one on his left. Then Jesus said, "Father, forgive them; for they do not know what they are doing." And they cast lots to divide his clothing. And the people stood by, watching; but the leaders scoffed at him, saying, "He saved others; let him save himself if he is the Messiah of God, his chosen one!" The soldiers also mocked him, coming up and offering him sour wine, and saying, "If you are the King of the Jews, save yourself!" There was also an inscription over him, "This is the King of the Jews."

**Silent or spoken reflection on the readings**

**Song**

So much wrong (SS84)
I love thee, Lord (H605)
Calvary (H249)
Why has God forsaken me? (H246)

**Philippians 2.5-8**

## Call to intercession

Do not hide your face from us, O God;
you have been our help.
***Do not leave us to the malice of our enemies,***
***O God of our salvation!***

Trustworthy God, we bring our prayers to you because we rely on you to protect and provide.
In your mercy,
***Lord, hear our prayer.***

Your Spirit helps us in our weakness. We pray for ourselves and those dear to us.
*(open prayers)*
In your mercy,
***Lord, hear our prayer.***

You are present in the darkest hour. We pray for our community and for our neighbors.
*(open prayers)*
In your mercy,
***Lord, hear our prayer.***

You deliver those who trust in you. We pray for the church in all places, that we may speak boldly for Christ.
*(open prayers)*
In your mercy,
***Lord, hear our prayer.***

You gave your beloved; you offer eternal life. We pray for the world, for all who do justice and love mercy.
*(open prayers)*
In your mercy,
***Lord, hear our prayer.***

We offer you other concerns we carry in our hearts.
*(open prayers)*
In your mercy,
***Lord, hear our prayer.***

God of strength in days of testing,
you deliver us from fear to love.
Pierce our vanity and empty us of pride,
that we may see your image in all humankind
and, like Christ,
embrace both neighbor and enemy.
In the name of Jesus our Savior, we pray:

***Our Father …***

**Benediction**

***Now may our Lord Jesus Christ himself***
***and God our Father,***
***who has loved us and through grace***
***has given us eternal comfort and good hope,***
***comfort and strengthen our hearts***
***in every good work and word. Amen.***

# He became obedient unto death

## HOLY WEEK FRIDAY EVENING

**Opening sentence**

He humbled himself,
***and he became obedient unto death.***

## Call to praise

To you, O Lord, I lift up my soul.
O my God, in you I trust.
***Do not let me be put to shame;***
***do not let my enemies exult over me.***

*Glory …*

**Psalm 22.10-22 [9-21]**

Yes, it was you who took me from the womb,
entrusted me to my mother's breast.
***To you I was committed from birth,***
***from my mother's womb you have been my God.***
Do not leave me alone in my distress;
Come close, there is none else to help.

***Many bulls have surrounded me,***
***fierce bulls of Bashan close me in.***
Against me they open wide their jaws,
like lions, rending and roaring.

***Like water I am poured out,***
***disjointed are all my bones.***
My heart has become like wax,
it is melted within my breast.
***Parched as burnt clay is my throat,***
***my tongue cleaves to my jaws.***

Many dogs have surrounded me,
a band of the wicked beset me.
***They tear holes in my hands and my feet,***
***and lay me in the dust of death.***

I can count every one of my bones.
These people stare at me and gloat;
***they divide my clothing among them.***
***They cast lots for my robe.***

O LORD, do not leave me alone,
my strength, make haste to help me!
***Rescue my soul from the sword,***
***my life from the grip of these dogs.***
***Save my life from the jaws of these lions,***
***my soul from the horns of these oxen.***

**Thanksgiving**

Blessed are you, Lord;
you hear the sound of my pleadings.
***You are my strength and my shield;***
***in you my heart trusts.***
*(free prayers of thanksgiving)*
You have helped me, and my heart exults,
***and with my song I give thanks to you. Amen.***

**Song**

My song is love unknown (H235)
O Lamb of God all holy (H146)
Christ, we do all adore thee (H105)
God moves in a mysterious way (SJ104, vv. 1–3, 6)
Kyrie eleison (H144)
Open are the gifts of God (H255)

**Confession**

My eyes keep looking to you, Lord,
***spring me from this trap.***
*(silence)*
Turn to me and be gracious to me,
***for I am lonely and afflicted. Amen.***

## Call to discipleship

Jesus said, This is my commandment,
that you love one another as I have loved you.
***No one has greater love than this,***
***to lay down one's life for one's friends.***

**Zephaniah 3.19**

I will deal with all your oppressors
at that time.
And I will save the lame
and gather the outcast,
and I will change their shame into praise
and renown in all the earth.

**Luke 23.39-48**

One of the criminals who were hanged there kept deriding [Jesus] and saying, "Are you not the Messiah? Save yourself and us!" But the other rebuked him, saying, "Do you not fear God, since you are under the same sentence of condemnation? And we indeed have been condemned justly, for we are getting what we deserve for our deeds, but this man has done nothing wrong." Then he said, "Jesus, remember me when you come into your kingdom." He replied, "Truly I tell you, today you will be with me in Paradise."

It was now about noon, and darkness came over the whole land until three in the afternoon, while the sun's light failed; and the curtain of the temple was torn in two. Then Jesus, crying with a loud voice, said, "Father, into your hands I commend my spirit." Having said this, he breathed his last. When the centurion saw what had taken place, he praised God and said, "Certainly this man was innocent." And when all the crowds who had gathered there for this spectacle saw what had taken place, they returned home, beating their breasts.

**Silent or spoken reflection on the readings**

**Song**

I love thee, Lord (H605)
Holy Spirit, Storm of love (H132, vv. 1–3)
How shallow former shadows (H251)
Beneath the cross of Jesus (H250)
Were you there (H257)
Jesus, remember me (H247)
Remember me (SS83)
Don't be afraid (SJ105)

**Philippians 2.5-8**

## Call to intercession

O God, our God, why are you so far from us?
***Do not stay far off. We have no other help.***

Compassionate God, we pour out our hearts before you, because you are a refuge for us. In your mercy,
***Lord, hear our prayer.***

Your Spirit helps us in our weakness. We pray for ourselves and those dear to us.
*(open prayers)*
In your mercy,
***Lord, hear our prayer.***

You are present in the darkest hour. We pray for our community and for our neighbors.
*(open prayers)*

In your mercy,
***Lord, hear our prayer.***

You deliver those who trust in you. We pray for the church in all places, that we may speak boldly for Christ.
*(open prayers)*
In your mercy,
***Lord, hear our prayer.***

You gave your beloved; you offer eternal life. We pray for the world, for all who do justice and love mercy.
*(open prayers)*
In your mercy,
***Lord, hear our prayer.***

We offer you other concerns we carry in our hearts.
*(open prayers)*
In your mercy,
***Lord, hear our prayer.***

God of all sorrows known,
you endured human rejection,
even to the death of your own Son.
Put the same mind in us
that was in Christ Jesus,
that we may walk his path of obedient love.
In his name we pray:

***Our Father ...***

**Benediction**

*Neither death, nor life, nor angels, nor rulers,*
*nor things present, nor things to come,*
*nor powers, nor height, nor depth,*
*nor anything else in all creation,*
*can separate us from the love of God*
*in Christ Jesus our Lord. Amen.*

# He became obedient unto death, even death on a cross

## HOLY WEEK SATURDAY MORNING

**Opening sentence**

He became obedient unto death,
***even death on a cross.***

## Call to praise

Lord, hear me when I cry aloud;
be gracious to me and answer me!
***"Come," my heart says, "seek God's face!"***
***Your face, Lord, do I seek.***

***Glory …***

**Psalm 17**

LORD, hear a cause that is just,
pay heed to my cry.
***Turn your ear to my prayer,***
***no deceit is on my lips.***

From you may my judgment come forth.
Your eyes discern the truth.

***You search my heart, you visit me by night.***
***You test me and you find in me no wrong.***
***My words are not sinful like human words.***

I kept from violence because of your word,
I kept my feet firmly in your paths;
there was no faltering in my steps.

***I am here and I call, you will hear me, O God.***
***Turn your ear to me; hear my words.***
Display your great love, you whose right hand saves
your friends from those who rebel against them.

***Guard me as the apple of your eye.***
***Hide me in the shadow of your wings***
***from the violent attack of the wicked.***

My foes encircle me with deadly intent.
Their hearts tight shut, their mouths speak proudly.
They advance against me, and now they surround me.

***Their eyes are watching to strike me to the ground,***
***as though they were lions ready to claw***
***or like some young lion crouched in hiding.***

LORD, arise, confront them, strike them down!
Let your sword rescue me from the wicked;
***let your hand, O LORD, rescue me,***
***from those whose reward is in this present life.***

You give them their fill of your treasures;
they rejoice in abundance of offspring
and leave their wealth to their children.

***As for me, in my justice I shall see your face
and be filled, when I awake, with the sight of
your glory.***

**Thanksgiving**

I pray to you, Lord;
my prayer rises with the sun.
***You hear my words, my groans,
my cries for help.***
*(free prayers of thanksgiving)*
Your grace surrounds those
who take refuge in you;
***you protect them
and crown them with your favor. Amen.***

**Song**

Christ, we do all adore thee (H105)
My song is love unknown (H235)

## Call to discipleship

Jesus said, If any want to become my followers,
let them deny themselves
and take up their cross and follow me.
***For those who want to save their life
will lose it,***

*and those who lose their life for my sake*
*will save it.*

**Song of Solomon 8.6-7**

Set me as a seal upon your heart,
as a seal upon your arm;
for love is strong as death,
passion fierce as the grave.
Its flashes are flashes of fire,
a raging flame.
Many waters cannot quench love,
neither can floods drown it.
If one offered for love
all the wealth of his house,
it would be utterly scorned.

**Luke 23.49**

But all [Jesus'] acquaintances, including the women who had followed him from Galilee, stood at a distance, watching these things.

**Silent or spoken reflection on the readings**

**Song**

So much wrong (SS84)
Open are the gifts of God (H255)
Kyrie (SS68)
Ah, holy Jesus (H254)

**Philippians 2.5-8**

## Call to intercession

Do not hide your face from us, O God;
you have been our help.
***Do not leave us to the malice of our enemies,***
***O God of our salvation!***

Trustworthy God, we bring our prayers to you because we rely on you to protect and provide.
In your mercy,
***Lord, hear our prayer.***

You hide us in the shadow of your wings. We pray for ourselves and those dear to us.
*(open prayers)*
In your mercy,
***Lord, hear our prayer.***

You consider and answer those who call on you. We pray for our community and for our neighbors.
*(open prayers)*
In your mercy,
***Lord, hear our prayer.***

You have dealt bountifully with your people. We pray for the church in all places, that we may be faithful in solidarity across generations and geography.
*(open prayers)*

In your mercy,
***Lord, hear our prayer.***

Your love shines in the darkest places. We pray for the world, for our enemies and for those who are in conflict.
*(open prayers)*
In your mercy,
***Lord, hear our prayer.***

We offer you other concerns we carry in our hearts.
*(open prayers)*
In your mercy,
***Lord, hear our prayer.***

God of strength in days of testing,
you deliver us from fear to love.
Pierce our vanity and empty us of pride,
that we may see your image in all humankind
and, like Christ,
embrace both neighbor and enemy.
In the name of Jesus our Savior, we pray:

***Our Father …***

**Benediction**

***Now may our Lord Jesus Christ himself***
***and God our Father,***
***who has loved us and through grace***
***has given us eternal comfort and good hope,***

*comfort and strengthen our hearts*
*in every good work and word.* Amen.

# He became obedient unto death, even death on a cross

## HOLY WEEK SATURDAY EVENING

**Opening sentence**

He became obedient unto death,
***even death on a cross.***

## Call to praise

To you, O Lord, I lift up my soul.
O my God, in you I trust.
***Do not let me be put to shame;***
***do not let my enemies exult over me.***

*Glory ...*

**Psalm 13**

How long, O LORD, will you forget me?
How long will you hide your face?
***How long must I bear grief in my soul,***
***this sorrow in my heart day and night?***
***How long shall my enemy prevail?***

Look at me, answer me, LORD my God!
Give light to my eyes lest I fall asleep in death,
***lest my enemy say: "I have prevailed";***
***lest my foes rejoice to see my fall.***

As for me, I trust in your merciful love.
Let my heart rejoice in your saving help.
***Let me sing to you LORD for your goodness to me,***
***sing psalms to your name, O Lord, Most High.***

**Thanksgiving**

Blessed are you, Lord;
you hear the sound of my pleadings.
***You are my strength and my shield;***
***in you my heart trusts.***
*(free prayers of thanksgiving)*
You have helped me, and my heart exults,
***and with my song I give thanks to you. Amen.***

**Song**

Christ, we do all adore thee (H105)
Man of sorrows (H258)
O praise the gracious power (H111, vv. 1–3, 6–7)
What wondrous love is this (H530)

**Confession**

My eyes keep looking to you, Lord,
***spring me from this trap.***
*(silence)*
Turn to me and be gracious to me,
***for I am lonely and afflicted. Amen.***

## Call to discipleship

Jesus said, This is my commandment,
that you love one another as I have loved you.
***No one has greater love than this,***
***to lay down one's life for one's friends.***

**Habakkuk 3.17-19**

Though the fig tree does not blossom,
and no fruit is on the vines;
though the produce of the olive fails
and the fields yield no food;
though the flock is cut off from the fold
and there is no herd in the stalls,
yet I will rejoice in the LORD;
I will exult in the God of my salvation.
GOD, the Lord, is my strength;
he makes my feet like the feet of a deer,
and makes me tread upon the heights.

**Luke 23.50-56**

Now there was a good and righteous man named Joseph, who, though a member of the council, had not agreed to their plan and action. He came from the Jewish town of Arimathea, and he was waiting expectantly for the kingdom of God. This man went to Pilate and asked for the body of Jesus. Then he took it down, wrapped it in a linen cloth, and laid it in a rock-hewn tomb where no one had ever been laid. It was the day of Preparation, and the sabbath was beginning. The women who had come with him from Galilee followed, and they saw the tomb and how his body was laid. Then they returned, and prepared spices and ointments.

On the sabbath they rested according to the commandment.

**Silent or spoken reflection on the readings**

**Song**

La ténèbre (Our darkness) (SJ101)
All will be well (SJ98)
Christ, who is in the form of God (H333)
The strife is o'er (H263; alternative verses in accompaniment book)

**Philippians 2.5-8**

## Call to intercession

O God, our God, why are you so far from us?
***Do not stay far off. We have no other help.***

Compassionate God, we pour out our hearts before you, because you are a refuge for us. In your mercy,
***Lord, hear our prayer.***

You hide us in the shadow of your wings. We pray for ourselves and those dear to us.
*(open prayers)*
In your mercy,
***Lord, hear our prayer.***

You consider and answer those who call on you. We pray for our community and for our neighbors.
*(open prayers)*
In your mercy,
***Lord, hear our prayer.***

You have dealt bountifully with your people. We pray for the church in all places, that we may be faithful in solidarity across generations and geography.
*(open prayers)*
In your mercy,
***Lord, hear our prayer.***

Your love shines in the darkest places. We pray for the world, for our enemies and for those who are in conflict.
*(open prayers)*
In your mercy,
***Lord, hear our prayer.***

We offer you other concerns we carry in our hearts.
*(open prayers)*

In your mercy,
***Lord, hear our prayer.***

God of all sorrows known,
you endured human rejection,
even to the death of your own Son.
Put the same mind in us
that was in Christ Jesus,
that we may walk his path of obedient love.
In his name we pray:

***Our Father …***

**Benediction**

***Neither death, nor life, nor angels, nor rulers,***
***nor things present, nor things to come,***
***nor powers, nor height, nor depth,***
***nor anything else in all creation,***
***can separate us from the love of God***
***in Christ Jesus our Lord. Amen.***

# Easter

## Introduction to the Easter prayers

In the early church, Christians considered every Sunday a little Easter, in which they celebrated the whole story of redemption. Some called the fifty days after Easter "one great Sunday." According to an early third-century Christian writer, Easter was the most joyous season, so Christians did not fast and in their worship services they stood to pray and often said Alleluia.

During the Easter season, we retell and ponder the joyful but often puzzling experiences of Jesus' first disciples in the days and weeks after his death and burial. As we pray these services, we imagine ourselves into the Gospel stories of disciples struggling to make sense of their experiences. In the Psalm readings we express our new song of joy in the resurrection. And throughout we ponder the questions the first Christians confronted, too: Who is this risen Lord? What is the meaning of his death and of God's vindication?

The fortieth day after Easter is Ascension day—always a Thursday—so the Thursday services include the ascension accounts.

The opening sentences, from the hymn in Philippians 2.8-11, form a continuity with—and reversal of—the early lines of the hymn that began services in Holy Week (Phil 2.5-7). As the week progresses, more and more of the hymn appears. The entire hymn serves as the canticle for the week. In the call to discipleship both morning and evening, Jesus beckons us to the abundant life that flows from following in his paradoxical way: in losing our lives for his sake, we will find life. The first readings are Gospel accounts of Jesus' post-resurrection appearances. The second readings extend the Christological affirmations of the opening sentences. The intercessions, too, are framed with the promise of "a new thing" that springs forth in the power of the resurrection. The benedictions overflow with joy and thanks to God, who in glorious power "makes us complete in everything good."

# God lifted him high

## EASTER SUNDAY MORNING

**Opening sentence**

He humbled himself,
and he became obedient unto death,
even death on a cross.
***Therefore God lifted him high.***

## Call to praise

We sing your praises, our God and king,
and bless your name forever and ever.
***Every day we will bless you,***
***and praise your name forever and ever.***
***Alleluia!***

*Glory ...*

**Psalm 118.14-29**

The LORD is my strength and my song;
and has been my savior.
***There are shouts of joy and victory***
***in the tents of the just.***

The LORD's right hand has triumphed;
God's right hand raised me.
***The LORD's right hand has triumphed;***
***I shall not die, I shall live***
***and recount God's deeds.***

I was punished, I was punished by the LORD,
but not doomed to die.

*Open to me the gates of holiness:*
*I will enter and give thanks.*
This is the LORD'S own gate
where the just may enter.
*I will thank you for you have answered*
*and you are my savior.*

The stone which the builders rejected
has become the corner stone.
*This is the work of the LORD,*
*a marvel in our eyes.*
This day was made by the LORD;
we rejoice and are glad.

*O LORD, grant us salvation;*
*O LORD, grant success.*
Blessed in the name of the LORD
is he who comes.
*We bless you from the house of the LORD;*
*the LORD God is our light.*

Go forward in procession with branches
even to the altar.
*You are my God, I thank you.*
*My God, I praise you.*
Give thanks to the LORD who is good;
*for God's love endures for ever.*

**Thanksgiving**

Happy are those
whose help is the God of Jacob,
whose hope is in the Lord their God:
***you made heaven and earth,***
***the sea and all that is in them;***
***you keep faith forever.***
*(free prayers of thanksgiving)*
You satisfy us in the morning
with your steadfast love;
***we rejoice and are glad all our days. Amen.***

**Song**

This is the day (H58)
This is the day the Lord has made (H642)
Christ has arisen (H267)
This is a day of new beginnings (H640)
Alleluia! Give the glory (SS93)

## Call to discipleship

Jesus said, I came that they may have life,
and have it abundantly.
***Whoever follows me***
***will never walk in darkness***
***but will have the light of life.***

**Matthew 28.1-10**

After the sabbath, as the first day of the week was dawning, Mary Magdalene and the other

Mary went to see the tomb. And suddenly there was a great earthquake; for an angel of the Lord, descending from heaven, came and rolled back the stone and sat on it. His appearance was like lightning, and his clothing white as snow. For fear of him the guards shook and became like dead men. But the angel said to the women, "Do not be afraid; I know that you are looking for Jesus who was crucified. He is not here; for he has been raised, as he said. Come, see the place where he lay. Then go quickly and tell his disciples, 'He has been raised from the dead, and indeed he is going ahead of you to Galilee; there you will see him.' This is my message for you." So they left the tomb quickly with fear and great joy, and ran to tell his disciples. Suddenly Jesus met them and said, "Greetings!" And they came to him, took hold of his feet, and worshiped him. Then Jesus said to them, "Do not be afraid; go and tell my brothers to go to Galilee; there they will see me."

**Galatians 2.19-20**

I have been crucified with Christ; and it is no longer I who live, but it is Christ who lives in me. And the life I now live in the flesh I live by faith in the Son of God, who loved me and gave himself for me.

**Silent or spoken reflection on the readings**

**Song**

See the splendor of the morning (H268)
O sons and daughters, let us sing (H274)
Christ is alive! Let Christians sing (H278)
For me to live is Christ (SS111)

**Philippians 2.5-11**

## Call to intercession

Lift up your eyes to the heavens,
and look at the earth beneath;
***The salvation of the Lord will be forever;***
***God's deliverance will never be ended.***

God of peace, you are making all things new.
In your mercy,
***Lord, hear our prayer.***

You satisfy us with your steadfast love. We pray for ourselves and those dear to us.
*(open prayers)*
In your mercy,
***Lord, hear our prayer.***

You come to us in many and various ways. We pray for our community and for our neighbors.
*(open prayers)*

In your mercy,
***Lord, hear our prayer.***

You are our strength and our song. We pray for the church in all places, that we may be one.
*(open prayers)*
In your mercy,
***Lord, hear our prayer.***

You hate wickedness and love righteousness. We pray for the world, that your reign may come and your will be done on earth.
*(open prayers)*
In your mercy,
***Lord, hear our prayer.***

We offer you other concerns we carry in our hearts.
*(open prayers)*
In your mercy,
***Lord, hear our prayer.***

God of glory beyond our comprehension,
you exalt the humble and raise the lowly.
Give us grace to know the mind of Jesus,
that we may follow him through death
and into new life.
We glorify your name,
praying as Jesus taught us:

***Our Father …***

**Benediction**

*Now may the God of peace,*
*who brought back from the dead*
*our Lord Jesus, the great shepherd of the sheep,*
*by the blood of the eternal covenant,*
*make us complete in everything good*
*so that we may do God's will,*
*through Jesus Christ,*
*to whom be the glory forever and ever. Amen.*

# God lifted him high

## EASTER SUNDAY EVENING

**Opening sentence**

He humbled himself,
and he became obedient unto death,
even death on a cross.
***Therefore God lifted him high.***

## Call to praise

Stay with us, Lord,
for evening draws near and daylight is fading.
***Open the scriptures to us***
***and open our eyes to recognize you.***

***Glory …***

**Psalm 110.1-4**

The LORD's revelation to my Master:
"Sit on my right;
your foes I will put beneath your feet."

***The LORD will wield from Zion***
***your scepter of power;***
***rule in the midst of all your foes.***

A prince from the day of your birth
on the holy mountains;
from the womb before the dawn I begot you.

*The* LORD *has sworn an oath and will not change.*
*"You are a priest for ever,*
*a priest like Melchizedek of old."*

**Thanksgiving**

Your steadfast love is established forever, O God;
***your faithfulness is as firm as the heavens.***
*(free prayers of thanksgiving)*
My mouth is filled with your praise,
***and with your glory all day long. Amen.***

**Song**

Christ is arisen (H271)
Sing with all the saints in glory (SS92)
I will sing the Lord's high triumph (H261)

**Confession**

Raised with Christ,
let us seek the things that are above,
***where Christ is,***
***seated at the right hand of God.***
*(silence)*
O God, draw our minds
to the things that are above,
***for we have died, and our life is hidden***
***with Christ in you. Amen.***

## Call to discipleship

Jesus said, Those who want to save their life will lose it,
***and those who lose their life for my sake will find it.***

**Luke 24.1-12**

But on the first day of the week, at early dawn, [the women] came to the tomb, taking the spices that they had prepared. They found the stone rolled away from the tomb, but when they went in, they did not find the body. While they were perplexed about this, suddenly two men in dazzling clothes stood beside them. The women were terrified and bowed their faces to the ground, but the men said to them, "Why do you look for the living among the dead? He is not here, but has risen. Remember how he told you, while he was still in Galilee, that the Son of Man must be handed over to sinners, and be crucified, and on the third day rise again." Then they remembered his words, and returning from the tomb, they told all this to the eleven and to all the rest. Now it was Mary Magdalene, Joanna, Mary the mother of James, and the other women with them who told this to the apostles. But these words seemed to them an idle tale, and they did not believe them. But Peter got up and ran to the tomb; stooping and looking in, he saw the linen cloths by themselves; then he went home, amazed at what had happened.

**Hebrews 1.1-9**

Long ago God spoke to our ancestors in many and various ways by the prophets, but in these last days he has spoken to us by a Son, whom he appointed heir of all things, through whom he also created the worlds. He is the reflection of God's glory and the exact imprint of God's very being, and he sustains all things by his powerful word. When he had made purification for sins, he sat down at the right hand of the Majesty on high, having become as much superior to angels as the name he has inherited is more excellent than theirs.

For to which of the angels did God ever say,
    "You are my Son;
    today I have begotten you"?
Or again,
    "I will be his Father,
    and he will be my Son"?
And again, when he brings the firstborn into the world, he says,
    "Let all God's angels worship him."
Of the angels he says,
    "He makes his angels winds,
    and his servants flames of fire."

But of the Son he says,

"Your throne, O God, is forever and ever,
and the righteous scepter is the scepter of your kingdom.
You have loved righteousness and hated wickedness;
therefore God, your God, has anointed you
with the oil of gladness beyond your companions."

**Silent or spoken reflection on the readings**

**Song**

All hail the power of Jesus' name (H106)
At the name of Jesus (H342)
Oh, qué bueno es Jesús (Oh, how good is Christ the Lord) (SS90)

**Philippians 2.5-11**

## Call to intercession

I am about to do a new thing;
now it springs forth, do you not perceive it?
***I will make a way in the wilderness***
***and rivers in the desert.***

God of new life, we look for your resurrection power. In your mercy,
***Lord, hear our prayer.***

You satisfy us with your steadfast love. We pray for ourselves and those dear to us.
*(open prayers)*
In your mercy,
***Lord, hear our prayer.***

You come to us in many and various ways. We pray for our community and for our neighbors.
*(open prayers)*
In your mercy,
***Lord, hear our prayer.***

You are our strength and our song. We pray for the church in all places, that we may be one.
*(open prayers)*
In your mercy,
***Lord, hear our prayer.***

You hate wickedness and love righteousness. We pray for the world, that your reign may come and your will be done on earth.
*(open prayers)*
In your mercy,
***Lord, hear our prayer.***

We offer you other concerns we carry in our hearts.
*(open prayers)*
In your mercy,
***Lord, hear our prayer.***

God of new beginnings,
you raise us from the grave
and draw us into your glory.
In your love, release us
from all that binds us to death,
that we may be eternally bound to you
through the resurrection of your son Jesus,
with whom we pray:

*Our Father ...*

**Benediction**

***May we be made strong with all the strength***
***that comes from God's glorious power,***
***enduring everything with patience,***
***while joyfully giving thanks to the Father,***
***who has enabled us to share in the inheritance***
***of the saints in the light. Amen.***

# God granted to him the name above every name

## EASTER MONDAY MORNING

**Opening sentence**

Therefore God lifted him high
***and granted freely to him***
***the name above every name.***

## Call to praise

We sing your praises, our God and king,
and bless your name forever and ever.
***Every day we will bless you,***
***and praise your name forever and ever.***
***Alleluia!***

*Glory …*

**Hosea 6.1-3**

"Come, let us return to the LORD;
for it is he who has torn, and he will heal us;
he has struck down, and he will bind us up.
***After two days he will revive us;***
***on the third day he will raise us up,***
***that we may live before him.***
Let us know, let us press on to know the LORD;
his appearing is as sure as the dawn;

*he will come to us like the showers,*
*like the spring rains that water the earth."*

**Thanksgiving**

Happy are those
whose help is the God of Jacob,
whose hope is in the Lord their God:
***you made heaven and earth,***
***the sea and all that is in them;***
***you keep faith forever.***
*(free prayers of thanksgiving)*
You satisfy us in the morning
with your steadfast love;
***we rejoice and are glad all our days. Amen.***

**Song**

Christ has arisen (H267)
Alleluia! Give the glory (SS93)
Proclaim the tidings near and far (H282)
Thine is the glory (H269)

## Call to discipleship

Jesus said, I came that they may have life,
and have it abundantly.
***Whoever follows me***
***will never walk in darkness***
***but will have the light of life.***

**Luke 24.13-27**

Now on that same day two of [the disciples] were going to a village called Emmaus, about seven miles from Jerusalem, and talking with each other about all these things that had happened. While they were talking and discussing, Jesus himself came near and went with them, but their eyes were kept from recognizing him. And he said to them, "What are you discussing with each other while you walk along?" They stood still, looking sad. Then one of them, whose name was Cleopas, answered him, "Are you the only stranger in Jerusalem who does not know the things that have taken place there in these days?" He asked them, "What things?" They replied, "The things about Jesus of Nazareth, who was a prophet mighty in deed and word before God and all the people, and how our chief priests and leaders handed him over to be condemned to death and crucified him. But we had hoped that he was the one to redeem Israel. Yes, and besides all this, it is now the third day since these things took place. Moreover, some women of our group astounded us. They were at the tomb early this morning, and when they did not find his body there, they came back and told us that they had indeed seen a vision of angels who said that he was alive. Some of those who were with us went to the tomb and found it just as the women had said; but they did not see him." Then he said to them, "Oh, how foolish you are, and how slow of heart to believe all that the prophets have declared! Was it not necessary that the Messiah should suffer these things and then enter into his glory?" Then beginning with Moses and all the prophets, he interpreted to them the things about himself in all the scriptures.

**Philippians 3.7-14**

Yet whatever gains I had, these I have come to regard as loss because of Christ. More than that, I regard everything as loss because of the surpassing value of knowing Christ Jesus my Lord. For his sake I have suffered the loss of all things, and I regard them as rubbish, in order that I may gain Christ and be found in him, not having a righteousness of my own that comes from the law, but one that comes through faith in Christ, the righteousness from God based on faith. I want to know Christ and the power of his resurrection and the sharing of his sufferings by becoming like him in his death, if somehow I may attain the resurrection from the dead.

Not that I have already obtained this or have already reached the goal; but I press on to make it my own, because Christ Jesus has made me his own. Beloved, I do not consider that I have made it my own; but this one thing I do: forgetting what lies behind and straining forward to what lies ahead, I press on toward the goal for the prize of the heavenly call of God in Christ Jesus.

**Silent or spoken reflection on the readings**

**Song**

Awake, my soul (H609)
On the journey to Emmaus (SS98)
Now go forward (H399)

**Philippians 2.5-11**

## Call to intercession

Lift up your eyes to the heavens,
and look at the earth beneath;
***The salvation of the Lord will be forever;***
***God's deliverance will never be ended.***

God of peace, you are making all things new.
In your mercy,
***Lord, hear our prayer.***

You are the source of our salvation. We pray for ourselves and those dear to us.
*(open prayers)*
In your mercy,
***Lord, hear our prayer.***

You will heal what is torn. We pray for our community and for our neighbors.
*(open prayers)*
In your mercy,
***Lord, hear our prayer.***

You are our God; we are led by your hand. We pray for the church in all places, that we may know the freedom of life in the Spirit.
*(open prayers)*
In your mercy,
***Lord, hear our prayer.***

You are able to bring life out of death. We pray for the world and for all who care for creation.
*(open prayers)*
In your mercy,
***Lord, hear our prayer.***

We offer you other concerns we carry in our hearts.
*(open prayers)*
In your mercy,
***Lord, hear our prayer.***

God of glory beyond our comprehension,
you exalt the humble and raise the lowly.
Give us grace to know the mind of Jesus,
that we may follow him through death
and into new life.
We glorify your name,
praying as Jesus taught us:

*Our Father ...*

**Benediction**

*Now may the God of peace,*
*who brought back from the dead*
*our Lord Jesus, the great shepherd of the sheep,*
*by the blood of the eternal covenant,*
*make us complete in everything good*
*so that we may do God's will,*
*through Jesus Christ,*
*to whom be the glory forever and ever. Amen.*

# God granted to him the name above every name

## EASTER MONDAY EVENING

**Opening sentence**

Therefore God lifted him high
***and granted freely to him***
***the name that is above every name.***

## Call to praise

Stay with us, Lord,
for evening draws near and daylight is fading.
***Open the scriptures to us***
***and open our eyes to recognize you.***

***Glory …***

**Psalm 95.1-7**

Come, ring out our joy to the LORD;
hail the rock who saves us.
***Let us come before God, giving thanks,***
***with songs let us hail the LORD.***

A mighty God is the LORD,
a great king above all gods,
***in whose hands are the depths of the earth;***
***the heights of the mountains as well.***

The sea belongs to God, who made it
and the dry land shaped by his hands.

***Come in; let us bow and bend low;***
***let us kneel before the God who made us***
for this is our God and we
the people who belong to his pasture,
the flock that is led by his hand.

***O that today you would listen to God's voice!***

**Thanksgiving**

Your steadfast love is established forever, O God;
***your faithfulness is as firm as the heavens.***
*(free prayers of thanksgiving)*
My mouth is filled with your praise,
***and with your glory all day long. Amen.***

**Song**

This joyful Eastertide (H276)
I will stand in the congregation (SS113)
All people that on earth do dwell (H42)

**Confession**

Raised with Christ,
let us seek the things that are above,
***where Christ is,***
***seated at the right hand of God.***
*(silence)*
O God, draw our minds
to the things that are above,

*for we have died, and our life is hidden with Christ in you. Amen.*

## Call to discipleship

Jesus said, Those who want to save their life will lose it,

***and those who lose their life for my sake will find it.***

**Luke 24.28-35**

As [the disciples] came near the village to which they were going, [Jesus] walked ahead as if he were going on. But they urged him strongly, saying, "Stay with us, because it is almost evening and the day is now nearly over." So he went in to stay with them. When he was at the table with them, he took bread, blessed and broke it, and gave it to them. Then their eyes were opened, and they recognized him; and he vanished from their sight. They said to each other, "Were not our hearts burning within us while he was talking to us on the road, while he was opening the scriptures to us?" That same hour they got up and returned to Jerusalem; and they found the eleven and their companions gathered together. They were saying, "The Lord has risen indeed, and he has appeared to Simon!" Then they told what had happened on the road, and how he had been made known to them in the breaking of the bread.

**Acts 4.1-12**

While Peter and John were speaking to the people, the priests, the captain of the temple, and the Sadducees came to them, much annoyed because they were teaching the people and proclaiming that in Jesus there is the resurrection of the dead. So they arrested them and put them in custody until the next day, for it was already evening. But many of those who heard the word believed; and they numbered about five thousand.

The next day their rulers, elders, and scribes assembled in Jerusalem, with Annas the high priest, Caiaphas, John, and Alexander, and all who were of the high-priestly family. When they had made the prisoners stand in their midst, they inquired, "By what power or by what name did you do this?" Then Peter, filled with the Holy Spirit, said to them, "Rulers of the people and elders, if we are questioned today because of a good deed done to someone who was sick and are asked how this man has been healed, let it be known to all of you, and to all the people of Israel, that this man is standing before you in good health by the name of Jesus Christ of Nazareth, whom you

crucified, whom God raised from the dead.
This Jesus is
'the stone that was rejected by you, the
builders;
it has become the cornerstone.'
There is salvation in no one else, for there is no other name under heaven given among mortals by which we must be saved."

**Silent or spoken reflection on the readings**

**Song**

I know that my Redeemer lives (H277)
Christ is our cornerstone (H43)
On the journey to Emmaus (SS98)

**Philippians 2.5-11**

## Call to intercession

I am about to do a new thing;
now it springs forth, do you not perceive it?
***I will make a way in the wilderness***
***and rivers in the desert.***

God of new life, we look for your resurrection power. In your mercy,
***Lord, hear our prayer.***

You are the source of our salvation. We pray for ourselves and those dear to us.

*(open prayers)*
In your mercy,
***Lord, hear our prayer.***

You will heal what is torn. We pray for our community and for our neighbors.
*(open prayers)*
In your mercy,
***Lord, hear our prayer.***

You are our God; we are led by your hand. We pray for the church in all places, that we may know the freedom of life in the Spirit.
*(open prayers)*
In your mercy,
***Lord, hear our prayer.***

You are able to bring life out of death. We pray for the world and for all who care for creation.
*(open prayers)*
In your mercy,
***Lord, hear our prayer.***

We offer you other concerns we carry in our hearts.
*(open prayers)*
In your mercy,
***Lord, hear our prayer.***

God of new beginnings,
you raise us from the grave
and draw us into your glory.

In your love, release us
from all that binds us to death,
that we may be eternally bound to you
through the resurrection of your son Jesus,
with whom we pray:

*Our Father ...*

**Benediction**

*May we be made strong with all the strength*
*that comes from God's glorious power,*
*enduring everything with patience,*
*while joyfully giving thanks to the Father,*
*who has enabled us to share in the inheritance*
*of the saints in the light. Amen.*

# In the name of Jesus every knee would bend

## EASTER TUESDAY MORNING

**Opening sentence**

Therefore God lifted him high
and granted freely to him
the name above every name,
***so that in the name of Jesus***
***every knee would bend.***

## Call to praise

We sing your praises, our God and king,
and bless your name forever and ever.
***Every day we will bless you,***
***and praise your name forever and ever.***
***Alleluia!***

***Glory ...***

**Psalm 2**

Why this tumult among nations,
among peoples this useless murmuring?
***They arise, the kings of the earth,***
***princes plot against the LORD and his***
***Anointed.***
"Come, let us break their fetters,
come, let us cast off their yoke."

*God who sits in the heavens laughs,*
*the* L*ORD* *is laughing them to scorn.*
Then God will speak in anger,
and in rage will strike them with terror.
*"It is I who have set up my king*
*on Zion, my holy mountain."*

(I will announce the decree of the LORD.)

*The* L*ORD* *said to me: "You are my Son.*
*It is I who have begotten you this day.*
Ask and I shall bequeath you the nations,
put the ends of the earth in your possession.
*With a rod of iron you will break them,*
*shatter them like a potter's jar.*

Now, O kings, understand,
take warning, rulers of the earth;
*serve the* L*ORD* *with awe*
*and trembling, pay your homage*
lest God be angry and you perish;
for suddenly God's anger will blaze.

***Blessed are they who put their trust in God.***

**Thanksgiving**

Happy are those
whose help is the God of Jacob,
whose hope is in the Lord their God:
*you made heaven and earth,*
*the sea and all that is in them;*
*you keep faith forever.*

*(free prayers of thanksgiving)*
You satisfy us in the morning
with your steadfast love;
***we rejoice and are glad all our days. Amen.***

**Song**

Christ is arisen (H271)
O bless the Lord, my soul (H600)
Alleluia! Give the glory (SS93)
Ask ye what great thing I know (H337)

## Call to discipleship

Jesus said, I came that they may have life,
and have it abundantly.
***Whoever follows me***
***will never walk in darkness***
***but will have the light of life.***

**Luke 24.36-43**

While [the disciples] were talking about this, Jesus himself stood among them and said to them, "Peace be with you." They were startled and terrified, and thought that they were seeing a ghost. He said to them, "Why are you frightened, and why do doubts arise in your hearts? Look at my hands and my feet; see that it is I myself. Touch me and see; for a ghost does not have flesh and bones as you see that I have." And when he had said this, he showed them his hands and his feet. While in their joy they were disbelieving and still wondering, he said to them, "Have you anything here to eat?" They gave him a piece of broiled fish, and he took it and ate in their presence.

**Ephesians 1.15-23**

I have heard of your faith in the Lord Jesus and your love toward all the saints, and for this reason I do not cease to give thanks for you as I remember you in my prayers. I pray that the God of our Lord Jesus Christ, the Father of glory, may give you a spirit of wisdom and revelation as you come to know him, so that, with the eyes of your heart enlightened, you may know what is the hope to which he has called you, what are the riches of his glorious inheritance among the saints, and what is the immeasurable greatness of his power for us who believe, according to the working of his great power. God put this power to work in Christ when he raised him from the dead and seated him at his right hand in the heavenly places, far above all rule and authority and power and dominion, and above every name that is named, not only in this age but also in the age to come. And he has put all things under his feet and has made him the head over all things for the church, which is his body, the fullness of him who fills all in all.

**Silent or spoken reflection on the readings**

**Song**

Jesus, stand among us (H25)
Confitemini Domino (Come and fill our hearts) (SJ59)
Rejoice, the Lord is King (H288)
Sing with all the saints in glory (SS92)

**Philippians 2.5-11**

## Call to intercession

Lift up your eyes to the heavens,
and look at the earth beneath;
***The salvation of the Lord will be forever;***
***God's deliverance will never be ended.***

God of peace, you are making all things new.
In your mercy,
***Lord, hear our prayer.***

You call us to hope. We pray for ourselves and those dear to us.
*(open prayers)*
In your mercy,
***Lord, hear our prayer.***

You speak peace to those who are frightened. We pray for our community and for our neighbors.
*(open prayers)*
In your mercy,
***Lord, hear our prayer.***

Your spirit of wisdom enlightens the hearts of your people. We pray for the church in all places, that we may reflect your faithful love.
*(open prayers)*
In your mercy,
***Lord, hear our prayer.***

Your rule is far above all other authority, dominion, and power. We pray for the world, for those who are in need.
*(open prayers)*
In your mercy,
***Lord, hear our prayer.***

We offer you other concerns we carry in our hearts.
*(open prayers)*
In your mercy,
***Lord, hear our prayer.***

God of glory beyond our comprehension,
you exalt the humble and raise the lowly.
Give us grace to know the mind of Jesus,
that we may follow him through death
and into new life.

We glorify your name,
praying as Jesus taught us:

*Our Father ...*

**Benediction**

*Now may the God of peace,*
*who brought back from the dead*
*our Lord Jesus, the great shepherd of the sheep,*
*by the blood of the eternal covenant,*
*make us complete in everything good*
*so that we may do God's will,*
*through Jesus Christ,*
*to whom be the glory forever and ever. Amen.*

# In the name of Jesus every knee would bend

## EASTER TUESDAY EVENING

**Opening sentence**

Therefore God lifted him high
and granted freely to him
the name above every name,
***so that in the name of Jesus***
***every knee would bend.***

## Call to praise

Stay with us, Lord,
for evening draws near and daylight is fading.
***Open the scriptures to us***
***and open our eyes to recognize you.***

***Glory …***

**Psalm 100**

Cry out with joy to the LORD, all the earth.
Serve the LORD with gladness.
Come before God, singing for joy.

***Know that the LORD is God,***
***Our Maker, to whom we belong.***
***We are God's people, sheep of the flock.***

Enter the gates with thanksgiving,
God's courts with songs of praise.
Give thanks to God and bless his name.

***Indeed, how good is the LORD,***
***whose merciful love is eternal,***
***whose faithfulness lasts forever.***

**Thanksgiving**

Your steadfast love is established forever, O God;
***your faithfulness is as firm as the heavens.***
*(free prayers of thanksgiving)*
My mouth is filled with your praise,
***and with your glory all day long. Amen.***

**Song**

Let the whole creation cry (H51)
Open now thy gates of beauty (H19)
Praise, praise, praise the Lord! (SJ11)
Cantai ao Senhor (O sing to the Lord) (SJ12)

**Confession**

Raised with Christ,
let us seek the things that are above,
***where Christ is,***
***seated at the right hand of God.***
*(silence)*
O God, draw our minds
to the things that are above,
***for we have died, and our life is hidden***
***with Christ in you. Amen.***

## Call to discipleship

Jesus said, Those who want to save their life will lose it,
***and those who lose their life for my sake will find it.***

**Luke 24.44-49**

Then [Jesus] said to [the disciples], "These are my words that I spoke to you while I was still with you—that everything written about me in the law of Moses, the prophets, and the psalms must be fulfilled." Then he opened their minds to understand the scriptures, and he said to them, "Thus it is written, that the Messiah is to suffer and to rise from the dead on the third day, and that repentance and forgiveness of sins is to be proclaimed in his name to all nations, beginning from Jerusalem. You are witnesses of these things. And see, I am sending upon you what my Father promised; so stay here in the city until you have been clothed with power from on high."

**Ephesians 3.7-13**

Of this gospel I have become a servant according to the gift of God's grace that was given me by the working of his power. Although I am the very least of all the saints, this grace was given to me to bring to the Gentiles the news of the boundless riches of Christ, and to make everyone see what is the plan of the mystery hidden for ages in God who created all things; so that through the church the wisdom of God in its rich variety might now be made known to the rulers and authorities in the heavenly places. This was in accordance with the eternal purpose that he has carried out in Christ Jesus our Lord, in whom we have access to God in boldness and confidence through faith in him. I pray therefore that you may not lose heart over my sufferings for you; they are your glory.

**Silent or spoken reflection on the readings**

**Song**

Christ who left his home in glory (H283)
Lift your glad voices (H275)
The church's one foundation (H311)
Jesus has done so much for me (SS95)

**Philippians 2.5-11**

## Call to intercession

I am about to do a new thing;
now it springs forth, do you not perceive it?
***I will make a way in the wilderness***
***and rivers in the desert.***

God of new life, we look for your resurrection power. In your mercy,
***Lord, hear our prayer.***

You call us to hope. We pray for ourselves and those dear to us.
*(open prayers)*
In your mercy,
***Lord, hear our prayer.***

You speak peace to those who are frightened. We pray for our community and for our neighbors.
*(open prayers)*
In your mercy,
***Lord, hear our prayer.***

Your spirit of wisdom enlightens the hearts of your people. We pray for the church in all places, that we may reflect your faithful love.
*(open prayers)*
In your mercy,
***Lord, hear our prayer.***

Your rule is far above all other authority, dominion, and power. We pray for the world, for those who are in need.
*(open prayers)*
In your mercy,
***Lord, hear our prayer.***

We offer you other concerns we carry in our hearts.
*(open prayers)*
In your mercy,
***Lord, hear our prayer.***

God of new beginnings,
you raise us from the grave
and draw us into your glory.
In your love, release us
from all that binds us to death,
that we may be eternally bound to you
through the resurrection of your son Jesus,
with whom we pray:

***Our Father ...***

**Benediction**

***May we be made strong with all the strength
that comes from God's glorious power,
enduring everything with patience,
while joyfully giving thanks to the Father,
who has enabled us to share in the inheritance
of the saints in the light. Amen.***

# Every knee would bend, in heaven, on earth, under the earth

## EASTER WEDNESDAY MORNING

**Opening sentence**

Therefore God lifted him high
and granted freely to him
the name above every name,
***so that in the name of Jesus***
***every knee would bend,***
***in heaven, on earth, under the earth.***

## Call to praise

We sing your praises, our God and king,
and bless your name forever and ever.
***Every day we will bless you,***
***and praise your name forever and ever.***
***Alleluia!***

*Glory ...*

**Isaiah 11.6-9**

The wolf shall live with the lamb,
the leopard shall lie down with the kid,
***the calf and the lion and the fatling together,***
***and a little child shall lead them.***

The cow and the bear shall graze,
their young shall lie down together;
and the lion shall eat straw like the ox.
***The nursing child shall play over the hole of the asp,***
***and the weaned child shall put its hand on the adder's den.***
They will not hurt or destroy
on all my holy mountain;
***for the earth will be full of the knowledge of the LORD***
***as the waters cover the sea.***

**Thanksgiving**

Happy are those
whose help is the God of Jacob,
whose hope is in the Lord their God:
***you made heaven and earth,***
***the sea and all that is in them;***
***you keep faith forever.***
*(free prayers of thanksgiving)*
You satisfy us in the morning
with your steadfast love;
***we rejoice and are glad all our days. Amen.***

**Song**

That Easter day with joy was bright (H281)
O day of peace (H408)

## Call to discipleship

Jesus said, I came that they may have life,
and have it abundantly.
***Whoever follows me***
***will never walk in darkness***
***but will have the light of life.***

**John 20.1-10**

Early on the first day of the week, while it was still dark, Mary Magdalene came to the tomb and saw that the stone had been removed from the tomb. So she ran and went to Simon Peter and the other disciple, the one whom Jesus loved, and said to them, "They have taken the Lord out of the tomb, and we do not know where they have laid him." Then Peter and the other disciple set out and went toward the tomb. The two were running together, but the other disciple outran Peter and reached the tomb first. He bent down to look in and saw the linen wrappings lying there, but he did not go in. Then Simon Peter came, following him, and went into the tomb. He saw the linen wrappings lying there, and the cloth that had been on Jesus' head, not lying with the linen wrappings but rolled up in a place by itself. Then the other disciple, who reached the tomb first, also went in, and he saw and believed;

for as yet they did not understand the scripture, that he must rise from the dead. Then the disciples returned to their homes.

**Revelation 5.1-10**

Then I saw in the right hand of the one seated on the throne a scroll written on the inside and on the back, sealed with seven seals; and I saw a mighty angel proclaiming with a loud voice, "Who is worthy to open the scroll and break its seals?" And no one in heaven or on earth or under the earth was able to open the scroll or to look into it. And I began to weep bitterly because no one was found worthy to open the scroll or to look into it. Then one of the elders said to me, "Do not weep. See, the Lion of the tribe of Judah, the Root of David, has conquered, so that he can open the scroll and its seven seals."

Then I saw between the throne and the four living creatures and among the elders a Lamb standing as if it had been slaughtered, having seven horns and seven eyes, which are the seven spirits of God sent out into all the earth. He went and took the scroll from the right hand of the one who was seated on the throne. When he had taken the scroll, the four living creatures and the twenty-four elders fell before the Lamb, each holding a harp and golden bowls full of incense, which are the prayers of the saints. They sing a new song:

"You are worthy to take the scroll
and to open its seals,
for you were slaughtered and by your
blood you ransomed for God
saints from every tribe and language and
people and nation;
you have made them to be a kingdom and
priests serving our God,
and they will reign on earth."

**Silent or spoken reflection on the readings**

**Song**

That Easter morn, at break of day (SS88)
Oh, for a thousand tongues to sing (H81)
Great is the Lord (H87)
Look, you saints (H286)

**Philippians 2.5-11**

## Call to intercession

Lift up your eyes to the heavens,
and look at the earth beneath;
***The salvation of the Lord will be forever;***
***God's deliverance will never be ended.***

God of peace, you are making all things new.
In your mercy,
***Lord, hear our prayer.***

You satisfy us with your steadfast love. We pray for ourselves and those dear to us.
*(open prayers)*
In your mercy,
***Lord, hear our prayer.***

Your love binds everything together. We pray for our community and for our neighbors.
*(open prayers)*
In your mercy,
***Lord, hear our prayer.***

You have ransomed saints from every tribe and language and people and nation. We pray for the church in all places, that we may bear witness to your reign of justice, peace, and joy.
*(open prayers)*
In your mercy,
***Lord, hear our prayer.***

Justice and right are your throne. We pray for the world, for all who are ensnared in greed, violence, and oppression.
*(open prayers)*
In your mercy,
***Lord, hear our prayer.***

We offer you other concerns we carry in our hearts.
*(open prayers)*
In your mercy,
***Lord, hear our prayer.***

God of glory beyond our comprehension,
you exalt the humble and raise the lowly.
Give us grace to know the mind of Jesus,
that we may follow him through death
and into new life.
We glorify your name,
praying as Jesus taught us:

***Our Father …***

**Benediction**

***Now may the God of peace,***
***who brought back from the dead***
***our Lord Jesus, the great shepherd of the sheep,***
***by the blood of the eternal covenant,***
***make us complete in everything good***
***so that we may do God's will,***
***through Jesus Christ,***
***to whom be the glory forever and ever. Amen.***

# Every knee would bend, in heaven, on earth, under the earth

## EASTER WEDNESDAY EVENING

**Opening sentence**

Therefore God lifted him high
and granted freely to him
the name above every name,
***so that in the name of Jesus***
***every knee would bend,***
***in heaven, on earth, under the earth.***

## Call to praise

Stay with us, Lord,
for evening draws near and daylight is fading.
***Open the scriptures to us***
***and open our eyes to recognize you.***

***Glory …***

**Psalm 97**

The LORD is king, let earth rejoice,
let all the coastlands be glad.
***Surrounded by cloud and darkness;***
***justice and right, God's throne.***

A fire prepares the way;
it burns up foes on every side.

***God's lightnings light up the world,***
***the earth trembles at the sight.***

The mountains melt like wax
before the LORD of all the earth.
***The skies proclaim God's justice;***
***all peoples see God's glory.***

Let those who serve idols be ashamed,
those who boast of their worthless gods.
All you spirits, worship the Lord.

***Zion hears and is glad;***
***the people of Judah rejoice***
***because of your judgments, O LORD.***

For you indeed are the LORD
most high above all the earth,
exalted far above all spirits.

***The LORD loves those who hate evil,***
***guards the souls of the saints,***
***and sets them free from the wicked.***

Light shines forth for the just
and joy for the upright of heart.
***Rejoice, you just, in the LORD;***
***give glory to God's holy name.***

**Thanksgiving**

Your steadfast love is established forever, O God;
***your faithfulness is as firm as the heavens.***
*(free prayers of thanksgiving)*

My mouth is filled with your praise,
***and with your glory all day long. Amen.***

**Song**

Come, ye faithful, raise the strain (H264)
The Lord is King (H69)

**Confession**

Raised with Christ,
let us seek the things that are above,
***where Christ is,***
***seated at the right hand of God.***
*(silence)*
O God, draw our minds
to the things that are above,
***for we have died, and our life is hidden***
***with Christ in you. Amen.***

## Call to discipleship

Jesus said, Those who want to save their life will lose it,
***and those who lose their life for my sake will find it.***

**John 20.11-18**

But Mary stood weeping outside the tomb. As she wept, she bent over to look into the tomb; and she saw two angels in white, sitting where the body of Jesus had been lying, one at the head and the other at the feet. They said to her, "Woman, why are you weeping?" She said to them, "They have taken away my Lord, and I do not know where they have laid him." When she had said this, she turned around and saw Jesus standing there, but she did not know that it was Jesus. Jesus said to her, "Woman, why are you weeping? Whom are you looking for?" Supposing him to be the gardener, she said to him, "Sir, if you have carried him away, tell me where you have laid him, and I will take him away." Jesus said to her, "Mary!" She turned and said to him in Hebrew, "Rabbouni!" (which means Teacher). Jesus said to her, "Do not hold on to me, because I have not yet ascended to the Father. But go to my brothers and say to them, 'I am ascending to my Father and your Father, to my God and your God.'" Mary Magdalene went and announced to the disciples, "I have seen the Lord"; and she told them that he had said these things to her.

**Revelation 5.11-14**

Then I looked, and I heard the voice of many angels surrounding the throne and the living creatures and the elders; they numbered myriads of myriads and thousands of thousands, singing with full voice,

"Worthy is the Lamb that was slaughtered
to receive power and wealth and wisdom
and might
and honor and glory and blessing!"

Then I heard every creature in heaven and on earth and under the earth and in the sea, and all that is in them, singing,

"To the one seated on the throne and to the
Lamb
be blessing and honor and glory and might
forever and ever!"

And the four living creatures said, "Amen!"
And the elders fell down and worshiped.

**Silent or spoken reflection on the readings**

**Song**

Holy God, we praise thy name (H121)
Amen (H643)
O worship the Lord (H124)
That Easter morn, at break of day (SS88)
Alleluia! Gracious Jesus! (SS110, vv. 1–3)

**Philippians 2.5-11**

## Call to intercession

I am about to do a new thing;
now it springs forth, do you not perceive it?

***I will make a way in the wilderness***
***and rivers in the desert.***

God of new life, we look for your resurrection power. In your mercy,
***Lord, hear our prayer.***

You satisfy us with your steadfast love. We pray for ourselves and those dear to us.
*(open prayers)*
In your mercy,
***Lord, hear our prayer.***

Your love binds everything together. We pray for our community and for our neighbors.
*(open prayers)*
In your mercy,
***Lord, hear our prayer.***

You have ransomed saints from every tribe and language and people and nation. We pray for the church in all places, that we may bear witness to your reign of justice, peace, and joy.
*(open prayers)*
In your mercy,
***Lord, hear our prayer.***

Justice and right are your throne. We pray for the world, for all who are ensnared in greed, violence, and oppression.
*(open prayers)*

In your mercy,
***Lord, hear our prayer.***

We offer you other concerns we carry in our hearts.
*(open prayers)*
In your mercy,
***Lord, hear our prayer.***

God of new beginnings,
you raise us from the grave
and draw us into your glory.
In your love, release us
from all that binds us to death,
that we may be eternally bound to you
through the resurrection of your son Jesus,
with whom we pray:

***Our Father ...***

**Benediction**

***May we be made strong with all the strength***
***that comes from God's glorious power,***
***enduring everything with patience,***
***while joyfully giving thanks to the Father,***
***who has enabled us to share in the inheritance***
***of the saints in the light. Amen.***

# And every tongue consent

## EASTER THURSDAY MORNING

**Opening sentence**

Therefore God lifted him high
and granted freely to him
the name above every name,
***so that in the name of Jesus***
***every knee would bend,***
***in heaven, on earth, under the earth,***
***and every tongue consent.***

## Call to praise

We sing your praises, our God and king,
and bless your name forever and ever.
***Every day we will bless you,***
***and praise your name forever and ever.***
***Alleluia!***

*Glory ...*

**Psalm 47**

All peoples, clap your hands,
cry to God with shouts of joy!
***For the LORD, the Most High, we must fear,***
***great king over all the earth.***

God subdues peoples under us
and nations under our feet.

***Our inheritance, our glory, is from God,***
***given to Jacob out of love.***

God goes up with shouts of joy;
the LORD goes up with trumpet blast.
***Sing praise for God, sing praise,***
***sing praise to our king, sing praise.***

God is king of all the earth,
sing praise with all your skill.
***God is king over the nations;***
***God reigns enthroned in holiness.***

The leaders of the people are assembled
with the people of Abraham's God.
***The rulers of the earth belong to God,***
***to God who reigns over all.***

**Thanksgiving**

Happy are those
whose help is the God of Jacob,
whose hope is in the Lord their God:
***you made heaven and earth,***
***the sea and all that is in them;***
***you keep faith forever.***
*(free prayers of thanksgiving)*
You satisfy us in the morning
with your steadfast love;
***we rejoice and are glad all our days. Amen.***

**Song**

All hail the power of Jesus' name (H285)

Alleluia! Give the glory (SS93)
Come away to the skies (H284)
Blessing and honor (SS109)

## Call to discipleship

Jesus said, I came that they may have life,
and have it abundantly.
***Whoever follows me***
***will never walk in darkness***
***but will have the light of life.***

**Luke 24.50-53**

Then [Jesus] led [the disciples] out as far as Bethany, and, lifting up his hands, he blessed them. While he was blessing them, he withdrew from them and was carried up into heaven. And they worshiped him, and returned to Jerusalem with great joy; and they were continually in the temple blessing God.

**Revelation 19.1-5**

After this I heard what seemed to be the loud voice of a great multitude in heaven, saying,

"Hallelujah!
Salvation and glory and power to our God,
for his judgments are true and just;
he has judged the great whore
who corrupted the earth with her
fornication,

and he has avenged on her the blood of his
servants."
Once more they said,
"Hallelujah!
The smoke goes up from her forever and
ever."
And the twenty-four elders and the four living creatures fell down and worshiped God who is seated on the throne, saying,
"Amen. Hallelujah!"

And from the throne came a voice saying,
"Praise our God,
all you his servants,
and all who fear him,
small and great."

**Silent or spoken reflection on the readings**

**Song**

Alleluia (SS87)
Look, ye saints (H286)
Praise the Lord, sing hallelujah (H50)
Alleluia! Gracious Jesus! (SS110)
For me to live is Christ (SS111)

**Philippians 2.5-11**

## Call to intercession

Lift up your eyes to the heavens,
and look at the earth beneath;
***The salvation of the Lord will be forever;***
***God's deliverance will never be ended.***

God of peace, you are making all things new.
In your mercy,
***Lord, hear our prayer.***

You keep faith forever. We pray for ourselves and those dear to us.
*(open prayers)*
In your mercy,
***Lord, hear our prayer.***

You are about to do a new thing. We pray for our community and for our neighbors.
*(open prayers)*
In your mercy,
***Lord, hear our prayer.***

You promise your faithfulness, firm as the heavens. We pray for the church in all places, that we may daily follow in the footsteps of Christ.
*(open prayers)*
In your mercy,
***Lord, hear our prayer.***

You will judge the nations with justice. We pray for the world, for those in positions of power and authority.
*(open prayers)*
In your mercy,
***Lord, hear our prayer.***

We offer you other concerns we carry in our hearts.
*(open prayers)*
In your mercy,
***Lord, hear our prayer.***

God of glory beyond our comprehension,
you exalt the humble and raise the lowly.
Give us grace to know the mind of Jesus,
that we may follow him through death
and into new life.
We glorify your name,
praying as Jesus taught us:

***Our Father …***

**Benediction**

***Now may the God of peace,***
***who brought back from the dead***
***our Lord Jesus, the great shepherd of the sheep,***
***by the blood of the eternal covenant,***
***make us complete in everything good***
***so that we may do God's will,***
***through Jesus Christ,***
***to whom be the glory forever and ever. Amen.***

# And every tongue consent

## EASTER THURSDAY EVENING

**Opening sentence**

Therefore God lifted him high
and granted freely to him
the name above every name,
***so that in the name of Jesus***
***every knee would bend,***
***in heaven, on earth, under the earth,***
***and every tongue consent.***

## Call to praise

Stay with us, Lord,
for evening draws near and daylight is fading.
***Open the scriptures to us***
***and open our eyes to recognize you.***

***Glory ...***

**Psalm 98**

Sing a new song to the LORD
who has worked wonders;
***whose right hand and holy arm***
***have brought salvation.***

The LORD has made known salvation;
has shown justice to the nations;

***has remembered truth and love***
***for the house of Israel.***

All the ends of the earth have seen
the salvation of our God.
***Shout to the LORD, all the earth,***
***ring out your joy.***

Sing psalms to the LORD with the harp
with the sound of music.
***With trumpets and the sound of the horn***
***acclaim the King, the LORD.***

Let the sea and all within it, thunder;
the world, and all its peoples.
***Let the rivers clap their hands***
***and the hills ring out their joy***

at the presence of the LORD, who comes,
who comes to rule the earth.
***God will rule the world with justice***
***and the peoples with fairness.***

**Thanksgiving**

Your steadfast love is established forever, O God;
***your faithfulness is as firm as the heavens.***
*(free prayers of thanksgiving)*
My mouth is filled with your praise,
***and with your glory all day long. Amen.***

**Song**

Rejoice, the Lord is King (H288)

Sithi bonga (We sing praise) (SS94)
Sing we triumphant hymns (H287)

**Confession**

Raised with Christ,
let us seek the things that are above,
***where Christ is,***
***seated at the right hand of God.***
*(silence)*
O God, draw our minds
to the things that are above,
***for we have died, and our life is hidden***
***with Christ in you. Amen.***

## Call to discipleship

Jesus said, Those who want to save their life will lose it,
***and those who lose their life for my sake will find it.***

**Acts 1.1-11**

In the first book, Theophilus, I wrote about all that Jesus did and taught from the beginning until the day when he was taken up to heaven, after giving instructions through the Holy Spirit to the apostles whom he had chosen. After his suffering he presented himself alive to them by many convincing proofs, appearing to them during forty days and speaking about the kingdom of God. While staying with them, he ordered them not to leave Jerusalem, but to wait there for the promise of the Father. "This," he said, "is what you have heard from me; for John baptized with water, but you will be baptized with the Holy Spirit not many days from now."

So when they had come together, they asked him, "Lord, is this the time when you will restore the kingdom to Israel?" He replied, "It is not for you to know the times or periods that the Father has set by his own authority. But you will receive power when the Holy Spirit has come upon you; and you will be my witnesses in Jerusalem, in all Judea and Samaria, and to the ends of the earth." When he had said this, as they were watching, he was lifted up, and a cloud took him out of their sight. While he was going and they were gazing up toward heaven, suddenly two men in white robes stood by them. They said, "Men of Galilee, why do you stand looking up toward heaven? This Jesus, who has been taken up from you into heaven, will come in the same way as you saw him go into heaven."

**Revelation 19.6-10**

Then I heard what seemed to be the voice of a great multitude, like the sound of many waters

and like the sound of mighty thunderpeals,
crying out,

"Hallelujah!
For the Lord our God
the Almighty reigns.
Let us rejoice and exult
and give him the glory,
for the marriage of the Lamb has come,
and his bride has made herself ready;
to her it has been granted to be clothed
with fine linen, bright and pure"—

for the fine linen is the righteous deeds of the saints.

And the angel said to me, "Write this: Blessed are those who are invited to the marriage supper of the Lamb." And he said to me, "These are true words of God." Then I fell down at his feet to worship him, but he said to me, "You must not do that! I am a fellow servant with you and your comrades who hold the testimony of Jesus. Worship God! For the testimony of Jesus is the spirit of prophecy."

**Silent or spoken reflection on the readings**

**Song**

Blessed Savior, we adore thee (H107)
The church of Christ in every age (H403)
View the present (SS108)
Christ is alive (SS89)

**Philippians 2.5-11**

## Call to intercession

I am about to do a new thing;
now it springs forth, do you not perceive it?
***I will make a way in the wilderness***
***and rivers in the desert.***

God of new life, we look for your resurrection power. In your mercy,
***Lord, hear our prayer.***

You keep faith forever. We pray for ourselves and those dear to us.
*(open prayers)*
In your mercy,
***Lord, hear our prayer.***

You are about to do a new thing. We pray for our community and for our neighbors.
*(open prayers)*
In your mercy,
***Lord, hear our prayer.***

You promise your faithfulness, firm as the heavens. We pray for the church in all places, that we may daily follow in the footsteps of Christ.
*(open prayers)*

In your mercy,
***Lord, hear our prayer.***

You will judge the nations with justice. We pray for the world, for those in positions of power and authority.
*(open prayers)*
In your mercy,
***Lord, hear our prayer.***

We offer you other concerns we carry in our hearts.
*(open prayers)*
In your mercy,
***Lord, hear our prayer.***

God of new beginnings,
you raise us from the grave
and draw us into your glory.
In your love, release us
from all that binds us to death,
that we may be eternally bound to you
through the resurrection of your son Jesus,
with whom we pray:

***Our Father …***

**Benediction**

***May we be made strong with all the strength***
***that comes from God's glorious power,***
***enduring everything with patience,***
***while joyfully giving thanks to the Father,***

*who has enabled us to share in the inheritance of the saints in the light. Amen.*

# Jesus Christ is Lord

## EASTER FRIDAY MORNING

**Opening sentence**

Therefore God lifted him high
and granted freely to him
the name above every name,
***so that in the name of Jesus***
***every knee would bend,***
***in heaven, on earth, under the earth,***
***and every tongue consent***
***that Jesus Christ is Lord.***

## Call to praise

We sing your praises, our God and king,
and bless your name forever and ever.
***Every day we will bless you,***
***and praise your name forever and ever.***
***Alleluia!***

***Glory …***

**Psalm 148**

Alleluia!

Praise the LORD from the heavens,
praise God in the heights.
***Praise God, all you angels,***
***praise him, all you host.***

Praise God, sun and moon,
praise him, shining stars.
***Praise God, highest heavens***
***and the waters above the heavens.***

Let them praise the name of the LORD.
The LORD commanded: they were made.
***God fixed them forever,***
***gave a law which shall not pass away.***

Praise the LORD from the earth,
sea creatures and all oceans,
***fire and hail, snow and mist,***
***stormy winds that obey God's word;***

all mountains and hills,
all fruit trees and cedars,
***beasts, wild and tame,***
***reptiles and birds on the wing;***

all earth's nations and peoples,
earth's leaders and rulers;
***young men and maidens,***
***the old together with children.***

Let them praise the name of the LORD
who alone is exalted.
***The splendor of God's name***
***reaches beyond heaven and earth.***

God exalts the strength of the people,
is the praise of all the saints,

***of the sons and daughters of Israel,***
***of the people to whom he comes close.***

***Alleluia!***

**Thanksgiving**

Happy are those
whose help is the God of Jacob,
whose hope is in the Lord their God:
***you made heaven and earth,***
***the sea and all that is in them;***
***you keep faith forever.***
*(free prayers of thanksgiving)*
You satisfy us in the morning
with your steadfast love;
***we rejoice and are glad all our days. Amen.***

**Song**

Christ is risen! Shout hosanna (H272)
Let all creation bless the Lord (H61)
Let all creation dance (SS122)
Praise the Lord, sing hallelujah (H50)

## Call to discipleship

Jesus said, I came that they may have life,
and have it abundantly.
***Whoever follows me***
***will never walk in darkness***
***but will have the light of life.***

**John 20.19-23**

When it was evening on that day, the first day of the week, and the doors of the house where the disciples had met were locked for fear of the Jews, Jesus came and stood among them and said, "Peace be with you." After he said this, he showed them his hands and his side. Then the disciples rejoiced when they saw the Lord. Jesus said to them again, "Peace be with you. As the Father has sent me, so I send you." When he had said this, he breathed on them and said to them, "Receive the Holy Spirit. If you forgive the sins of any, they are forgiven them; if you retain the sins of any, they are retained."

**Acts 2.32-39**

This Jesus God raised up, and of that all of us are witnesses. Being therefore exalted at the right hand of God, and having received from the Father the promise of the Holy Spirit, he has poured out this that you both see and hear. For David did not ascend into the heavens, but he himself says,

'The Lord said to my Lord,
"Sit at my right hand,
until I make your enemies your footstool."'

Therefore let the entire house of Israel know with certainty that God has made him both

Lord and Messiah, this Jesus whom you crucified."

Now when they heard this, they were cut to the heart and said to Peter and to the other apostles, "Brothers, what should we do?" Peter said to them, "Repent, and be baptized every one of you in the name of Jesus Christ so that your sins may be forgiven; and you will receive the gift of the Holy Spirit. For the promise is for you, for your children, and for all who are far away, everyone whom the Lord our God calls to him."

**Silent or spoken reflection on the readings**

**Song**

Christ, who is in the form of God (H333)
Lift high the cross (H321)
All who believe and are baptized (H436)
Comme un souffle fragile (Like a tender
  breath, stirring) (SS106)
Jesus has done so much for me (SS95)
O blessed spring (SS100)

**Philippians 2.5-11**

## Call to intercession

Lift up your eyes to the heavens,
and look at the earth beneath;

***The salvation of the Lord will be forever; God's deliverance will never be ended.***

God of peace, you are making all things new.
In your mercy,
***Lord, hear our prayer.***

You show no partiality. We pray for ourselves and those dear to us.
*(open prayers)*
In your mercy,
***Lord, hear our prayer.***

You establish equity, justice, and right.
We pray for our community and for our neighbors.
*(open prayers)*
In your mercy,
***Lord, hear our prayer.***

Your gospel is peace for all people. We pray for the church in all places, that we may speak boldly for Christ.
*(open prayers)*
In your mercy,
***Lord, hear our prayer.***

You give your Spirit, power for forgiveness and reconciliation. We pray for the world, for all who do justice and love mercy.
*(open prayers)*

In your mercy,
***Lord, hear our prayer.***

We offer you other concerns we carry in our hearts.
*(open prayers)*
In your mercy,
***Lord, hear our prayer.***

God of glory beyond our comprehension,
you exalt the humble and raise the lowly.
Give us grace to know the mind of Jesus,
that we may follow him through death
and into new life.
We glorify your name,
praying as Jesus taught us:

***Our Father …***

**Benediction**

***Now may the God of peace,***
***who brought back from the dead***
***our Lord Jesus, the great shepherd of the sheep,***
***by the blood of the eternal covenant,***
***make us complete in everything good***
***so that we may do God's will,***
***through Jesus Christ,***
***to whom be the glory forever and ever. Amen.***

# Jesus Christ is Lord

## EASTER FRIDAY EVENING

**Opening sentence**

Therefore God lifted him high
and granted freely to him
the name above every name,
***so that in the name of Jesus***
***every knee would bend,***
***in heaven, on earth, under the earth,***
***and every tongue consent***
***that Jesus Christ is Lord.***

## Call to praise

Stay with us, Lord,
for evening draws near and daylight is fading.
***Open the scriptures to us***
***and open our eyes to recognize you.***

***Glory …***

**Psalm 99**

The LORD is king; the peoples tremble.
He is throned on the cherubim; the earth
quakes.
The LORD is great in Zion;

*You are supreme over all the peoples.*
*Let them praise your name, so terrible and great,*
*so holy, full of power.*

You are a king who loves what is right;
you have established equity, justice and right;
you have established them in Jacob.

*Exalt the LORD our God;*
*bow down before God's footstool.*
*The LORD our God is holy.*

Among the priests were Aaron and Moses,
among those who invoked the LORD's name was Samuel.
They invoked the LORD who answered.

*The LORD spoke to them in the pillar of cloud.*
*They did God's will; they kept the law,*
*which the LORD our God had given.*

O LORD our God, you answered them.
For them you were a God who forgives;
yet you punished all their offenses.

*Exalt the LORD our God;*
*bow down before God's holy mountain*
*for the LORD our God is holy.*

**Thanksgiving**

Your steadfast love is established forever, O God;
*your faithfulness is as firm as the heavens.*

*(free prayers of thanksgiving)*
My mouth is filled with your praise,
***and with your glory all day long. Amen.***

**Song**

Lift your glad voices (H275)
Had God brought us out (SS96)
Heilig, heilig, heilig (Holy, holy, holy) (H75)
Fill now our life, O Lord (SS107)

**Confession**

Raised with Christ,
let us seek the things that are above,
***where Christ is,***
***seated at the right hand of God.***
*(silence)*
O God, draw our minds
to the things that are above,
***for we have died, and our life is hidden***
***with Christ in you. Amen.***

## Call to discipleship

Jesus said, Those who want to save their life will lose it,
***and those who lose their life for my sake will find it.***

**John 20.24-29**

But Thomas (who was called the Twin), one of the twelve, was not with them when Jesus came. So the other disciples told him, "We have seen the Lord." But he said to them, "Unless I see the mark of the nails in his hands, and put my finger in the mark of the nails and my hand in his side, I will not believe."

A week later his disciples were again in the house, and Thomas was with them. Although the doors were shut, Jesus came and stood among them and said, "Peace be with you." Then he said to Thomas, "Put your finger here and see my hands. Reach out your hand and put it in my side. Do not doubt but believe." Thomas answered him, "My Lord and my God!" Jesus said to him, "Have you believed because you have seen me? Blessed are those who have not seen and yet have come to believe."

**Acts 10.34-43**

Then Peter began to speak to [Cornelius and his friends]: "I truly understand that God shows no partiality, but in every nation anyone who fears him and does what is right is acceptable to him. You know the message he sent to the people of Israel, preaching peace by Jesus Christ—he is Lord of all. That message spread throughout Judea, beginning in Galilee after the baptism that John announced: how God anointed Jesus of Nazareth with the Holy Spirit and with power; how he went about doing good and healing all who were oppressed by the devil, for God was with him. We are witnesses to all that he did both in Judea and in Jerusalem. They put him to death by hanging him on a tree; but God raised him on the third day and allowed him to appear, not to all the people but to us who were chosen by God as witnesses, and who ate and drank with him after he rose from the dead. He commanded us to preach to the people and to testify that he is the one ordained by God as judge of the living and the dead. All the prophets testify about him that everyone who believes in him receives forgiveness of sins through his name."

**Silent or spoken reflection on the readings**

**Song**

The strife is o'er (H263)
We walk by faith (H570)
Hail to the Lord's anointed (H185)
Oh, qué bueno es Jesús (Oh, how good is Christ the Lord) (SS90)
This is the threefold truth (H335)

**Philippians 2.5-11**

## Call to intercession

I am about to do a new thing;
now it springs forth, do you not perceive it?
***I will make a way in the wilderness
and rivers in the desert.***

God of new life, we look for your resurrection power. In your mercy,
***Lord, hear our prayer.***

You show no partiality. We pray for ourselves and those dear to us.
*(open prayers)*
In your mercy,
***Lord, hear our prayer.***

You establish equity, justice, and right. We pray for our community and for our neighbors.
*(open prayers)*
In your mercy,
***Lord, hear our prayer.***

Your gospel is peace for all people. We pray for the church in all places, that we may speak boldly for Christ.
*(open prayers)*

In your mercy,
***Lord, hear our prayer.***

You give your Spirit, power for forgiveness and reconciliation. We pray for the world, for all who do justice and love mercy.
*(open prayers)*
In your mercy,
***Lord, hear our prayer.***

We offer you other concerns we carry in our hearts.
*(open prayers)*
In your mercy,
***Lord, hear our prayer.***

God of new beginnings,
you raise us from the grave
and draw us into your glory.
In your love, release us
from all that binds us to death,
that we may be eternally bound to you
through the resurrection of your son Jesus,
with whom we pray:

***Our Father …***

**Benediction**

***May we be made strong with all the strength***
***that comes from God's glorious power,***
***enduring everything with patience,***
***while joyfully giving thanks to the Father,***

*who has enabled us to share in the inheritance of the saints in the light. Amen.*

# To the glory of God the Father

## EASTER SATURDAY MORNING

**Opening sentence**

Therefore God lifted him high
and granted freely to him
the name above every name,
***so that in the name of Jesus***
***every knee would bend,***
***in heaven, on earth, under the earth,***
***and every tongue consent***
***that Jesus Christ is Lord—***
***to the glory of God the Father.***

## Call to praise

We sing your praises, our God and king,
and bless your name forever and ever.
***Every day we will bless you,***
***and praise your name forever and ever.***
***Alleluia!***

***Glory …***

**Psalm 145.1-13, 21**

I will give you glory, O God my king,
I will bless your name for ever.

***I will bless you day after day***
***and praise your name for ever.***

You are great, LORD, highly to be praised,
your greatness cannot be measured.

***Age to age shall proclaim your works,***
***shall declare your mighty deeds,***
shall speak of your splendor and glory,
tell the tale of your wonderful works.
***They will speak of your terrible deeds,***
***recount your greatness and might.***
They will recall your abundant goodness;
age to age shall ring out your justice.

***You are kind and full of compassion,***
***slow to anger, abounding in love.***
How good you are, LORD, to all,
compassionate to all your creatures.

***All your creatures shall thank you, O LORD,***
***and your friends shall repeat their blessing.***
They shall speak of the glory of your reign
and declare your might, O God,

***to make known to all your mighty deeds***
***and the glorious splendor of your reign.***
Yours is an everlasting kingdom;
your rule lasts from age to age.

***You are faithful in all your words***
***and loving in all your deeds.***

Let me speak your praise, O LORD,
***let all peoples bless your holy name***
***for ever, for ages unending.***

**Thanksgiving**

Happy are those
whose help is the God of Jacob,
whose hope is in the Lord their God:
***you made heaven and earth,***
***the sea and all that is in them;***
***you keep faith forever.***
*(free prayers of thanksgiving)*
You satisfy us in the morning
with your steadfast love;
***we rejoice and are glad all our days. Amen.***

**Song**

At the Lamb's high feast (H262)
Great is thy faithfulness (H327)
Well met, dear friends (SS102)
Nothing is lost on the breath of God (SS121)

## Call to discipleship

Jesus said, I came that they may have life,
and have it abundantly.
***Whoever follows me***
***will never walk in darkness***
***but will have the light of life.***

**John 21.3-14**

Simon Peter said to [the other disciples], "I am going fishing." They said to him, "We will go with you." They went out and got into the boat, but that night they caught nothing.

Just after daybreak, Jesus stood on the beach; but the disciples did not know that it was Jesus. Jesus said to them, "Children, you have no fish, have you?" They answered him, "No." He said to them, "Cast the net to the right side of the boat, and you will find some." So they cast it, and now they were not able to haul it in because there were so many fish. That disciple whom Jesus loved said to Peter, "It is the Lord!" When Simon Peter heard that it was the Lord, he put on some clothes, for he was naked, and jumped into the sea. But the other disciples came in the boat, dragging the net full of fish, for they were not far from the land, only about a hundred yards off.

When they had gone ashore, they saw a charcoal fire there, with fish on it, and bread. Jesus said to them, "Bring some of the fish that you have just caught." So Simon Peter went aboard and hauled the net ashore, full of large fish, a hundred fifty-three of them; and though there were so many, the net was not torn. Jesus said to them, "Come and have breakfast." Now none of the disciples dared to ask him, "Who are you?" because they knew it was the Lord. Jesus came and took the bread and gave it to them, and did the same with the fish. This was now the third time that Jesus appeared to the disciples after he was raised from the dead.

**1 Peter 1.3-9**

Blessed be the God and Father of our Lord Jesus Christ! By his great mercy he has given us a new birth into a living hope through the resurrection of Jesus Christ from the dead, and into an inheritance that is imperishable, undefiled, and unfading, kept in heaven for you, who are being protected by the power of God through faith for a salvation ready to be revealed in the last time. In this you rejoice, even if now for a little while you have had to suffer various trials, so that the genuineness of your faith—being more precious than gold that, though perishable, is tested by fire—may be found to result in praise and glory and honor when Jesus Christ is revealed. Although you have not seen him, you love him; and even though you do not see him now, you believe in him and rejoice with an indescribable and glorious joy, for you are receiving the outcome of your faith, the salvation of your souls.

**Silent or spoken reflection on the readings**

**Song**

Christ is alive! Let Christians sing (H278)
Let us talents and tongues employ (SS123)

At the name of Jesus (H342)
I know that my Redeemer lives (H277, H279)
Who are these (H270)

**Philippians 2.5-11**

## Call to intercession

Lift up your eyes to the heavens,
and look at the earth beneath;
***The salvation of the Lord will be forever;***
***God's deliverance will never be ended.***

God of peace, you are making all things new.
In your mercy,
***Lord, hear our prayer.***

You are faithful and gracious. We pray for ourselves and those dear to us.
*(open prayers)*
In your mercy,
***Lord, hear our prayer.***

You have compassion for all that you have made. We pray for our community and for our neighbors.
*(open prayers)*
In your mercy,
***Lord, hear our prayer.***

You desire to fill us with the fullness of your love. We pray for the church in all places, that

we may be faithful in solidarity across generations and geography.
*(open prayers)*
In your mercy,
***Lord, hear our prayer.***

From you every family on earth takes its name. We pray for the world, for our enemies and for those who are in conflict.
*(open prayers)*
In your mercy,
***Lord, hear our prayer.***

We offer you other concerns we carry in our hearts.
*(open prayers)*
In your mercy,
***Lord, hear our prayer.***

God of glory beyond our comprehension,
you exalt the humble and raise the lowly.
Give us grace to know the mind of Jesus,
that we may follow him through death
and into new life.
We glorify your name,
praying as Jesus taught us:

***Our Father …***

**Benediction**

***Now may the God of peace,***
***who brought back from the dead***

*our Lord Jesus, the great shepherd of the sheep,*
*by the blood of the eternal covenant,*
*make us complete in everything good*
*so that we may do God's will,*
*through Jesus Christ,*
*to whom be the glory forever and ever. Amen.*

# To the glory of God the Father

## EASTER SATURDAY EVENING

**Opening sentence**

Therefore God lifted him high
and granted freely to him
the name above every name,
***so that in the name of Jesus***
***every knee would bend,***
***in heaven, on earth, under the earth,***
***and every tongue consent***
***that Jesus Christ is Lord—***
***to the glory of God the Father.***

## Call to praise

Stay with us, Lord,
for evening draws near and daylight is fading.
***Open the scriptures to us***
***and open our eyes to recognize you.***

***Glory …***

**Psalm 96.9-13**

Worship the LORD in the temple.
O earth, stand in fear of the LORD.

***Proclaim to the nations: "God is king."***
***The world was made firm in its place;***
***God will judge the people in fairness.***

Let the heavens rejoice and earth be glad,
let the sea and all within it thunder praise,
***let the land and all it bears rejoice,***
***all the trees of the wood shout for joy***

at the presence of the LORD who comes,
who comes to rule the earth,
***comes with justice to rule the world,***
***and to judge the peoples with truth.***

**Thanksgiving**

Your steadfast love is established forever, O God;
***your faithfulness is as firm as the heavens.***
*(free prayers of thanksgiving)*
My mouth is filled with your praise,
***and with your glory all day long. Amen.***

**Song**

Proclaim the tidings near and far (H282)
Sing we triumphant hymns (H287)
Oh, that I had a thousand voices (H84)
Let the heavens be glad (H187)
We believe, as one by one (SS119)

**Confession**

Raised with Christ,
let us seek the things that are above,
***where Christ is,***
***seated at the right hand of God.***
*(silence)*

O God, draw our minds
to the things that are above,
***for we have died, and our life is hidden
with Christ in you. Amen.***

## Call to discipleship

Jesus said, Those who want to save their life will lose it,
***and those who lose their life for my sake will find it.***

**John 21.15-19**

When they had finished breakfast, Jesus said to Simon Peter, "Simon son of John, do you love me more than these?" He said to him, "Yes, Lord; you know that I love you." Jesus said to him, "Feed my lambs." A second time he said to him, "Simon son of John, do you love me?" He said to him, "Yes, Lord; you know that I love you." Jesus said to him, "Tend my sheep." He said to him the third time, "Simon son of John, do you love me?" Peter felt hurt because he said to him the third time, "Do you love me?" And he said to him, "Lord, you know everything; you know that I love you." Jesus said to him, "Feed my sheep. Very truly, I tell you, when you were younger, you used to fasten your own belt and to go wherever you wished. But when you grow old, you will stretch out your hands, and someone else will fasten a belt around you and take you where you do not wish to go." (He said this to indicate the kind of death by which he would glorify God.) After this he said to him, "Follow me."

**Ephesians 3.14-19**

For this reason I bow my knees before the Father, from whom every family in heaven and on earth takes its name. I pray that, according to the riches of his glory, he may grant that you may be strengthened in your inner being with power through his Spirit, and that Christ may dwell in your hearts through faith, as you are being rooted and grounded in love. I pray that you may have the power to comprehend, with all the saints, what is the breadth and length and height and depth, and to know the love of Christ that surpasses knowledge, so that you may be filled with all the fullness of God.

**Silent or spoken reflection on the readings**

**Song**

We know that Christ is raised (H443)
How can I say (SS117)
Heart with loving heart united (H420)
In the bulb there is a flower (H614)
I love thee, Lord (H605)

**Philippians 2.5-11**

## Call to intercession

I am about to do a new thing;
now it springs forth, do you not perceive it?
***I will make a way in the wilderness***
***and rivers in the desert.***

God of new life, we look for your resurrection power. In your mercy,
***Lord, hear our prayer.***

You are faithful and gracious. We pray for ourselves and those dear to us.
*(open prayers)*
In your mercy,
***Lord, hear our prayer.***

You have compassion for all that you have made. We pray for our community and for our neighbors.
*(open prayers)*
In your mercy,
***Lord, hear our prayer.***

You desire to fill us with the fullness of your love. We pray for the church in all places, that we may be faithful in solidarity across generations and geography.
*(open prayers)*

In your mercy,
***Lord, hear our prayer.***

From you every family on earth takes its name. We pray for the world, for our enemies and for those who are in conflict.
*(open prayers)*
In your mercy,
***Lord, hear our prayer.***

We offer you other concerns we carry in our hearts.
*(open prayers)*
In your mercy,
***Lord, hear our prayer.***

God of new beginnings,
you raise us from the grave
and draw us into your glory.
In your love, release us
from all that binds us to death,
that we may be eternally bound to you
through the resurrection of your son Jesus,
with whom we pray:

***Our Father …***

**Benediction**

***May we be made strong with all the strength***
***that comes from God's glorious power,***
***enduring everything with patience,***
***while joyfully giving thanks to the Father,***

*who has enabled us to share in the inheritance of the saints in the light. Amen.*

# Pentecost

## Introduction to the Pentecost prayers: Week 1

*Pentecost* is the Greek name given to the Jewish Feast of Weeks; it was celebrated fifty days after Passover and was initially the festival at which the first-fruits of the grain harvest were presented (Dt 16.9). Later in Israel's history, Pentecost also commemorated the giving of the Law at Sinai.

Christian celebration of Pentecost marks the birth of the church fifty days after Jesus' resurrection. According to Acts 2.1, Jesus' followers were in Jerusalem when the day of Pentecost came. On that occasion, the Holy Spirit descended on the apostles, empowering them to be Jesus' witnesses in Jerusalem, in all Judea and Samaria, and to the ends of the earth" (1.8). As incarnation was wrought of God's grace and Mary's courage, so Pentecost is a unique partnership of divine and human energy, as the gospel takes wing through the determined tread of the disciples' feet—and goes out to all nations.

For this week of Pentecost services, we drew on Old Testament texts about the Spirit coming on the Messiah, in particular, but also about God's spirit refreshing God's people more generally. The Psalms and the Prophets often yearn toward the Spirit as source of healing and holiness.

In light of the Old Testament Spirit texts, Pentecost is, or should be, utterly predictable. God bestows on Jesus' covenant people the same lively Spirit that anointed Jesus for his messianic ministry. Acts 2.22-24, 32-33, the first words we hear from Peter after his denial—in themselves a compelling witness to the power of the Spirit—becomes the morning confession of faith. Title lines, opening sentences, and canticle from Ephesians 2.17-22 remind us that the Spirit we celebrate in this season of Pentecost is the Spirit of the one who came proclaiming peace; that Spirit now reconciles strangers and aliens, making of them a dwelling place for God.

Scripture readings and Psalms for this week span the times: Old Testament promises that God will pour out the Spirit, and New Testament declarations that God's Spirit inspired Jesus' ministry, and that of his followers in the Acts of the Apostles. Evening selections from Jesus' Upper Room discourse highlight Jesus' promise of the Spirit to teach and guide his disciples, then and now. Selections from the Epistles emphasize the fruit of the Spirit in making life new and holy, uniting us with God and Jesus. The blessed Holy Spirit also leads us in prayer, as we, in sorrow and struggle, hunger for the fullness of the new creation (Romans 8).

# Christ Jesus came and proclaimed peace

## PENTECOST SUNDAY MORNING

**Opening sentence**

Christ Jesus came and proclaimed peace
to you who were far off
***and peace to those who were near.***

## Call to praise

I will sing to the Lord as long as I live;
***I will sing praise to my God***
***while I have being.***

***Glory …***

**Isaiah 57.15-19**

For thus says the high and lofty one
who inhabits eternity, whose name is Holy:
***I dwell in the high and holy place,***
***and also with those who are contrite and humble in spirit,***
to revive the spirit of the humble,
and to revive the heart of the contrite.
***For I will not continually accuse,***
***nor will I always be angry;***

for then the spirits would grow faint before me,
even the souls that I have made.
***Because of their wicked covetousness I was angry;***
***I struck them, I hid and was angry;***
***but they kept turning back to their own ways.***
I have seen their ways, but I will heal them;
I will lead them and repay them with comfort,
creating for their mourners the fruit of the lips.
***Peace, peace, to the far and the near, says the LORD;***
***and I will heal them.***

**Thanksgiving**

Bless the Lord, O my soul.
O my God, you are very great.
***You are clothed with honor and majesty,***
***wrapped in light as with a garment.***
*(free prayers of thanksgiving)*
You make the winds your messengers,
***fire and flame your ministers. Amen.***

**Song**

From all that dwell below the skies (H49)
O bless the Lord, my soul (H80, H600)
Cantai ao Senhor (O sing to the Lord) (SJ12)
Asithi: Amen (Sing amen) (H64)
Alleluia (SS24)

**Confession of faith**

Jesus of Nazareth was a man
commended to us by God
***through the powerful acts, wonders, and signs***
***God did through him in our midst—***
***as we ourselves know well.***
This man, according to the declared purpose
and foreknowledge of God,
was handed over, crucified and killed
by the hands of lawless ones.
***Yet God raised him up,***
***releasing him from the birth pangs of death***
***because it was not possible for him***
***to be taken over by it.***
This Jesus God raised up,
and of that we are all witnesses.
***Being therefore lifted high***
***at the right hand of God,***
***having received the promise of the Holy Spirit***
***from the Father,***
***he has poured out this***
***that we both see and hear.***

## Call to discipleship

Let us hold to the standard of sound teaching
that we have heard,
***in the faith and love that are in Christ Jesus.***

**Acts 1.1-8**

In the first book, Theophilus, I [Luke] wrote about all that Jesus did and taught from the beginning until the day when he was taken up to heaven, after giving instructions through the Holy Spirit to the apostles whom he had chosen. After his suffering he presented himself alive to them by many convincing proofs, appearing to them during forty days and speaking about the kingdom of God. While staying with them, he ordered them not to leave Jerusalem, but to wait there for the promise of the Father. "This," he said, "is what you have heard from me; for John baptized with water, but you will be baptized with the Holy Spirit not many days from now."

So when they had come together, they asked him, "Lord, is this the time when you will restore the kingdom to Israel?" He replied, "It is not for you to know the times or periods that the Father has set by his own authority. But you will receive power when the Holy Spirit has come upon you; and you will be my witnesses in Jerusalem, in all Judea and Samaria, and to the ends of the earth."

**Romans 15.7-13**

Welcome one another, therefore, just as Christ has welcomed you, for the glory of God. For

I tell you that Christ has become a servant of the circumcised on behalf of the truth of God in order that he might confirm the promises given to the patriarchs, and in order that the Gentiles might glorify God for his mercy. As it is written,

"Therefore I will confess you among the
Gentiles,
and sing praises to your name";

and again he says,

"Rejoice, O Gentiles, with his people";

and again,

"Praise the Lord, all you Gentiles,
and let all the peoples praise him";

and again Isaiah says,

"The root of Jesse shall come,
the one who rises to rule the Gentiles;
in him the Gentiles shall hope."

May the God of hope fill you with all joy and peace in believing, so that you may abound in hope by the power of the Holy Spirit.

**Silent or spoken reflection on the readings**

**Song**

Fill now our life, O Lord (SS107)
Filled with the Spirit's power (H289)
Christ, who is in the form of God (H333)
Amen (H643)

**Ephesians 2.17-22**

## Call to intercession

Beloved, let us build ourselves up
on our most holy faith,
***and let us pray in the Holy Spirit.***

God of hope, you promise peace to all, both far and near. In your mercy,
***Lord, hear our prayer.***

You are the source of comfort and healing. We pray for ourselves and those dear to us.
*(open prayers)*
In your mercy,
***Lord, hear our prayer.***

You revive the hearts of the humble. We pray for our community and for our neighbors.
*(open prayers)*
In your mercy,
***Lord, hear our prayer.***

You send your Spirit to give us power to witness. We pray for the church in all places, that we may be one.
*(open prayers)*
In your mercy,
***Lord, hear our prayer.***

The ends of the earth will see your salvation. We pray for the world, that your reign may come and your will be done on earth.

*(open prayers)*
In your mercy,
***Lord, hear our prayer.***

We offer you other concerns we carry in our hearts.
*(open prayers)*
In your mercy,
***Lord, hear our prayer.***

God of convincing power,
you pour out your Spirit
on all who call on you.
Restore us with the breath
of your holy presence,
that we may see the vision of your shalom
and proclaim your good news to the world.
Through Jesus, who taught us,
we pray for the coming of your reign:

***Our Father …***

**Charge**

Do not worry about how you are to speak
or what you are to say;
for what you are to say
will be given to you at that time;
for it is not you who speak,
but the Spirit of your Father
speaking through you. ***Amen.***

# Christ Jesus came and proclaimed peace

## PENTECOST SUNDAY EVENING

**Opening sentence**

Christ Jesus came and proclaimed peace
to you who were far off
***and peace to those who were near.***

## Call to praise

Come, bless the Lord,
all you servants of the Lord,
who stand by night in the house of the Lord!
***Lift up your hands to the holy place,***
***and bless the Lord.***

***Alleluia!***

*Glory …*

**Isaiah 52.7-10**

How beautiful upon the mountains
are the feet of the messenger who announces
peace,
***who brings good news,***
***who announces salvation,***
***who says to Zion, "Your God reigns."***

Listen! Your sentinels lift up their voices,
together they sing for joy;
***for in plain sight they see***
***the return of the LORD to Zion.***
Break forth together into singing,
you ruins of Jerusalem;
***for the LORD has comforted his people,***
***he has redeemed Jerusalem.***
The LORD has bared his holy arm
before the eyes of all the nations;
***and all the ends of the earth shall see***
***the salvation of our God.***

**Thanksgiving**

Lord, how manifold are your works!
The earth is full of your creatures.
***When you give to them, they gather it up;***
***when you open your hand,***
***they are filled with good things.***
*(free prayers of thanksgiving)*
O Lord, may your glory endure forever;
may you rejoice in your works.
***When you send forth your spirit,***
***they are created;***
***and you renew the face of the ground. Amen.***

**Song**

Great is the Lord (H87)
Glorious things of thee are spoken (H619)

Come, we that love the Lord (H14)
Sing praise to God who reigns (H59)

**Confession**

In goodness and loving kindness, you save us,
***not because of anything we have done,***
***but in mercy,***
***through the water of rebirth and renewal***
***by the Holy Spirit.***
*(silence)*
This Spirit you pour out on us richly, O God,
through Jesus Christ our Savior,
***so that, having been justified by grace,***
***we might become heirs***
***according to the hope of eternal life. Amen.***

## Call to discipleship

God chose us as the first fruits for salvation
through sanctification by the Spirit
and belief in the truth.
***Then let us stand firm***
***and hold fast to the traditions we were taught.***

**John 14.15-17**

"If you love me, you will keep my commandments. And I will ask the Father, and he will give you another Advocate, to be with you forever. This is the Spirit of truth, whom the world cannot receive, because it neither sees him nor knows him. You know him, because he abides with you, and he will be in you."

**Ephesians 6.14-18**

Stand therefore, and fasten the belt of truth around your waist, and put on the breastplate of righteousness. As shoes for your feet put on whatever will make you ready to proclaim the gospel of peace. With all of these, take the shield of faith, with which you will be able to quench all the flaming arrows of the evil one. Take the helmet of salvation, and the sword of the Spirit, which is the word of God.

Pray in the Spirit at all times in every prayer and supplication. To that end keep alert and always persevere in supplication for all the saints.

**Silent or spoken reflection on the readings**

**Song**

Filled with the Spirit's power (H289)
Fire of God, undying flame (SS103)
Holy Spirit, Truth divine (H508, SS105)
Holy Spirit, come to us (SS79)

**Ephesians 2.17-22**

## Call to intercession

The whole creation has been groaning,
and not only the creation,
***but we ourselves,***
***who have the first fruits of the Spirit,***
***groan inwardly while we wait***
***for the redemption of our bodies.***

God of hope, you promise peace to all, both far and near. In your mercy,
***Lord, hear our prayer.***

You are the source of comfort and healing. We pray for ourselves and those dear to us.
*(open prayers)*
In your mercy,
***Lord, hear our prayer.***

You revive the hearts of the humble. We pray for our community and for our neighbors.
*(open prayers)*
In your mercy,
***Lord, hear our prayer.***

You send your Spirit to give us power to witness. We pray for the church in all places, that we may be one.
*(open prayers)*
In your mercy,
***Lord, hear our prayer.***

The ends of the earth will see your salvation. We pray for the world, that your reign may come and your will be done on earth.
*(open prayers)*
In your mercy,
***Lord, hear our prayer.***

We offer you other concerns we carry in our hearts.
*(open prayers)*
In your mercy,
***Lord, hear our prayer.***

God of abiding presence,
you lead us by your Spirit
and claim us as your children.
Call us in righteousness,
and renew us in hope and joy,
that we may be messengers of your peace,
fearlessly announcing your salvation.
Through Jesus, who taught us,
we pray for the coming of your reign:

***Our Father …***

**Benediction**

***May the God of peace sanctify us entirely;***
***and may our spirit and soul and body***
***be kept sound and blameless***
***at the coming of our Lord Jesus Christ.***
***The one who calls us is faithful***
***and will do this. Amen.***

# In one Spirit

## PENTECOST MONDAY MORNING

**Opening sentence**

Christ Jesus came and proclaimed peace
to you who were far off
and peace to those who were near;
***for through him both of us have access***
***in one Spirit to the Father.***

## Call to praise

I will sing to the Lord as long as I live;
***I will sing praise to my God***
***while I have being.***

***Glory …***

**Isaiah 11.1-4, 10-12**

A shoot shall come out from the stump of
 Jesse,
and a branch shall grow out of his roots.
***The spirit of the LORD shall rest on him,***
***the spirit of wisdom and understanding,***
the spirit of counsel and might,
the spirit of knowledge and the fear of the
 LORD.
***His delight shall be in the fear of the LORD.***

He shall not judge by what his eyes see,
or decide by what his ears hear;
***but with righteousness he shall judge the poor,***
***and decide with equity for the meek of the earth....***

On that day the root of Jesse shall stand
as a signal to the peoples;
***the nations shall inquire of him,***
***and his dwelling shall be glorious.***

On that day the Lord will extend his hand
yet a second time
to recover the remnant
that is left of his people,
***from Assyria, from Egypt, from Pathros, from Ethiopia,***
***from Elam, from Shinar, from Hamath,***
***and from the coastlands of the sea.***
He will raise a signal for the nations,
and will assemble the outcasts of Israel,
***and gather the dispersed of Judah***
***from the four corners of the earth.***

**Thanksgiving**

Bless the Lord, O my soul.
O my God, you are very great.
***You are clothed with honor and majesty,***
***wrapped in light as with a garment.***
*(free prayers of thanksgiving)*

You make the winds your messengers,
***fire and flame your ministers. Amen.***

**Song**

God is working his purpose out (H638)
Comfort, comfort, O my people (H176)
O day of peace (H408)
My soul cries out (SS124)

**Confession of faith**

Jesus of Nazareth was a man
commended to us by God
***through the powerful acts, wonders, and signs***
***God did through him in our midst—***
***as we ourselves know well.***
This man, according to the declared purpose
and foreknowledge of God,
was handed over, crucified and killed
by the hands of lawless ones.
***Yet God raised him up,***
***releasing him from the birth pangs of death***
***because it was not possible for him***
***to be taken over by it.***
This Jesus God raised up,
and of that we are all witnesses.
***Being therefore lifted high***
***at the right hand of God,***
***having received the promise of the Holy Spirit***
***from the Father,***

***he has poured out this***
***that we both see and hear.***

## Call to discipleship

Let us hold to the standard of sound teaching that we have heard,
***in the faith and love that are in Christ Jesus.***

**Acts 2.1-13**

When the day of Pentecost had come, [the disciples] were all together in one place. And suddenly from heaven there came a sound like the rush of a violent wind, and it filled the entire house where they were sitting. Divided tongues, as of fire, appeared among them, and a tongue rested on each of them. All of them were filled with the Holy Spirit and began to speak in other languages, as the Spirit gave them ability.

Now there were devout Jews from every nation under heaven living in Jerusalem. And at this sound the crowd gathered and was bewildered, because each one heard them speaking in the native language of each. Amazed and astonished, they asked, "Are not all these who are speaking Galileans? And how is it that we hear, each of us, in our own native language? Parthians, Medes, Elamites, and residents of Mesopotamia, Judea and Cappadocia, Pontus and Asia, Phrygia and Pamphylia, Egypt and the parts of Libya belonging to Cyrene, and visitors from Rome, both Jews and proselytes, Cretans and Arabs—in our own languages we hear them speaking about God's deeds of power." All were amazed and perplexed, saying to one another, "What does this mean?" But others sneered and said, "They are filled with new wine."

**Acts 10.(34-43), 44-48**

While Peter was still speaking, the Holy Spirit fell upon all who heard the word. The circumcised believers who had come with Peter were astounded that the gift of the Holy Spirit had been poured out even on the Gentiles, for they heard them speaking in tongues and extolling God. Then Peter said, "Can anyone withhold the water for baptizing these people who have received the Holy Spirit just as we have?" So he ordered them to be baptized in the name of Jesus Christ. Then they invited him to stay for several days.

**Silent or spoken reflection on the readings**

**Song**

Filled with the Spirit's power (H289)
Come, O Spirit, come (SS104, vv. 1–5)
All who believe and are baptized (H436)

**Ephesians 2.17-22**

## Call to intercession

Beloved, let us build ourselves up
on our most holy faith,
***and let us pray in the Holy Spirit.***

God of wind and word, you send your Spirit of power. In your mercy,
***Lord, hear our prayer.***

You show mercy and an abundance of steadfast love. We pray for ourselves and those dear to us.
*(open prayers)*
In your mercy,
***Lord, hear our prayer.***

You bring an end to division and enmity between people. We pray for our community and for our neighbors.
*(open prayers)*
In your mercy,
***Lord, hear our prayer.***

Your Spirit bears witness with our spirit that we are your children. We pray for the church in all places, that we may know the freedom of life in the Spirit.
*(open prayers)*

In your mercy,
***Lord, hear our prayer.***

You decide with equity for the meek of the earth. We pray for the world and for all who care for creation.
*(open prayers)*
In your mercy,
***Lord, hear our prayer.***

We offer you other concerns we carry in our hearts.
*(open prayers)*
In your mercy,
***Lord, hear our prayer.***

God of convincing power,
you pour out your Spirit
on all who call on you.
Restore us with the breath
of your holy presence,
that we may see the vision of your shalom
and proclaim your good news to the world.
Through Jesus, who taught us,
we pray for the coming of your reign:

***Our Father …***

**Charge**

And Jesus came and said to them,
"All authority in heaven and on earth
has been given to me.

Go therefore and make disciples of all nations,
baptizing them in the name of the Father
and of the Son and of the Holy Spirit,
and teaching them to obey
everything that I have commanded you.
And remember, I am with you always,
to the end of the age." ***Amen.***

# In one Spirit

## PENTECOST MONDAY EVENING

**Opening sentence**

Christ Jesus came and proclaimed peace
to you who were far off
and peace to those who were near;
***for through him both of us have access***
***in one Spirit to the Father.***

## Call to praise

Come, bless the Lord,
all you servants of the Lord,
who stand by night in the house of the Lord!
***Lift up your hands to the holy place,***
***and bless the Lord.***

*Glory ...*

**Isaiah 63.7-16**

I will recount the gracious deeds of the LORD,
the praiseworthy acts of the LORD,
***because of all that the LORD has done for us,***
***and the great favor to the house of Israel***
that he has shown them according to his
mercy,
according to the abundance of his steadfast
love.

***For he said, "Surely they are my people,***
***children who will not deal falsely";***
and he became their savior
in all their distress.
It was no messenger or angel
but his presence that saved them;
***in his love and in his pity he redeemed them;***
***he lifted them up and carried them all the days of old.***

But they rebelled
and grieved his holy spirit;
therefore he became their enemy;
he himself fought against them.
***Then they remembered the days of old,***
***of Moses his servant.***
Where is the one who brought them up out of the sea
with the shepherds of his flock?
***Where is the one who put within them***
***his holy spirit,***
who caused his glorious arm
to march at the right hand of Moses,
***who divided the waters before them***
***to make for himself an everlasting name,***
who led them through the depths?
***Like a horse in the desert,***
***they did not stumble.***
Like cattle that go down into the valley,
the spirit of the LORD gave them rest.

***Thus you led your people,***
***to make for yourself a glorious name.***
Look down from heaven and see,
from your holy and glorious habitation.
Where are your zeal and your might?
***The yearning of your heart and your compassion?***
***They are withheld from me.***
For you are our father,
though Abraham does not know us
and Israel does not acknowledge us;
***you, O Lord, are our father;***
***our Redeemer from of old is your name.***

**Thanksgiving**

Lord, how manifold are your works!
The earth is full of your creatures.
***When you give to them, they gather it up;***
***when you open your hand,***
***they are filled with good things.***
*(free prayers of thanksgiving)*
O Lord, may your glory endure forever;
may you rejoice in your works.
***When you send forth your spirit,***
***they are created;***
***and you renew the face of the ground. Amen.***

**Song**

We give thanks unto you (H161)

Had God brought us out (SS96)
Praise, my soul, the God of heaven (H63)

**Confession**

In goodness and loving kindness, you save us,
***not because of anything we have done,***
***but in mercy,***
***through the water of rebirth and renewal***
***by the Holy Spirit.***
*(silence)*
This Spirit you pour out on us richly, O God,
through Jesus Christ our Savior,
***so that, having been justified by grace,***
***we might become heirs***
***according to the hope of eternal life. Amen.***

## Call to discipleship

God chose us as the first fruits for salvation
through sanctification by the Spirit
and belief in the truth.
***Then let us stand firm***
***and hold fast to the traditions we were taught.***

**John 14.18-21**

"I will not leave you orphaned; I am coming to you. In a little while the world will no longer see me, but you will see me; because I live, you also will live. On that day you will know that I am in my Father, and you in me, and I in you. They who have my commandments and keep them are those who love me; and those who love me will be loved by my Father, and I will love them and reveal myself to them."

**Romans 8.14-17**

For all who are led by the Spirit of God are children of God. For you did not receive a spirit of slavery to fall back into fear, but you have received a spirit of adoption. When we cry, "Abba! Father!" it is that very Spirit bearing witness with our spirit that we are children of God, and if children, then heirs, heirs of God and joint heirs with Christ—if, in fact, we suffer with him so that we may also be glorified with him.

**Silent or spoken reflection on the readings**

**Song**

Holy Spirit, come to us (SS79)
Filled with the Spirit's power (H289)
Come, O Spirit, come (SS104, vv. 1, 6–7)
Away with our fears (H292)

**Ephesians 2.17-22**

## Call to intercession

The whole creation has been groaning,
and not only the creation,
***but we ourselves,***
***who have the first fruits of the Spirit,***
***groan inwardly while we wait***
***for the redemption of our bodies.***

God of wind and word, you send your Spirit of power. In your mercy,
***Lord, hear our prayer.***

You show mercy and an abundance of steadfast love. We pray for ourselves and those dear to us.
*(open prayers)*
In your mercy,
***Lord, hear our prayer.***

You bring an end to division and enmity between people. We pray for our community and for our neighbors.
*(open prayers)*
In your mercy,
***Lord, hear our prayer.***

Your Spirit bears witness with our spirit that we are your children. We pray for the church in all places, that we may know the freedom of life in the Spirit.

*(open prayers)*
In your mercy,
***Lord, hear our prayer.***

You decide with equity for the meek of the earth. We pray for the world and for all who care for creation.
*(open prayers)*
In your mercy,
***Lord, hear our prayer.***

We offer you other concerns we carry in our hearts.
*(open prayers)*
In your mercy,
***Lord, hear our prayer.***

God of abiding presence,
you lead us by your Spirit
and claim us as your children.
Call us in righteousness,
and renew us in hope and joy,
that we may be messengers of your peace,
fearlessly announcing your salvation.
Through Jesus, who taught us,
we pray for the coming of your reign:

***Our Father …***

**Benediction**

***According to the riches of his glory***
***may God grant that we may be strengthened***

*in our inner being*
*with power through the Spirit,*
*and that Christ may dwell in our hearts*
*through faith,*
*as we are being rooted and grounded in love.*
*Amen.*

# No longer strangers

## PENTECOST TUESDAY MORNING

**Opening sentence**

Through him both of us have access
in one Spirit to the Father.
***So then you are no longer strangers and aliens.***

## Call to praise

I will sing to the Lord as long as I live;
***I will sing praise to my God***
***while I have being.***

*Glory ...*

**Joel 2.26-32**

You shall eat in plenty and be satisfied,
and praise the name of the LORD your God,
who has dealt wondrously with you.
***And my people shall never again be put to shame.***
You shall know that I am in the midst of Israel,
and that I, the LORD, am your God and there is no other.
***And my people shall never again be put to shame.***

Then afterward
I will pour out my spirit on all flesh;
your sons and your daughters shall prophesy,
***your old men shall dream dreams,***
***and your young men shall see visions.***
Even on the male and female slaves,
in those days, I will pour out my spirit.

***I will show portents in the heavens***
***and on the earth,***
***blood and fire and columns of smoke.***
The sun shall be turned to darkness,
and the moon to blood,
before the great and terrible day of the LORD comes.
***Then everyone who calls on the name of the LORD shall be saved;***
for in Mount Zion and in Jerusalem
there shall be those who escape,
as the LORD has said,
***and among the survivors***
***shall be those whom the LORD calls.***

**Thanksgiving**

Bless the Lord, O my soul.
O my God, you are very great.
***You are clothed with honor and majesty,***
***wrapped in light as with a garment.***
*(free prayers of thanksgiving)*
You make the winds your messengers,
***fire and flame your ministers. Amen.***

**Song**

O Holy Spirit, by whose breath (H291)
I will stand in the congregation (SS113)
Praise with joy the world's Creator (SJ16)

**Confession of faith**

Jesus of Nazareth was a man
commended to us by God
***through the powerful acts, wonders, and signs***
***God did through him in our midst—***
***as we ourselves know well.***
This man, according to the declared purpose
and foreknowledge of God,
was handed over, crucified and killed
by the hands of lawless ones.
***Yet God raised him up,***
***releasing him from the birth pangs of death***
***because it was not possible for him***
***to be taken over by it.***
This Jesus God raised up,
and of that we are all witnesses.
***Being therefore lifted high***
***at the right hand of God,***
***having received the promise of the Holy Spirit***
***from the Father,***
***he has poured out this***
***that we both see and hear.***

## Call to discipleship

Let us hold to the standard of sound teaching that we have heard,
***in the faith and love that are in Christ Jesus.***

**Acts 2.14-21**

But Peter, standing with the eleven, raised his voice and addressed them, "Men of Judea and all who live in Jerusalem, let this be known to you, and listen to what I say. Indeed, these are not drunk, as you suppose, for it is only nine o'clock in the morning. No, this is what was spoken through the prophet Joel:

'In the last days it will be, God declares,
that I will pour out my Spirit upon all
flesh,
and your sons and your daughters shall
prophesy,
and your young men shall see visions,
and your old men shall dream dreams.
Even upon my slaves, both men and
women,
in those days I will pour out my Spirit;
and they shall prophesy.
And I will show portents in the heaven
above
and signs on the earth below,
blood, and fire, and smoky mist.

The sun shall be turned to darkness
and the moon to blood,
before the coming of the Lord's great and
glorious day.
Then everyone who calls on the name of
the Lord shall be saved.'"

**Romans 10.9-18**

If you confess with your lips that Jesus is Lord and believe in your heart that God raised him from the dead, you will be saved. For one believes with the heart and so is justified, and one confesses with the mouth and so is saved. The scripture says, "No one who believes in him will be put to shame." For there is no distinction between Jew and Greek; the same Lord is Lord of all and is generous to all who call on him. For, "Everyone who calls on the name of the Lord shall be saved."

But how are they to call on one in whom they have not believed? And how are they to believe in one of whom they have never heard? And how are they to hear without someone to proclaim him? And how are they to proclaim him unless they are sent? As it is written, "How beautiful are the feet of those who bring good news!" But not all have obeyed the good news; for Isaiah says, "Lord, who has believed our message?" So faith comes from what is heard, and what is heard comes through the word of Christ.

But I ask, have they not heard? Indeed they have; for

> "Their voice has gone out to all the earth,
> and their words to the ends of the world."

**Silent or spoken reflection on the readings**

**Song**

Santo, santo, santo (Holy, holy, holy) (H400)
God has chosen me (SS114)
God sends us the Spirit (H293)
New earth, heavens new (H299)

**Ephesians 2.17-22**

## Call to intercession

Beloved, let us build ourselves up
on our most holy faith,
***and let us pray in the Holy Spirit.***

Lord of all, you are generous to all who call on you. In your mercy,
***Lord, hear our prayer.***

You offer us a peace that the world cannot give. We pray for ourselves and those dear to us.
*(open prayers)*

In your mercy,
***Lord, hear our prayer.***

The breath of your Spirit is the life of all people. We pray for our community and for our neighbors.
*(open prayers)*
In your mercy,
***Lord, hear our prayer.***

You have given your people as a light to the nations. We pray for the church in all places, that we may reflect your faithful love.
*(open prayers)*
In your mercy,
***Lord, hear our prayer.***

You delight in the one through whom your Spirit brings justice. We pray for the world, for those who are in need.
*(open prayers)*
In your mercy,
***Lord, hear our prayer.***

We offer you other concerns we carry in our hearts.
*(open prayers)*
In your mercy,
***Lord, hear our prayer.***

God of convincing power,
you pour out your Spirit

on all who call on you.
Restore us with the breath
of your holy presence,
that we may see the vision of your shalom
and proclaim your good news to the world.
Through Jesus, who taught us,
we pray for the coming of your reign:

***Our Father ...***

**Charge**

If we sow to the Spirit,
we will reap eternal life from the Spirit.
So let us not grow weary
in doing what is right,
for we will reap at harvest-time,
if we do not give up.
So then, whenever we have an opportunity,
let us work for the good of all,
and especially for those of the family of faith.
***Amen.***

# No longer strangers

## PENTECOST TUESDAY EVENING

**Opening sentence**

Through him both of us have access
in one Spirit to the Father.
***So then you are no longer strangers and aliens.***

## Call to praise

Come, bless the Lord,
all you servants of the Lord,
who stand by night in the house of the Lord!
***Lift up your hands to the holy place,***
***and bless the Lord.***

*Glory ...*

**Isaiah 42.1-6**

Here is my servant, whom I uphold,
my chosen, in whom my soul delights;
***I have put my spirit upon him;***
***he will bring forth justice to the nations.***
He will not cry or lift up his voice,
or make it heard in the street;
***a bruised reed he will not break,***
***and a dimly burning wick he will not quench;***
he will faithfully bring forth justice.

*He will not grow faint or be crushed*
*until he has established justice in the earth;*
*and the coastlands wait for his teaching.*

Thus says God, the LORD,
who created the heavens and stretched them out,
who spread out the earth and what comes from it,
*who gives breath to the people upon it*
*and spirit to those who walk in it:*
I am the LORD, I have called you in righteousness,
I have taken you by the hand and kept you;
*I have given you as a covenant to the people,*
*a light to the nations.*

**Thanksgiving**

Lord, how manifold are your works!
The earth is full of your creatures.
*When you give to them, they gather it up;*
*when you open your hand,*
*they are filled with good things.*
*(free prayers of thanksgiving)*
O Lord, may your glory endure forever;
may you rejoice in your works.
*When you send forth your spirit,*
*they are created;*
*and you renew the face of the ground. Amen.*

**Song**

Hail to the Lord's anointed (H185)
My soul is filled with joy (SJ13)

**Confession**

In goodness and loving kindness, you save us,
***not because of anything we have done,***
***but in mercy,***
***through the water of rebirth and renewal***
***by the Holy Spirit.***
*(silence)*
This Spirit you pour out on us richly, O God,
through Jesus Christ our Savior,
***so that, having been justified by grace,***
***we might become heirs***
***according to the hope of eternal life. Amen.***

# Call to discipleship

God chose us as the first fruits for salvation
through sanctification by the Spirit
and belief in the truth.
***Then let us stand firm***
***and hold fast to the traditions we were taught.***

**John 14.25-27**

"I have said these things to you while I am still with you. But the Advocate, the Holy Spirit, whom the Father will send in my name, will teach you everything, and remind you of all that I have said to you. Peace I leave with you; my peace I give to you. I do not give to you as the world gives. Do not let your hearts be troubled, and do not let them be afraid."

**Galatians 5.16-25**

Live by the Spirit, I say, and do not gratify the desires of the flesh. For what the flesh desires is opposed to the Spirit, and what the Spirit desires is opposed to the flesh; for these are opposed to each other, to prevent you from doing what you want. But if you are led by the Spirit, you are not subject to the law. Now the works of the flesh are obvious: fornication, impurity, licentiousness, idolatry, sorcery, enmities, strife, jealousy, anger, quarrels, dissensions, factions, envy, drunkenness, carousing, and things like these. I am warning you, as I warned you before: those who do such things will not inherit the kingdom of God.

By contrast, the fruit of the Spirit is love, joy, peace, patience, kindness, generosity, faithfulness, gentleness, and self-control. There is no law against such things. And those who belong to Christ Jesus have crucified the flesh with its passions and desires. If we live by the Spirit, let us also be guided by the Spirit.

**Silent or spoken reflection on the readings**

**Song**

The risen Christ (SS101)
Awake, awake, fling off the night (H448)
I will come to you in the silence (SS49)
Beloved, God's chosen (SJ38)
Spirit, working in creation (SJ10)
Herr, füll mich neu (God, fill me now) (SS63)

**Ephesians 2.17-22**

## Call to intercession

The whole creation has been groaning,
and not only the creation,
***but we ourselves,***
***who have the first fruits of the Spirit,***
***groan inwardly while we wait***
***for the redemption of our bodies.***

Lord of all, you are generous to all who call on you. In your mercy,
***Lord, hear our prayer.***

You offer us a peace that the world cannot give. We pray for ourselves and those dear to us.
*(open prayers)*
In your mercy,
***Lord, hear our prayer.***

The breath of your Spirit is the life of all people. We pray for our community and for our neighbors.
*(open prayers)*
In your mercy,
***Lord, hear our prayer.***

You have given your people as a light to the nations. We pray for the church in all places, that we may reflect your faithful love.
*(open prayers)*
In your mercy,
***Lord, hear our prayer.***

You delight in the one through whom your Spirit brings justice. We pray for the world, for those who are in need.
*(open prayers)*
In your mercy,
***Lord, hear our prayer.***

We offer you other concerns we carry in our hearts.
*(open prayers)*
In your mercy,
***Lord, hear our prayer.***

God of abiding presence,
you lead us by your Spirit
and claim us as your children.
Call us in righteousness,
and renew us in hope and joy,

that we may be messengers of your peace,
fearlessly announcing your salvation.
Through Jesus, who taught us,
we pray for the coming of your reign:

*Our Father ...*

**Benediction**

*May we have the power to comprehend,
with all the saints,
what is the breadth and length
and height and depth,
and to know the love of Christ
that surpasses knowledge,
so that we may be filled
with all the fullness of God. Amen.*

# Members of the household of God

## PENTECOST WEDNESDAY MORNING

**Opening sentence**

So then you are no longer strangers and aliens,
***but you are citizens with the saints***
***and also members of the household of God.***

## Call to praise

I will sing to the Lord as long as I live;
***I will sing praise to my God***
***while I have being.***

*Glory …*

**Psalm 16.7-11**

I will bless you, LORD, you give me counsel,
and even at night direct my heart.
***I keep you, LORD, ever in my sight;***
***since you are at my right hand, I shall stand firm.***

And so my heart rejoices, my soul is glad;
even my body shall rest in safety.
***For you will not leave my soul among the dead,***
***nor let your beloved know decay.***

You will show me the path of life,
the fullness of joy in your presence,
***at your right hand happiness for ever.***

**Thanksgiving**

Bless the Lord, O my soul.
O my God, you are very great.
***You are clothed with honor and majesty,***
***wrapped in light as with a garment.***
*(free prayers of thanksgiving)*
You make the winds your messengers,
***fire and flame your ministers. Amen.***

**Song**

I to the hills will lift my eyes (H169, H563)
Make music to the Lord most high (H73)
Je louerai l'Eternel (Praise, I will praise you,
Lord) (H76)
Love the Lord your God (SS55)

**Confession of faith**

Jesus of Nazareth was a man
commended to us by God
***through the powerful acts, wonders, and signs***
***God did through him in our midst—***
***as we ourselves know well.***
This man, according to the declared purpose
and foreknowledge of God,
was handed over, crucified and killed
by the hands of lawless ones.

***Yet God raised him up,***
***releasing him from the birth pangs of death***
***because it was not possible for him***
***to be taken over by it.***
This Jesus God raised up,
and of that we are all witnesses.
***Being therefore lifted high***
***at the right hand of God,***
***having received the promise of the Holy Spirit***
***from the Father,***
***he has poured out this***
***that we both see and hear.***

## Call to discipleship

Let us hold to the standard of sound teaching
that we have heard,
***in the faith and love that are in Christ Jesus.***

**Acts 2.22-28**

[Peter said,] "You that are Israelites, listen to what I have to say: Jesus of Nazareth, a man attested to you by God with deeds of power, wonders, and signs that God did through him among you, as you yourselves know—this man, handed over to you according to the definite plan and foreknowledge of God, you crucified and killed by the hands of those outside the law. But God raised him up, having freed him from death, because it was impossible for him to be held in its power. For David says concerning him,

'I saw the Lord always before me,
for he is at my right hand so that I will not
be shaken;
therefore my heart was glad, and my
tongue rejoiced;
moreover my flesh will live in hope.
For you will not abandon my soul to
Hades,
or let your Holy One experience
corruption.
You have made known to me the ways of
life;
you will make me full of gladness with
your presence.'"

**Acts 11.11-18**

[Peter said,] "At that very moment three men, sent to me from Caesarea, arrived at the house where we were. The Spirit told me to go with them and not to make a distinction between them and us. These six brothers also accompanied me, and we entered the man's house. He told us how he had seen the angel standing in his house and saying, 'Send to Joppa and bring Simon, who is called Peter; he will give you a message by which you and your entire household will be saved.' And as I began to speak, the Holy Spirit fell upon them just as it had upon us at the beginning. And I remembered the word of the Lord, how he had said, 'John baptized with water, but you will be baptized with the Holy Spirit.' If then God gave them the same gift that he gave us when we believed in the Lord Jesus Christ, who was I that I could hinder God?" When they heard this, they were silenced. And they praised God, saying, "Then God has given even to the Gentiles the repentance that leads to life."

**Silent or spoken reflection on the readings**

**Song**

This is the threefold truth (H335)
Holy Spirit, truth divine (SS105, H508)
O Holy Spirit, making whole (H300)
Abre mis ojos (Open my eyes) (SS65)

**Ephesians 2.17-22**

## Call to intercession

Beloved, let us build ourselves up
on our most holy faith,
***and let us pray in the Holy Spirit.***

God of blessing, you are very great. In your mercy,
***Lord, hear our prayer.***

You show us the path of life. We pray for ourselves and those dear to us.
*(open prayers)*
In your mercy,
***Lord, hear our prayer.***

The Spirit you send renews the face of the earth. We pray for our community and for our neighbors.
*(open prayers)*
In your mercy,
***Lord, hear our prayer.***

You offer to all peoples the repentance that leads to life. We pray for the church in all places, that we may bear witness to your reign of justice, peace, and joy.
*(open prayers)*
In your mercy,
***Lord, hear our prayer.***

Your power is stronger than the power of death. We pray for the world, for all who are ensnared in greed, violence, and oppression.
*(open prayers)*
In your mercy,
***Lord, hear our prayer.***

We offer you other concerns we carry in our hearts.
*(open prayers)*

In your mercy,
***Lord, hear our prayer.***

God of convincing power,
you pour out your Spirit
on all who call on you.
Restore us with the breath
of your holy presence,
that we may see the vision of your shalom
and proclaim your good news to the world.
Through Jesus, who taught us,
we pray for the coming of your reign:

***Our Father ...***

**Charge**

If then there is any encouragement in Christ,
any consolation from love,
any sharing in the Spirit,
any compassion and sympathy,
be of the same mind, having the same love,
being in full accord and of one mind. ***Amen.***

# Members of the household of God

## PENTECOST WEDNESDAY EVENING

**Opening sentence**

So then you are no longer strangers and aliens,
***but you are citizens with the saints***
***and also members of the household of God.***

## Call to praise

Come, bless the Lord,
all you servants of the Lord,
who stand by night in the house of the Lord!
***Lift up your hands to the holy place,***
***and bless the Lord.***

*Glory …*

**Psalm 143.5-10**

I remember the days that are past;
I ponder all your works.
***I muse on what your hand has wrought***
***and to you I stretch out my hands.***
Like a parched land my soul thirsts for you.

***LORD, make haste and answer;***
***for my spirit fails within me.***
Do not hide your face
lest I become like those in the grave.

***In the morning let me know your love***
***for I put my trust in you.***
Make me know the way I should walk;
to you I lift up my soul.

***Rescue me, LORD, from my enemies;***
***I have fled to you for refuge.***
Teach me to do your will
for you, O Lord, are my God.
***Let your good spirit guide me***
***in ways that are level and smooth.***

**Thanksgiving**

Lord, how manifold are your works!
The earth is full of your creatures.
***When you give to them, they gather it up;***
***when you open your hand,***
***they are filled with good things.***
*(free prayers of thanksgiving)*
O Lord, may your glory endure forever;
may you rejoice in your works.
***When you send forth your spirit,***
***they are created;***
***and you renew the face of the ground. Amen.***

**Song**

When all thy mercies, O my God (H72)
From time beyond my memory (H484)
We are often tossed and driv'n (SS72)
O God, to whom then shall I turn? (SS61)

**Confession**

In goodness and loving kindness, you save us,
***not because of anything we have done,***
***but in mercy,***
***through the water of rebirth and renewal***
***by the Holy Spirit.***
*(silence)*
This Spirit you pour out on us richly, O God,
through Jesus Christ our Savior,
***so that, having been justified by grace,***
***we might become heirs***
***according to the hope of eternal life. Amen.***

## Call to discipleship

God chose us as the first fruits for salvation
through sanctification by the Spirit
and belief in the truth.
***Then let us stand firm***
***and hold fast to the traditions we were taught.***

**John 15.4-5**

"Abide in me as I abide in you. Just as the branch cannot bear fruit by itself unless it abides in the vine, neither can you unless you abide in me. I am the vine, you are the branches. Those who abide in me and I in them bear much fruit, because apart from me you can do nothing."

**2 Corinthians 3.17-18**

Now the Lord is the Spirit, and where the Spirit of the Lord is, there is freedom. And all of us, with unveiled faces, seeing the glory of the Lord as though reflected in a mirror, are being transformed into the same image from one degree of glory to another; for this comes from the Lord, the Spirit.

**Silent or spoken reflection on the readings**

**Song**

Star of the morning (SS91)
Gracious Spirit, dwell with me (H507)
O blessed spring (SS100)
Thou true Vine, that heals (H373)
Love divine, all loves excelling (H592)

**Ephesians 2.17-22**

## Call to intercession

The whole creation has been groaning,
and not only the creation,
***but we ourselves,***
***who have the first fruits of the Spirit,***
***groan inwardly while we wait***
***for the redemption of our bodies.***

God of blessing, you are very great. In your mercy,
***Lord, hear our prayer.***

You show us the path of life. We pray for ourselves and those dear to us.
*(open prayers)*
In your mercy,
***Lord, hear our prayer.***

The Spirit you send renews the face of the earth. We pray for our community and for our neighbors.
*(open prayers)*
In your mercy,
***Lord, hear our prayer.***

You offer to all peoples the repentance that leads to life. We pray for the church in all places, that we may bear witness to your reign of justice, peace, and joy.
*(open prayers)*
In your mercy,
***Lord, hear our prayer.***

Your power is stronger than the power of death. We pray for the world, for all who are ensnared in greed, violence, and oppression.
*(open prayers)*
In your mercy,
***Lord, hear our prayer.***

We offer you other concerns we carry in our hearts.
*(open prayers)*
In your mercy,
***Lord, hear our prayer.***

God of abiding presence,
you lead us by your Spirit
and claim us as your children.
Call us in righteousness,
and renew us in hope and joy,
that we may be messengers of your peace,
fearlessly announcing your salvation.
Through Jesus, who taught us,
we pray for the coming of your reign:

***Our Father …***

**Benediction**

***The grace of the Lord Jesus Christ,***
***the love of God,***
***and the communion of the Holy Spirit***
***be with all of us. Amen.***

# On the foundation of the apostles and prophets

## PENTECOST THURSDAY MORNING

**Opening sentence**

So then you are no longer strangers and aliens,
but you are citizens with the saints
and also members of the household of God,
***built upon the foundation***
***of the apostles and prophets,***
***with Christ Jesus himself as the cornerstone.***

## Call to praise

I will sing to the Lord as long as I live;
***I will sing praise to my God***
***while I have being.***

*Glory ...*

**Ezekiel 37.9-14**

Then he said to me,
"Prophesy to the breath,
prophesy, mortal, and say to the breath:
***Thus says the Lord GOD:***
***Come from the four winds, O breath,***
***and breathe upon these slain,***
***that they may live."***

I prophesied as he commanded me,
and the breath came into them,
and they lived, and stood on their feet,
a vast multitude.

***Then he said to me, "Mortal,***
***these bones are the whole house of Israel.***
They say, 'Our bones are dried up,
and our hope is lost;
we are cut off completely.'
***Therefore prophesy, and say to them,***
***Thus says the Lord GOD:***
I am going to open your graves,
and bring you up from your graves,
O my people;
and I will bring you back to the land of Israel.
***And you shall know that I am the LORD,***
***when I open your graves,***
***and bring you up from your graves,***
***O my people.***
I will put my spirit within you,
and you shall live,
and I will place you on your own soil;
***then you shall know***
***that I, the LORD, have spoken and will act,"***
***says the LORD.***

**Thanksgiving**

Bless the Lord, O my soul.
O my God, you are very great.

***You are clothed with honor and majesty,***
***wrapped in light as with a garment.***
*(free prayers of thanksgiving)*
You make the winds your messengers,
***fire and flame your ministers. Amen.***

**Song**

Veni Sancte Spiritus (H298)
O breathe on me, O breath of God (SJ46)

**Confession of faith**

Jesus of Nazareth was a man
commended to us by God
***through the powerful acts, wonders, and signs***
***God did through him in our midst—***
***as we ourselves know well.***
This man, according to the declared purpose
and foreknowledge of God,
was handed over, crucified and killed
by the hands of lawless ones.
***Yet God raised him up,***
***releasing him from the birth pangs of death***
***because it was not possible for him***
***to be taken over by it.***
This Jesus God raised up,
and of that we are all witnesses.
***Being therefore lifted high***
***at the right hand of God,***
***having received the promise of the Holy Spirit***
***from the Father,***

***he has poured out this***
***that we both see and hear.***

## Call to discipleship

Let us hold to the standard of sound teaching that we have heard,
***in the faith and love that are in Christ Jesus.***

**Acts 2.29-36**

[Peter said,] "Fellow Israelites, I may say to you confidently of our ancestor David that he both died and was buried, and his tomb is with us to this day. Since he was a prophet, he knew that God had sworn with an oath to him that he would put one of his descendants on his throne. Foreseeing this, David spoke of the resurrection of the Messiah, saying,

'He was not abandoned to Hades,
nor did his flesh experience corruption.'

This Jesus God raised up, and of that all of us are witnesses. Being therefore exalted at the right hand of God, and having received from the Father the promise of the Holy Spirit, he has poured out this that you both see and hear. For David did not ascend into the heavens, but he himself says,

'The Lord said to my Lord,
"Sit at my right hand,
until I make your enemies your footstool."'

Therefore let the entire house of Israel know with certainty that God has made him both Lord and Messiah, this Jesus whom you crucified."

**1 Corinthians 12.3-11**

No one speaking by the Spirit of God ever says "Let Jesus be cursed!" and no one can say "Jesus is Lord" except by the Holy Spirit.

Now there are varieties of gifts, but the same Spirit; and there are varieties of services, but the same Lord; and there are varieties of activities, but it is the same God who activates all of them in everyone. To each is given the manifestation of the Spirit for the common good. To one is given through the Spirit the utterance of wisdom, and to another the utterance of knowledge according to the same Spirit, to another faith by the same Spirit, to another gifts of healing by the one Spirit, to another the working of miracles, to another prophecy, to another the discernment of spirits, to another various kinds of tongues, to another the interpretation of tongues. All these are activated by one and the same Spirit, who allots to each one individually just as the Spirit chooses.

**Silent or spoken reflection on the readings**

**Song**

Low in the grave he lay (H273)
Rejoice, the Lord is King (H288)
There are many gifts (H304)
The risen Christ (SS101)

**Ephesians 2.17-22**

## Call to intercession

Beloved, let us build ourselves up
on our most holy faith,
***and let us pray in the Holy Spirit.***

God of the apostles and prophets, the breath of your Spirit revives dry bones. In your mercy,
***Lord, hear our prayer.***

You bind up the brokenhearted. We pray for ourselves and those dear to us.
*(open prayers)*
In your mercy,
***Lord, hear our prayer.***

Your good news is for the oppressed. We pray for our community and for our neighbors.
*(open prayers)*
In your mercy,
***Lord, hear our prayer.***

To each you give gifts of the Spirit for the common good. We pray for the church in all plac-

es, that we may daily follow in the footsteps of Christ.
*(open prayers)*
In your mercy,
***Lord, hear our prayer.***

You have made Jesus who was crucified both Lord and Messiah. We pray for the world, for those in positions of power and authority.
*(open prayers)*
In your mercy,
***Lord, hear our prayer.***

We offer you other concerns we carry in our hearts.
*(open prayers)*
In your mercy,
***Lord, hear our prayer.***

God of convincing power,
you pour out your Spirit
on all who call on you.
Restore us with the breath
of your holy presence,
that we may see the vision of your shalom
and proclaim your good news to the world.
Through Jesus, who taught us,
we pray for the coming of your reign:

***Our Father …***

**Charge**

Be filled with the Spirit,
as you sing psalms and hymns
and spiritual songs among yourselves,
singing and making melody
to the Lord in your hearts,
giving thanks to God the Father
at all times and for everything
in the name of our Lord Jesus Christ. ***Amen.***

# On the foundation of the apostles and prophets

## PENTECOST THURSDAY EVENING

**Opening sentence**

So then you are no longer strangers and aliens,
but you are citizens with the saints
and also members of the household of God,
***built upon the foundation***
***of the apostles and prophets,***
***with Christ Jesus himself as the cornerstone.***

## Call to praise

Come, bless the Lord,
all you servants of the Lord,
who stand by night in the house of the Lord!
***Lift up your hands to the holy place,***
***and bless the Lord.***

***Glory …***

**Isaiah 61.1-3**

The spirit of the Lord GOD is upon me,
because the LORD has anointed me;
***he has sent me to bring good news to the***
***oppressed,***
***to bind up the brokenhearted,***

to proclaim liberty to the captives,
and release to the prisoners;
***to proclaim the year of the LORD's favor,***
***and the day of vengeance of our God;***
to comfort all who mourn;
to provide for those who mourn in Zion—
***to give them a garland instead of ashes,***
***the oil of gladness instead of mourning,***
***the mantle of praise instead of a faint spirit.***
They will be called oaks of righteousness,
***the planting of the LORD, to display his glory.***

**Thanksgiving**

Lord, how manifold are your works!
The earth is full of your creatures.
***When you give to them, they gather it up;***
***when you open your hand,***
***they are filled with good things.***
*(free prayers of thanksgiving)*
O Lord, may your glory endure forever;
may you rejoice in your works.
***When you send forth your spirit,***
***they are created;***
***and you renew the face of the ground. Amen.***

**Song**

Praise the One who breaks the darkness (SS1)
I'll praise my Maker (H166)
God of the Bible (SJ27, vv. 1–3, 5)
When Jesus worked here on earth (SS38)

## Confession

In goodness and loving kindness, you save us,
***not because of anything we have done,***
***but in mercy,***
***through the water of rebirth and renewal***
***by the Holy Spirit.***
*(silence)*
This Spirit you pour out on us richly, O God,
through Jesus Christ our Savior,
***so that, having been justified by grace,***
***we might become heirs***
***according to the hope of eternal life. Amen.***

# Call to discipleship

God chose us as the first fruits for salvation
through sanctification by the Spirit
and belief in the truth.
***Then let us stand firm***
***and hold fast to the traditions we were taught.***

## John 15.11-15

"I have said these things to you so that my joy may be in you, and that your joy may be complete.

"This is my commandment, that you love one another as I have loved you. No one has greater love than this, to lay down one's life for one's friends. You are my friends if you do what I command you. I do not call you servants any longer, because the servant does not know what the master is doing; but I have called you friends, because I have made known to you everything that I have heard from my Father."

**1 John 3.16-24**

We know love by this, that he laid down his life for us—and we ought to lay down our lives for one another. How does God's love abide in anyone who has the world's goods and sees a brother or sister in need and yet refuses help?

Little children, let us love, not in word or speech, but in truth and action. And by this we will know that we are from the truth and will reassure our hearts before him whenever our hearts condemn us; for God is greater than our hearts, and he knows everything. Beloved, if our hearts do not condemn us, we have boldness before God; and we receive from him whatever we ask, because we obey his commandments and do what pleases him.

And this is his commandment, that we should believe in the name of his Son Jesus Christ and love one another, just as he has commanded us. All who obey his commandments abide in him, and he abides in them. And by this we know that he abides in us, by the Spirit that he has given us.

**Silent or spoken reflection on the readings**

**Song**

Holy Spirit, come to us (SS79)
Where charity and love prevail (H305)
All praise to our redeeming Lord (H21)
Will you let me be your servant (H307)
How can I say (SS117)

**Ephesians 2.17-22**

# Call to intercession

The whole creation has been groaning,
and not only the creation,
***but we ourselves,***
***who have the first fruits of the Spirit,***
***groan inwardly while we wait***
***for the redemption of our bodies.***

God of the apostles and prophets, the breath of your Spirit revives dry bones. In your mercy,
***Lord, hear our prayer.***

You bind up the brokenhearted. We pray for ourselves and those dear to us.
*(open prayers)*

In your mercy,
***Lord, hear our prayer.***

Your good news is for the oppressed. We pray for our community and for our neighbors.
*(open prayers)*
In your mercy,
***Lord, hear our prayer.***

To each you give gifts of the Spirit for the common good. We pray for the church in all places, that we may daily follow in the footsteps of Christ.
*(open prayers)*
In your mercy,
***Lord, hear our prayer.***

You have made Jesus who was crucified both Lord and Messiah. We pray for the world, for those in positions of power and authority.
*(open prayers)*
In your mercy,
***Lord, hear our prayer.***

We offer you other concerns we carry in our hearts.
*(open prayers)*
In your mercy,
***Lord, hear our prayer.***

God of abiding presence,
you lead us by your Spirit

and claim us as your children.
Call us in righteousness,
and renew us in hope and joy,
that we may be messengers of your peace,
fearlessly announcing your salvation.
Through Jesus, who taught us,
we pray for the coming of your reign:

*Our Father ...*

**Benediction**

*May the God of steadfastness*
*and encouragement*
*grant us to live in harmony with one another,*
*in accordance with Christ Jesus,*
*so that together we may with one voice*
*glorify the God and Father*
*of our Lord Jesus Christ. Amen.*

# In him the whole structure is joined

## PENTECOST FRIDAY MORNING

**Opening sentence**

In him the whole structure is joined together
***and grows into a holy temple in the Lord.***

## Call to praise

I will sing to the Lord as long as I live;
***I will sing praise to my God***
***while I have being.***

*Glory …*

**Psalm 68.18-21 [17-20]**

The chariots of God are thousands upon thousands.
The Lord has come from Sinai to the holy place.
***You have gone up on high; you have taken captives,***
***receiving people in tribute, O God,***
***even those who rebel, into your dwelling, O LORD.***

May the Lord be blessed day after day.
God our savior bears our burdens;
***this God of ours is a God who saves.***
***The LORD our God holds the keys of death.***

**Thanksgiving**

Bless the Lord, O my soul.
O my God, you are very great.
***You are clothed with honor and majesty,***
***wrapped in light as with a garment.***
*(free prayers of thanksgiving)*
You make the winds your messengers,
***fire and flame your ministers. Amen.***

**Song**

Praise, praise, praise the Lord! (SJ11)
O worship the King (H66)
Who is so great a God (H62)
Blessing and honor (SS109)

**Confession of faith**

Jesus of Nazareth was a man
commended to us by God
***through the powerful acts, wonders, and signs***
***God did through him in our midst—***
***as we ourselves know well.***
This man, according to the declared purpose
and foreknowledge of God,
was handed over, crucified and killed
by the hands of lawless ones.
***Yet God raised him up,***
***releasing him from the birth pangs of death***
***because it was not possible for him***
***to be taken over by it.***

This Jesus God raised up,
and of that we are all witnesses.
***Being therefore lifted high***
***at the right hand of God,***
***having received the promise of the Holy Spirit***
***from the Father,***
***he has poured out this***
***that we both see and hear.***

## Call to discipleship

Let us hold to the standard of sound teaching
that we have heard,
***in the faith and love that are in Christ Jesus.***

**Acts 2.37-41**

Now when they heard this, [the people] were cut to the heart and said to Peter and to the other apostles, "Brothers, what should we do?" Peter said to them, "Repent, and be baptized every one of you in the name of Jesus Christ so that your sins may be forgiven; and you will receive the gift of the Holy Spirit. For the promise is for you, for your children, and for all who are far away, everyone whom the Lord our God calls to him." And he testified with many other arguments and exhorted them, saying, "Save yourselves from this corrupt generation." So those who welcomed his message were baptized, and that day about three thousand persons were added.

**Ephesians 4.1-13**

I therefore, the prisoner in the Lord, beg you to lead a life worthy of the calling to which you have been called, with all humility and gentleness, with patience, bearing with one another in love, making every effort to maintain the unity of the Spirit in the bond of peace. There is one body and one Spirit, just as you were called to the one hope of your calling, one Lord, one faith, one baptism, one God and Father of all, who is above all and through all and in all.

But each of us was given grace according to the measure of Christ's gift. Therefore it is said,

> "When he ascended on high he made captivity itself a captive;
> he gave gifts to his people."

(When it says, "He ascended," what does it mean but that he had also descended into the lower parts of the earth? He who descended is the same one who ascended far above all the heavens, so that he might fill all things.) The gifts he gave were that some would be apostles, some prophets, some evangelists, some pastors and teachers, to equip the saints for the work of ministry, for building up the body of Christ, until all of us come to the unity of the faith and of the knowledge of the Son of God, to maturity, to the measure of the full stature of Christ.

**Silent or spoken reflection on the readings**

**Song**

Som'landela (We will follow) (SS40)
One is the body (SJ72)
I believe in you, Lord Jesus (H440)
I sing with exultation (H438)

**Ephesians 2.17-22**

## Call to intercession

Beloved, let us build ourselves up
on our most holy faith,
***and let us pray in the Holy Spirit.***

God our savior, you bear our burdens. In your mercy,
***Lord, hear our prayer.***

Your spirit of fervor sustains us. We pray for ourselves and those dear to us.
*(open prayers)*
In your mercy,
***Lord, hear our prayer.***

You love truth and integrity. We pray for our community and for our neighbors.
*(open prayers)*
In your mercy,
***Lord, hear our prayer.***

You equip the saints for the work of ministry. We pray for the church in all places, that we may speak boldly for Christ.
*(open prayers)*
In your mercy,
***Lord, hear our prayer.***

You are above all and through all and in all. We pray for the world, for all who do justice and love mercy.
*(open prayers)*
In your mercy,
***Lord, hear our prayer.***

We offer you other concerns we carry in our hearts.
*(open prayers)*
In your mercy,
***Lord, hear our prayer.***

God of convincing power,
you pour out your Spirit
on all who call on you.
Restore us with the breath
of your holy presence,
that we may see the vision of your shalom

and proclaim your good news to the world.
Through Jesus, who taught us,
we pray for the coming of your reign:

***Our Father …***

**Charge**

Lead a life worthy of the calling
to which you have been called,
with all humility and gentleness,
with patience,
bearing with one another in love,
making every effort
to maintain the unity of the Spirit
in the bond of peace. ***Amen.***

# In him the whole structure is joined

## PENTECOST FRIDAY EVENING

**Opening sentence**

In him the whole structure is joined together
***and grows into a holy temple in the Lord.***

## Call to praise

Come, bless the Lord,
all you servants of the Lord,
who stand by night in the house of the Lord!
***Lift up your hands to the holy place,***
***and bless the Lord.***

***Glory …***

**Psalm 51.8-15 [6-13]**

Indeed you love truth in the heart;
then in the secret of my heart teach me
wisdom.
***O purify me, then I shall be clean;***
***O wash me, I shall be whiter than snow.***

Make me hear rejoicing and gladness
that the bones you have crushed may revive.
***From my sins turn away your face***
***and blot out all my guilt.***

A pure heart create for me, O God,
put a steadfast spirit within me.
***Do not cast me away from your presence,***
***nor deprive me of your holy spirit.***

Give me again the joy of your help;
with a spirit of fervor sustain me,
***that I may teach transgressors your ways***
***and sinners may return to you.***

**Thanksgiving**

Lord, how manifold are your works!
The earth is full of your creatures.
***When you give to them, they gather it up;***
***when you open your hand,***
***they are filled with good things.***
*(free prayers of thanksgiving)*
O Lord, may your glory endure forever;
may you rejoice in your works.
***When you send forth your spirit,***
***they are created;***
***and you renew the face of the ground. Amen.***

**Song**

Take, O take me as I am (SJ81)
Create in me a clean heart (SS62)
Open, Lord, my inward ear (H140)
When in the hour of deepest need (H131)

**Confession**

In goodness and loving kindness, you save us,
***not because of anything we have done,***
***but in mercy,***
***through the water of rebirth and renewal***
***by the Holy Spirit.***
*(silence)*
This Spirit you pour out on us richly, O God,
through Jesus Christ our Savior,
***so that, having been justified by grace,***
***we might become heirs***
***according to the hope of eternal life. Amen.***

## Call to discipleship

God chose us as the first fruits for salvation
through sanctification by the Spirit
and belief in the truth.
***Then let us stand firm***
***and hold fast to the traditions we were taught.***

**John 15.26-27**

"When the Advocate comes, whom I will send to you from the Father, the Spirit of truth who comes from the Father, he will testify on my behalf. You also are to testify because you have been with me from the beginning."

**Ephesians 4.14-21**

We must no longer be children, tossed to and fro and blown about by every wind of doctrine, by people's trickery, by their craftiness in deceitful scheming. But speaking the truth in love, we must grow up in every way into him who is the head, into Christ, from whom the whole body, joined and knit together by every ligament with which it is equipped, as each part is working properly, promotes the body's growth in building itself up in love.

Now this I affirm and insist on in the Lord: you must no longer live as the Gentiles live, in the futility of their minds. They are darkened in their understanding, alienated from the life of God because of their ignorance and hardness of heart. They have lost all sensitivity and have abandoned themselves to licentiousness, greedy to practice every kind of impurity. That is not the way you learned Christ! For surely you have heard about him and were taught in him, as truth is in Jesus.

**Silent or spoken reflection on the readings**

**Song**

Comme un souffle fragile (Like a tender breath, stirring) (SS106)
Ask ye what great thing I know (H337)

I know not why God's wondrous (H338)
Fire of God, undying Flame (H129, SS103)

**Ephesians 2.17-22**

## Call to intercession

The whole creation has been groaning,
and not only the creation,
***but we ourselves,***
***who have the first fruits of the Spirit,***
***groan inwardly while we wait***
***for the redemption of our bodies.***

God our savior, you bear our burdens. In your mercy,
***Lord, hear our prayer.***

Your spirit of fervor sustains us. We pray for ourselves and those dear to us.
*(open prayers)*
In your mercy,
***Lord, hear our prayer.***

You love truth and integrity. We pray for our community and for our neighbors.
*(open prayers)*
In your mercy,
***Lord, hear our prayer.***

You equip the saints for the work of ministry. We pray for the church in all places, that we may speak boldly for Christ.
*(open prayers)*
In your mercy,
***Lord, hear our prayer.***

You are above all and through all and in all. We pray for the world, for all who do justice and love mercy.
*(open prayers)*
In your mercy,
***Lord, hear our prayer.***

We offer you other concerns we carry in our hearts.
*(open prayers)*
In your mercy,
***Lord, hear our prayer.***

God of abiding presence,
you lead us by your Spirit
and claim us as your children.
Call us in righteousness,
and renew us in hope and joy,
that we may be messengers of your peace,
fearlessly announcing your salvation.
Through Jesus, who taught us,
we pray for the coming of your reign:

***Our Father …***

**Closing affirmation**

*Now the Lord is the Spirit,*
*and where the Spirit of the Lord is,*
*there is freedom.*
*And all of us, with unveiled faces,*
*seeing the glory of the Lord*
*as though reflected in a mirror,*
*are being transformed into the same image*
*from one degree of glory to another;*
*for this comes from the Lord, the Spirit. Amen.*

# A dwelling place for God

## PENTECOST SATURDAY MORNING

**Opening sentence**

In him the whole structure is joined together
and grows into a holy temple in the Lord;
***in whom you also are built together spiritually***
***into a dwelling place for God.***

## Call to praise

I will sing to the Lord as long as I live;
***I will sing praise to my God***
***while I have being.***

***Glory ...***

**Isaiah 55.1-6**

Ho, everyone who thirsts,
come to the waters;
and you that have no money,
come, buy and eat!
***Come, buy wine and milk***
***without money and without price.***
Why do you spend your money for that which
is not bread,
and your labor for that which does not satisfy?
***Listen carefully to me, and eat what is good,***
***and delight yourselves in rich food.***

Incline your ear, and come to me;
listen, so that you may live.
***I will make with you an everlasting covenant,***
***my steadfast, sure love for David.***
See, I made him a witness to the peoples,
a leader and commander for the peoples.
***See, you shall call nations that you do not know,***
***and nations that do not know you shall run to you,***
because of the LORD your God, the Holy One of Israel,
for he has glorified you.

***Seek the LORD while he may be found,***
***call upon him while he is near.***

**Thanksgiving**

Bless the Lord, O my soul.
O my God, you are very great.
***You are clothed with honor and majesty,***
***wrapped in light as with a garment.***
*(free prayers of thanksgiving)*
You make the winds your messengers,
***fire and flame your ministers. Amen.***

**Song**

Taste and see (SJ86)
Come to me, come to us (SS60)
Sing praise to God who reigns (H59)

Bless'd be the God of Israel (H174)
There is a well (Un pozo hay) (SS64)

**Confession of faith**

Jesus of Nazareth was a man
commended to us by God
***through the powerful acts, wonders, and signs***
***God did through him in our midst—***
***as we ourselves know well.***
This man, according to the declared purpose
and foreknowledge of God,
was handed over, crucified and killed
by the hands of lawless ones.
***Yet God raised him up,***
***releasing him from the birth pangs of death***
***because it was not possible for him***
***to be taken over by it.***
This Jesus God raised up,
and of that we are all witnesses.
***Being therefore lifted high***
***at the right hand of God,***
***having received the promise of the Holy Spirit***
***from the Father,***
***he has poured out this***
***that we both see and hear.***

## Call to discipleship

Let us hold to the standard of sound teaching that we have heard,
***in the faith and love that are in Christ Jesus.***

**Acts 2.42-47**

[The believers] devoted themselves to the apostles' teaching and fellowship, to the breaking of bread and the prayers.

Awe came upon everyone, because many wonders and signs were being done by the apostles. All who believed were together and had all things in common; they would sell their possessions and goods and distribute the proceeds to all, as any had need. Day by day, as they spent much time together in the temple, they broke bread at home and ate their food with glad and generous hearts, praising God and having the goodwill of all the people. And day by day the Lord added to their number those who were being saved.

**Romans 15.25-33**

At present, however, I am going to Jerusalem in a ministry to the saints; for Macedonia and Achaia have been pleased to share their resources with the poor among the saints at Jerusalem. They were pleased to do this, and indeed they owe it to them; for if the Gentiles have come to share in their spiritual blessings, they ought also to be of service to them in material things. So, when I have completed this, and have delivered to them what has been collected, I will set out by way of you to Spain; and I know that when I come to you, I will come in the fullness of the blessing of Christ.

I appeal to you, brothers and sisters, by our Lord Jesus Christ and by the love of the Spirit, to join me in earnest prayer to God on my behalf, that I may be rescued from the unbelievers in Judea, and that my ministry to Jerusalem may be acceptable to the saints, so that by God's will I may come to you with joy and be refreshed in your company. The God of peace be with all of you. Amen.

**Silent or spoken reflection on the readings**

**Song**

Prepare a room for me (SS76)
Help us to help each other (H362)
We give thee but thine own (H384)
Here is the bread (SS77)
Fill now our life, O Lord (SS107)

**Ephesians 2.17-22**

## Call to intercession

Beloved, let us build ourselves up
on our most holy faith,
***and let us pray in the Holy Spirit.***

Awe-inspiring God, your ways are higher than our ways, yet you invite us to come to you. In your mercy,
***Lord, hear our prayer.***

Your love is steadfast and sure. We pray for ourselves and those dear to us.
*(open prayers)*
In your mercy,
***Lord, hear our prayer.***

You call all to seek you while you may be found. We pray for our community and for our neighbors.
*(open prayers)*
In your mercy,
***Lord, hear our prayer.***

You give us sisters and brothers whose company refreshes our spirits. We pray for the church in all places, that we may be faithful in solidarity across generations and geography.
*(open prayers)*
In your mercy,
***Lord, hear our prayer.***

Your Spirit breaks walls of division and inspires us to share resources with those in need. We pray for the world, for our enemies and for those who are in conflict.
*(open prayers)*
In your mercy,
***Lord, hear our prayer.***

We offer you other concerns we carry in our hearts.
*(open prayers)*
In your mercy,
***Lord, hear our prayer.***

God of convincing power,
you pour out your Spirit
on all who call on you.
Restore us with the breath
of your holy presence,
that we may see the vision of your shalom
and proclaim your good news to the world.
Through Jesus, who taught us,
we pray for the coming of your reign:

***Our Father ...***

## Charge

See that none of you repays evil for evil,
but always seek to do good
to one another and to all.
Rejoice always, pray without ceasing,
give thanks in all circumstances;

for this is the will of God
in Christ Jesus for you.
Do not quench the Spirit. ***Amen.***

# A dwelling place for God

## PENTECOST SATURDAY EVENING

**Opening sentence**

In him the whole structure is joined together
and grows into a holy temple in the Lord;
***in whom you also are built together spiritually***
***into a dwelling place for God.***

## Call to praise

Come, bless the Lord,
all you servants of the Lord,
who stand by night in the house of the Lord!
***Lift up your hands to the holy place,***
***and bless the Lord.***

*Glory ...*

**Isaiah 55.6-13**

Seek the LORD while he may be found,
call upon him while he is near;
***let the wicked forsake their way,***
***and the unrighteous their thoughts;***
let them return to the LORD, that he may have mercy on them,
***and to our God, for he will abundantly pardon.***

For my thoughts are not your thoughts,
nor are your ways my ways, says the LORD.
***For as the heavens are higher than the earth,***
***so are my ways higher than your ways***
***and my thoughts than your thoughts.***

For as the rain and the snow come down from heaven,
and do not return there until they have watered the earth,
***making it bring forth and sprout,***
***giving seed to the sower and bread to the eater,***
so shall my word be that goes out from my mouth;
it shall not return to me empty,
***but it shall accomplish that which I purpose,***
***and succeed in the thing for which I sent it.***

For you shall go out in joy,
and be led back in peace;
***the mountains and the hills before you***
***shall burst into song,***
***and all the trees of the field shall clap their hands.***
Instead of the thorn shall come up the cypress;
instead of the brier shall come up the myrtle;
***and it shall be to the LORD for a memorial,***
***for an everlasting sign that shall not be cut off.***

**Thanksgiving**

Lord, how manifold are your works!
The earth is full of your creatures.
***When you give to them, they gather it up;***
***when you open your hand,***
***they are filled with good things.***
*(free prayers of thanksgiving)*
O Lord, may your glory endure forever;
may you rejoice in your works.
***When you send forth your spirit,***
***they are created;***
***and you renew the face of the ground. Amen.***

**Song**

Let the heavens be glad (H187)
Let all creation dance (SS122)
Joyful, joyful, we adore thee (H71)
O bless the Lord, my soul (H80)
Heri ni jina (Blessed be the name) (SS75)

**Confession**

In goodness and loving kindness, you save us,
***not because of anything we have done,***
***but in mercy,***
***through the water of rebirth and renewal***
***by the Holy Spirit.***
*(silence)*
This Spirit you pour out on us richly, O God,
through Jesus Christ our Savior,

***so that, having been justified by grace,***
***we might become heirs***
***according to the hope of eternal life. Amen.***

## Call to discipleship

God chose us as the first fruits for salvation
through sanctification by the Spirit
and belief in the truth.
***Then let us stand firm***
***and hold fast to the traditions we were taught.***

**John 16.13-14**

"When the Spirit of truth comes, he will guide you into all the truth; for he will not speak on his own, but will speak whatever he hears, and he will declare to you the things that are to come. He will glorify me, because he will take what is mine and declare it to you."

**Ephesians 1.11-17**

In Christ we have also obtained an inheritance, having been destined according to the purpose of him who accomplishes all things according to his counsel and will, so that we, who were the first to set our hope on Christ, might live for the praise of his glory. In him you also, when you had heard the word of truth, the gospel of your salvation, and had believed in him, were marked with the seal of the promised Holy Spirit; this is the pledge of our inheritance toward redemption as God's own people, to the praise of his glory.

I have heard of your faith in the Lord Jesus and your love toward all the saints, and for this reason I do not cease to give thanks for you as I remember you in my prayers. I pray that the God of our Lord Jesus Christ, the Father of glory, may give you a spirit of wisdom and revelation as you come to know him.

**Silent or spoken reflection on the readings**

**Song**

Spirit of the living God (H349)
Come, divine Interpreter (H302)
O Breath of Life (SJ35)
We know that Christ is raised (H443)
Sing with all the saints in glory (SS92)

**Ephesians 2.17-22**

## Call to intercession

The whole creation has been groaning,
and not only the creation,
***but we ourselves,***
***who have the first fruits of the Spirit,***
***groan inwardly while we wait***
***for the redemption of our bodies.***

Awe-inspiring God, your ways are higher than our ways, yet you invite us to come to you. In your mercy,
***Lord, hear our prayer.***

Your love is steadfast and sure. We pray for ourselves and those dear to us.
*(open prayers)*
In your mercy,
***Lord, hear our prayer.***

You call all to seek you while you may be found. We pray for our community and for our neighbors.
*(open prayers)*
In your mercy,
***Lord, hear our prayer.***

You give us sisters and brothers whose company refreshes our spirits. We pray for the church in all places, that we may be faithful in solidarity across generations and geography.
*(open prayers)*
In your mercy,
***Lord, hear our prayer.***

Your Spirit breaks walls of division and inspires us to share resources with those in need. We pray for the world, for our enemies and for those who are in conflict.
*(open prayers)*

In your mercy,
***Lord, hear our prayer.***

We offer you other concerns we carry in our hearts.
*(open prayers)*
In your mercy,
***Lord, hear our prayer.***

God of abiding presence,
you lead us by your Spirit
and claim us as your children.
Call us in righteousness,
and renew us in hope and joy,
that we may be messengers of your peace,
fearlessly announcing your salvation.
Through Jesus, who taught us,
we pray for the coming of your reign:

***Our Father …***

**Closing affirmation**

***Jesus Christ was not "Yes and No";***
***but in him it is always "Yes."***
***For in him***
***every one of God's promises is a "Yes."***
***For this reason***
***it is through him that we say the "Amen,"***
***to the glory of God.***
***But it is God who establishes us in Christ***
***and has anointed us, by putting his seal on us***

*and giving us his Spirit in our hearts*
*as a first installment. Amen.*

# Pentecost 2

# Introduction to the Pentecost prayers: Week 2

In a thoroughly Anabaptist enthusiasm for the importance of the Spirit in the life of the church, we have extended our celebration of Pentecost beyond a single day, not just to a week's services, but to two. As you pray during this season, we suggest alternating weeks 1 and 2, for perhaps a total of four weeks, before returning to prayers for ordinary time.

Pentecost is the Greek name given to the Jewish Feast of Weeks; it was celebrated fifty days after Passover and was initially the feast at which the first-fruits of the grain harvest were presented (Dt 16.9). The scriptures selected for this second week of Pentecost season services connect with this Old Testament celebration, a time of great rejoicing and gratitude for God's gifts to the people. In the mornings we linger with ancient rhythms of work and worship, as we read from the Pentateuch God's directions for observing the first-fruits festival. In the evenings, the readings from 2 Corinthians 8–9 feature Paul's appeal to Corinthian believers to emulate God's grace and generosity by contributing from their abundance to the relief gift for the poor in Jerusalem.

In the Jewish sense, God's abundance, God's providential generosity in liberating Israel and claiming a people from the desert stragglers, is synthesized most profoundly in God's giving of the Law. Torah as pure grace was the historical event that came to be commemorated on Pentecost. The Psalm selections for both morning and evening prayers celebrate this gift of God extended now also to us Gentiles.

It was during their observance of this Jewish festival that the Holy Spirit descended on those gathered in Jerusalem. Thus, Christian celebration of Pentecost marks the birth of the church fifty days after Jesus' resurrection. Pentecost becomes a rich and multi-layered celebration of God's goodness: the first-fruits of the harvest and our delight in God's bountiful earth; the graceful gifts of freedom and peoplehood embodied in law; the flame of the Spirit unlocking tongues and minds and hearts, giving wings to feet.

The Acts readings for both morning and evening prayers describe these dynamic days of the Spirit's work in the early church, stirring our imaginations and inviting our own boldness for Christ. The title lines, opening sentences, and canticle for this week's services come from 1 Thessalonians 5.16-24, surely one of the most exuberant texts in our biblical canon and a firm reminder that above all the Spirit of Christ is life-giving. The work of the Spirit we celebrate in this season is paradoxical, holding together

Spirit and letter, law and gospel, the inner life of the spirit and the outer life of discipleship.

# Rejoice always

## PENTECOST 2 SUNDAY MORNING

**Opening sentence**

Rejoice always,
***pray without ceasing.***

## Call to praise

Rejoice in the Lord always;
***again I will say, Rejoice.***

*Glory …*

**Psalm 1**

Happy indeed are those
who follow not the counsel of the wicked,
nor linger in the way of sinners
***nor sit in the company of scorners,***
***but whose delight is in the law of the LORD***
***and who ponder God's law day and night.***

They are like a tree that is planted
beside the flowing waters,
that yields its fruit in due season
***and whose leaves shall never fade;***
***and all that they do shall prosper.***
***Not so are the wicked, not so!***

For they like winnowed chaff
shall be driven away by the wind.
When the wicked are judged they shall not stand,
***nor find room among those who are just;***
***for the LORD guards the way of the just***
***but the way of the wicked leads to doom.***

**Thanksgiving**

O God, we give thanks to you
at all times and for everything
***in the name of our Lord Jesus Christ.***
*(free prayers of thanksgiving)*
We sing psalms and hymns
and spiritual songs,
***making melody to you in our hearts, O Lord.***
***Amen.***

**Song**

I long for your commandments (H543)
How bless'd are they (H525)
I saw a tree by the riverside (SS116)

**Confession of faith**

Jesus of Nazareth was a man
commended to us by God
***through the powerful acts, wonders, and signs***
***God did through him in our midst—***
***as we ourselves know well.***
This man, according to the declared purpose
and foreknowledge of God,

was handed over, crucified and killed
by the hands of lawless ones.
***Yet God raised him up,***
***releasing him from the birth pangs of death***
***because it was not possible for him***
***to be taken over by it.***
This Jesus God raised up,
and of that we are all witnesses.
***Being therefore lifted high***
***at the right hand of God,***
***having received the promise of the Holy Spirit***
***from the Father,***
***he has poured out this***
***that we both see and hear.***

## Call to discipleship

Let us guard the good treasure entrusted to us,
***with the help of the Holy Spirit living in us.***

**Deuteronomy 16.9-12**

You shall count seven weeks; begin to count the seven weeks from the time the sickle is first put to the standing grain. Then you shall keep the festival of weeks for the LORD your God, contributing a freewill offering in proportion to the blessing that you have received from the LORD your God. Rejoice before the LORD your God—you and your sons and your daughters, your male and female slaves, the

Levites resident in your towns, as well as the strangers, the orphans, and the widows who are among you—at the place that the LORD your God will choose as a dwelling for his name. Remember that you were a slave in Egypt, and diligently observe these statutes.

**Acts 2.29-37**

"Fellow Israelites, I [Peter] may say to you confidently of our ancestor David that he both died and was buried, and his tomb is with us to this day. Since he was a prophet, he knew that God had sworn with an oath to him that he would put one of his descendants on his throne. Foreseeing this, David spoke of the resurrection of the Messiah, saying,

'He was not abandoned to Hades,
nor did his flesh experience corruption.'

This Jesus God raised up, and of that all of us are witnesses. Being therefore exalted at the right hand of God, and having received from the Father the promise of the Holy Spirit, he has poured out this that you both see and hear. For David did not ascend into the heavens, but he himself says,

'The Lord said to my Lord,
"Sit at my right hand,
until I make your enemies your footstool."'

Therefore let the entire house of Israel know with certainty that God has made him both

Lord and Messiah, this Jesus whom you crucified."

Now when they heard this, they were cut to the heart and said to Peter and to the other apostles, "Brothers, what should we do?"

**Silent or spoken reflection on the readings**

**Song**

Look, you saints (H286)
As saints of old (H386)
Lord of all good (SJ60)

**1 Thessalonians 5.16-24**

## Call to intercession

Beloved,
let us keep ourselves in the love of God,
***looking forward to the mercy***
***of our Lord Jesus Christ that leads to life.***

God of bountiful harvest, your Spirit pours out gifts on your people. In your mercy,
***Lord, hear our prayer.***

Your grace can bring joy even in the midst of affliction. We pray for ourselves and those dear to us.
*(open prayers)*

In your mercy,
***Lord, hear our prayer.***

Your desire is that we provide for those in need. We pray for our community and for our neighbors.
*(open prayers)*
In your mercy,
***Lord, hear our prayer.***

You make our footsteps firm to walk in your paths. We pray for the church in all places, that we may be one.
*(open prayers)*
In your mercy,
***Lord, hear our prayer.***

You guard the ways of the just. We pray for the world, that your reign may come and your will be done on earth.
*(open prayers)*
In your mercy,
***Lord, hear our prayer.***

We offer you other concerns we carry in our hearts.
*(open prayers)*
In your mercy,
***Lord, hear our prayer.***

God of every gift,
you provide for us, body and soul,

through the bounty of creation
and the gift of your own Holy Spirit.
Hold us fast to your ways,
so that our delight will be
to join your work this day.
In the example of Jesus, who taught us,
we pray:

***Our Father …***

**Charge**

And Jesus came and said to them,
"All authority in heaven and on earth
has been given to me.
Go therefore and make disciples of all nations,
baptizing them in the name of the Father
and of the Son and of the Holy Spirit,
and teaching them to obey
everything that I have commanded you.
And remember, I am with you always,
to the end of the age." ***Amen.***

# Pray without ceasing

## PENTECOST 2 SUNDAY EVENING

**Opening sentence**

Rejoice always,
***pray without ceasing.***

## Call to praise

What should I do then?
I will pray with the spirit,
but I will pray with the mind also.
***I will sing praise with the spirit,***
***but I will sing praise with the mind also.***

*Glory …*

**Psalm 119.1-8**

They are happy whose life is blameless,
who follow God's law!
***They are happy who do God's will,***
***seeking God with all their hearts,***
who never do anything evil
but walk in God's ways.
***You have laid down your precepts***
***to be obeyed with care.***
May my footsteps be firm
to obey your statutes.

***Then I shall not be put to shame***
***as I heed your commands.***
I will thank you with an upright heart
as I learn your decrees.
***I will obey your statutes;***
***do not forsake me.***

**Thanksgiving**

O God, you provide us with every good gift;
we have ample means to meet our need
***and enough to share abundantly***
***in every good work.***
*(free prayers of thanksgiving)*
You lavish your gifts on those in need;
***your goodness stands fast forever. Amen.***

**Song**

I long for your commandments (H543)
The God of Abraham praise (H162)
Come, divine Interpreter (H302)
Lead me, Lord (H538)

**Confession**

O God, clothe us with compassion,
kindness, humility, patience.
***Enfold us in love,***
***which binds everything together in harmony.***
*(silence)*
You have forgiven us; may we also forgive.
***And may Christ's peace rule in our hearts.***
***Amen.***

## Call to discipleship

Friends, let us not love with words
but with actions and in truth.
***This is how we know***
***that Jesus Christ lives in us,***
***by the Spirit he gave us.***

**Acts 6.1-6**

Now during those days, when the disciples were increasing in number, the Hellenists complained against the Hebrews because their widows were being neglected in the daily distribution of food. And the twelve called together the whole community of the disciples and said, "It is not right that we should neglect the word of God in order to wait on tables. Therefore, friends, select from among yourselves seven men of good standing, full of the Spirit and of wisdom, whom we may appoint to this task, while we, for our part, will devote ourselves to prayer and to serving the word." What they said pleased the whole community, and they chose Stephen, a man full of faith and the Holy Spirit, together with Philip, Prochorus, Nicanor, Timon, Parmenas, and Nicolaus, a proselyte of Antioch. They had these men stand before the apostles, who prayed and laid their hands on them.

**2 Corinthians 8.1-6**

We want you to know, brothers and sisters, about the grace of God that has been granted to the churches of Macedonia; for during a severe ordeal of affliction, their abundant joy and their extreme poverty have overflowed in a wealth of generosity on their part. For, as I can testify, they voluntarily gave according to their means, and even beyond their means, begging us earnestly for the privilege of sharing in this ministry to the saints—and this, not merely as we expected; they gave themselves first to the Lord and, by the will of God, to us, so that we might urge Titus that, as he had already made a beginning, so he should also complete this generous undertaking among you.

**Silent or spoken reflection on the readings**

**Song**

We give thee but thine own (H384)
How good a thing it is (H310)
As tranquil streams (SJ51)
Lord of all good (SJ60)

**1 Thessalonians 5.16-24**

## Call to intercession

God, who searches the heart,
knows what is the mind of the Spirit,
***because the Spirit intercedes for the saints according to the will of God.***

God of bountiful harvest, your Spirit pours out gifts on your people. In your mercy,
***Lord, hear our prayer.***

Your grace can bring joy even in the midst of affliction. We pray for ourselves and those dear to us.
*(open prayers)*
In your mercy,
***Lord, hear our prayer.***

Your desire is that we provide for those in need. We pray for our community and for our neighbors.
*(open prayers)*
In your mercy,
***Lord, hear our prayer.***

You make our footsteps firm to walk in your paths. We pray for the church in all places, that we may be one.
*(open prayers)*
In your mercy,
***Lord, hear our prayer.***

You guard the ways of the just. We pray for the world, that your reign may come and your will be done on earth.
*(open prayers)*
In your mercy,
***Lord, hear our prayer.***

We offer you other concerns we carry in our hearts.
*(open prayers)*
In your mercy,
***Lord, hear our prayer.***

Extravagant God,
you do not hold back anything,
but pour out your Spirit
for the sake of your creation.
Transform our stony hearts
so that our generosity toward those in need
will match your own.
In the company of Jesus, who taught us,
we pray:

***Our Father …***

**Benediction**

***May the God of peace sanctify us entirely;***
***and may our spirit and soul and body***
***be kept sound and blameless***
***at the coming of our Lord Jesus Christ.***
***The one who calls us is faithful***
***and will do this. Amen.***

# Give thanks in all circumstances

## PENTECOST 2 MONDAY MORNING

**Opening sentence**

Rejoice always, pray without ceasing,
***give thanks in all circumstances;***
***for this is the will of God***
***in Christ Jesus for you.***

## Call to praise

Rejoice in the Lord always;
***again I will say, Rejoice.***

*Glory …*

**Psalm 119.9-16**

How shall the young remain sinless?
By obeying your word.
***I have sought you with all my heart;***
***let me not stray from your commands.***
I treasure your promise in my heart
lest I sin against you.
***Blessed are you, O LORD;***
***teach me your statutes.***
With my tongue I have recounted
the decrees of your lips.
***I rejoiced to do your will***
***as though all riches were mine.***

I will ponder all your precepts
and consider your paths.
***I take delight in your statutes;***
***I will not forget your word.***

**Thanksgiving**

O God, we give thanks to you
at all times and for everything
***in the name of our Lord Jesus Christ.***
*(free prayers of thanksgiving)*
We sing psalms and hymns
and spiritual songs,
***making melody to you in our hearts, O Lord.***
***Amen.***

**Song**

I long for your commandments (H543)
Rejoice, rejoice in God (H313)
Lamp of our feet (H312)

**Confession of faith**

Jesus of Nazareth was a man
commended to us by God
***through the powerful acts, wonders, and signs***
***God did through him in our midst—***
***as we ourselves know well.***
This man, according to the declared purpose
and foreknowledge of God,
was handed over, crucified and killed
by the hands of lawless ones.

*Yet God raised him up,*
*releasing him from the birth pangs of death*
*because it was not possible for him*
*to be taken over by it.*
This Jesus God raised up,
and of that we are all witnesses.
*Being therefore lifted high*
*at the right hand of God,*
*having received the promise of the Holy Spirit*
*from the Father,*
*he has poured out this*
*that we both see and hear.*

## Call to discipleship

Let us guard the good treasure entrusted to us,
***with the help of the Holy Spirit living in us.***

**Exodus 34.21-26**

Six days you shall work, but on the seventh day you shall rest; even in plowing time and in harvest time you shall rest. You shall observe the festival of weeks, the first fruits of wheat harvest, and the festival of ingathering at the turn of the year. Three times in the year all your males shall appear before the LORD God, the God of Israel. For I will cast out nations before you, and enlarge your borders; no one shall covet your land when you go up to appear before the LORD your God three times in the year.

You shall not offer the blood of my sacrifice with leaven, and the sacrifice of the festival of the passover shall not be left until the morning.

The best of the first fruits of your ground you shall bring to the house of the LORD your God.

**Acts 9.10-20**

Now there was a disciple in Damascus named Ananias. The Lord said to him in a vision, "Ananias." He answered, "Here I am, Lord." The Lord said to him, "Get up and go to the street called Straight, and at the house of Judas look for a man of Tarsus named Saul. At this moment he is praying, and he has seen in a vision a man named Ananias come in and lay his hands on him so that he might regain his sight." But Ananias answered, "Lord, I have heard from many about this man, how much evil he has done to your saints in Jerusalem; and here he has authority from the chief priests to bind all who invoke your name." But the Lord said to him, "Go, for he is an instrument whom I have chosen to bring my name before Gentiles and kings and before the people of Israel; I myself will show him how much he must suffer for the sake of my name."

So Ananias went and entered the house. He laid his hands on Saul and said, "Brother Saul, the Lord Jesus, who appeared to you on your way here, has sent me so that you may regain your sight and be filled with the Holy Spirit." And immediately something like scales fell from his eyes, and his sight was restored. Then he got up and was baptized, and after taking some food, he regained his strength.

For several days he was with the disciples in Damascus, and immediately he began to proclaim Jesus in the synagogues, saying, "He is the Son of God."

**Silent or spoken reflection on the readings**

**Song**

As saints of old (H386)
Take my life (H389)
'Tis not with eyes of flesh we see (H571)

**1 Thessalonians 5.16-24**

## Call to intercession

Beloved,
let us keep ourselves in the love of God,
***looking forward to the mercy***
***of our Lord Jesus Christ that leads to life.***

God of grace, you have given us your law to lead us into life. In your mercy,
***Lord, hear our prayer.***

You promise us rebirth and renewal. We pray for ourselves and those dear to us.
*(open prayers)*
In your mercy,
***Lord, hear our prayer.***

You invite us to give generously to those in need. We pray for our community and for our neighbors.
*(open prayers)*
In your mercy,
***Lord, hear our prayer.***

You became poor so that we may be rich. We pray for the church in all places, that we may know the freedom of life in the Spirit.
*(open prayers)*
In your mercy,
***Lord, hear our prayer.***

Your law guides us in our pilgrimage on earth. We pray for the world and for all who care for creation.
*(open prayers)*
In your mercy,
***Lord, hear our prayer.***

We offer you other concerns we carry in our hearts.
*(open prayers)*
In your mercy,
***Lord, hear our prayer.***

God of every gift,
you provide for us, body and soul,
through the bounty of creation
and the gift of your own Holy Spirit.
Hold us fast to your ways,
so that our delight will be
to join your work this day.
In the example of Jesus, who taught us,
we pray:

***Our Father ...***

**Charge**

Let the peace of Christ rule in your hearts,
to which indeed you were called
in the one body.
And be thankful.
Let the word of Christ dwell in you richly;
And whatever you do, in word or deed,
do everything in the name of the Lord Jesus,
giving thanks to God the Father through him.
***Amen.***

# This is the will of God in Christ Jesus

## PENTECOST 2 MONDAY EVENING

**Opening sentence**

Rejoice always, pray without ceasing,
*give thanks in all circumstances;*
*for this is the will of God*
*in Christ Jesus for you.*

## Call to praise

What should I do then?
I will pray with the spirit,
but I will pray with the mind also.
*I will sing praise with the spirit,*
*but I will sing praise with the mind also.*

*Glory ...*

**Psalm 119.17-24**

Bless your servant and I shall live
and obey your word.
*Open my eyes that I may see*
*the wonders of your law.*
I am a pilgrim on the earth;
show me your commands.
*My soul is ever consumed*
*as I long for your decrees.*

You threaten the proud, the accursed,
who turn from your commands.
***Relieve me from scorn and contempt***
***for I do your will.***
Though the powerful sit plotting against me
I ponder on your statutes.
***Your will is my delight;***
***your statutes are my counselors.***

**Thanksgiving**

O God, you provide us with every good gift;
we have ample means to meet our need
***and enough to share abundantly***
***in every good work.***
*(free prayers of thanksgiving)*
You lavish your gifts on those in need;
***your goodness stands fast forever. Amen.***

**Song**

I long for your commandments (H543)
Open my ears, open my eyes (SS5)
You are all we have (SJ29)

**Confession**

O God, clothe us with compassion,
kindness, humility, patience.
***Enfold us in love,***
***which binds everything together in harmony.***
*(silence)*

You have forgiven us; may we also forgive.
***And may Christ's peace rule in our hearts. Amen.***

## Call to discipleship

Friends, let us not love with words
but with actions and in truth.
***This is how we know***
***that Jesus Christ lives in us,***
***by the Spirit he gave us.***

**Acts 9.26-31**

When [Saul] had come to Jerusalem, he attempted to join the disciples; and they were all afraid of him, for they did not believe that he was a disciple. But Barnabas took him, brought him to the apostles, and described for them how on the road he had seen the Lord, who had spoken to him, and how in Damascus he had spoken boldly in the name of Jesus. So he went in and out among them in Jerusalem, speaking boldly in the name of the Lord. He spoke and argued with the Hellenists; but they were attempting to kill him. When the believers learned of it, they brought him down to Caesarea and sent him off to Tarsus.

Meanwhile the church throughout Judea, Galilee, and Samaria had peace and was built up. Living in the fear of the Lord and in the comfort of the Holy Spirit, it increased in numbers.

**2 Corinthians 8.7-9**

Now as you excel in everything—in faith, in speech, in knowledge, in utmost eagerness, and in our love for you—so we want you to excel also in this generous undertaking.

I do not say this as a command, but I am testing the genuineness of your love against the earnestness of others. For you know the generous act of our Lord Jesus Christ, that though he was rich, yet for your sakes he became poor, so that by his poverty you might become rich.

**Silent or spoken reflection on the readings**

**Song**

If all you want, Lord (H512)
For me to live is Christ (SS111)
Lord, speak to me (H499)
Take, O take me as I am (SJ81)

**1 Thessalonians 5.16-24**

## Call to intercession

God, who searches the heart,
knows what is the mind of the Spirit,

***because the Spirit intercedes for the saints according to the will of God.***

God of grace, you have given us your law to lead us into life. In your mercy,
***Lord, hear our prayer.***

You promise us rebirth and renewal. We pray for ourselves and those dear to us.
*(open prayers)*
In your mercy,
***Lord, hear our prayer.***

You invite us to give generously to those in need. We pray for our community and for our neighbors.
*(open prayers)*
In your mercy,
***Lord, hear our prayer.***

You became poor so that we may be rich. We pray for the church in all places, that we may know the freedom of life in the Spirit.
*(open prayers)*
In your mercy,
***Lord, hear our prayer.***

Your law guides us in our pilgrimage on earth. We pray for the world and for all who care for creation.
*(open prayers)*

In your mercy,
***Lord, hear our prayer.***

We offer you other concerns we carry in our hearts.
*(open prayers)*
In your mercy,
***Lord, hear our prayer.***

Extravagant God,
you do not hold back anything,
but pour out your Spirit
for the sake of your creation.
Transform our stony hearts
so that our generosity toward those in need
will match your own.
In the company of Jesus, who taught us,
we pray:

***Our Father …***

**Benediction**

***May our love overflow more and more***
***with knowledge and full insight***
***to help us to determine what is best,***
***so that in the day of Christ***
***we may be pure and blameless,***
***having produced the harvest of righteousness***
***that comes through Jesus Christ***
***for the glory and praise of God. Amen.***

# Do not quench the Spirit

## PENTECOST 2 TUESDAY MORNING

**Opening sentence**

Do not quench the Spirit.
***Do not despise the words of prophets.***

## Call to praise

Rejoice in the Lord always;
***again I will say, Rejoice.***

***Glory …***

**Psalm 119.33-40**

Teach me the demands of your statutes
and I will keep them to the end.
***Train me to observe your law,***
***to keep it with my heart.***
Guide me in the path of your commands;
for there is my delight.
***Bend my heart to your will***
***and not to love of gain.***
Keep my eyes from what is false;
by your word, give me life.
***Keep the promise you have made***
***to the servant who fears you.***
Keep me from the scorn I dread,
for your decrees are good.

***See, I long for your precepts;***
***then in your justice, give me life.***

**Thanksgiving**

O God, we give thanks to you
at all times and for everything
***in the name of our Lord Jesus Christ.***
*(free prayers of thanksgiving)*
We sing psalms and hymns
and spiritual songs,
***making melody to you in our hearts, O Lord.***
***Amen.***

**Song**

Teach me, O Lord (H487)
Lord, I have made thy word (H317)
Lead me, Lord (H538)

**Confession of faith**

Jesus of Nazareth was a man
commended to us by God
***through the powerful acts, wonders, and signs***
***God did through him in our midst—***
***as we ourselves know well.***
This man, according to the declared purpose
and foreknowledge of God,
was handed over, crucified and killed
by the hands of lawless ones.
***Yet God raised him up,***
***releasing him from the birth pangs of death***

***because it was not possible for him***
***to be taken over by it.***
This Jesus God raised up,
and of that we are all witnesses.
***Being therefore lifted high***
***at the right hand of God,***
***having received the promise of the Holy Spirit***
***from the Father,***
***he has poured out this***
***that we both see and hear.***

## Call to discipleship

Let us guard the good treasure entrusted to us,
***with the help of the Holy Spirit living in us.***

**Numbers 11.23-29**

The LORD said to Moses, "Is the LORD's power limited? Now you shall see whether my word will come true for you or not."

So Moses went out and told the people the words of the LORD; and he gathered seventy elders of the people, and placed them all around the tent. Then the LORD came down in the cloud and spoke to him, and took some of the spirit that was on him and put it on the seventy elders; and when the spirit rested upon them, they prophesied. But they did not do so again.

Two men remained in the camp, one named Eldad, and the other named Medad, and the spirit rested on them; they were among those registered, but they had not gone out to the tent, and so they prophesied in the camp. And a young man ran and told Moses, "Eldad and Medad are prophesying in the camp." And Joshua son of Nun, the assistant of Moses, one of his chosen men, said, "My lord Moses, stop them!" But Moses said to him, "Are you jealous for my sake? Would that all the Lord's people were prophets, and that the LORD would put his spirit on them!"

**Acts 8.14-25**

Now when the apostles at Jerusalem heard that Samaria had accepted the word of God, they sent Peter and John to them. The two went down and prayed for them that they might receive the Holy Spirit (for as yet the Spirit had not come upon any of them; they had only been baptized in the name of the Lord Jesus). Then Peter and John laid their hands on them, and they received the Holy Spirit. Now when Simon saw that the Spirit was given through the laying on of the apostles' hands, he offered them money, saying, "Give me also this power so that anyone on whom I lay my hands may receive the Holy Spirit." But Peter said to him, "May your silver perish with you, because you thought you could obtain God's gift with money! You have no part or share in this, for your heart is not right before God. Repent therefore of this wickedness of yours, and pray to the Lord that, if possible, the intent of your heart may be forgiven you. For I see that you are in the gall of bitterness and the chains of wickedness." Simon answered, "Pray for me to the Lord, that nothing of what you have said may happen to me."

Now after Peter and John had testified and spoken the word of the Lord, they returned to Jerusalem, proclaiming the good news to many villages of the Samaritans.

**Silent or spoken reflection on the readings**

**Song**

Come, O Spirit, come (SS104)
Spirit of the living God (H349)
O Spirit of the living God (H361)
O Breath of Life (SJ35)

**1 Thessalonians 5.16-24**

## Call to intercession

Beloved,
let us keep ourselves in the love of God,

***looking forward to the mercy***
***of our Lord Jesus Christ that leads to life.***

God of law and grace, the path of your commands is a source of delight. In your mercy,
***Lord, hear our prayer.***

It was your hand that shaped us. We pray for ourselves and those dear to us.
*(open prayers)*
In your mercy,
***Lord, hear our prayer.***

You desire to bring release from bitterness and wrong. We pray for our community and for our neighbors.
*(open prayers)*
In your mercy,
***Lord, hear our prayer.***

You seek a fair balance between our abundance and others' need. We pray for the church in all places, that we may reflect your faithful love.
*(open prayers)*
In your mercy,
***Lord, hear our prayer.***

In your justice you give life. We pray for the world, for those who are in need.
*(open prayers)*

In your mercy,
***Lord, hear our prayer.***

We offer you other concerns we carry in our hearts.
*(open prayers)*
In your mercy,
***Lord, hear our prayer.***

God of every gift,
you provide for us, body and soul,
through the bounty of creation
and the gift of your own Holy Spirit.
Hold us fast to your ways,
so that our delight will be
to join your work this day.
In the example of Jesus, who taught us,
we pray:

***Our Father …***

**Charge**

Do not worry about how you are to speak
or what you are to say;
for what you are to say
will be given to you at that time;
for it is not you who speak,
but the Spirit of your Father
speaking through you. ***Amen.***

# Do not despise the words of prophets

PENTECOST 2 TUESDAY EVENING

**Opening sentence**

Do not quench the Spirit.
*Do not despise the words of prophets.*

## Call to praise

What should I do then?
I will pray with the spirit,
but I will pray with the mind also.
***I will sing praise with the spirit,***
***but I will sing praise with the mind also.***

*Glory ...*

**Psalm 119.73-80**

It was your hands that made me and shaped me:
help me to learn your commands.
***Your faithful will see me and rejoice***
***for I trust in your word.***
LORD, I know that your decrees are right,
that you afflict me justly.
***Let your love be ready to console me***
***by your promise to your servant.***

Let your love come and I shall live
for your law is my delight.
***Shame the proud who harm me with lies***
***while I ponder your precepts.***
Let your faithful turn to me,
those who know your will.
***Let my heart be blameless in your statutes***
***lest I be ashamed.***

**Thanksgiving**

O God, you provide us with every good gift;
we have ample means to meet our need
***and enough to share abundantly***
***in every good work.***
*(free prayers of thanksgiving)*
You lavish your gifts on those in need;
***your goodness stands fast forever. Amen.***

**Song**

Teach me, O Lord (H487)
We would extol thee (H74)
You are all we have (SJ29)

**Confession**

O God, clothe us with compassion,
kindness, humility, patience.
***Enfold us in love,***
***which binds everything together in harmony.***
*(silence)*

You have forgiven us; may we also forgive.
***And may Christ's peace rule in our hearts. Amen.***

## Call to discipleship

Friends, let us not love with words
but with actions and in truth.
***This is how we know***
***that Jesus Christ lives in us,***
***by the Spirit he gave us.***

**Acts 8.26-39**

Then an angel of the Lord said to Philip, "Get up and go toward the south to the road that goes down from Jerusalem to Gaza." (This is a wilderness road.) So he got up and went. Now there was an Ethiopian eunuch, a court official of the Candace, queen of the Ethiopians, in charge of her entire treasury. He had come to Jerusalem to worship and was returning home; seated in his chariot, he was reading the prophet Isaiah. Then the Spirit said to Philip, "Go over to this chariot and join it." So Philip ran up to it and heard him reading the prophet Isaiah. He asked, "Do you understand what you are reading?" He replied, "How can I, unless someone guides me?" And he invited Philip to get in and sit beside him. Now the passage of the scripture that he was reading was this:

"Like a sheep he was led to the slaughter,
and like a lamb silent before its shearer,
so he does not open his mouth.
In his humiliation justice was denied him.
Who can describe his generation?
For his life is taken away from the earth."

The eunuch asked Philip, "About whom, may I ask you, does the prophet say this, about himself or about someone else?" Then Philip began to speak, and starting with this scripture, he proclaimed to him the good news about Jesus. As they were going along the road, they came to some water; and the eunuch said, "Look, here is water! What is to prevent me from being baptized?" He commanded the chariot to stop, and both of them, Philip and the eunuch, went down into the water, and Philip baptized him. When they came up out of the water, the Spirit of the Lord snatched Philip away; the eunuch saw him no more, and went on his way rejoicing.

**2 Corinthians 8.10-15**

And in this matter I am giving my advice: it is appropriate for you who began last year not only to do something but even to desire to do something—now finish doing it, so that your eagerness may be matched by completing it according to your means. For if the eagerness is there, the gift is acceptable according to what one has—not according to what one does not have. I do not mean that there should be relief for others and pressure on you, but it is a question of a fair balance between your present abundance and their need, so that their abundance may be for your need, in order that there may be a fair balance. As it is written,

"The one who had much did not have too much,
and the one who had little did not have too little."

**Silent or spoken reflection on the readings**

**Song**

Spirit of God, unleashed on earth (H364)
Lord, speak to me (H499, vv. 1–2, 4–6)
Heart and mind, possessions, Lord (H392)

**1 Thessalonians 5.16-24**

## Call to intercession

God, who searches the heart,
knows what is the mind of the Spirit,
***because the Spirit intercedes for the saints according to the will of God.***

God of law and grace, the path of your commands is a source of delight. In your mercy,
***Lord, hear our prayer.***

It was your hand that shaped us. We pray for ourselves and those dear to us.
*(open prayers)*
In your mercy,
***Lord, hear our prayer.***

You desire to bring release from bitterness and wrong. We pray for our community and for our neighbors.
*(open prayers)*
In your mercy,
***Lord, hear our prayer.***

You seek a fair balance between our abundance and others' need. We pray for the church in all places, that we may reflect your faithful love.
*(open prayers)*
In your mercy,
***Lord, hear our prayer.***

In your justice you give life. We pray for the world, for those who are in need.
*(open prayers)*
In your mercy,
***Lord, hear our prayer.***

We offer you other concerns we carry in our hearts.
*(open prayers)*
In your mercy,
***Lord, hear our prayer.***

Extravagant God,
you do not hold back anything,
but pour out your Spirit
for the sake of your creation.
Transform our stony hearts
so that our generosity toward those in need
will match your own.
In the company of Jesus, who taught us,
we pray:

***Our Father …***

**Benediction**

***May we have the power to comprehend,***
***with all the saints,***
***what is the breadth and length***
***and height and depth,***
***and to know the love of Christ***
***that surpasses knowledge,***
***so that we may be filled***
***with all the fullness of God. Amen.***

# But test everything

## PENTECOST 2 WEDNESDAY MORNING

**Opening sentence**

Do not quench the Spirit.
Do not despise the words of prophets,
***but test everything;***
***hold fast to what is good.***

## Call to praise

Rejoice in the Lord always;
***again I will say, Rejoice.***

***Glory …***

**Psalm 119.89-96**

Your word, O LORD, for ever
stands firm in the heavens:
***your truth lasts from age to age,***
***like the earth you created.***
By your decree it endures to this day;
for all things serve you.
***Had your law not been my delight***
***I would have died in my affliction.***
I will never forget your precepts
for with them you give me life.
***Save me, for I am yours***
***since I seek your precepts.***

Though the wicked lie in wait to destroy me
yet I ponder your will.
***I have seen that all perfection has an end***
***but your command is boundless.***

**Thanksgiving**

O God, we give thanks to you
at all times and for everything
***in the name of our Lord Jesus Christ.***
*(free prayers of thanksgiving)*
We sing psalms and hymns
and spiritual songs,
***making melody to you in our hearts, O Lord.***
***Amen.***

**Song**

O God, our help in ages past (H328)
Teach me, O Lord (H487)
Lord, thou hast searched me (H556)

**Confession of faith**

Jesus of Nazareth was a man
commended to us by God
***through the powerful acts, wonders, and signs***
***God did through him in our midst—***
***as we ourselves know well.***
This man, according to the declared purpose
and foreknowledge of God,
was handed over, crucified and killed
by the hands of lawless ones.

***Yet God raised him up,***
***releasing him from the birth pangs of death***
***because it was not possible for him***
***to be taken over by it.***
This Jesus God raised up,
and of that we are all witnesses.
***Being therefore lifted high***
***at the right hand of God,***
***having received the promise of the Holy Spirit***
***from the Father,***
***he has poured out this***
***that we both see and hear.***

## Call to discipleship

Let us guard the good treasure entrusted to us,
***with the help of the Holy Spirit living in us.***

**Leviticus 23.9-16**

The LORD spoke to Moses: Speak to the people of Israel and say to them: When you enter the land that I am giving you and you reap its harvest, you shall bring the sheaf of the first fruits of your harvest to the priest. He shall raise the sheaf before the LORD, that you may find acceptance; on the day after the sabbath the priest shall raise it. On the day when you raise the sheaf, you shall offer a lamb a year old, without blemish, as a burnt offering to the LORD. And the grain offering with it shall be two-tenths of an ephah of choice flour mixed with oil, an offering by fire of pleasing odor to the LORD; and the drink offering with it shall be of wine, one-fourth of a hin. You shall eat no bread or parched grain or fresh ears until that very day, until you have brought the offering of your God: it is a statute forever throughout your generations in all your settlements.

And from the day after the sabbath, from the day on which you bring the sheaf of the elevation offering, you shall count off seven weeks; they shall be complete. You shall count until the day after the seventh sabbath, fifty days; then you shall present an offering of new grain to the LORD.

**Acts 11.11-18**

At that very moment three men, sent to me [Peter] from Caesarea, arrived at the house where we were. The Spirit told me to go with them and not to make a distinction between them and us. These six brothers also accompanied me, and we entered the man's house. He told us how he had seen the angel standing in his house and saying, 'Send to Joppa and bring Simon, who is called Peter; he will give you a message by which you and your entire household will be saved.' And as I began to speak, the Holy Spirit fell upon them just as it had upon us at the beginning. And I remembered the word of the Lord, how he had said, 'John baptized with water, but you will be baptized with the Holy Spirit.' If then God gave them the same gift that he gave us when we believed in the Lord Jesus Christ, who was I that I could hinder God?" When they heard this, they were silenced. And they praised God, saying, "Then God has given even to the Gentiles the repentance that leads to life."

**Silent or spoken reflection on the readings**

**Song**

For the fruit of all creation (H90)
Spirit of God, unleashed on earth (H364)
O Holy Spirit, making whole (H300)

**1 Thessalonians 5.16-24**

## Call to intercession

Beloved,
let us keep ourselves in the love of God,
***looking forward to the mercy***
***of our Lord Jesus Christ that leads to life.***

Trustworthy God, with your law you give us life. In your mercy,
***Lord, hear our prayer.***

You are our rock and rescuer. We pray for ourselves and those dear to us.
*(open prayers)*
In your mercy,
***Lord, hear our prayer.***

Your decrees bring wisdom, clarity, and justice. We pray for our community and for our neighbors.
*(open prayers)*
In your mercy,
***Lord, hear our prayer.***

You offer to all the repentance that leads to life. We pray for the church in all places, that we may bear witness to your reign of justice, peace, and joy.
*(open prayers)*
In your mercy,
***Lord, hear our prayer.***

Your truth lasts from age to age. We pray for the world, for all who are ensnared in greed, violence, and oppression.
*(open prayers)*
In your mercy,
***Lord, hear our prayer.***

We offer you other concerns we carry in our hearts.
*(open prayers)*

In your mercy,
***Lord, hear our prayer.***

God of every gift,
you provide for us, body and soul,
through the bounty of creation
and the gift of your own Holy Spirit.
Hold us fast to your ways,
so that our delight will be
to join your work this day.
In the example of Jesus, who taught us,
we pray:

***Our Father …***

**Charge**

If then there is any encouragement in Christ,
any consolation from love,
any sharing in the Spirit,
any compassion and sympathy,
be of the same mind, having the same love,
being in full accord and of one mind. ***Amen.***

# Hold fast to what is good

## PENTECOST 2 WEDNESDAY EVENING

**Opening sentence**

Do not quench the Spirit.
Do not despise the words of prophets,
***but test everything;***
***hold fast to what is good.***

## Call to praise

What should I do then?
I will pray with the spirit,
but I will pray with the mind also.
***I will sing praise with the spirit,***
***but I will sing praise with the mind also.***

***Glory …***

**Psalm 19.8-15 [7-14]**

The law of the LORD is perfect,
it revives the soul;
***the rule of the LORD is to be trusted,***
***it gives wisdom to the simple.***

The precepts of the LORD are right,
they gladden the heart.
***The command of the LORD is clear,***
***it gives light to the eyes.***

The fear of the LORD is holy,
abiding for ever.
***The decrees of the LORD are truth***
***and all of them just.***

They are more to be desired than gold,
than the purest of gold
***and sweeter are they than honey,***
***than honey from the comb.***

So in them your servant finds instruction;
great reward is in their keeping.
***But can we discern all our errors?***
***From hidden faults acquit us.***

From presumption restrain your servant
and let it not rule me.
***Then shall I be blameless,***
***clean from grave sin.***

May the spoken words of my mouth,
the thoughts of my heart,
***win favor in your sight, O LORD,***
***my rescuer, my rock!***

**Thanksgiving**

O God, you provide us with every good gift;
we have ample means to meet our need
***and enough to share abundantly***
***in every good work.***
*(free prayers of thanksgiving)*

You lavish your gifts on those in need;
***your goodness stands fast forever. Amen.***

**Song**

Lamp of our feet (H312)
You are all we have (SJ29)

**Confession**

O God, clothe us with compassion,
kindness, humility, patience.
***Enfold us in love,***
***which binds everything together in harmony.***
*(silence)*
You have forgiven us; may we also forgive.
***And may Christ's peace rule in our hearts.***
***Amen.***

## Call to discipleship

Friends, let us not love with words
but with actions and in truth.
***This is how we know***
***that Jesus Christ lives in us,***
***by the Spirit he gave us.***

**Acts 11.19-26**

Now those who were scattered because of the persecution that took place over Stephen traveled as far as Phoenicia, Cyprus, and Antioch, and they spoke the word to no one except Jews. But among them were some men of Cyprus and Cyrene who, on coming to Antioch, spoke to the Hellenists also, proclaiming the Lord Jesus. The hand of the Lord was with them, and a great number became believers and turned to the Lord. News of this came to the ears of the church in Jerusalem, and they sent Barnabas to Antioch. When he came and saw the grace of God, he rejoiced, and he exhorted them all to remain faithful to the Lord with steadfast devotion; for he was a good man, full of the Holy Spirit and of faith. And a great many people were brought to the Lord. Then Barnabas went to Tarsus to look for Saul, and when he had found him, he brought him to Antioch. So it was that for an entire year they met with the church and taught a great many people, and it was in Antioch that the disciples were first called "Christians."

**2 Corinthians 8.16-19**

But thanks be to God who put in the heart of Titus the same eagerness for you that I myself have. For he not only accepted our appeal, but since he is more eager than ever, he is going to you of his own accord. With him we are sending the brother who is famous among all the churches for his proclaiming the good news; and not only that, but he has also been appointed by the churches to travel with us while we are administering this generous undertaking for the glory of the Lord himself and to show our goodwill.

**Silent or spoken reflection on the readings**

**Song**

The work is thine, O Christ (H396)
In Christ there is no East or West (H306)

**1 Thessalonians 5.16-24**

## Call to intercession

God, who searches the heart,
knows what is the mind of the Spirit,
***because the Spirit intercedes for the saints according to the will of God.***

Trustworthy God, with your law you give us life. In your mercy,
***Lord, hear our prayer.***

You are our rock and rescuer. We pray for ourselves and those dear to us.
*(open prayers)*
In your mercy,
***Lord, hear our prayer.***

Your decrees bring wisdom, clarity, and justice. We pray for our community and for our neighbors.

*(open prayers)*
In your mercy,
***Lord, hear our prayer.***

You offer to all the repentance that leads to life. We pray for the church in all places, that we may bear witness to your reign of justice, peace, and joy.
*(open prayers)*
In your mercy,
***Lord, hear our prayer.***

Your truth lasts from age to age. We pray for the world, for all who are ensnared in greed, violence, and oppression.
*(open prayers)*
In your mercy,
***Lord, hear our prayer.***

We offer you other concerns we carry in our hearts.
*(open prayers)*
In your mercy,
***Lord, hear our prayer.***

Extravagant God,
you do not hold back anything,
but pour out your Spirit
for the sake of your creation.
Transform our stony hearts
so that our generosity toward those in need
will match your own.

In the company of Jesus, who taught us,
we pray:

*Our Father ...*

**Benediction**

*The grace of the Lord Jesus Christ,
the love of God,
and the communion of the Holy Spirit
be with all of us. Amen.*

# Abstain from every form of evil

## PENTECOST 2 THURSDAY MORNING

**Opening sentence**

Do not quench the Spirit.
Do not despise the words of prophets,
but test everything;
hold fast to what is good;
***abstain from every form of evil.***
***May the God of peace sanctify you entirely.***

## Call to praise

Rejoice in the Lord always;
***again I will say, Rejoice.***

*Glory …*

**Psalm 119.97-104**

Lord, how I love your law!
It is ever in my mind.
***Your command makes me wiser than my foes;***
***for it is mine for ever.***
I have more insight than all who teach me
for I ponder your will.
***I have more understanding than the old***
***for I keep your precepts.***
I turn my feet from evil paths
to obey your word.

***I have not turned from your decrees;***
***you yourself have taught me.***
Your promise is sweeter to my taste
than honey in the mouth.
***I gain understanding from your precepts***
***and so I hate false ways.***

**Thanksgiving**

O God, we give thanks to you
at all times and for everything
***in the name of our Lord Jesus Christ.***
*(free prayers of thanksgiving)*
We sing psalms and hymns
and spiritual songs,
***making melody to you in our hearts, O Lord.***
***Amen.***

**Song**

Make music to the Lord most high (H73)
In this world abound scrolls (H316)
Lord, I have made thy word (H317)

**Confession of faith**

Jesus of Nazareth was a man
commended to us by God
***through the powerful acts, wonders, and signs***
***God did through him in our midst—***
***as we ourselves know well.***
This man, according to the declared purpose
and foreknowledge of God,

was handed over, crucified and killed
by the hands of lawless ones.
***Yet God raised him up,***
***releasing him from the birth pangs of death***
***because it was not possible for him***
***to be taken over by it.***
This Jesus God raised up,
and of that we are all witnesses.
***Being therefore lifted high***
***at the right hand of God,***
***having received the promise of the Holy Spirit***
***from the Father,***
***he has poured out this***
***that we both see and hear.***

## Call to discipleship

Let us guard the good treasure entrusted to us,
***with the help of the Holy Spirit living in us.***

**Zechariah 4.1-7**

The angel who talked with me came again, and wakened me, as one is wakened from sleep. He said to me, "What do you see?" And I said, "I see a lampstand all of gold, with a bowl on the top of it; there are seven lamps on it, with seven lips on each of the lamps that are on the top of it. And by it there are two olive trees, one on the right of the bowl and the other on its left." I said to the angel who talked with me, "What are these, my lord?" Then the angel who talked with me answered me, "Do you not know what these are?" I said, "No, my lord." He said to me, "This is the word of the LORD to Zerubbabel: Not by might, nor by power, but by my spirit, says the LORD of hosts. What are you, O great mountain? Before Zerubbabel you shall become a plain; and he shall bring out the top stone amid shouts of 'Grace, grace to it!'"

**John 20.19-23**

When it was evening on that day, the first day of the week, and the doors of the house where the disciples had met were locked for fear of the Jews, Jesus came and stood among them and said, "Peace be with you." After he said this, he showed them his hands and his side. Then the disciples rejoiced when they saw the Lord. Jesus said to them again, "Peace be with you. As the Father has sent me, so I send you." When he had said this, he breathed on them and said to them, "Receive the Holy Spirit. If you forgive the sins of any, they are forgiven them; if you retain the sins of any, they are retained."

**Silent or spoken reflection on the readings**

**Song**

Comme un souffle fragile (Like a tender breath, stirring) (SS106)
Breathe upon us, Holy Spirit (H28)
If you believe and I believe (SJ32)
Forgive our sins as we forgive (H137)

**1 Thessalonians 5.16-24**

## Call to intercession

Beloved,
let us keep ourselves in the love of God,
***looking forward to the mercy***
***of our Lord Jesus Christ that leads to life.***

Sustaining God, your promise upholds us and gives us life. In your mercy,
***Lord, hear our prayer.***

You are our shelter and shield. We pray for ourselves and those dear to us.
*(open prayers)*
In your mercy,
***Lord, hear our prayer.***

You call us to hold fast to what is good. We pray for our community and for our neighbors.
*(open prayers)*

In your mercy,
***Lord, hear our prayer.***

In your Spirit's presence is the power of forgiveness. We pray for the church in all places, that we may daily follow in the footsteps of Christ.
*(open prayers)*
In your mercy,
***Lord, hear our prayer.***

You teach us to hate what is false. We pray for the world, for those in positions of power and authority.
*(open prayers)*
In your mercy,
***Lord, hear our prayer.***

We offer you other concerns we carry in our hearts.
*(open prayers)*
In your mercy,
***Lord, hear our prayer.***

God of every gift,
you provide for us, body and soul,
through the bounty of creation
and the gift of your own Holy Spirit.
Hold us fast to your ways,
so that our delight will be
to join your work this day.

In the example of Jesus, who taught us,
we pray:

***Our Father …***

**Charge**

Be filled with the Spirit,
as you sing psalms and hymns
and spiritual songs among yourselves,
singing and making melody to the Lord
in your hearts,
giving thanks to God the Father
at all times and for everything
in the name of our Lord Jesus Christ. ***Amen.***

# May the God of peace sanctify you

## PENTECOST 2 THURSDAY EVENING

**Opening sentence**

Do not quench the Spirit.
Do not despise the words of prophets,
but test everything;
hold fast to what is good;
*abstain from every form of evil.*
*May the God of peace sanctify you entirely.*

## Call to praise

What should I do then?
I will pray with the spirit,
but I will pray with the mind also.
*I will sing praise with the spirit,*
*but I will sing praise with the mind also.*

*Glory ...*

**Psalm 119.113-120**

I have no love for the halfhearted;
my love is for your law.
*You are my shelter, my shield;*
*I hope in your word.*
Leave me, you who do evil;
I will keep God's command.

***If you uphold me by your promise I shall live;***
***let my hopes not be in vain.***
Sustain me and I shall be saved
and ever observe your statutes.
***You spurn all who swerve from your statutes;***
***their cunning is in vain.***
You throw away the wicked like dross;
so I love your will.
***I tremble before you in terror;***
***I fear your decrees.***

**Thanksgiving**

O God, you provide us with every good gift;
we have ample means to meet our need
***and enough to share abundantly***
***in every good work.***
*(free prayers of thanksgiving)*
You lavish your gifts on those in need;
***your goodness stands fast forever. Amen.***

**Song**

Lord, I have made thy word (H317)
You are all we have (SJ29)
In this world abound scrolls (H316)

**Confession**

O God, clothe us with compassion,
kindness, humility, patience.
***Enfold us in love,***
***which binds everything together in harmony.***
*(silence)*

You have forgiven us; may we also forgive.
***And may Christ's peace rule in our hearts. Amen.***

## Call to discipleship

Friends, let us not love with words
but with actions and in truth.
***This is how we know***
***that Jesus Christ lives in us,***
***by the Spirit he gave us.***

**Acts 13.1-5**

Now in the church at Antioch there were prophets and teachers: Barnabas, Simeon who was called Niger, Lucius of Cyrene, Manaen a member of the court of Herod the ruler, and Saul. While they were worshiping the Lord and fasting, the Holy Spirit said, "Set apart for me Barnabas and Saul for the work to which I have called them." Then after fasting and praying they laid their hands on them and sent them off.

So, being sent out by the Holy Spirit, they went down to Seleucia; and from there they sailed to Cyprus. When they arrived at Salamis, they proclaimed the word of God in the synagogues of the Jews. And they had John also to assist them.

**2 Corinthians 8.20-24**

We [Paul and Silas] intend that no one should blame us about this generous gift that we are administering, for we intend to do what is right not only in the Lord's sight but also in the sight of others. And with them we are sending our brother whom we have often tested and found eager in many matters, but who is now more eager than ever because of his great confidence in you. As for Titus, he is my partner and co-worker in your service; as for our brothers, they are messengers of the churches, the glory of Christ. Therefore openly before the churches, show them the proof of your love and of our reason for boasting about you.

**Silent or spoken reflection on the readings**

**Song**

How buoyant and bold the stride (H394, vv. 1–2, 5)
Lord, you give the great commission (SJ63, vv. 1–2, 5)
Now go forward (H399)

**1 Thessalonians 5.16-24**

## Call to intercession

God, who searches the heart,
knows what is the mind of the Spirit,
***because the Spirit intercedes for the saints according to the will of God.***

Sustaining God, your promise upholds us and gives us life. In your mercy,
***Lord, hear our prayer.***

You are our shelter and shield. We pray for ourselves and those dear to us.
*(open prayers)*
In your mercy,
***Lord, hear our prayer.***

You call us to hold fast to what is good. We pray for our community and for our neighbors.
*(open prayers)*
In your mercy,
***Lord, hear our prayer.***

In your Spirit's presence is the power of forgiveness. We pray for the church in all places, that we may daily follow in the footsteps of Christ.
*(open prayers)*
In your mercy,
***Lord, hear our prayer.***

You teach us to hate what is false. We pray for the world, for those in positions of power and authority.
*(open prayers)*
In your mercy,
***Lord, hear our prayer.***

We offer you other concerns we carry in our hearts.
*(open prayers)*
In your mercy,
***Lord, hear our prayer.***

Extravagant God,
you do not hold back anything,
but pour out your Spirit
for the sake of your creation.
Transform our stony hearts
so that our generosity toward those in need
will match your own.
In the company of Jesus, who taught us,
we pray:

***Our Father …***

**Benediction**

***May the God of steadfastness***
***and encouragement***
***grant us to live in harmony with one another,***
***in accordance with Christ Jesus,***
***so that together we may with one voice***

*glorify the God and Father*
*of our Lord Jesus Christ. Amen.*

# May your spirit and soul and body be kept sound

## PENTECOST 2 FRIDAY MORNING

**Opening sentence**

May the God of peace sanctify you entirely;
***and may your spirit and soul and body***
***be kept sound and blameless***
***at the coming of our Lord Jesus.***

## Call to praise

Rejoice in the Lord always;
***again I will say, Rejoice.***

*Glory …*

**Psalm 119.129-136**

Your will is wonderful indeed;
therefore I obey it.
***The unfolding of your word gives light***
***and teaches the simple.***
I open my mouth and I sigh
as I yearn for your commands.
***Turn and show me your mercy;***
***show justice to your friends.***
Let my steps be guided by your promise;
let no evil rule me.

*Redeem me from those who oppress me*
*and I will keep your precepts.*
Let your face shine on your servant
and teach me your decrees.
*Tears stream from my eyes*
*because your law is disobeyed.*

**Thanksgiving**

O God, we give thanks to you
at all times and for everything
*in the name of our Lord Jesus Christ.*
*(free prayers of thanksgiving)*
We sing psalms and hymns
and spiritual songs,
*making melody to you in our hearts, O Lord.*
*Amen.*

**Song**

Lord, I have made thy word (H317)
O bless the Lord, my soul (H80)
Lamp of our feet (H312)

**Confession of faith**

Jesus of Nazareth was a man
commended to us by God
*through the powerful acts, wonders, and signs*
*God did through him in our midst—*
*as we ourselves know well.*
This man, according to the declared purpose
and foreknowledge of God,

was handed over, crucified and killed
by the hands of lawless ones.
***Yet God raised him up,***
***releasing him from the birth pangs of death***
***because it was not possible for him***
***to be taken over by it.***
This Jesus God raised up,
and of that we are all witnesses.
***Being therefore lifted high***
***at the right hand of God,***
***having received the promise of the Holy Spirit***
***from the Father,***
***he has poured out this***
***that we both see and hear.***

## Call to discipleship

Let us guard the good treasure entrusted to us,
***with the help of the Holy Spirit living in us.***

**Isaiah 59.21**

And as for me, this is my covenant with them, says the LORD: my spirit that is upon you, and my words that I have put in your mouth, shall not depart out of your mouth, or out of the mouths of your children, or out of the mouths of your children's children, says the LORD, from now on and forever.

**Acts 19.1-7**

While Apollos was in Corinth, Paul passed through the interior regions and came to Ephesus, where he found some disciples. He said to them, "Did you receive the Holy Spirit when you became believers?" They replied, "No, we have not even heard that there is a Holy Spirit." Then he said, "Into what then were you baptized?" They answered, "Into John's baptism." Paul said, "John baptized with the baptism of repentance, telling the people to believe in the one who was to come after him, that is, in Jesus." On hearing this, they were baptized in the name of the Lord Jesus. When Paul had laid his hands on them, the Holy Spirit came upon them, and they spoke in tongues and prophesied—altogether there were about twelve of them.

**Silent or spoken reflection on the readings**

**Song**

Spirit of God, unleashed on earth (H364)
Filled with the Spirit's power (H289)
Come, O Spirit, come (SS104, vv. 1, 5–7)

**1 Thessalonians 5.16-24**

## Call to intercession

Beloved,
let us keep ourselves in the love of God,
***looking forward to the mercy***
***of our Lord Jesus Christ that leads to life.***

God of peace, in love you hear us when we call. In your mercy,
***Lord, hear our prayer.***

You are close; your commands are true. We pray for ourselves and those dear to us.
*(open prayers)*
In your mercy,
***Lord, hear our prayer.***

You love those who give cheerfully. We pray for our community and for our neighbors.
*(open prayers)*
In your mercy,
***Lord, hear our prayer.***

You give your people the gift of your Spirit. We pray for the church in all places, that we may speak boldly for Christ.
*(open prayers)*
In your mercy,
***Lord, hear our prayer.***

Your law is far from the unjust who bring harm. We pray for the world, for all who do justice and love mercy.
*(open prayers)*
In your mercy,
***Lord, hear our prayer.***

We offer you other concerns we carry in our hearts.
*(open prayers)*
In your mercy,
***Lord, hear our prayer.***

God of every gift,
you provide for us, body and soul,
through the bounty of creation
and the gift of your own Holy Spirit.
Hold us fast to your ways,
so that our delight will be
to join your work this day.
In the example of Jesus, who taught us,
we pray:

***Our Father …***

**Charge**

Lead a life worthy of the calling
to which you have been called,
with all humility and gentleness,
with patience,
bearing with one another in love,
making every effort

to maintain the unity of the Spirit
in the bond of peace. ***Amen.***

# At the coming of our Lord Jesus

PENTECOST 2 FRIDAY EVENING

**Opening sentence**

May the God of peace sanctify you entirely;
***and may your spirit and soul and body***
***be kept sound and blameless***
***at the coming of our Lord Jesus.***

## Call to praise

What should I do then?
I will pray with the spirit,
but I will pray with the mind also.
***I will sing praise with the spirit,***
***but I will sing praise with the mind also.***

*Glory ...*

**Psalm 119.145-152**

I call with all my heart; LORD, hear me,
I will keep your statutes.
***I call upon you, save me***
***and I will do your will.***
I rise before dawn and cry for help,
I hope in your word.
***My eyes watch through the night***
***to ponder your promise.***

In your love hear my voice, O LORD;
give me life by your decrees.
***Those who harm me unjustly draw near;***
***they are far from your law.***
But you, O LORD, are close,
your commands are truth.
***Long have I known that your will***
***is established for ever.***

**Thanksgiving**

O God, you provide us with every good gift;
we have ample means to meet our need
***and enough to share abundantly***
***in every good work.***
*(free prayers of thanksgiving)*
You lavish your gifts on those in need;
***your goodness stands fast forever. Amen.***

**Song**

Lord, I have made thy word (H317)
You are all we have (SJ29)

**Confession**

O God, clothe us with compassion,
kindness, humility, patience.
***Enfold us in love,***
***which binds everything together in harmony.***
*(silence)*
You have forgiven us; may we also forgive.
***And may Christ's peace rule in our hearts.***
***Amen.***

## Call to discipleship

Friends, let us not love with words
but with actions and in truth.
***This is how we know***
***that Jesus Christ lives in us,***
***by the Spirit he gave us.***

**Acts 21.7-14**

When we [Paul and Luke] had finished the voyage from Tyre, we arrived at Ptolemais; and we greeted the believers and stayed with them for one day. The next day we left and came to Caesarea; and we went into the house of Philip the evangelist, one of the seven, and stayed with him. He had four unmarried daughters who had the gift of prophecy. While we were staying there for several days, a prophet named Agabus came down from Judea. He came to us and took Paul's belt, bound his own feet and hands with it, and said, "Thus says the Holy Spirit, 'This is the way the Jews in Jerusalem will bind the man who owns this belt and will hand him over to the Gentiles.'" When we heard this, we and the people there urged him not to go up to Jerusalem. Then Paul answered, "What are you doing, weeping and breaking my heart? For I am ready not only to be bound but even to die in Jerusalem for the name of the Lord Jesus." Since he would not be persuaded, we remained silent except to say, "The Lord's will be done."

**2 Corinthians 9.5-7**

So I thought it necessary to urge the brothers to go on ahead to you, and arrange in advance for this bountiful gift that you have promised, so that it may be ready as a voluntary gift and not as an extortion.

The point is this: the one who sows sparingly will also reap sparingly, and the one who sows bountifully will also reap bountifully. Each of you must give as you have made up your mind, not reluctantly or under compulsion, for God loves a cheerful giver.

**Silent or spoken reflection on the readings**

**Song**

Lord, thou dost love (H387)
How clear is our vocation, Lord (H541)
Living and dying with Jesus (H550)

**1 Thessalonians 5.16-24**

## Call to intercession

God, who searches the heart,
knows what is the mind of the Spirit,
***because the Spirit intercedes for the saints according to the will of God.***

God of peace, in love you hear us when we call. In your mercy,
***Lord, hear our prayer.***

You are close; your commands are true. We pray for ourselves and those dear to us.
*(open prayers)*
In your mercy,
***Lord, hear our prayer.***

You love those who give cheerfully. We pray for our community and for our neighbors.
*(open prayers)*
In your mercy,
***Lord, hear our prayer.***

You give your people the gift of your Spirit. We pray for the church in all places, that we may speak boldly for Christ.
*(open prayers)*
In your mercy,
***Lord, hear our prayer.***

Your law is far from the unjust who bring harm. We pray for the world, for all who do justice and love mercy.
*(open prayers)*
In your mercy,
***Lord, hear our prayer.***

We offer you other concerns we carry in our hearts.
*(open prayers)*
In your mercy,
***Lord, hear our prayer.***

Extravagant God,
you do not hold back anything,
but pour out your Spirit
for the sake of your creation.
Transform our stony hearts
so that our generosity toward those in need
will match your own.
In the company of Jesus, who taught us,
we pray:

***Our Father …***

**Closing affirmation**

***Now the Lord is the Spirit,***
***and where the Spirit of the Lord is,***
***there is freedom.***
***And all of us, with unveiled faces,***
***seeing the glory of the Lord***
***as though reflected in a mirror,***

*are being transformed into the same image*
*from one degree of glory to another;*
*for this comes from the Lord, the Spirit. Amen.*

# The one who calls you is faithful

## PENTECOST 2 SATURDAY MORNING

**Opening sentence**

May the God of peace sanctify you entirely;
and may your spirit and soul and body
be kept sound and blameless
at the coming of our Lord Jesus.
***The one who calls you is faithful***
***and will do this.***

## Call to praise

Rejoice in the Lord always;
***again I will say, Rejoice.***

***Glory …***

**Psalm 119.161-168**

Though the powerful oppress me unjustly,
I stand in awe of your word.
***I take delight in your promise***
***like one who finds a treasure.***
Lies I hate and detest
but your law is my love.
***Seven times a day I praise you***
***for your just decrees.***
The lovers of your law have great peace;
they never stumble.

***I await your saving help, O Lord,***
***I fulfill your commands.***
My soul obeys your will
and loves it dearly.
***I obey your precepts and your will;***
***all that I do is before you.***

### Thanksgiving

O God, we give thanks to you
at all times and for everything
***in the name of our Lord Jesus Christ.***
*(free prayers of thanksgiving)*
We sing psalms and hymns
and spiritual songs,
***making melody to you in our hearts, O Lord.***
***Amen.***

### Song

Lamp of our feet (H312)
Obey my voice (H163)

### Confession of faith

Jesus of Nazareth was a man
commended to us by God
***through the powerful acts, wonders, and signs***
***God did through him in our midst—***
***as we ourselves know well.***
This man, according to the declared purpose
and foreknowledge of God,
was handed over, crucified and killed
by the hands of lawless ones.

***Yet God raised him up,***
***releasing him from the birth pangs of death***
***because it was not possible for him***
***to be taken over by it.***
This Jesus God raised up,
and of that we are all witnesses.
***Being therefore lifted high***
***at the right hand of God,***
***having received the promise of the Holy Spirit***
***from the Father,***
***he has poured out this***
***that we both see and hear.***

## Call to discipleship

Let us guard the good treasure entrusted to us,
***with the help of the Holy Spirit living in us.***

**Exodus 34.4-8**

So Moses cut two tablets of stone like the former ones; and he rose early in the morning and went up on Mount Sinai, as the LORD had commanded him, and took in his hand the two tablets of stone. The LORD descended in the cloud and stood with him there, and proclaimed the name, "The LORD." The LORD passed before him, and proclaimed,

"The LORD, the LORD,
a God merciful and gracious,
slow to anger,

and abounding in steadfast love and
faithfulness,
keeping steadfast love for the thousandth
generation,
forgiving iniquity and transgression and
sin,
yet by no means clearing the guilty,
but visiting the iniquity of the parents
upon the children
and the children's children,
to the third and the fourth generation."

And Moses quickly bowed his head toward the earth, and worshiped.

**Acts 20.16-24**

Paul had decided to sail past Ephesus, so that he might not have to spend time in Asia; he was eager to be in Jerusalem, if possible, on the day of Pentecost.

From Miletus he sent a message to Ephesus, asking the elders of the church to meet him. When they came to him, he said to them:

"You yourselves know how I lived among you the entire time from the first day that I set foot in Asia, serving the Lord with all humility and with tears, enduring the trials that came to me through the plots of the Jews. I did not shrink from doing anything helpful, proclaiming the message to you and teaching you publicly and from house to house, as I testified to both Jews and Greeks about repentance toward God and faith toward our Lord Jesus. And now, as a captive to the Spirit, I am on my way to Jerusalem, not knowing what will happen to me there, except that the Holy Spirit testifies to me in every city that imprisonment and persecutions are waiting for me. But I do not count my life of any value to myself, if only I may finish my course and the ministry that I received from the Lord Jesus, to testify to the good news of God's grace."

**Silent or spoken reflection on the readings**

**Song**

Praise, my soul, the God of heaven (H63)
Praise, my soul, the King of heaven (H65)
Who now would follow Christ (H535)
When we are tempted (SS81)

**1 Thessalonians 5.16-24**

## Call to intercession

Beloved,
let us keep ourselves in the love of God,
***looking forward to the mercy***
***of our Lord Jesus Christ that leads to life.***

Merciful and gracious God, you teach us by your word. In your mercy,
***Lord, hear our prayer.***

Your hand is ready to help us. We pray for ourselves and those dear to us.
*(open prayers)*
In your mercy,
***Lord, hear our prayer.***

You abound in steadfast love and faithfulness. We pray for our community and for our neighbors.
*(open prayers)*
In your mercy,
***Lord, hear our prayer.***

You give us the ministry of testifying to the good news of your grace. We pray for the church in all places, that we may be faithful in solidarity across generations and geography.
*(open prayers)*
In your mercy,
***Lord, hear our prayer.***

You forgive iniquity and transgression. We pray for the world, for our enemies and for those who are in conflict.
*(open prayers)*
In your mercy,
***Lord, hear our prayer.***

We offer you other concerns we carry in our hearts.
*(open prayers)*
In your mercy,
***Lord, hear our prayer.***

God of every gift,
you provide for us, body and soul,
through the bounty of creation
and the gift of your own Holy Spirit.
Hold us fast to your ways,
so that our delight will be
to join your work this day.
In the example of Jesus, who taught us,
we pray:

***Our Father …***

**Charge**

Do not worry about how you are to speak
or what you are to say;
for what you are to say
will be given to you at that time;
for it is not you who speak.
but the Spirit of your Father
speaking through you. ***Amen.***

# The one who calls you will do this

## PENTECOST 2 SATURDAY EVENING

**Opening sentence**

May the God of peace sanctify you entirely;
and may your spirit and soul and body
be kept sound and blameless
at the coming of our Lord Jesus.
***The one who calls you is faithful***
***and will do this.***

## Call to praise

What should I do then?
I will pray with the spirit,
but I will pray with the mind also.
***I will sing praise with the spirit,***
***but I will sing praise with the mind also.***

*Glory …*

**Psalm 119.169-176**

LORD, let my cry come before you:
teach me by your word.
***Let my pleading come before you:***
***save me by your promise.***
Let my lips proclaim your praise
because you teach me your statutes.

***Let my tongue sing your promise***
***for your commands are just.***
Let your hand be ready to help me,
since I have chosen your precepts.
***LORD, I long for your saving help***
***and your law is my delight.***
Give life to my soul that I may praise you.
Let your decrees give me help.
***I am lost like a sheep; seek your servant***
***for I remember your commands.***

**Thanksgiving**

O God, you provide us with every good gift;
we have ample means to meet our need
***and enough to share abundantly***
***in every good work.***
*(free prayers of thanksgiving)*
You lavish your gifts on those in need;
***your goodness stands fast forever. Amen.***

**Song**

You are all we have (SJ29)
From all that dwell below the skies (H49)
The God of Abraham praise (H162)

**Confession**

O God, clothe us with compassion,
kindness, humility, patience.
***Enfold us in love,***
***which binds everything together in harmony.***
*(silence)*

You have forgiven us; may we also forgive.
***And may Christ's peace rule in our hearts. Amen.***

## Call to discipleship

Friends, let us not love with words
but with actions and in truth.
***This is how we know***
***that Jesus Christ lives in us,***
***by the Spirit he gave us.***

**Acts 20.25-32**

"And now I [Paul] know that none of you, among whom I have gone about proclaiming the kingdom, will ever see my face again. Therefore I declare to you this day that I am not responsible for the blood of any of you, for I did not shrink from declaring to you the whole purpose of God. Keep watch over yourselves and over all the flock, of which the Holy Spirit has made you overseers, to shepherd the church of God that he obtained with the blood of his own Son. I know that after I have gone, savage wolves will come in among you, not sparing the flock. Some even from your own group will come distorting the truth in order to entice the disciples to follow them. Therefore be alert, remembering that for three years I did not cease night or day to warn everyone with tears. And now I commend you to God and to the message of his grace, a message that is able to build you up and to give you the inheritance among all who are sanctified."

**2 Corinthians 9.8-15**

And God is able to provide you with every blessing in abundance, so that by always having enough of everything, you may share abundantly in every good work. As it is written,

"He scatters abroad, he gives to the poor;
his righteousness endures forever."

He who supplies seed to the sower and bread for food will supply and multiply your seed for sowing and increase the harvest of your righteousness. You will be enriched in every way for your great generosity, which will produce thanksgiving to God through us; for the rendering of this ministry not only supplies the needs of the saints but also overflows with many thanksgivings to God. Through the testing of this ministry you glorify God by your obedience to the confession of the gospel of Christ and by the generosity of your sharing with them and with all others, while they long for you and pray for you because of the surpassing grace of God that he has given you. Thanks be to God for his indescribable gift!

**Silent or spoken reflection on the readings**

**Song**

God the Spirit, Guide and Guardian (H632)
The church of Christ in every age (H403)
God, whose giving (H383)
Cuando el pobre (When the poor ones) (SJ69)

**1 Thessalonians 5.16-24**

## Call to intercession

God, who searches the heart,
knows what is the mind of the Spirit,
***because the Spirit intercedes for the saints according to the will of God.***

Merciful and gracious God, you teach us by your word. In your mercy,
***Lord, hear our prayer.***

Your hand is ready to help us. We pray for ourselves and those dear to us.
*(open prayers)*
In your mercy,
***Lord, hear our prayer.***

You abound in steadfast love and faithfulness. We pray for our community and for our neighbors.
*(open prayers)*

In your mercy,
***Lord, hear our prayer.***

You give us the ministry of testifying to the good news of your grace. We pray for the church in all places, that we may be faithful in solidarity across generations and geography.
*(open prayers)*
In your mercy,
***Lord, hear our prayer.***

You forgive iniquity and transgression. We pray for the world, for our enemies and for those who are in conflict.
*(open prayers)*
In your mercy,
***Lord, hear our prayer.***

We offer you other concerns we carry in our hearts.
*(open prayers)*
In your mercy,
***Lord, hear our prayer.***

Extravagant God,
you do not hold back anything,
but pour out your Spirit
for the sake of your creation.
Transform our stony hearts
so that our generosity toward those in need
will match your own.

In the company of Jesus, who taught us,
we pray:

*Our Father ...*

**Closing affirmation**

*Jesus Christ was not "Yes and No";*
*but in him it is always "Yes."*
*For in him*
*every one of God's promises is a "Yes."*
*For this reason*
*it is through him that we say the "Amen,"*
*to the glory of God.*
*But it is God who establishes us in Christ*
*and has anointed us, by putting his seal on us*
*and giving us his Spirit in our hearts*
*as a first installment. Amen.*

# Scripture index: Readings and Psalms



---

This scripture index includes entries for both Volume 1 (*Ordinary Time*) and Volume 2 (*Advent through Pentecost*) of *Take Our Moments and Our Days: An Anabaptist Prayer Book.*

| | | | | |
|---|---|---|---|---|
| 22.19-24 | Ordinary 4 | Friday | evening | Psalm |
| 24.1-6 | Ordinary 2 | Thursday | evening | Psalm |
| 25.1-7 | Ordinary 3 | Friday | morning | Psalm |
| 25.8-14 | Ordinary 2 | Tuesday | evening | Psalm |
| 25.16-21 | Ordinary 1 | Thursday | morning | Psalm |
| 26 | Holy week | Thursday | evening | Psalm |
| 27 | Holy week | Thursday | morning | Psalm |
| 29 | Epiphany | Tuesday | morning | Psalm |
| 30.2-5 | Ordinary 2 | Monday | evening | Psalm |
| 31.9-15 | Ordinary 1 | Thursday | evening | Psalm |
| 31.19-24 | Ordinary 2 | Saturday | morning | Psalm |
| 32.1-5 | Ordinary 3 | Sunday | morning | Psalm |
| 33.1-5 | Ordinary 3 | Tuesday | evening | Psalm |
| 34.11-18 | Ordinary 2 | Friday | evening | Psalm |
| 36.5-9 | Ordinary 2 | Wednesday | morning | Psalm |
| 37.3-11 | Ordinary 2 | Tuesday | morning | Psalm |
| 41 | Holy week | Tuesday | evening | Psalm |
| 43 | Ordinary 2 | Saturday | evening | Psalm |
| | Lent | Sunday | evening | Psalm |
| 46 | Lent | Saturday | evening | Psalm |
| 47 | Easter | Thursday | morning | Psalm |
| 48.9-14 | Ordinary 3 | Wednesday | evening | Psalm |
| 50.1-6 | Epiphany | Sunday | evening | Psalm |
| 51.1-12 | Lent | Monday | morning | Psalm |
| 51.6-13 | Pentecost | Friday | evening | Psalm |
| 51.12-17 | Ordinary 3 | Tuesday | morning | Psalm |
| 53 | Lent | Tuesday | evening | Psalm |
| 61.1-5 | Ordinary 4 | Friday | morning | Psalm |
| 65.1-4 | Ordinary 1 | Wednesday | evening | Psalm |
| 65.9-13 | Ordinary 3 | Monday | morning | Psalm |
| 66.1-9 | Ordinary 4 | Monday | evening | Psalm |
| 67 | Epiphany | Thursday | evening | Psalm |
| 68.4-11 | Christmas 1 | Dec 24 | evening | Psalm |
| 68.17-20 | Pentecost | Friday | morning | Psalm |
| 71.1-4 | Ordinary 1 | Friday | evening | Psalm |
| 71.5-8 | Ordinary 3 | Saturday | morning | Psalm |
| 71.15-19 | Ordinary 3 | Friday | evening | Psalm |
| 72.12-14 | Ordinary 4 | Tuesday | morning | Psalm |
| 75 | Lent | Thursday | morning | Psalm |

| | | | | |
|---|---|---|---|---|
| 77.4-15 | Epiphany | Tuesday | evening | Psalm |
| 78.18-26 | Ordinary 1 | Tuesday | morning | Psalm |
| 82 | Lent | Sunday | morning | Psalm |
| 84 | Lent | Thursday | evening | Psalm |
| 85.1-7 | Christmas 1 | Dec 29 | morning | Psalm |
| 85.7-13 | Ordinary 2 | Friday | morning | Psalm |
| 86.1-8 | Ordinary 2 | Thursday | morning | Psalm |
| 90.11-14 | Christmas 2 | Dec 31 | morning | Psalm |
| 90.15-17 | Christmas 2 | Jan 1 | evening | Psalm |
| 91 | Lent | Friday | morning | Psalm |
| 91.1-6 | Christmas 2 | Jan 2 | morning | Psalm |
| 91.8-17 | Christmas 2 | Jan 2 | evening | Psalm |
| 95.1-7 | Christmas 2 | Jan 3 | morning | Psalm |
| | Easter | Monday | evening | Psalm |
| 96 | Christmas 1 | Dec 25 | evening | Psalm |
| 96.9-13 | Easter | Saturday | evening | Psalm |
| 96.10-13 | Ordinary 2 | Wednesday | evening | Psalm |
| 97 | Easter | Wednesday | evening | Psalm |
| 97.1-6 | Christmas 2 | Jan 4 | evening | Psalm |
| 97.6-12 | Christmas 1 | Dec 29 | evening | Psalm |
| 98 | Easter | Thursday | evening | Psalm |
| 98.1-4 | Christmas 2 | Jan 5 | morning | Psalm |
| 99 | Easter | Friday | evening | Psalm |
| 99.1-5 | Ordinary 1 | Monday | morning | Psalm |
| 100 | Easter | Tuesday | evening | Psalm |
| 101 | Lent | Wednesday | evening | Psalm |
| 102.15-22 | Christmas 1 | Dec 27 | morning | Psalm |
| 102.24-28 | Christmas 2 | Jan 1 | morning | Psalm |
| 103.1-7 | Ordinary 1 | Sunday | evening | Psalm |
| 103.6-15 | Christmas 2 | Dec 31 | evening | Psalm |
| 103.8-14 | Ordinary 1 | Wednesday | morning | Psalm |
| 103.19-22 | Ordinary 1 | Monday | evening | Psalm |
| 104.1-4, 10-15 | Ordinary 1 | Sunday | morning | Psalm |
| 104.27-30 | Ordinary 1 | Tuesday | evening | Psalm |
| 105.1-5, 40-43 | Ordinary 4 | Monday | morning | Psalm |
| 107.10-16 | Ordinary 4 | Wednesday | morning | Psalm |
| 110.1-4 | Easter | Sunday | evening | Psalm |
| 111.1-4 | Ordinary 4 | Thursday | morning | Psalm |
| 114 | Christmas 1 | Dec 28 | morning | Psalm |

| | | | | |
|---|---|---|---|---|
| 116.2-9 | Ordinary 3 | Saturday | evening | Psalm |
| 118.13-17 | Ordinary 4 | Sunday | evening | Psalm |
| 118.14-29 | Easter | Sunday | morning | Psalm |
| 118.19-29 | Holy week | Sunday | morning | Psalm |
| 119.1-8 | Pentecost 2 | Sunday | evening | Psalm |
| 119.9-16 | Pentecost 2 | Monday | morning | Psalm |
| 119.17-24 | Pentecost 2 | Monday | evening | Psalm |
| 119.33-40 | Pentecost 2 | Tuesday | morning | Psalm |
| 119.41-48 | Holy week | Sunday | evening | Psalm |
| 119.49-56 | Holy week | Monday | morning | Psalm |
| 119.57-64 | Ordinary 3 | Thursday | morning | Psalm |
| | Holy week | Monday | evening | Psalm |
| 119.73-80 | Pentecost 2 | Tuesday | evening | Psalm |
| 119.89-96 | Pentecost 2 | Wednesday | morning | Psalm |
| 119.97-104 | Pentecost 2 | Thursday | morning | Psalm |
| 119.113-120 | Pentecost 2 | Thursday | evening | Psalm |
| 119.129-136 | Ordinary 3 | Thursday | evening | Psalm |
| | Pentecost 2 | Friday | morning | Psalm |
| 119.145-152 | Pentecost 2 | Friday | evening | Psalm |
| 119.161-168 | Pentecost 2 | Saturday | morning | Psalm |
| 119.169-176 | Pentecost 2 | Saturday | evening | Psalm |
| 126 | Ordinary 2 | Monday | morning | Psalm |
| 131.1-2 | Ordinary 2 | Sunday | evening | Psalm |
| 133 | Epiphany | Wednesday | morning | Psalm |
| 135.1-7 | Christmas 2 | Jan 4 | morning | Psalm |
| 136.1-9 | Christmas 2 | Jan 3 | evening | Psalm |
| 138.1-5 | Epiphany | Thursday | morning | Psalm |
| 139.1-6 | Ordinary 3 | Sunday | evening | Psalm |
| 139.13-18 | Epiphany | Sunday | morning | Psalm |
| 140.1-7 | Ordinary 1 | Friday | morning | Psalm |
| 143.5-10 | Pentecost | Wednesday | evening | Psalm |
| 145.1-9 | Ordinary 1 | Saturday | evening | Psalm |
| 145.1-13, 21 | Easter | Saturday | morning | Psalm |
| 145.10-14 | Ordinary 1 | Saturday | morning | Psalm |
| 145.15-21 | Ordinary 3 | Wednesday | morning | Psalm |
| 146 | Lent | Saturday | morning | Psalm |
| 146.1-9 | Ordinary 4 | Thursday | evening | Psalm |
| 147.1-7 | Ordinary 4 | Wednesday | evening | Psalm |
| 148 | Easter | Friday | morning | Psalm |

| | | | | |
|---|---|---|---|---|
| 150 | Christmas 2 | Jan 5 | evening | Psalm |
| **Song of Solomon** | | | | |
| 8.6-7 | Holy week | Saturday | morning | Reading 1 |
| **Isaiah** | | | | |
| 2.1-5 | Holy week | Tuesday | morning | Psalm |
| 2.2-4 | Epiphany | Friday | evening | Psalm |
| 6.1-8 | Epiphany | Thursday | evening | Reading 1 |
| 7.14-15 | Advent | Wednesday | evening | Psalm |
| 9.1-5 | Christmas 1 | Dec 30 | morning | Psalm |
| 9.2-7 | Advent | Thursday | morning | Psalm |
| 9.6-7 | Christmas 1 | Dec 30 | evening | Psalm |
| 11.1-9 | Advent | Wednesday | morning | Psalm |
| 11.1-4, 10-12 | Pentecost | Monday | morning | Psalm |
| 11.6-9 | Easter | Wednesday | morning | Psalm |
| 12.1-2 | Christmas 1 | Dec 27 | evening | Reading 2 |
| 12.2-6 | Advent | Tuesday | morning | Psalm |
| 25.6-9 | Ordinary 3 | Saturday | evening | Reading 2 |
| 25.9 | Christmas 2 | Jan 4 | evening | Reading 2 |
| 30.18-21 | Christmas 1 | Dec 26 | evening | Psalm |
| 32.15-18 | Ordinary 2 | Friday | evening | Reading 2 |
| 35.1-6 | Advent | Sunday | evening | Psalm |
| 40.1-2 | Ordinary 2 | Monday | evening | Reading 2 |
| 40.3 | Christmas 2 | Jan 2 | evening | Reading 2 |
| 40.9-11 | Advent | Thursday | evening | Psalm |
| 42.1-6 | Pentecost | Tuesday | evening | Psalm |
| 42.6-9 | Christmas 1 | Dec 26 | evening | Reading 2 |
| 43.1-3 | Epiphany | Saturday | morning | Psalm |
| 43.15-21 | Advent | Tuesday | evening | Psalm |
| 49.1-6 | Epiphany | Monday | morning | Psalm |
| 49.6 | Christmas 1 | Dec 27 | morning | Reading 2 |
| 49.8-11 | Advent | Friday | morning | Psalm |
| 49.13-15 | Christmas 1 | Dec 28 | morning | Reading 2 |
| 52.7-10 | Advent | Sunday | morning | Psalm |
| | Pentecost | Sunday | evening | Psalm |
| 52.10-15 | Lent | Friday | evening | Psalm |
| 53.1-9 | Lent | Monday | evening | Psalm |
| 54.11-14 | Advent | Saturday | evening | Psalm |
| 55.1-6 | Pentecost | Saturday | morning | Psalm |

| | | | | |
|---|---|---|---|---|
| 55.6-11 | Advent | Friday | evening | Psalm |
| 55.6-13 | Pentecost | Saturday | evening | Psalm |
| 57.14-15 | Ordinary 2 | Sunday | morning | Psalm |
| 57.15-19 | Pentecost | Sunday | morning | Psalm |
| 58.6-9 | Ordinary 4 | Friday | morning | Reading 2 |
| 58.9-11 | Ordinary 3 | Wednesday | evening | Reading 2 |
| 59.21 | Pentecost 2 | Friday | morning | Reading 1 |
| 60.1-3 | Epiphany | Jan 6 | morning | Psalm |
| 60.4-5 | Advent | Saturday | morning | Psalm |
| 60.4-6 | Epiphany | Jan 6 | evening | Psalm |
| 61.1-3 | Ordinary 4 | Saturday | morning | Psalm |
| | Pentecost | Thursday | evening | Psalm |
| 61.10-11 | Advent | Monday | morning | Psalm |
| 63.7-9 | Christmas 1 | Dec 27 | evening | Psalm |
| 63.7-16 | Pentecost | Monday | evening | Psalm |
| 65.17-19, 24-25 | Ordinary 4 | Saturday | evening | Psalm |
| 66.10-16 | Advent | Monday | evening | Psalm |

**Jeremiah**

| | | | | |
|---|---|---|---|---|
| 1.4-10 | Epiphany | Sunday | morning | Reading 2 |
| 31.15-17 | Christmas 1 | Dec 28 | evening | Psalm |

**Ezekiel**

| | | | | |
|---|---|---|---|---|
| 18.29-32 | Ordinary 3 | Saturday | morning | Reading 2 |
| 34.25-28 | Christmas 1 | Dec 25 | morning | Psalm |
| 37.9-14 | Pentecost | Thursday | morning | Psalm |
| 37.26-28 | Christmas 2 | Jan 2 | morning | Reading 2 |
| 43.1-7 | Epiphany | Friday | morning | Reading 1 |

**Daniel**

| | | | | |
|---|---|---|---|---|
| 3.16-18 | Holy week | Friday | morning | Reading 1 |
| 7.13-14 | Epiphany | Friday | evening | Reading 1 |
| 9.3-6, 17-19 | Lent | Monday | morning | Reading 2 |
| 9.20-23 | Advent | Tuesday | morning | Reading 2 |

**Hosea**

| | | | | |
|---|---|---|---|---|
| 6.1-3 | Christmas 1 | Dec 29 | evening | Reading 2 |
| | Easter | Monday | morning | Psalm |

**Joel**

| | | | | |
|---|---|---|---|---|
| 2.26-32 | Pentecost | Tuesday | morning | Psalm |

| | | | | |
|---|---|---|---|---|
| 12.15-20 | Ordinary 4 | Sunday | morning | Reading 1 |
| 13.31-33 | Advent | Tuesday | evening | Reading 2 |
| 13.44-46 | Ordinary 3 | Friday | evening | Reading 1 |
| 17.1-8 | Epiphany | Saturday | morning | Reading 1 |
| 17.9-13 | Epiphany | Saturday | evening | Reading 1 |
| 18.1-5 | Ordinary 2 | Sunday | evening | Reading 1 |
| 20.8-16 | Ordinary 3 | Saturday | morning | Reading 1 |
| 21.28-31 | Ordinary 3 | Thursday | morning | Reading 1 |
| 25.34-40 | Ordinary 3 | Wednesday | evening | Reading 1 |
| 26.36-39 | Ordinary 1 | Thursday | morning | Reading 1 |
| 26.40-46 | Ordinary 1 | Thursday | evening | Reading 1 |
| 28.1-10 | Easter | Sunday | morning | Reading 1 |

**Mark**

| | | | | |
|---|---|---|---|---|
| 1.4-11 | Epiphany | Sunday | morning | Reading 1 |
| 1.14-15 | Ordinary 1 | Saturday | morning | Reading 1 |
| 1.40-45 | Ordinary 4 | Tuesday | morning | Reading 1 |
| 3.1-6 | Ordinary 4 | Friday | morning | Reading 1 |
| 4.1-9 | Ordinary 3 | Monday | morning | Reading 1 |
| 6.39-44 | Ordinary 4 | Monday | evening | Reading 1 |
| 8.22-26 | Ordinary 4 | Thursday | evening | Reading 1 |
| 9.14-29 | Ordinary 4 | Wednesday | morning | Reading 1 |
| 9.33-37 | Ordinary 2 | Tuesday | evening | Reading 1 |
| 10.46-52 | Ordinary 4 | Thursday | morning | Reading 1 |
| 11.25 | Ordinary 1 | Wednesday | morning | Reading 1 |
| 13.32-37 | Ordinary 3 | Friday | morning | Reading 1 |
| 15.47-16.8 | Ordinary 2 | Sunday | morning | Reading 1 |

**Luke**

| | | | | |
|---|---|---|---|---|
| 1.5-7 | Advent | Monday | morning | Reading 1 |
| 1.8-17 | Advent | Monday | evening | Reading 1 |
| 1.18-20 | Advent | Tuesday | morning | Reading 1 |
| 1.21-25 | Advent | Tuesday | evening | Reading 1 |
| 1.26-38 | Advent | Wednesday | morning | Reading 1 |
| 1.39-45 | Advent | Thursday | morning | Reading 1 |
| 1.57-67, 80 | Advent | Thursday | evening | Reading 1 |
| 2.1-7 | Christmas 1 | Dec 24 | evening | Reading 1 |
| 2.8-14 | Christmas 1 | Dec 25 | morning | Reading 1 |
| 2.15-20 | Christmas 1 | Dec 25 | evening | Reading 1 |
| 2.21-24 | Christmas 1 | Dec 26 | morning | Reading 1 |

| | | | | |
|---|---|---|---|---|
| 2.21-30 | Holy week | Monday | evening | Reading 2 |
| 2.25-32 | Christmas 1 | Dec 26 | evening | Reading 1 |
| 2.33-35 | Christmas 1 | Dec 27 | morning | Reading 1 |
| 2.36-38 | Christmas 1 | Dec 27 | evening | Reading 1 |
| 2.39-40 | Christmas 1 | Dec 29 | evening | Reading 1 |
| 2.41-47 | Christmas 1 | Dec 30 | morning | Reading 1 |
| 2.48-52 | Christmas 1 | Dec 30 | evening | Reading 1 |
| 3.1-6 | Advent | Friday | morning | Reading 1 |
| 3.7-18 | Advent | Friday | evening | Reading 1 |
| 4.17-19 | Lent | Sunday | morning | Reading 1 |
| 4.24-30 | Lent | Sunday | evening | Reading 1 |
| 5.18-26 | Lent | Monday | morning | Reading 1 |
| 6.20-26 | Lent | Tuesday | morning | Reading 1 |
| 6.27-31 | Lent | Thursday | morning | Reading 1 |
| 6.32-36 | Lent | Thursday | evening | Reading 1 |
| 6.32-38 | Ordinary 2 | Thursday | morning | Reading 1 |
| 7.18-23 | Advent | Sunday | evening | Reading 1 |
| 7.36-50 | Lent | Tuesday | evening | Reading 1 |
| 7.40-50 | Ordinary 1 | Wednesday | evening | Reading 1 |
| 8.41-42, 49-55 | Ordinary 4 | Saturday | evening | Reading 1 |
| 8.43-48 | Ordinary 4 | Tuesday | evening | Reading 1 |
| 9.23-27 | Lent | Friday | evening | Reading 1 |
| 9.51-56 | Lent | Monday | evening | Reading 1 |
| 10.5-11 | Ordinary 1 | Monday | evening | Reading 1 |
| 10.29-37 | Ordinary 3 | Tuesday | evening | Reading 1 |
| 11.1-4, 9-13 | Ordinary 1 | Sunday | morning | Reading 1 |
| 12.22-31 | Ordinary 1 | Tuesday | evening | Reading 1 |
| 12.29-34 | Lent | Friday | morning | Reading 1 |
| 12.35-40 | Ordinary 3 | Thursday | evening | Reading 1 |
| 13.18-21 | Ordinary 3 | Monday | evening | Reading 1 |
| 14.7-11 | Ordinary 2 | Tuesday | morning | Reading 1 |
| 14.12-14 | Lent | Wednesday | morning | Reading 1 |
| 14.16-24 | Ordinary 3 | Saturday | evening | Reading 1 |
| 15.11-19 | Ordinary 3 | Sunday | morning | Reading 1 |
| 15.20-24 | Ordinary 3 | Sunday | evening | Reading 1 |
| 17.20-21 | Ordinary 1 | Monday | morning | Reading 1 |
| 18.1-8 | Ordinary 3 | Wednesday | morning | Reading 1 |
| 18.9-14 | Ordinary 3 | Tuesday | morning | Reading 1 |

| | | | | |
|---|---|---|---|---|
| 18.15-17 | Lent | Wednesday | evening | Reading 1 |
| 19.1-10 | Ordinary 2 | Wednesday | morning | Reading 1 |
| | Lent | Saturday | morning | Reading 1 |
| 19.29-44 | Holy week | Sunday | morning | Reading 1 |
| 21.5-11 | Advent | Saturday | morning | Reading 1 |
| 21.25-36 | Advent | Saturday | evening | Reading 1 |
| 21.37–22.13 | Holy week | Sunday | evening | Reading 2 |
| 22.14-20 | Holy week | Monday | morning | Reading 2 |
| 22.21-30 | Holy week | Monday | evening | Reading 2 |
| 22.31-53 | Holy week | Tuesday | morning | Reading 2 |
| 22.54-62 | Holy week | Tuesday | evening | Reading 2 |
| 22.63-71 | Holy week | Wednesday | morning | Reading 2 |
| 23.1-12 | Holy week | Wednesday | evening | Reading 2 |
| 23.13-25 | Holy week | Thursday | morning | Reading 2 |
| 23.26-31 | Holy week | Thursday | evening | Reading 2 |
| 23.32-38 | Holy week | Friday | morning | Reading 2 |
| 23.39-43 | Lent | Saturday | evening | Reading 1 |
| 23.39-48 | Holy week | Friday | evening | Reading 2 |
| 23.42-43 | Ordinary 1 | Saturday | evening | Reading 1 |
| 23.49 | Holy week | Saturday | morning | Reading 2 |
| 23.50-56 | Holy week | Saturday | evening | Reading 2 |
| 24.1-11 | Epiphany | Sunday | evening | Reading 1 |
| 24.1-12 | Easter | Sunday | evening | Reading 1 |
| 24.13-27 | Easter | Monday | morning | Reading 1 |
| 24.28-35 | Easter | Monday | evening | Reading 1 |
| 24.36-43 | Easter | Tuesday | morning | Reading 1 |
| 24.44-49 | Easter | Tuesday | evening | Reading 1 |
| 24.50-53 | Easter | Thursday | morning | Reading 1 |

**John**

| | | | | |
|---|---|---|---|---|
| 1.1-9 | Christmas 2 | Jan 1 | morning | Reading 1 |
| 1.9-13 | Christmas 2 | Jan 1 | evening | Reading 1 |
| 1.14-18 | Christmas 2 | Jan 2 | morning | Reading 1 |
| 1.19-23 | Christmas 2 | Jan 2 | evening | Reading 1 |
| 1.25-28 | Christmas 2 | Jan 3 | morning | Reading 1 |
| 1.29-34 | Christmas 2 | Jan 3 | evening | Reading 1 |
| 1.35-39 | Christmas 2 | Jan 4 | morning | Reading 1 |
| 1.40-41 | Christmas 2 | Jan 4 | evening | Reading 1 |
| 1.42-44 | Christmas 2 | Jan 5 | morning | Reading 1 |

| | | | | |
|---|---|---|---|---|
| 1.45-51 | Christmas 2 | Jan 5 | evening | Reading 1 |
| 1.47-51 | Ordinary 2 | Thursday | evening | Reading 1 |
| 2.1-11 | Ordinary 4 | Monday | morning | Reading 1 |
| 5.1-9 | Ordinary 4 | Wednesday | evening | Reading 1 |
| 6.8-14 | Ordinary 1 | Tuesday | morning | Reading 1 |
| 11.28-36 | Ordinary 2 | Monday | evening | Reading 1 |
| 11.38-44 | Ordinary 4 | Saturday | morning | Reading 1 |
| 12.27-32 | Epiphany | Tuesday | evening | Reading 2 |
| 13.31-35 | Epiphany | Wednesday | morning | Reading 2 |
| 14.15-17 | Pentecost | Sunday | evening | Reading 1 |
| 14.18-21 | Pentecost | Monday | evening | Reading 1 |
| 14.25-27 | Ordinary 2 | Friday | evening | Reading 1 |
| | Pentecost | Tuesday | evening | Reading 1 |
| 15.4-5 | Pentecost | Wednesday | evening | Reading 1 |
| 15.11-15 | Pentecost | Thursday | evening | Reading 1 |
| 15.18-20 | Ordinary 2 | Saturday | morning | Reading 1 |
| 15.26-27 | Pentecost | Friday | evening | Reading 1 |
| 16.13-14 | Pentecost | Saturday | evening | Reading 1 |
| 16.20-22 | Ordinary 2 | Monday | morning | Reading 1 |
| 17.20-24 | Epiphany | Tuesday | morning | Reading 2 |
| 20.1-10 | Easter | Wednesday | morning | Reading 1 |
| 20.11-18 | Ordinary 1 | Sunday | evening | Reading 1 |
| | Easter | Wednesday | evening | Reading 1 |
| 20.19-23 | Ordinary 4 | Sunday | evening | Reading 1 |
| | Easter | Friday | morning | Reading 1 |
| | Pentecost 2 | Thursday | morning | Reading 2 |
| 20.24-29 | Easter | Friday | evening | Reading 1 |
| 21.3-14 | Easter | Saturday | morning | Reading 1 |
| 21.15-19 | Easter | Saturday | evening | Reading 1 |

**Acts of the Apostles**

| | | | | |
|---|---|---|---|---|
| 1.1-8 | Pentecost | Sunday | morning | Reading 1 |
| 1.1-11 | Easter | Thursday | evening | Reading 1 |
| 2.1-13 | Pentecost | Monday | morning | Reading 1 |
| 2.14-21 | Pentecost | Tuesday | morning | Reading 1 |
| 2.22-28 | Pentecost | Wednesday | morning | Reading 1 |
| 2.29-36 | Pentecost | Thursday | morning | Reading 1 |
| 2.29-37 | Pentecost 2 | Sunday | morning | Reading 2 |
| 2.32-39 | Easter | Friday | morning | Reading 2 |

| | | | | |
|---|---|---|---|---|
| 12.9-16 | Ordinary 2 | Thursday | morning | Reading 2 |
| 13.11-14 | Advent | Saturday | evening | Reading 2 |
| 14.15-17 | Ordinary 1 | Monday | morning | Reading 2 |
| 15.7-13 | Pentecost | Sunday | morning | Reading 2 |
| 15.25-33 | Pentecost | Saturday | morning | Reading 2 |
| 16.25-27 | Advent | Thursday | morning | Reading 2 |
| **1 Corinthians** | | | | |
| 1.18-25 | Lent | Sunday | evening | Reading 2 |
| 1.26-31 | Ordinary 2 | Sunday | evening | Reading 2 |
| 10.12-13 | Ordinary 1 | Thursday | morning | Reading 2 |
| 12.3-11 | Pentecost | Thursday | morning | Reading 2 |
| 12.12-26 | Lent | Tuesday | morning | Reading 2 |
| 15.54-57 | Ordinary 4 | Saturday | morning | Reading 2 |
| **2 Corinthians** | | | | |
| 2.5-11 | Ordinary 1 | Wednesday | evening | Reading 2 |
| 3.12-13, 16-18 | | | | |
| | Epiphany | Wednesday | evening | Reading 2 |
| 3.17-18 | Ordinary 4 | Sunday | evening | Reading 2 |
| | Pentecost | Wednesday | evening | Reading 2 |
| 4.5-15 | Epiphany | Friday | morning | Reading 2 |
| 4.6 | Ordinary 4 | Monday | morning | Reading 2 |
| 8.1-6 | Pentecost 2 | Sunday | evening | Reading 2 |
| 8.7-9 | Pentecost 2 | Monday | evening | Reading 2 |
| 8.9 | Christmas 1 | Dec 24 | evening | Reading 2 |
| 8.10-15 | Pentecost 2 | Tuesday | evening | Reading 2 |
| 8.16-19 | Pentecost 2 | Wednesday | evening | Reading 2 |
| 8.20-24 | Pentecost 2 | Thursday | evening | Reading 2 |
| 9.5-7 | Pentecost 2 | Friday | evening | Reading 2 |
| 9.8-15 | Pentecost 2 | Saturday | evening | Reading 2 |
| 12.7-10 | Ordinary 4 | Wednesday | morning | Reading 2 |
| **Galatians** | | | | |
| 3.6-14 | Epiphany | Monday | morning | Reading 2 |
| 5.16-25 | Pentecost | Tuesday | evening | Reading 2 |
| **Ephesians** | | | | |
| 1.3-10 | Christmas 1 | Dec 29 | morning | Reading 2 |
| 1.11-17 | Pentecost | Saturday | evening | Reading 2 |
| 1.15-23 | Easter | Tuesday | morning | Reading 2 |
| 1.17-23 | Christmas 2 | Jan 5 | evening | Reading 2 |

# Scripture index: Other elements

**Theme**

| | |
|---|---|
| Advent | Lk 1.46-55 |
| Christmas 1 | Lk 1.68-79 |
| New Year's eve | Mt 6.20-21, 30 |
| Christmas 2 | Col 1.15-20 |
| Epiphany | Lk 2.29-32 |
| Ash Wednesday | Joel 2.13 |
| Lent | 1 Pt 2.21-24 |
| Holy week | Phil 2.5-8 |
| Easter | Phil 2.8-11 |
| Pentecost | Eph 2.17-22 |
| Pentecost 2 | 1 Thes 5.16-24 |

**Call 1**

| | | |
|---|---|---|
| Advent | morning | Ps 130.5-6 |
| | evening | Is 40.5 |
| Christmas 1 | morning | Jn 1.4, 14 |
| | evening | Mt 1.23 |
| | | Lk 2.14 |
| New Year's eve | | Ps 90.1-2 |
| Christmas 2 | morning | Ps 67.2-3 |
| | evening | Ps 149.1, 5 |
| Epiphany | morning | Is 60.1, 3 |
| | | Jn 1.5 |
| | evening | Ti 2.11 |
| Lent | morning | Ps 27.1 |
| | evening | Ps 25.5 |
| Holy week | morning | Ps 27.7-8 |
| | evening | Ps 25.1, 2 |
| Easter | morning | Ps 145.1-2 |
| | evening | Lk 24.29, 31-32 |
| Pentecost | morning | Ps 104.33 |
| | evening | Ps 134.1-2 |
| Pentecost 2 | morning | Phil 4.4 |
| | evening | 1 Cor 14.15 |

**Thanksgiving**

| | | |
|---|---|---|
| Advent | morning | Is 12.3-4 |
| | | Is 25.9 |
| | evening | Is 63.7 |
| | | Is 25.9 |
| Christmas 1 | morning | Is 63.7,9 |
| | evening | Ps 118.24, 29 |
| New Year's eve | morning | Ps 50.14, 23 |
| | evening | Ps 42.8, 11 |
| Christmas 2 | morning | Jn 1.5, 14 |
| | evening | Gal 4.4; 2 Cor 9.15 |
| Epiphany | morning | Ps 68.3 |
| | | Ps 59.16 |
| | evening | Ps 71.8 |
| | | Lam 3.22 |
| Lent | morning | Ps 33.20-22 |
| | evening | Ps 56.12-13 |
| Holy week | morning | Ps 5.1, 2, 3, 11, 12 |
| | evening | Ps 28.6-7 |
| Easter | morning | Ps 146.5-6 |
| | | Ps 90.14 |
| | evening | Ps 89.2 |
| | | Ps 71.8 |
| Pentecost | morning | Ps 104.1-2, 4 |
| | evening | Ps 104.24, 28, 30, 31 |
| Pentecost 2 | morning | Eph 5.19-20 |
| | evening | 2 Cor 9.8-9 |

**Confession**

| | | |
|---|---|---|
| Advent | evening | Ps 51.1, 6 |
| Christmas 1 | evening | Is 30.18 |
| New Year's eve | evening | Ps 139.1, 3, 7, 23-24 |
| Christmas 2 | evening | Ps 25.8, 9, 11 |
| Epiphany | evening | 1 Jn 1.7, 9 |
| Lent | evening | Ps 25.6, 17, 18 |
| Holy week | evening | Ps 25.15-16 |
| Easter | evening | Col 3.1-3 |
| Pentecost | evening | Ti 3.4-7 |
| Pentecost 2 | evening | Col 3.12-14 |

| | | |
|---|---|---|
| **Confession of faith** | | |
| Pentecost | morning | Acts 2.22-24, 32-33 |
| Pentecost 2 | morning | Acts 2.22-24, 32-33 |
| **Call 2** | | |
| Advent | morning | 1 Cor 3.11 |
| | evening | Mt 11.28 |
| Christmas 1 | morning | 1 Jn 4.7 |
| | evening | Jas 1.17 |
| New Year's eve | | Mt 6.25 |
| Christmas 2 | morning | 1 Jn 4.9, 11 |
| | evening | Col 3.16 |
| Epiphany | morning | Eph 5.8-9 |
| | evening | Jn 8.12 |
| Lent | morning | Mt 4.4, 10 |
| | evening | Jn 12.24, 26 |
| Holy week | morning | Mk 8.34-35 |
| | evening | Jn 15.12-13 |
| Easter | morning | Jn 10.10 |
| | | Jn 8.12 |
| | evening | Mt 16.25 |
| Pentecost | morning | 2 Tm 1.14 |
| | evening | 2 Thes 2.13, 15 |
| Pentecost 2 | morning | 2 Tm 1.13-14 |
| | evening | 1 Jn 3.18, 24 |
| **Canticle** | | |
| Advent | | Lk 1.46-55 |
| Christmas 1 | | Lk 1.68-79 |
| New Year's eve | morning | Lk 1.68-79 |
| | evening | Lk 1.46-55 |
| | | Lk 2.29-32 |
| Christmas 2 | | Col 1.15-20 |
| Epiphany | | Lk 2.29-32 |
| Lent | | 1 Pt 2.21-24 |
| Holy week | | Phil 2.5-8 |
| Easter | | Phil 2.5-11 |
| Pentecost | | Eph 2.17-22 |
| Pentecost 2 | | 1 Thes 5.16-24 |

**Call 3**

| | | |
|---|---|---|
| Advent | morning | Ps 5.2-3 |
| | evening | Is 55.6 |
| Christmas 1 | morning | Ps 145.19 |
| | evening | Lk 18.1, 7, 8 |
| New Year's eve | | Is 49.15-16 |
| Christmas 2 | morning | Ps 55.16, 17, 18, 22 |
| | evening | Jn 15.7, 16 |
| Epiphany | morning | Mal 3.10; 4.2 |
| | evening | Lk 18.1, 7, 8 |
| Lent | morning | Ps 27.7, 14 |
| | evening | Rom 8.26 |
| Holy week | morning | Ps 27.9 |
| | evening | Ps 22.1, 11 |
| Easter | morning | Is 51.6 |
| | evening | Is 43.19 |
| Pentecost | morning | Jude 20 |
| | evening | Rom 8.22-23 |
| Pentecost 2 | morning | Jude 21 |
| | evening | Rom 8.27 |

**Benediction**

| | | | |
|---|---|---|---|
| Advent | | morning | Rom 15.13 |
| | | evening | 1 Thes 5.23-24 |
| Christmas 1 | | morning | 2 Pt 1.2 |
| | | evening | Rom 16.25-26 |
| New Year's eve | | | Ps 121.7-8 |
| Christmas 2 | | morning | 2 Pt 1.2 |
| | | evening | Ps 121.7-8 |
| Epiphany | | morning | Lk 1.78-79 |
| | | evening | Nm 6.24-26 |
| Ash Wednesday | | | 2 Thes 2.16-17 |
| Lent | Sunday | | Jude 24-25 |
| | Monday | | Jude 24-25 |
| | Tuesday | | Ps 121.7-8 |
| | Wednesday | | 2 Thes 2.16-17 |
| | Thursday | | 2 Cor 9.10 |
| | Friday | | 1 Pt 5.10 |
| | Saturday | | Rom 8.38-39 |

| | | | |
|---|---|---|---|
| Holy week | | morning | 2 Thes 2.16-17 |
| | | evening | Rom 8.38-39 |
| Easter | | morning | Heb 13.20-21 |
| | | evening | Col 1.11-12 |
| Pentecost | Sunday | morning | Mt 10.19-20 |
| | | evening | 1 Thes 5.23-24 |
| | Monday | morning | Mt 28.18-20 |
| | | evening | Eph 3.16-17 |
| | Tuesday | morning | Gal 6.8-10 |
| | | evening | Eph 3.18-19 |
| | Wednesday | morning | Phil 2.1-2 |
| | | evening | 2 Cor 13.13 |
| | Thursday | morning | Eph 5.18-20 |
| | | evening | Rom 15.5-6 |
| | Friday | morning | Eph 4.1-3 |
| | | evening | 2 Cor 3.17-18 |
| | Saturday | morning | 1 Thes 5.15-19 |
| | | evening | 2 Cor 1.19-22 |
| **Pentecost 2** | | | |
| | Sunday | morning | Mt 28.18-20 |
| | | evening | 1 Thes 5.23-24 |
| | Monday | morning | Col 3.15, 16, 17 |
| | | evening | Phil 1.9-11 |
| | Tuesday | morning | Mt 10.19-20 |
| | | evening | Eph 3.18-19 |
| | Wednesday | morning | Phil 2.1-2 |
| | | evening | 2 Cor 13.13 |
| | Thursday | morning | Eph 5.18-20 |
| | | evening | Rom 15.5-6 |
| | Friday | morning | Eph 4.1-3 |
| | | evening | 2 Cor 3.17-18 |
| | Saturday | morning | Mt 10.19-20 |
| | | evening | 2 Cor 1.19-22 |